In Search of KINGS

WHAT BECAME OF THE
PASSENGERS OF THE *RE D'ITALIA*

In Search of
KINGS

TONY DE BOLFO

HarperCollins*Publishers*

HarperCollins*Publishers*

First published in 2002
Reprinted in 2002
by HarperCollins*Publishers* Pty Limited
ABN 36 009 913 517
A member of the HarperCollins*Publishers* (Australia) Pty Limited Group
www.harpercollins.com.au

HarperCollinsPublishers
25 Ryde Road, Pymble, Sydney, NSW 2073, Australia
31 View Road, Glenfield, Auckland 10, New Zealand
77–85 Fulham Palace Road, London, W6 8JB, United Kingdom
Hazelton Lanes, 55 Avenue Road, Suite 2900, Toronto, Ontario M5R 3L2
and 1995 Markham Road, Scarborough, Ontario M1B 5M8, Canada
10 East 53rd Street, New York NY 10022, USA

National Library of Australia Cataloguing-in-Publication data:

De Bolfo, Tony.
   In search of kings: what became of the passengers of the
   re d'Italia.
   ISBN 0 7322 7573 3.
   1. Re d'italia (Ship). 2. Italians – Australia.
   3. Immigrants – Australia. 4. Italians – Travel. 5. Italy –
   Emigration and immigration. 6. Australia – Emigration and
   immigration. I. Title.
325.2450994

Front cover images courtesy The Herald & Weekly Times, Ray Massacavallo and the National
Archives of Australia
Back cover images by Melanie Calabretta
Cover and internal design by Melanie Calabretta, HarperCollins Design Studio
Typeset in 10/15.5 Sabon by HarperCollins Design Studio
Printed and bound in Australia by Griffin Press on 80gsm Bulky Book Ivory

8 7 6 5 4 3 2   02 03 04 05

For my family

Name	Class	Occupation	Sex	Age	Status	ITALY	Λ	ITALIAN	AUSTRALIA
Da Vinchie GioBatta	3ᵃ	farm. lab.	m	28	S	ITALY	Λ	ITALIAN	AUSTRALIA
Beltrame Valentino	„	„	„	m	39	m	·	Λ	·	·
Formentini Pietro	„	„	„	m	38	m	„	Λ	„	„
Basso Eugenio	„	„	„	m	24	S	„	Λ	„	„
Borgnolo Vittorio	„	„	„	m	26	S	„	Λ	„	„
Benani Ettore	„	mason	m	30	m	„	Λ	„	„
Dorzi Luigi	„	farm. lab.	m	25	m	·	Λ	„	„
Campara Domenico	„	„	„	m	28	m	„	Λ	„	„
Zanimarchi Giuseppe	„	„	„	m	26	S	„	Λ	„	„
Tagliaferri Luigi	„	„	„	m	21	S	„	Λ	„	„
Deppi Girolamo	„	„	„	m	30	m	„	Λ	„	„
Brotto Angelo	„	„	„	m	29	S	„	Λ	„	„
Lago Ernesto	„	„	„	m	28	m	„	Λ	„	„
Cisinato Giovanni	„	„	„	m	37	m	„	Λ	„	„
Bonanni Vittorio	„	mason	m	30	m	„	Λ	„	„
Fogliato Valentino	„	farm. labor	m	28	S	„	Λ	„	„
Tonita Ermenegildo	„	carpenter	m	29	m	„	Λ	„	„
Cengia Antonio	„	farm. labor	m	23	m	„	Λ	„	„
Menegazzo Angelo	„	„	„	m	22	S	„	Λ	„	„
Querin Antonio	„	„	„	m	28	S	„	Λ	„	„
Sartore Gaetano	„	„	„	m	25	S	„	Λ	„	„
Caffaro Domenico	„	„	„	m	25	S	„	Λ	„	„
Carbonetto Maria	„	domestic	f	28	m	„	Λ	„	„
Costello Giovanni	„	children	m	4	—	„	Λ	„	„
Benvenuto Rameso	„	farm. lab.	m	36	m	„	Λ	„	„
Segat Luigi	„	„	„	m	40	m	„	Λ	„	„

Part of the list of incoming passengers who disembarked from the steamship *Re d'Italia* in Melbourne.
LIST COURTESY NATIONAL ARCHIVES OF AUSTRALIA, MELBOURNE OFFICE.

CONTENTS

ACKNOWLEDGMENTS

WHAT YOU ARE about to read is the culmination of eight years of research, which brought me into contact with many wonderful people, too numerous to thank individually, including some who sadly have not lived long enough to see these stories in print.

I am indebted to my late great-uncle, Igino De Bolfo, the inspiration for this story. I would also like to honour the memory of Igino's brothers, Benedetto, Francesco and my grandfather, Silvio De Bolfo. Great men, gone but not forgotten.

To all the tireless workers of the National Archives of Australia I am greatly indebted, particularly Lil Mangoni and Doreen Mahony in the Melbourne office. Lil and Doreen arranged my first access to the glorious sepia-coloured, pen-and-ink-blotched pages of the *Re d'Italia*'s passenger list, as well as the *atti di chiamata* (nomination forms), containing vital details of all but two of the 108 disembarkees. The Public Records Office in Melbourne also allowed me to view precious archival documents, not the least significant of which was the suicide note penned by the passenger Antonio Gnata.

I take my hat off to Laura Mecca and Lorenzo Iozzi of the Italian Historical Society in Melbourne, for whom nothing was too much trouble, and Iole Simeonato of the Bellunese del Mondo club in Adelaide, who was instrumental in locating the final resting place of the first-listed passenger, GioBatta Da Vinchie.

Thanks also to F.I.L.E.F., the Federazione Italiana di Lavatori Emigrati e loro Famiglie (Italian Federation of Migrant Workers and their Families), for kind permission to reprint excerpts from *With Courage in their Cases: The Experiences of Thirty-five Italian Immigrant Workers and their Families in Australia,* collected and edited by Morag Loh (F.I.L.E.F., Melbourne, 1980). (F.I.L.E.F. is a community-based organisation involved in welfare rights and language and cultural activities.) Morag Loh in turn was quoting from an interview with the ninth passenger on the list, Guiseppe Alfonso Maria Zammarchi, conducted during the late 1970s by her colleague, Wendy Lowenstein, and originally published in *Weevils in the Flour: An Oral Record of the 1930s Depression in Australia* (Highland House, Melbourne, 1978). I extend my gratitude to both authors for their interest in my project and for generously allowing me to make use of their work.

To Brigid Donovan and Vince Tucci, whose immense skills were truly reflected in the ABC's glorious presentation of 'In Search of Kings' for the 'Australian Story' television series, I am truly grateful. Filming took place on location in Stawell and at North Wharf where the old steamer came in, with footage shot over a fortnight in May 1999.

Paolo Coniglio and Maria Monaco generously offered their time and energies as interpreters, whenever late-night phone calls needed to be placed to the various *comuni* (municipal offices) scattered throughout Italy, or indeed to the homes of descendants whose forebears had returned to the old country many years before.

Their efforts were rewarded with interest by the kindly people, mostly volunteers, of the *comuni,* who were only too willing to provide vital documentation relating to the disembarkees, after the operators from both Telstra and Telecom Italia had made the right connections.

My cousins Giada and Edy De Bolfo, who live in the town of Borsea in the Veneto region, also served admirably as interpreters through my eight weeks in northern Italy from December 1999, while their father, Ettore, also gave of his time to chauffeur me to and from the houses of many of the descendants.

Amalia Salent deserves special commendation for her extensive interviewing of her beloved father for the purposes of this book, as do Yvonne Mogorovich (née Stella) and John Sculli who, during their respective visits to the northern and southern Italian towns of Asiago and Brancaleone, located information on the lives of Angelo Rigoni, Giuseppe Benavoli and Annunziato Guida.

Ray Massacavallo, whose father disembarked from the *Re d'Italia* in Adelaide in 1927, kindly provided the precious postcard images of the old steamship, few of which now remain, while Guy Puglia, the great-nephew of the passenger Michele Pisa, sent me a poem penned by Michele aboard the *Re d'Italia* in October 1927. The poem had remained in the memory of Michele's cousin, Antonio Pisa, some fifty years after Michele's death.

Ellenor Musumeci, of the Stawell Biarri Genealogical Society, and Father Wally Tudor, the parish priest of St Patrick's Roman Catholic Church in Stawell, were responsible for what was an unforgettable tribute to the memory of Antonio Gnata. Peter Morrissy kindly led my wife and me on a terrific tour of Redrock and Glen Alvie in Victoria's western districts as we retraced the footsteps of another of the passengers, Giuseppe ('Uncle Joe') Violi.

Special thanks to Lina Cecchin for the home-grown lettuce cut fresh from the Lago market garden in Werribee, to Antonia Dasin (née Bellò) for the freshly plucked chicken and chunk of beef from her sharefarm in Fonte, Provincia di Treviso, and to John Sculli, who filled a cardboard carton to the brim with the fruits of his Strathmore greengrocery.

To Tony Dal Sasso — 'thumbs up' for the home-made *vino* (I await next year's vintage with particular interest!), and to Dr Ray Lanteri — never has a bottle of Asti tasted as sweet as yours.

To all the descendants of the passengers of the *Re d'Italia* who invited me into their lives, my heart goes out to you. And to the passengers themselves — particularly Annunziata Faralla (née Picone), Ampelio Acquasaliente (Salent) and Igino De Bolfo — may you rest in peace.

THIS IMPORTANT DEADLINE of November 2002, coinciding with the seventy-fifth anniversary of the *Re d'Italia*'s arrival, was only reached with the tremendous input of James Weston, a great friend and true professional who gave up much of his time to cast a perceptive eye over the manuscript and whose editorial expertise was greatly valued. My father's cousin, Joan Miskin (née De Bolfo), also gave graciously of her time to get the manuscript into a presentable form for the capable team at HarperCollins — most notably Emma Kelso, who throughout the process was an absolute joy, Alison Urquhart, who always kept the faith, typesetter Amanda Goodsir, for all her hard work and Melanie Calabretta, whose design of this book beautifully captures the essence of the story.

The families of the passengers have provided me with hundreds of wonderful photographs, many of which are reproduced within these pages. Editorial constraints have unfortunately meant that not all the photos could be included here, but the families can rest assured that it is my intention to submit the entire photographic collection to the Italian Historical Society's archives, so that future generations may share in this glorious visual record.

I would like to thank my father and mother, John and Maureen, for every piece of good fortune that they have dealt me in life, and my three younger brothers, Paul, Greg and Richard, and their families, for their ongoing support.

Finally, I save the greatest thank you for my dear wife Kate, who, through no fault of hers, has had to live with this obsession of mine, and whose selfless attitude has allowed me to somehow reach the end of this journey; and for Carlo, my son, who may one day see fit to read this story — I hope he feels the same deep sense of pride in his family history that I have discovered through writing this book.

FOREWORD

WHAT BEGAN FOR Tony De Bolfo as a limited search for the story of his grandfather's arrival in 1927 grew into an epic search for the stories of the other passengers who also disembarked from the *Re d'Italia* at North Wharf. In a remarkable piece of patient detective work in the best journalistic tradition, Tony De Bolfo managed to track down — after a lapse of nearly seventy years — the relatives of almost all the 108 passengers who had made Melbourne their landfall. In a few precious interviews he even managed to meet some of the passengers themselves.

De Bolfo sets out the story of each of these pioneers, describing the small towns or countryside they left, their ambitions and their brave struggle to survive and even prosper in a difficult environment. Although most gave their occupation as labourers, they filled many roles in their new land. Unlike the postwar flood of immigrants, there was little factory work and most had to seek work in Victoria's rural areas, often in isolated localities. There was not the multicultural diversity and tolerance that came to characterise postwar Melbourne, nor did they have the assistance of chaplains, the Italian Assistance Association, and a large, supportive, Italian community.

There are many touching images in the short stories of each of these admirable settlers, illustrating the hardships overcome and the satisfaction of acceptance and success.

One of the most interesting insights for the current age, in which international travel is invariably completed in less than twenty four hours, is the picture of the long-drawn-out sea voyage of some six weeks. Hardworking adults were unaccustomed to such leisure and complained of the boredom and endless card games. For the children it would have been otherwise for, as a seven year-old, I travelled the same route on a similar ship in 1938 and found it fascinating, with so many parts of the ship to pry into and so many colourful ports of call.

For some there will be much nostalgia reawakened by this book, and for all there will be a valuable treasure trove of insights into the minds of an interesting group of settlers. This book bears witness to much care and affection in the way it has been prepared and its portrayal of a very human story.

Sir James Gobbo
Italian Historical Society — Co. As. It.
Melbourne

The Hon. Sir James Gobbo (b. 1931) served as a Judge of the Supreme Court of Victoria from 1978 to 1994 and as Governor of Victoria from 1997 to 2000, among his many illustrious achievements. Since 2001 he has acted as Commissioner for Italy in the Department of State and Regional Development of Victoria. He also holds the Gran Croce dell'Ordine al Merito della Repubblica Italiana (Grand Cross of the Order of Merit of the Republic of Italy). Apart from his patronage of the Italian Historical Society, he has a personal connection with the events depicted in this book: his father, Antonio, acted as best man at the wedding of passenger nineteen, Angelo Menegazzo, who would later become Sir James's godfather. Angelo Menegazzo, Sir James's parents and his elder brother Flavio all feature in a photograph included in the book.

INTRODUCTION

ONE SATURDAY AFTERNOON late in October 1997, I sat down at the kitchen table and cast my eyes once again over a passenger list I had first perused three years earlier. This list carried the names of the 110 men, women and children who disembarked from the steamship *Re d'Italia* (*King of Italy*) in Melbourne on the afternoon of Thursday, 24 November 1927.

Little did I realise that this simple act would set me on a five-year search to determine what had become of the old steamship's inhabitants in the seven decades since their forty-six day voyage from Genoa ended at 19 North Wharf, Victoria Dock.

I already knew what had become of my grandfather and his two brothers. Although my grandfather had died a number of years earlier, my great-uncle Igino (Nino) De Bolfo was still alive when I became interested in their experiences. In fact, it was Nino's vivid recollections of their journey and new lives in Australia that had compelled me to seek out the passenger list of the *Re d'Italia* at the Australian Archives' Melbourne office in the first place, back in 1994.

Although I had known that the three De Bolfo brothers were passengers on this ship and would naturally be on this list, actually seeing their names beautifully handwritten in blue ink made their journey so real for me. On seeing those names, my thoughts turned to their courage, conviction and yearnings to succeed, which in turn filled me with a deep sense of pride and admiration.

Three years later, when I again held the passenger list in my hands, I thought about all those other brave men, women and children who had sought a better life in Australia.

Why did they leave, and what did they leave behind? Was this country what they had hoped for? Did their life-changing decision prove to be the right one?

It was at this point that the idea of a book began to form in my mind.

I slowly but surely worked my way through the phone book, making more and more family connections with the passengers on the list. Based on the ages given upon boarding, I already knew that most of the passengers were probably dead by now, but I was buoyed by the hope that a few of the younger passengers could still be alive, such as Giovanni Costella, who was only a boy of four when he boarded the ship in Genoa.

It wasn't until October 1997, when I telephoned a Mr F. Lanza of Gladstone Park, that I located the first surviving passenger other than my great-uncle Nino. When I asked the man who answered if he had ever heard the name Francesco Lanza, a heavily accented voice replied, 'It's me!'

I could hardly breathe. Here was not just a link with the list, but an actual passenger — someone else who could tell me their story. And all I had to do was ask. I could barely disguise my excitement as arrangements were made to meet. But it was a meeting that was never to take place, for fate played a cruel trick, as is revealed in the later pages of this book.

My search for these passengers and their descendants has allowed me to forge great friendships, as we have all shared wonderful memories of another time — a time of great hope underscored by political unrest, warfare, economic hardship and racism. For me, these stories have highlighted the strength and courage of ordinary men and women, and have proved over and over again that everybody has a story to tell.

My research has unearthed stories dotted with triumph and tragedy. Some passengers became murderers or murder victims; others had Mafia connections, or were Fascists or anti-Fascists. But the *Re d'Italia* also ferried farmers and fishermen, musicians and craftsmen, philanderers and great family men — all of whom sacrificed everything for a better life so far away.

The search has taken me around metropolitan Melbourne and Victoria — including Drysdale, where I searched for and eventually found a passenger's grave whilst on my honeymoon! — and on to Sydney, then to Europe and the United States. I have made countless domestic and international phone calls — to anywhere and everywhere from Bunyip to Bari, Archie's Creek to Buenos Aires and Phillip Island to Philadelphia.

It is my greatest hope that this book will inspire others to look at their own family histories and come to understand and value the choices made by their own relatives. If my experience has taught me anything, it's that when a person dies an encyclopaedia of information dies with them.

The life stories of all 110 passengers (including Anselmo Sist and Carmelo Spadaro, who actually disembarked in the respective ports of Adelaide and Sydney) are documented in the same order in which they appeared on the original list. These 110 passengers are only a handful of the countless thousands of migrants who set foot in Australia in search of a better life. Maybe their stories are, in part, indicative of and similar to the experiences of each and every new Australian who has ever called this great country home.

Perhaps this book will encourage people to tell their own stories and ask others about theirs.

Tony De Bolfo
Melbourne, November 2002

Ho Gesù fateci buon tempo,
Nessun vento fate soffiare,
Tenete alle catene
Ogni momento i venti
Che colpiscono il mare.

Oh Jesus, give us fine weather,
Let no wind blow,
Keep chained
Every moment those winds
That beat upon the sea.

—Michele Pisa's prayer, as the *Re d'Italia* departed from his native Messina for Melbourne, 14 October 1927.

CHAPTER ONE

Last Respects

AT EIGHTEEN MINUTES past eight on the night of Monday, 14 January 2002, the telephone rang at my Preston home. While it was always a pleasure to talk to Amalia Salent, something in her voice suggested all was not well.

'Hello, Tony?' she said. 'I'm afraid I've got some terrible news. Dad died last night.'

Ampelio Acquasaliente (Salent) was dead at age ninety-seven. The news stunned me, as much because of its timing as its magnitude. Just twenty days earlier, on Christmas Eve 2001, my great-uncle Igino De Bolfo had passed away at ninety.

In the time it took to celebrate a Christmas and usher in a New Year, the dual living links to my search had gone. Ampelio and Igino were the last surviving members of the core of 108 men, women and children who had disembarked from the *Re d'Italia* on a November afternoon in 1927. They were my final living ties to a story that had tantalised me for eight years, a tale of late-night phone calls, cemetery visits, archival searches and country drives — even a pilgrimage back to Italy, where the story began. All in the quest to unravel the stories behind the pioneers of seventy-five years past.

While the search could often be as satisfying as the discovery, there was no thrill to match the unveiling of a passenger's path in his new land, or, indeed, his return to the mother country. Finally, as soon as I had them all, they were gone.

At St Patrick's Roman Catholic Church in the eastern Melbourne suburb of Murrumbeena, my great-uncle Igino's memory had been honoured by the R.S.L. with the playing of the last post. This was because he had served his adopted country in Borneo and New Guinea during the Second World War. I remember once asking Igino why he enlisted and he simply replied, 'Australia gave me a chance. I wanted to repay the faith it had in me.'

During the funeral service, my first-born son, Carlo, at that time five months old, broke the silence with his intermittent giggles and grunts. Carlo's playful noises were not lost on Igino's wife Armida, his son Peter and his daughters Joan and Susan. As Susan said afterwards, 'Dad would have loved that, because he loved children. Whenever he came to this church in the past he always made a point of sitting behind a baby, and by the end of the service he'd be cradling the baby in his arms.'

Igino's death had prompted me to call Amalia Salent in Sydney. Three weeks later it was her task to convey the sad tidings about her father.

I wanted to be there to pay my last respects, so I pledged my attendance at Ampelio's funeral at St Patrick's Roman Catholic Church in the Sydney suburb of Kogarah, not far from the Salent family home. That Friday morning, the 18th, found me on a flight to Sydney, and a short cab ride through Sydney's suburbs took me to St Patrick's.

One of Amalia's cousins, Anne, greeted me and — to my surprise — comforted me, and it was only then that the reality of it all hit home. Not only had a great, honourable man been taken from our midst; with Ampelio's passing came a close to the great journey undertaken by those passengers who bravely ventured down the gangway all those years ago.

Anne had asked if I would like to act as one of the pallbearers. While it would have been an honour, I politely declined, for the emotion of the occasion had bettered me. Anne then handed me a small white envelope that contained a bereavement card bearing a photograph of a beaming Ampelio, plus the following inscription that, in seven simple lines, somehow said all there was to know about him:

Una parola cara
Aveva per tutti.
È morto come ha vissuto,
Amando tutti.
Il suo sorriso allegro,
Il suo cuore d'oro,
La persona più cara
Di questo mondo.

A kind word for everyone,
He died as he lived.
Everyone's friend.
His cheerful smile,
His heart of gold,
The dearest person
This world could hold.

The back of the card carried an image of a ship on the seas, its sails adorned with a cross, surely escorting Ampelio on his final journey home.

Amalia's brother, John, fulfilled the difficult task of delivering the eulogy. John told the gathering that whether you had known Ampelio for a lifetime or for a brief period, you could not be left untouched by the kindness of the man, a sentiment that certainly rang true to me. But, he stressed, there were three people most affected of all: himself, Amalia and their mother, Rosa, Ampelio's wife of forty-seven years, with whom he had never had so much as an argument.

I stood six rows back as Ampelio's coffin went by. The symbolism of it all proved particularly painful, for I knew that here and now an era was ending before my very eyes, that the last of the 'Kings of Italy' had now completed the longest journey of all. His journey had embraced two World Wars, the Great Depression, the introduction of the talking movie and the television and man's first tentative step on the moon. And through his eyes, the old world and the new had become one.

Following Ampelio's burial, family and friends returned to his home in Rockdale. Soon afterwards, I had a flight to catch, and bid them a sad farewell.

'How's your little boy Carlo?' asked Rosa, as we prepared to part.

'He's well,' I responded.

She smiled, and led me to a small colour photograph in a nearby cabinet. It was a picture I had mailed some months before of myself cradling Carlo, who was proudly modelling the little jump suit Ampelio and his family had sent as a celebration of his birth in July 2001. Such was the warmth of this family, who had recognised my passion for Ampelio's story and repaid me many times over.

It was an ingredient common to all 108 chains of descendants, each family proud and eager to celebrate their roots and, in some cases, discover them for the first time. Slowly their connections to the past grew, link by link, through uncaptioned pictures, stories related by grandchildren, letters from Italy in broken but proud English, birth and death certificates — bookending lives not so remarkable on face value, but lives that reconfirmed the basic thread that bound them all together: the fact that everyone has a story to tell.

Take, for example, the first telephone conversation I had with Ampelio. To his astonishment, I addressed him by his surname of birth, 'Acquasaliente', a title he had not heard for forty-odd years since shortening his name by deed poll.

Nor shall I ever forget our first meeting, when I presented him with the passenger list and his nomination form for admission into his new country. They were accompanied by a photograph of the *Re d'Italia*, which later took pride of place on the wall facing him when he dined. 'All the time I look up there and see the old ship — the *Re d'Italia*,' he later enthused.

On Ampelio's ninety-seventh birthday the previous April, I had stopped in to surprise him with the small gift of a navy-blue sleeveless jumper, which he proudly donned. The bespectacled man with the deep voice responded with that trademark smile of approval.

Sadly, it is a smile that will beam no more.

Una parola cara
aveva per tutti.
È morto come ha vissuto
amando tutti.
Il suo sorriso allegro.
Il suo cuore d'oro.
La persona più cara
di questo mondo.

A kind word for everyone,
he died as he lived.
Everyone's friend.
His cheerful smile.
His heart of gold,
the dearest person
this world could hold.

Ampelio Salent
(Acquasaliente)

Nato a Sarbarro di Sant Ulderico
(Trento-Italia)
il 4 Aprile 1904
Deceduto a Sydney (Australia)
il 13 Gennaio 2002

Lascia nel profondo dolore la moglie
Rosa, I figli John ed Amalia, la nuora
Christine, I nipoti Sarah, Elizabeth,
Kathy, Alex e Michael, parenti
ed amici tutti vicini e lontani.

The kindness of our friends who
shared our sorrow, has comforted
and sustained us in the loss of one
so dear and we thank you sincerely
for your expressions of sympathy.

Never was a truer word said of Ampelio than what was spelled out on his funeral card. Fittingly, the back of the card carried an image of a blessed ship, taking the old man on the final journey home.

BEREAVEMENT CARD COURTESY OF THE AUTHOR.

CHAPTER TWO

Recollections

I HAVE LIVED all of my life in Melbourne. My formative years were, for the most part, typically Australian. Unlike some of the Italian kids in primary school, such as Joey Nardella or Enrico 'Fatty' Fisacaro, I somehow escaped most of the racial taunts. I felt 'Aussie' in the Anglo-Saxon sense. And yet my Italian-sounding surname has always somehow connected me with another place and another time, even if the 'where' and 'when' of my link with Italy took me more than thirty years to truly identify.

Regrettably, I cannot speak Italian. *Pizza*, *pasta* and *cassata* are familiar enough words, but put that down to a ravenous appetite rather than any linguistic ability. Surnames like Barassi, Silvagni, DiPierdomenico and Liberatore all roll off the tongue too, but as any self-respecting supporter will tell you, these are as firmly entrenched in the Australian Rules football vernacular as Whitten, Nicholls and Matthews.

I have often wondered why my father, John, didn't teach me the fundamentals of Italian. Maybe Dad didn't see the need, particularly since my mother, Maureen, was not Italian. Plus, we lived in the tree-lined streets of the Garden State rather than the romantic canals of old Venice.

In any event, Dad was born in Melbourne too, a year after his father, Silvio De Bolfo, and mother, Maria (née Cincotta), married in the northern Victorian country town of Kerang. For whatever reason, Dad did not converse with his parents in Italian, quite probably because Silvio and Maria were speakers of vastly different northern and southern Italian dialects and English was seen as the only means of assimilation into the Australian way of life. Silvio De Bolfo hailed from a tiny town in northern Italy's majestic Dolomites, called San Nicolò, where he was born 100 years ago, on 18 June 1902. His future wife, Maria Cincotta, was born on the Aeolian island of Filicudi in 1915, but at just six years of age she left the island with her mother and sister, never to return. In fact, her only memory of life on Filicudi was of gathering periwinkles from the island's shores to eat.

The tiny towns from which Silvio and Maria hailed were separated by the length of Italy, which made for what might be construed as a 'mixed marriage' within the Italian community. But fate brought the new Australians together in St Kilda around 1934, then they married in 1935 and their only son, John, was born in Caulfield the following year.

Although his parents Silvio and Maria conversed in English, Dad disciplined himself to learn the Italian language anyway — motivated by a serious need to communicate with an old Italian lady living next door. The lady had no command of English, but was a dab hand at making *crostoli*, and the little kid with the big appetite loved those sugar-sweet, melt-in-the-mouth pastries. Still does.

MUM AND DAD met at the Heidelberg Town Hall, a popular dance venue where many matches were made. The meeting occurred between the barn dance and the foxtrot (only joking!) on the Monday night of the Queen's Birthday long weekend in 1959. The day before, Mum had spotted Dad at the Holy Spirit Church in Thornbury, and had been particularly taken with the cut of his overcoat as she sat behind him. On the night of the dance Dad said to Mum, 'I know you, you were sitting behind me in church yesterday!'

Dad was working as a teller in the English, Scottish & Australian Bank Limited (now the A.N.Z.) opposite the Victoria Market in Victoria Street, North Melbourne, when Mum gave birth to me in East Melbourne's since-demolished St Vincent's Maternity Hospital on 16 February 1962. My brother Paul was born the following year, then came Greg in 1970 and

Richard in 1972. We were blessed with two wonderful parents who loved us very much, which means that our memories of childhood are happy ones, often rekindled through the flickering Super 8 film reels of our old movie projector.

Our house was built on a block fronting a relatively quiet thoroughfare, but by 1979, when the traffic had finally taken over, Mum and Dad thought it in everyone's interest for the family to relocate to the more tranquil environs of Heidelberg, where Roberts, McCubbin and Condor once set up their easels.

Heidelberg's vast parkland would be the envy of most local municipalities, and it was here, at a local sports ground known as Warringal Park, that my younger brother Paul and I saw out the light on most weekday afternoons. After school we'd both converge on the park proudly sporting our navy blue Carlton jumpers — Paul with the number two of John Nicholls on his back, yours truly with Alex Jesaulenko's number twenty-five — and we'd partake in epic battles of footy with the other kids in the neighbourhood.

The influence of my grandfather on me can be seen in many ways. For example, the significance of the Carlton Football Club in my life — and indeed the lives of my father and three younger brothers — is his legacy, since he became an Australian Rules football 'convert' seven decades ago.

Silvio, so the story goes, had only just taken up lodgings in an old boarding house in Canning Street upon arriving in the country when an acquaintance encouraged him to make the short walk to the Princes Park ground to see old-time Carlton footballers like 'Soapy' Vallence and 'Mocca' Johnson sporting the navy blue.

Silvio might have been weaned on Italian soccer, but by the time he filed out of Princes Park on that particular afternoon around 1930, he had lost interest in the round ball forever. As he completed the short walk back to Canning Street my grandfather became convinced that what he had just seen was the greatest game in the world.

A measure of Silvio's love for both Carlton and his grandchildren was seen in 1971, after my father decided that Paul and I were old enough to accompany him and our *nonno* (grandfather) to Princes Park. Silvio, a cabinetmaker whose skills had been honed back in the days of his apprenticeship in San Nicolò, fashioned a small collapsible stool of long-lasting Baltic pine. That stool remains a treasured heirloom in the family, for it was on that stool, at a game between Carlton and Geelong in '71, that Paul and I first took our place on the terraces.

Suddenly you are head and shoulders above the crowd, watching luminaries of the game like Nicholls, Silvagni, Jesaulenko and Jackson strutting their stuff on the 'field of dreams'. That first game is a moment I will never forget. Likewise the 1972 Grand Final — my first Grand Final — when three generations of the De Bolfo family filed into the Melbourne Cricket Ground to see the Carlton players turn on a display of near-perfect football, appropriately enough against arch-rival Richmond.

At one point during the second quarter of the Grand Final, when 'Big Nick', Robert Walls and 'Jezza' were turning it on for the Blues, Nonno advised my wildly animated father to 'Sit down and act your age.' Dad was thirty-six at the time, and the incident goes a long way towards explaining what this great game can do to you!

Silvio's immense passion for the Carlton Football Club rubbed off on all of us, including Mum, even though she had no say in the matter. I can admit now that my allegiance to the Blues somewhat tainted my objectivity in a ten-year career as a football writer with the *Herald Sun* newspaper, for not once did I tip against the Blues. How could I? Those years with the newspaper enabled me to fulfil a boyhood dream of being involved with Australian Rules football in some capacity, even if a severe lack of on-field ability prevented me from ever taking to the field myself.

IF SATURDAYS WITH Silvio at Princes Park served as a reminder of another time and place, then so too did Sundays at his home in Raglan Street, Preston. Every second or third Sunday the family would have lunch with Nanna and Nonno, who would take up most of the morning preparing the meal. We used to laugh at their idle banter, when funny-sounding words like '*polpette*' (meatballs) and '*sugo*' (sauce) caught our ears. But how sweet the *polpette* in *sugo* tasted, and the delectable *gnocchi* that Silvio would roll and cut before our eyes — to be followed by Nanna's mandatory rice pudding, which usually completed the feast.

Nonno was an expert cook, the legacy of his years back home in Italy. As his mother had always been preoccupied with running the family bakery in San Nicolò, he was left to prepare dishes of *gnocchi*, *ravioli* and *polenta* for the family, and I've never tasted roast chicken and rabbit like he used to make.

Nonno's specialty was a hearty dish called *'canederli'*, unique to the northern Italian region from which he hailed. *Canederli* basically comprise pieces of bread, salami and beef, all bound together with egg yolk and parmesan cheese to form dumplings, which are poached in a rich, clear, beefy soup or broth, known as *'brodo'*.

I quickly came to appreciate Nonno's cooking as the stuff of legend, just as my father had found it in his childhood — once to his own detriment, as he revealed to me:

> Dad put up a magnificent pigeon loft behind the garage of the family home at Raglan Street, Preston, which prompted me to start collecting pigeons. After a while I was developing quite an impressive collection, swapping plain ones for those with white wings, real beauties. But at some point I remember saying to my father, 'My pigeons are going missing', and it wasn't until I found out what I'd been eating with my polenta for tea that the penny finally dropped and my appetite suddenly waned!

Sharing the collapsible Baltic pine stool's heirloom status is the 1962 E.K. Holden sedan, registration number HOT 377. The E.K., with its maroon-coloured body, white rounded roof, big bench seats and distinctive tailfins, was bought as new by Silvio in 1962. It was lovingly maintained by Nonno until a stroke cut him down around 1975. The stroke, suffered by Silvio one day while his younger brother Igino was visiting him at his Preston home, adversely affected his speech, left him paralysed down one side and forced a change in lifestyle, including an end to his driving days. Coincidentally, I was nearing my eighteenth birthday at the time, and Nonno thought it best to pass on his pride and joy to his oldest grandson. The car sat unused in his garage until I had obtained my licence. It was early in 1980 when I took the keys — remarkably, the old Holden had covered just 18,000 kilometres in eighteen years. It is now in the possession of my youngest brother Richard, and is going strong and still in mint condition.

That E.K. has provided me with some of my most enduring memories — of taxiing schoolmates to class in my H.S.C. year, of late nights at the drive-ins, and of memorable road trips to coastal towns like Anglesea and Barwon Heads. And of the short drive from the Austin Hospital, having just bid a final farewell to my dying grandfather, on the afternoon of 29 April 1981. A one- or two-kilometre journey, and easily the most difficult of my life.

At the time of Nonno's death I was barely a year out of school. His passing had a dramatic impact upon me, for it was the first time I had experienced the pain of losing a very close loved one. Silvio De Bolfo was seventy-eight when he died, having survived his older brother, Benedetto, by one year.

Benedetto, who died in Melbourne's St Vincent's Hospital on 28 April 1980, came to Australia alone, disembarking from the steamship *Palermo* in Melbourne on 20 May 1927. A third brother, Francesco, died at his home in West Brunswick on 10 August 1987, leaving Igino, then ninety, as the sole surviving brother in Australia. (The last surviving siblings — younger brother Andrea, now ninety, and sister Anna, eighty-eight — are still living in San Nicolò.)

I will speak more of Igino a little later, but for the moment here are a few observations about Francesco and Benedetto.

I didn't see a lot of Uncle Frank over the years, but I do recall seeing him at quite an advanced age in his three-piece suit peddling his push-bike down Royal Parade. Francesco spent most of his working life on the Melbourne waterfront and married a lovely lady named Alba, whom he met in a boarding house in Fitzroy managed by her mother.

Uncle Frank and Aunty Alba had four children — Frances, Benedict, Anne and Gina — all of whom were raised in the family home in West Brunswick. Frank lived in the house until his death.

Benedetto — Uncle Ben, as my younger brothers Paul, Greg and Richard and I fondly knew him — was a bachelor all his life. It was he who acted as guarantor of work and lodgings to Silvio, Francesco and Igino in 1927, when the four brothers were reunited in Melbourne. In the years prior to the Second World War, Ben, Silvio, Frank and Nino ran a fish shop in Koornang Road, Carnegie. Ben later settled in Werribee. He lived in a little cottage by the pier at Werribee South, where he fished for flounder.

Following the War Uncle Ben moved from farm to farm, and it was on a property at Newstead that my first memories of the man were forged. Though doubled over through a back injury suffered in his early years, which left him with a pronounced limp and a walking stick, Uncle Ben worked and cleared land, first at Werribee, then Toolangi and Newstead.

Uncle Ben used to wear braces to hold up his old baggy shorts, got around in gum boots with their toes cut out and always smoked a pipe jam-packed with aromatic Havelock tobacco. His sinewy biceps, with their bulging veins almost bursting through the skin, were a testament to the limits to which Uncle Ben pushed his body. There was little time for personal luxuries, although he always had a library book handy. He was a hard-working man with a heart of gold, boasting little in the way of treasured possessions, and what money he had was always given to charity. For example, when Uncle Ben learnt that a new church was being erected not far from his home town of San Nicolò, he forwarded regular donations to be put towards the building of the bell tower.

One day in the early 1970s, during his time in his little cottage in Newstead, Uncle Ben was found by the local priest face up on the kitchen floor and in a great deal of pain. He was quickly whisked away by ambulance to nearby Maldon Hospital, where doctors confirmed pneumonia. By the time my father and grandfather got there, Uncle Ben was given little hope of pulling through. He pulled through all right, just enough to discharge himself from hospital and drive off in his old Falcon ute — only to lose control and hit a lamppost on the way home! He survived the accident, but knew he was nearing the end. He even wrote a letter to my father and mother, requesting that he be admitted to a home for the elderly.

Dad then asked Uncle Ben if he might be interested in taking up lodgings in a bungalow on the family's five-acre (two-hectare) bushland property at Hoddles Creek, barely an hour's drive from Melbourne. Dad had expected the proposal to fall on deaf ears, for this was a man who had lived alone most of his life. But to his great surprise and delight, Uncle Ben graciously accepted — on the proviso that he be allowed to build a small tin shed around the wood-fired stove that would accompany him from his Newstead cottage kitchen.

Uncle Ben slept in the bungalow, but spent most of his waking hours in the shed, which was barely a quarter of the size of your standard single bedroom. This was Uncle Ben's inner sanctum, for it was here — when not clearing the Hoddles Creek property of its fallen logs — that he could cook his meals in the old oven, listen to the world news on his mantelpiece radio, puff away on his pipe and say his prayers.

My younger brothers and I got to know Uncle Ben very well in his last few years, through the regular weekend trips we made to Hoddles Creek with Mum and Dad. Uncle Ben once tried to teach me the language of the old country and I recall the times he would hand me a notepad containing his beautifully handwritten letters of the Italian alphabet, which I used to recite to him.

Uncle Ben used to put his wood-fired stove to excellent use. He would lovingly prepare thick slabs of toasted bread, which he'd smother in home-made apricot jam for us — providing, of course, that we assured him we had helped Mum and Dad with the timber clearing on the property. On one particular occasion my youngest brother, Richard, approached the tiny shed seeking one of Uncle Ben's tasty morsels, but when the little fellow was forced to admit he hadn't helped with the timber clearing, Uncle Ben promptly bellowed, 'Richard! No work, no toast!' Uncle Ben sent him away with nothing. Richard was four years old at the time.

Every second or third Sunday at Hoddles Creek, a car would pull up in the driveway and four solidly built, elderly men — all wearing three-piece suits and fedora hats — would emerge. They were Uncle Ben's younger brothers Silvio, Francesco and Igino, along with Andrea Mattea (Uncle Andy), Uncle Ben's first cousin and a great friend from the San Nicolò years.

The four men would walk down to Uncle Ben's shed and knock at the door. Uncle Ben would invariably take one, two or even three brothers to task over some trivial issue, and Andy — as gentle a man as there ever was — did not escape his wrath either. But while Uncle Ben might have been stubborn and rigid in his thinking, he never bore a grudge and was forever grateful to see the four visitors. The men would take off their fedoras, pull up timber fruit boxes by the doorway of Uncle Ben's shed and sit there for an hour or two talking about times long gone.

While Uncle Frank is buried in Fawkner Cemetery, Uncle Ben, Nonno and Uncle Andy are all buried within close proximity of each other in Springvale. Following Uncle Ben's funeral, the cross on his casket was given to the surviving brother, Igino, and later taken back to San Nicolò by their sister-in-law, Rita, who visited Australia in 1995. Rita positioned the cross in a roadside shrine about 100 metres from where Uncle Ben was born.

Rita's husband was Gilberto (Bert) De Bolfo, who was reunited with his brothers in Melbourne when he disembarked from the *Esquilino* in 1937. As Bert did not become naturalised, he was interned as an enemy alien in the Victorian timber town of Trentham during the Second World War. Bert returned to San Nicolò five days before his mother died, in 1947. He returned to Australia not long afterwards, but in 1952 again went back to Italy. He later married Rita, whom he had known since childhood, and remained in San Nicolò with her until his death in 1994.

As close as I was to my grandfather and to Uncle Ben, never once did I think to ask either of them about the old days. About why they all left their home town, never to return. Maybe I was too young to understand or appreciate what they must have gone through to start afresh in this sunburnt country.

It wasn't until 1994, with Benedetto, Silvio and Francesco all departed and Igino the only surviving sibling, that any urgency to record their stories became apparent to me. All I can say is that it suddenly dawned on me that Igino was the last of the brothers to have embarked on that journey and I was horrified by the reality that I did not know their story — why they left, what they were leaving behind and what they were coming to. I also felt some sort of moral obligation, not only for my own peace of mind, but also for future generations of the De Bolfo family, who would otherwise never know these precious gems of family history.

I called Igino — affectionately known as 'Uncle Nino' to his family, and as 'Jim' to his friends at the local bowling club — to be greeted by his beloved wife, Armida. Aunty Armida, who had herself migrated to Australia from Italy under trying circumstances, said Nino would be happy to talk about the brothers' epic voyage.

And so, on the afternoon of Friday, 13 May 1994, I drove to the family home in Melbourne's southeast, equipped with a tape recorder and a multitude of questions. The subsequent interview with Uncle Nino would act as the catalyst for this long-term project, which has ultimately had a marked impact on my life. Uncle Nino, then eighty-three, was only a boy when he, Silvio and Francesco boarded the steamship *Re d'Italia*. While I am sure that he would have passed on the stories of the past to his children Joan, Peter and Susan, I had never heard them before.

For me, Uncle Nino's stories were revelations.

The son of Giovanni Battista De Bolfo and Giovanna Zandonella, Igino was the fourth of eight children to survive into adulthood. The others were Benedetto, Silvio, Francesco, Gilberto, Andrea, Anna and Cornelio. Within a twenty-year time frame, Giovanna gave birth to thirteen children in all, including two sets of twins. The twins — Teresa and Andrea, Lino and Andrea — all died after a few months. Another girl, Linda, died four months short of her second birthday. Cornelio, the youngest child, lived to adulthood but died of peritonitis in Sicily at the outbreak of the Second World War in 1939. On Cornelio's death, his grieving parents instructed Andrea to venture south to retrieve his body for a proper home burial.

San Nicolò is a tiny town populated by just a few hundred people, nestled amongst the imposing snow-capped peaks of the Dolomites, not far from the Austrian border in the Veneto region of northern Italy. It was here that Giovanni and Giovanna ran a bakery from the basement of their imposing three-storey stone-walled home, which was built early last century and divided equally between the families of Giovanni and his brother, Valentino.

Towards the end of the First World War, when the Austrian soldiers were advancing across the northern Italian border, Giovanni's boys were instructed to hide the family cow in a camouflaged shed high up in the mountains to prevent what was virtually their only food source from being confiscated. Day after day the brothers trekked miles across the mountains, risking their lives amid the volley of gunshots to milk the cow.

The bakery was eventually taken over by the Italian army and used day and night to bake for a nearby barracks, while the front room of the house was used as an officers' mess and the kitchen to prepare meals for the officers. While Giovanni grew vegetables, tended the cow and chopped down trees (each of the original families in the region had an allotment), Giovanna somehow had to fend for her sizeable family, and at the same time work in the bakery for the army. She would start at one in the morning and work eighteen- to twenty-hour days. Such sacrifice was enormous, and yet the matriarch was always there to offer free bread to those less fortunate. (Giovanna's generosity and good-hearted nature were not lost on the town of San Nicolò, who turned out in droves for her funeral when she died on 19 December 1947.)

There was little relief for Giovanni, Giovanna and the eight children in the between-war years either. Towards the end of the 1920s, Italy was drawn into the worldwide economic downward spiral, ending with the Great Depression. At the same time, the Blackshirts and their menacing ideologies were also holding sway under the dictatorship of Benito Mussolini. The depth of support for 'Il Duce' during this period was encapsulated by Vahda Jeanne Bordeaux, in her preface to *Benito Mussolini — The Man*: 'He it is who is modernising Italy, making her grander day by day: clean, orderly, prosperous.'

Benedetto, Silvio, Francesco and Igino would not be part of this envisaged prosperity. For them, prosperity could only be afforded to their parents if there were fewer mouths to feed. Silvio, with his socialist sympathies, probably wanted out anyway. For them, prosperity beckoned in a faraway land — but unlike so many of their compatriots, fate would have them follow the light of the Southern Cross rather than the beam of the Statue of Liberty's beacon.

Silvio was twenty-five years of age, Francesco twenty-four and Igino just sixteen when, amid a climate of increasing tumult and instability, they embarked on their long and arduous voyage from Italy to Australia. They had resolved that the best course of action was to follow in the footsteps of the older Benedetto. On the day they were to leave their home forever, the brothers' belongings were packed into three pine trunks, all handmade by Silvio. A fourth trunk exceeded the ship's size regulations and still sits in the attic of the old family home in San Nicolò. The other trunks survive in Melbourne, a testament to Silvio's workmanship and the hardy, slow-growing Alpine pines used in their construction.

Those three trunks were taken away by truck as the boys headed off on foot towards the neighbouring town of Santo Stefano on their journey to the port of Genoa. Their beloved mother, Giovanna, left behind with their father and the remaining five De Bolfo children, was stricken with grief as she watched her boys walk down the road, rightly sensing that she would never see them again.

'Mum broke down very badly. It was tough, very tough,' Uncle Nino told me. 'I was like that [*crosses fingers*] with my dad and mum, and I broke down very badly too ... the first thing you do when you leave home is say, "I'll see you in twelve months' time" ... [but] it was tough, very tough. I was sixteen at the time and I cried ... I suppose I got to Belluno [about 60 kilometres away] before I stopped.'

At Genoa, the brothers boarded a crude twin-screw (double-propeller) steamer, the SS *Re d'Italia*. They were just three of the 523 emigrants (506 Italians, one Austrian and sixteen Greeks) who boarded the ship at the three key Italian ports — Genoa, Naples and Messina — for what proved a horrific seven-week ordeal at sea.

The tired old vessel trudged its way through the Tyrrhenian and Mediterranean Seas, the Suez Canal, the Red and Arabian Seas, and the Indian Ocean. It pulled in at the ports of Port Said (in Egypt), Suez (the port of what is now South Yemen), Colombo (capital of what is now Sri Lanka), Fremantle, Adelaide, Melbourne and finally Sydney. Card games on deck were the only activity to help passengers pass the time, and they also had to contend with warm drinking water and rancid food. Little wonder Uncle Nino, to the day he died, saw the whole experience as 'a terrible blot' on the record of his life.

'We were lucky, because Dad gave Silvio a little bit of money — 50,000 *lire* each — in case of need, which we put towards a cabin for four on the ship, sharing with another fellow from Torino, whose name I can't remember. But others slept on the floor, with about fifty or sixty in each area ... and they'd sit there all day and play cards. Nothing to do, nothing to do.'

Uncle Nino remembered that the *Re d'Italia* and its human cargo completed the arduous trip in forty-six days. On Thursday, 24 November the now-defunct Melbourne evening newspaper the *Herald*, briefly reported the ship's impending arrival as follows:

> *Re d'Italia* (W. Heale), is due to berth at 19 North Wharf at 4.00 p.m. today with passengers, including migrants, and general cargo from Southern European ports. She will continue her voyage to Sydney on Monday.

The *Re d'Italia* berthed at Victoria Dock, but there was no-one to greet Silvio, Francesco and Igino as the young men took their first few steps down the battered gangway, not even brother Ben. With Ben working day and night in a North Melbourne bakery, and Andy hard at work in a fish shop in Bridge Road, Richmond, neither was able to greet the worn-out trio.

This was a real worry for the three De Bolfos, who also had to contend with the vitriol heaped on them from striking members of the Waterside Workers' Union 'welcoming committee'. Unbeknown to the brothers, the workers were off the job as a result of a long-running dispute with the Commonwealth Steamship Owners' Association, and so treated incoming migrant 'scabs' with unbridled scorn. Thankfully a fellow passenger, Giuseppe Bosa, who had previously spent some time abroad, was on hand, as Uncle Nino explained to me.

'We came to know Bosa through Silvio, who was in the Italian grenadier guards with this fellow and who stuck with him all the time. When we got to Victoria Dock they put our three chests out on the wharf. Bosa had been to America and knew a bit of English, so he arranged for a horse and cart, which took us up Flinders Street, along Bridge Road and out to Ozzie's place. And that was the last time we brothers were together for a long time.'

I left Uncle Nino's home that day deeply touched by what I had heard. His recollections of life in years past only served to deepen my interest in my heritage, and I wanted to discover more about the voyage.

Perhaps it was also at this point that I really began to utilise and hone whatever journalistic skills I had. By the time of my important get-together with Uncle Nino in 1994 I had already spent fourteen years working as a sports writer. I was one whose brief was confined to reporting injured knees, hamstrings and the like. Accordingly, my interest in discovering more about my origins only served to nurture a style of investigative journalism not called on before — particularly in the tabloid world, where editors can seldom afford to allow their journalists a week or three to get their teeth into a ripping yarn.

Not long after meeting with Uncle Nino, I ventured into the Melbourne Archives Centre in Casselden Place, where two very kind ladies, Lil and Doreen, assisted with my inquiry. In no time, these two women were able to locate one of a multitude of microfilms which carried the names of those passengers who disembarked from the *Re d'Italia* on 24 November, seventy-five years ago.

Lil fed the film onto the spool and turned the handle. In no time, beautifully hand-written names, including those of my grandfather and great-uncles, appeared like magic on the screen before me:

> De Bolfo Igino, carpenter, male, 16, single, Italian
> De Bolfo Francesco, upholsterer, male, 24, single, Italian
> De Bolfo Silvio, joiner, male, 25, single, Italian

Excitedly I obtained black and white print-outs of the list, which carried 110 names — two of which had been ruled out. I later learned that the deleted passengers — Anselmo Sist and Carmelo Spadaro — actually disembarked in Port Adelaide and Sydney respectively, as the *Re d'Italia* wound its way from Fremantle to Port Adelaide, Melbourne and finally the Harbour City.

My interest was in the list of 108 who disembarked in Melbourne — the 103 men (including my grandfather and two great-uncles), three women and two young boys who set foot on the jetty at 19 North Wharf, Victoria Dock.

The passenger list was an important find for me — so important, in fact, that I persuaded a friendly *Herald Sun* photographer, George Salpigtidis, to take shots of all five pages of the original inventory. Later, I locked George's prints away in a lounge-room cupboard for safekeeping, thrilled with my newly acquired souvenir.

Three years later, in October 1997, I took three weeks' holiday. I hadn't planned to go anywhere, and the days became long, as I just hung around the house. On one of those days I decided, for no particular reason, to rummage through the cupboard, only to rediscover the list I had essentially forgotten.

Armed with the list, I ventured into the kitchen and took a seat at my old timber table which, as it happened, was previously owned by Uncle Ben. I again began to cast my eye down the list of disembarkees, and once more looked with pride at the names of the three brothers De Bolfo. I then started to peer at the names of the other passengers, and for whatever reason, curiosity overcame me. I began to ask myself, 'What has happened to these other people in the seventy years since their arrival?'

Just for the sake of it I randomly selected a name, that of Ernesto Lago, the thirteenth listed passenger. I then grabbed a copy of the Melbourne *White Pages* and looked up 'Lago'. There were about a dozen listings. After three or four calls a man referred me to a lady by the name of Lina Cecchin in Werribee, who was Ernesto Lago's daughter.

I called Lina, told her who I was and asked if her father had sailed to Melbourne on the *Re d'Italia*. Lina confirmed that her father had indeed made that voyage, and told me about what became of him in the years following. She told me that, like so many of the Italians, he settled in the farming community of Werribee, toiled hard to make a living for his wife and young family, and overcame the inevitable cultural and language barriers that befall the migrant.

So inspiring was Lina's story, and so obvious her pride in her father, that I felt compelled to begin what would become my own personal odyssey: determining what became of all 110 passengers on that list.

The author with his great uncle Igino in the lounge room of Igino's house at Murrumbeena, July 1997.
PHOTO COURTESY MAUREEN DE BOLFO, HEIDELBERG, VICTORIA.

CHAPTER THREE

Italy in the 1920s

*Fascism conceives of the State as an absolute, in comparison
with which all individuals or groups are relative, only to be
conceived of in their relation to the State.*

— Benito Mussolini's definition of Fascism, *Italian Encyclopaedia*, 1932

THE YEARS IMMEDIATELY following the First World War, which were among
the most turbulent in Italian history, ushered in an overwhelming political
seachange well before the *Re d'Italia* set sail for Australia in October 1927.

Italy emerged from the Great War in a far inferior position to that in
which it had entered. The country was heavily in debt at the start of the
1920s, 460,000 soldiers had been killed in battle, and inflation was rampant.
While Italy had been promised extra land by Britain and France during the
War, this arrangement did not eventuate, and a fractured government's lack
of unity meant an absence of direction at the highest level. The public also
felt betrayed by this broken promise, believing it had received little reward
for its wartime sacrifices. These factors, when combined with rising
unemployment, ensured that the environment was ripe for major change.

Benito Mussolini established the Fascist movement in 1919 and
advertised himself as a strong leader who could solve Italy's problems.

Mussolini had returned from the First World War a disenchanted character, who saw the evolution of Fascism as Italy's only answer. Five different governments presided over Italy between 1919 and 1922.

In an atmosphere of strikes and riots, the charismatic Mussolini threatened to March on Rome with his 'army' of 300,000 followers if he were not made Prime Minister. The King of Italy, Victor Emmanuel III, a Mussolini adherent, refused to back the existing government and on 31 October 1922 invited Mussolini to become Prime Minister.

Mussolini had promised to rebuild Italy and recreate the might of the Roman Empire — precisely the emotive promise the populace had been searching for, and a precedent for Adolf Hitler's rise to power in Germany the following decade. Mussolini sought to bring order out of chaos when the liberal democratic state could not. The Fascist government used such minor achievements as making trains run on time and draining swamps to obtain support and respect for its cause.

In his newspaper, *Il Popolo d'Italia* (*The People of Italy*), founded in 1914, Mussolini carried his message to the masses. It was not surprising that in April 1924 the Fascists won sixty per cent of the votes and gained 375 seats out of 535. A trained journalist, Mussolini had read the climate perfectly and, given the usually splintered nature of Italian government, his power base was cemented by this landslide result.

While it should have been a watershed for Italy, the fallout was immediately disturbing. When the reformist socialist Giacomo Matteotti, spoke out against the Fascists, he was kidnapped and murdered. In the years that followed, Mussolini created a secret police force, the O.V.R.A., and built concentration camps on the Lipari Islands for his banished opponents.

To be anti-Fascist was to court danger.

Mussolini soon assumed dictatorial powers and dissolved rival political parties, which effectively rendered Italy a police state by 1926. He rewrote laws and, incredibly, all teachers in schools and universities had to swear an oath to defend the Fascist regime. Even newspaper editors had to be personally approved by him, such was his paranoia about projecting a consistent message to the people. A final, telling blow was the stripping of powers of the unions.

Ultimately, Mussolini strove to make Italy self-sufficient, but although he pitched his country forward with an emphasis on heavy industry, it lacked the resources to achieve this self-sufficiency. In fact, his image of a forward-thinking, industrialised country could not have been further from the reality he achieved.

'Things were tough back then, because Italy in the 1920s was not that far removed from medieval times,' Pio Bosa, son of Giuseppe Bosa (passenger forty-two), told me. 'Dad came from a poor family and had four kids to feed, and worked very hard as a coach builder. He was also anti-Fascist and saw some of his best friends get belted up, so for a number of reasons he decided to come to Australia.'

It was a common theme amongst the passengers aboard the *Re d'Italia*. They may not all have been forced from their homeland, but many had seen first-hand the oppressive nature of *Il Duce*'s reign and its consequences for their everyday lives.

No single force embodied the quantum shift in culture as much as the Blackshirts, Mussolini's organised gangs which, in some cities such as Bologna, actually assumed the role of the police force. Designed to deal with 'troublemakers' and criminals, they also broke up strikes, and the fear they struck into sectors of the general public was palpable.

One of the *Re d'Italia*'s Melbourne disembarkees, Francesco Benvenuti, attributed his departure from his home town of Udine to their presence. His great-granddaughter, Simonne, explained his ordeal in a letter to me:

> Francesco was concerned with the growing number of Blackshirts who walked the streets of Udine, and held no sympathies for them. One night at a tavern, he drank too much and began voicing his opinions and fears about the Blackshirts. At the time there were severe consequences for that sort of behaviour, but despite the fact that he knew this, Francesco didn't seem to withhold his opinion from those who were drinking with him.
>
> Nothing happened until later, at about one o'clock in the morning, when he had already returned home. Francesco was forced to hide in the attic of the house as my great-

grandmother Nicolina refused the Blackshirts entry, claiming he had not returned from the tavern. This answer did not satisfy the Blackshirt officers, and when they asked to search the house she replied, 'And what do you think the rest of the village will say when they find out strange men have entered in the middle of the night?' There were more protests, but eventually the men left, leaving Francesco undiscovered.

Soon after, Francesco collected a few of his possessions and fled Italy over the Alps, leaving behind his wife, Nicolina, and three children, Rita, Giovanni [Simonne's grandfather] and Maria. Francesco managed to get a job in Germany for a while as a brick maker and was able to support himself and send the rest of the money to his family.

Francesco's story underlines a common saying among the anti-Fascists of the time, whose oppression was forcing them into chosen exile: 'Today, what are the Italian people? Nothing. What should they be? Everything.' Had Italy's economic situation improved markedly, Mussolini's excesses might have been excused. As it was, the 'medieval', hand-to-mouth nature of existence was driving people from their homes in search of a better life.

Livio Cusinato's father, Giovanni, was also aboard the *Re d'Italia*. 'You have to remember they were poor times, and if it had been good up there [in Italy] he wouldn't have come here ... we were very hard up against it,' Livio said to me.

'I came to Australia at the age of sixteen, having worked full days for just milk and *polenta*. And what about my sisters? They worked at a silkwear factory making the silk from the worm, and they did so under the names of other eighteen-year-old girls because they were too young. There was a real famine, and that's why we all decided to get away.'

Mussolini's oppression ... the Blackshirts ... unemployment ... lack of opportunity. The combination was crippling. My own ancestors came for all of these reasons.

I discovered many years after the death of my grandfather Silvio that he was actually a member of the anti-Fascist Matteotti Club in Melbourne. I have a wonderful sepia photograph of Silvio rubbing shoulders with members of the club at a May Day rally in Melbourne in 1931. Not long before this book went to print, I visited the premises of the old club, opposite Trades Hall in Victoria Street, in the Melbourne C.B.D. The words 'Matteotti Club' are still visible in flaking paint on the outside wall, near which games of *bocce* were once played.

The hall itself is capable of holding many hundreds of people. As I cast my eyes around its walls, I tried to imagine what this place was like in the early 1930s, when the Matteotti Club was teeming with idealistic Italians like my grandfather, who waltzed to the wonderful strains of the accordion whilst defiantly wielding copies of the anarchist newspaper *La Riscossa* (*The Revolt*).

For some of the passengers of the *Re d'Italia*, the woes of the old world remained with them forever. For most, though, the new land fulfilled the fundamental *speranza* (hope) that each and every migrant harbours.

A better life.

Italian May Day rally by the Yarra River, Melbourne, circa 1931. The tall man with the white hat standing beneath the 'Workers Of The World Unite' banner is Silvio De Bolfo.

CHAPTER FOUR

The Voyage

A FLIGHT FROM Messina, Italy, to Melbourne, Australia, takes about twenty-four hours, give or take a delayed connection here or stopover there. If you're lucky you can indulge in a little shopping in Singapore or Hong Kong, and maybe catch some sleep on the final leg to Australia. The biggest hurdle might involve being held up in Customs, or sitting next to someone who snores. Or worse still — Heaven forbid — a bumpy flight and the risk of spilling that bag of peanuts in your lap.

So turn again to the front of the book and ponder Michele Pisa's words of hope as the *Re d'Italia* pulled slowly out of the port of Messina on 14 October 1927. At the same time, contemplate Michele's words of fear, which somewhat temper his aspirations:

> *Il 14 ottobre son partito*
> *La mia bella Messina ho lasciato*
> *Un gran dolor al cuor ho sentito*
> *Quando le corde al vapor hanno levato*
> *Io guardavo la città e la banchina*
> *Quando ho visto il vapor che se alontanava*
> *Mi voltai in dietro e scomparve Messina.*

On 14 October I departed
I left my beloved Messina
I could feel my heart break
As the ropes to the tug were released
I was looking at the city and the wharf
When I noticed the tug at a distance
I turned around and Messina had disappeared.

Michele died in the tiny Gippsland town of Bunyip in 1952, and it was only with the help of his descendants that I was able to obtain his writings of seventy-five years ago. In these few lines, Michele's feelings of trepidation in leaving home, never to return, emerge. They were feelings shared by the last survivors of the *Re d'Italia's* voyage of late 1927 — Annunziata Faralla (née Picone), Ampelio Salent (Acquasaliente) and my great-uncle Igino.

Only they — together, indirectly, with Giuseppe Zammarchi, who conveyed his thoughts to author Wendy Lowenstein for her book *Weevils in the Flour*, published in 1978 (later quoted in *With Courage in their Cases*) — could provide me with precious first-hand accounts of their journey aboard the old steamship.

Ships have more than personalities — they have souls. Not one of the surviving passengers I spoke to from the 1927 trip failed to remember the *Re d'Italia*, its existence having played such an important part in their lives. While ships are a conglomeration of steel and timber, powered by enormous engines and willing engineers, in truth they are often driven by the dreams of those they spirit to a new life.

So it was with the *Re d'Italia*.

Yet the passengers on that forty-six day trek were neither the first nor the last to grace her decks. She had already survived countless adventures, and faced challenges even greater than those encountered on that voyage from Italy to Australia.

The *Re d'Italia* was one of three ships, along with the *Regina d'Italia* (*Queen of Italy*) and the *Principe di Piemonte* (*Prince of Piedmont*), built by James Laing & Sons (based in the port of Sunderland in the northeast of

England), under contract to the Prince Line of Newcastle upon Tyne. The contract was then acquired by Lloyd Sabaudo Società Anonima di Navigazione of Turin. The *Regina d'Italia* sailed the oceans for twenty-one years until she was broken up in 1928. The *Principe di Piemonte* — later sold to the Cunard Line and renamed the *Folia* — was torpedoed and sunk by a German submarine off the coast of Youghal, Ireland, in March 1917, resulting in the loss of 103 lives.

Which leaves the flagship. The *Re d'Italia* had a speed of fifteen knots and was 430 feet (131 metres) in length with a beam (breadth) of fifty-two feet, eight inches (sixteen metres). She boasted two funnels and two masts and could accommodate 120 first-class and 1900 third-class passengers.

She was launched on 22 December 1906 — in the same year as the ill-fated *Lusitania* — and left Genoa on her maiden voyage, to Naples, Palermo and New York, on 6 April 1907. The *Regina d'Italia* and *Principe di Piemonte* followed her at monthly intervals on their respective maiden voyages.

In December 1908, the *Re d'Italia* served as a hospital ship at Messina in the wake of one of Europe's most powerful earthquakes, which claimed the lives of an estimated 200,000 people and devastated southern Italy. On Boxing Day 1911, she embarked on what would be a fourteen-month mission as a hospital ship during the Italo–Turkish war. Boasting thirteen medical staff and accommodation for 116 patients, the *Re d'Italia* served between Italy and Libya and evacuated 36,983 sick and wounded. Following the First World War Armistice, in April 1919, she also assisted with the transportation of American soldiers from Marseilles to New York.

In 1920 the ship was refitted to carry second- and third-class passengers only. She continued her Mediterranean Sea–New York voyages until 1922, when she began making passages to South America. On 26 October 1923 she resumed her Genoa–Naples–Palermo–New York route for one round-the-world voyage.

In 1925 the old ship transferred to the Australian migrant trade along the Genoa–Suez–Fremantle–Melbourne–Sydney route. As a direct result of the Great Depression, the *Re d'Italia* was sold and broken up for scrap in the port of Genoa in 1930.

ON 10 OCTOBER 1927, the *Re d'Italia* set sail from that very port with a billet of 523 emigrants. The tired, twenty-one year old steamer, at this point three years away from being broken down for scrap, was never designed for ferrying human cargo. In this age of jet travel — indeed, in this age of increased knowledge — there is no way to encapsulate the emotional and physical experience they endured. In 1994, Uncle Nino told me the tale of what proved a harrowing expedition for the *Re d'Italia*'s passengers:

We travelled to Genoa and spent three or four days in hostel accommodation provided by the shipping company while we completed all the necessary interviews and paperwork before our departure.

The *Re d'Italia* left Genoa and pulled in at Livorno, where she remained for four days while they loaded marble. The ship then went down to Naples and stayed there for another four days, as they loaded up with more people. The same thing happened again at Messina.

After we got out into the Mediterranean, things started to go bad. Before that, they used to look after you hand and foot — tablecloths and everything else — and you'd eat your meals and walk away. But the moment we left the coast of Italy that was the end of it. We were stripped of everything ... the rest of this story is going to take a bit of telling.

People started to complain that the food wasn't so good, and when we got into the Red Sea after stopping at Port Said, it only got worse. The water was no better. People wanted water to drink, then in the Red Sea it was hot, and they started to complain. Conditions were terrible. Shocking. Silvio, a fellow passenger, Giuseppe Bosa, and another chap from Genoa formed a committee of three, along with another three from Naples and another three from Messina. They all got together, with Mr S. De Bolfo as chairman [*laughs*], and decided that three of them (a representative from each committee) would approach this captain and hand over their respective meals — one, two, three.

The captain said, 'Who's in charge of this?' and the two others nominated my brother. So the captain took my brother up to his cabin. He went in on his own with the captain, and a big burly bloke went in and put his back against the door, as much as to say, 'You want to go out, you've got to go through me.'

Silvio turned to the captain and said, 'Captain, sir, that man does not belong here. If you don't put him out the door, I'll put him out the porthole!' The captain replied, 'Do you think you could?' and he said, 'Don't worry about it, I can!' From then on Silvio was respected, the other fellow cleared out and Silvio told the captain man to man that it wasn't right what they were doing.

The captain called out something over the loudspeaker, and when my brother came down there were demijohns of cool water out there waiting. And whenever anything went wrong, Silvio went in and worked it through.

One time there was gravy beef that smelled. Silvio got the captain and said, 'Have a look at that.' He said, 'What's wrong with it?' and my brother said, 'Smell it.' The captain smelled it and he got his fellows to throw it overboard, no trouble at all. And from then on my brother and the eight representatives were respected and we had peace.

But when we got out to Australia, pulled in at Fremantle, berthed at Adelaide then pulled in at Melbourne, not one seaman left the ship. It was there for days, but none of them left the ship, because the passengers were waiting for them. They said, 'We'll pay you back! You go out at your own risk!'

On the ship, other than cards, there was no entertainment at all. I was only a kid, and I used to walk around and poke my nose into different things. The northerners rarely mixed with the southerners. They kept to themselves, we kept to ourselves and there were no problems.

I can't remember the ship stopping at Suez, but it stopped at Aden — a very short stop. The only thing I can remember about Port Said was that there was a chap who used to come around the side of the boat, swimming, and he'd sing out for coins. So you'd throw the coins down into the water, and he'd dive under and come up with the coins. If they were silver or aluminium it was all right. If they were copper, he'd come up with the copper coins to show that he'd got them, then throw them away — they weren't what he wanted.

By the time we left Messina I was already counting the days, and by the time we got to Colombo we were only halfway. In Colombo, the port was a lagoon. In order to transfer the necessary coal for the voyage, a fleet of small boats stretched from the shore to the *Re d'Italia*. Men in each of the boats passed containers of coal from one small boat to the next until it reached the *Re d'Italia*. It took three or four days to complete this operation. During this time the passengers had access to a small boat and were able to visit the city. As the weather was very hot, we were grateful to sit under a fan and sip a cool drink. We were able to purchase fresh fruits, such as hands of bananas, from the local markets.

From Colombo to Fremantle was ten days in one little old boat. We could see English boats in the morning, twenty or thirty miles back, but by two or three o'clock in the afternoon they were twenty or thirty miles in front! I wasn't sick all the time. It only happened this side of the equator, when the weather started to get bad.

Ampelio Acquasaliente (Salent) also spoke of difficulties on the voyage from Genoa to Melbourne:

My military pay-out, coupled with the money I made from my work, covered the cost of my trip — 1500 *lire*. People talked a lot about Australia, that it was a new land with plenty of work and basically a good place to live. It was also felt that

Australia was a place where people could make a lot of money, but this was not so in the early years.

I left Italy for political reasons. Fascism was on the rise, and I didn't like the disciplines that were being placed upon me. Also, as my brothers Giovanni and Pietro were always getting into trouble with the political parties they opposed, my idea was to make the move and send for them, to escape the political unrest that was occurring.

A close friend of mine, Giuseppe Raumer, who had already left for Australia a year earlier, in 1926, had also promised to be guarantor for me on my arrival. Giuseppe's father and brother had arrived in Australia in 1923. I was very much looking forward to the trip here and the start of a new life.

Although the decision to leave my family upset me deeply, it was a decision I had to make. My mother was very sorry to see me leave for a place neither she nor I knew anything about.

Before we said goodbye, she gave me a crucifix she had received from the local priest, to ensure my safe passage. I gave her a kiss, and I brought the cross with me.

I did not say goodbye to my father. He had abandoned his family after my younger brother Pietro was born, and was living his own life without the responsibility of supporting us — which of course made it very hard on all of us, particularly my mother.

I boarded the *Re d'Italia* in Genoa, with two men I knew from a neighbouring village, Santa Caterina, whose names I do not remember. The voyage was very, very bad; the food was awful and I was sick the whole time. As everything was rationed for the long and arduous journey, we were fed a lot of soup but hardly any pasta, which was awful, and as the ship was loaded with heavy cargo there were almost no individual cabins, and my sleeping quarters comprised a very large room of thirty people or more.

The first, second and third decks of the ship contained the sleeping areas, and the bottom deck was where the cargo was placed to balance the ship. But the seas were very rough and sometimes you couldn't even eat because the *Re d'Italia* rocked so much. At one point there was an announcement made on the ship that the *Principessa Mafalda* — another Italian vessel, bound for South America — had sunk en route[1] I remember seeing the *Principessa Mafalda* docked beside the *Re d'Italia* in Genoa — she set sail an hour before we did!

We were at sea for about fifty days. One port-of-call out of Italian waters was Colombo, where a day was spent taking on water and coal for the ship. Our next ports were Fremantle, the port of Adelaide and finally the port of Melbourne. Only a few people disembarked at the other ports, with most passengers disembarking at Victoria Dock.

Most of us had spent the entire journey on deck looking out over the sea, searching for land, and we were all glad to finally see it. When the *Re d'Italia* was coming into dock I remember wondering whether it was actually going to make it through what was a very small opening in the bay.

Just before the docking, officers came around to ensure we all had enough money on us. When you arrived in Australia you had to have at least £35 or £40 to maintain yourself for one year, since the government did not have the finances to pay unemployment benefits as they do today. The officers also checked our hands, although I do not know why they did this,[2] and they provided us with a book of common English words to help us converse in the language.

I brought with me one suitcase and a trunk, which my mother had filled with lots of things. She even included a pair of shoes with nails protruding from the soles, which I had used when I went walking in the hills back home. Of course they were no good to me in Australia, and I didn't even use half the clothes she packed.

My passport allowed me to sail as far as the port of Melbourne. Once the ship had docked we all began to disembark and make for different destinations. A man walked up to me and said, 'You look lost', to which I replied, 'Everyone is either going or being met by someone, but I'm here on my own ... yes, I am lost.' I had arranged to meet Giuseppe Raumer, but unfortunately he was not there when I arrived, as he was living in Queanbeyan at the time. I ended up leaving Melbourne for Sydney and later Queensland, and it wasn't until some fourteen years later that we met up with one another. From that time on we stayed in very close touch until Giuseppe died, in March 1998.[3]

Annunziata Faralla (née Picone) was only nineteen years of age when she made the voyage from Messina to Melbourne. The majority of the *Re d'Italia*'s passengers during both war service and migrant trade duties were men; a women's experience is understandably different from that of the opposite gender.

I wasn't too sure I'd be able to come to Australia, because I never went to school and I couldn't read or write. The others all went to school and they used to say, 'You didn't go to school, you don't know what you're talking about.' So I shut up and kept quietly praying, 'God, help me.'

As soon as I left the house, everybody cried. Some of the little ones said, 'Go get her, she was good to us, where has she gone?' And my mother said, 'She's gone far away, she won't be back no more.'

An aunty in Australia sent the trip money to me, because she knew what sort of a girl I was. She reckoned I would be able to pay her back, so she gave me the fare — 5000 *lire*[4] — and for two and a half years I would work hard to pay my fare, to the last penny!

I took with me a suitcase with two pairs of sheets, a pillow and a few dresses and underwear. There were no photographs, nothing. Just the pillow, sheets and a couple of other things.

I was nineteen, I think, when I got on the ship. I was given a guardian to look after me, Nicola Bastiana — a man. But I said, 'Bugger the man, I'll look after myself. I don't want them to send anyone with me. I want to be free.' First they put me in a big room with the other people. Because of some of the things I saw, I said, 'I don't want to stay here.' And all of a sudden, one of the men in the ship came in and said, 'Who brought you to this room?' 'I don't know,' I said. But the man said, 'You come with me', and he took me straight to a cabin, with another lady with a little boy. So we sailed together.

The lady had come to find her husband. Her name was Giovannina Casella and her son was Giuseppe Famularo [passengers 101 and 102]. We came out together.

Some days were nice. We'd go out on top, have a look and see, you know. Some days the ship wobbled too much [*laughs*] and we couldn't do anything. I was sometimes sick, but for most of the time I was all right. I took some fancy work with me, and when it was a nice day I had a little chair, sat down there and did some needlework. I made some pillowcases with some nice patterns, and I still have some of them. Some people asked me for them as presents, and I made them something beautiful.

The man I've talked about worked in the kitchen. He got us some water and some bread rolls and he brought them up to us to make us happy. There was no trouble with the men and I never got mixed up with anybody in the cabins. Two or three cabins up, there was a wife with another man, you know, but I didn't have anything to do with anybody [*laughs*]. No, no, no, no, I never got mixed up with anybody in the cabins.

The ship stopped at Colombo, but I never did much because I was frightened of all the black people. I remember the lady [Giovannina Casella] telling me at Colombo, 'We'll get off', so we went for a bit of a walk, but when we saw these black men and some of the things we thought, 'Oh, we're not staying here.' In the end I think I bought a couple of bananas there. At Colombo they stopped to get some charcoal [coal] for the ship. They also stopped at Port Said to get a passenger, and that's all.

The ship landed at Victoria Dock, and there were a lot of people there — Italianos and Greeks. When I got to Victoria Dock, an uncle, Giuseppe Fonti [her sponsor, a fruiterer of 167 Acland Street, St Kilda], was there to call my name. He said, 'Are you Annunziata?' I said, 'Yes' and he asked me what I had brought with me, and I said, 'A suitcase.'

I wasn't afraid at all on the voyage — it was an adventure, the chance to do something. After a while I started to miss my mother. I thought that if I could get work, I'd go back to see her. I used to say, 'I wish I was a bird — I'd fly back.' But I never went back.

The *Re d'Italia* reached Australian shores in late 1927. The steamship was cleared by customs in Fremantle on 13 November, and eleven days later docked at the port of Melbourne, via Port Adelaide, on Thursday, 24 November 1927. There, 103 men, three women and two male children — all of whom had travelled third class — disembarked from the tired old steamer. Fifty-nine of them had boarded the ship at Genoa, eight at Naples, 40 at Messina and one at Port Said. The passengers averaged twenty-nine years and one month in age, ranging from Giovanni Costella at four years, eight months and three days, through to Vincenzo Di Gregorio, at fifty-one years, one month and two days.

Giuseppe Bosa's daughter, Pia Benetti, remembered her father once telling her that during the voyage 'a huge albatross landed on the top deck — which in Italy was either a sign of good luck or bad luck, I'm not sure'.

I have come to appreciate the open-endedness of this comment, for, as I was soon to discover, while some passengers found good fortune in their new country, others were not so lucky.

The menu onboard the *Re d'Italia* on its voyage from Italy to Australia in October and November 1927.

CHAPTER FIVE

Australia in the 1920s

The history of Australia is a chapter in the history of migration ... Seven seas may divide the migrant from his homeland, but he will never quite shake its dust from his feet.

— R.M. (Max) Crawford, O.B.E (b. 1906) (Professor of History, University of Melbourne, 1937–1970), in *Australia* (Hutchinson, London, 1952)

THE *RE D'ITALIA* and her sister steamers did not, of course, dispatch the first Italians onto Australian soil. Antonio Ponto, a Venetian, reportedly sailed with Captain James Cook on the *Endeavour* and reached Australia in 1770. The First Fleet carried with it one Giuseppe Tusa, who stayed in Sydney, married, had four children and acquired fifty acres (twenty hectares) before his death in 1825.

By the mid-nineteenth century, Italians had begun to be recognised as a growing portion of Australian society. From the area of Ticino, near the Swiss border, 2000 men were induced to the Australian goldfields during a time of agricultural depression, beginning a trickle, rather than a stream, until later in the century. Following the arrival of the first Italian immigrants to Australia from southern Italy in the 1890s, the Italian migrant population grew steadily to form the largest non-British migrant group recorded in the 1933 census.

Granted, this figure is not enormous — the census of 1921 recorded an Italian-born population of 8135, spread fairly evenly across the three eastern states and Western Australia. But consider that in 1922 the entire population of Canberra was just 2500, and five years later, when Parliament House opened, it had only increased to 5700.

IF AUSTRALIA IN the nineteenth and early twentieth centuries was not exactly the land of milk and honey, it was certainly the land of sheep and wheat. This was the era that built the country's reputation for 'riding on the sheep's back', and indeed at the start of the twentieth century Australia had possibly the highest per capita income in the world. But a devastating, fall was just around the corner. Primary produce, and the industries that supported it, were about to take a nose dive.

Australian export prices fell continuously from 1925 to the end of the decade. While America and Canada had the resources to stockpile and artificially maintain their wheat and wool prices, Australia had no such ability. Farmers sold whatever they could, wherever they could, thus driving prices down, and Australia's reliance on international credit was increasing dramatically as its primary export market eroded despite boom production years from 1925 to 1928.

In short, a substantial trade deficit became less able to be managed by international borrowing, such that by 1928 the country had an enormous burden of debt. The following year, Australia found it impossible to borrow further funds from its major partners in the U.S. and England — indeed both countries were suspicious of our national debt, and foreign investment petered out. This was a catastrophe, since 200,000 men had been employed on public works projects financed largely by foreign loans.

Next came the break in wheat and wool prices in June and August 1929. The stockpiling eventually caught up with the international market, so that by the time the Great Crash arrived in October 1929, the Australian economy was already in free fall. And nowhere was it felt more harshly than on the land. In all of this country's rich history of rural prosperity, there might never have been a worse moment to find one's feet here than in the five years that followed the *Re d'Italia*'s berthing in 1927.

So why choose Australia? For many, the United States was the more likely choice, given that many had relatives already safely landed in America. Many entered through New York City's fabled Ellis Island — from 1882 to 1924 more than 22 million immigrants crossed the threshold there to begin a new life. Ellis Island was, for many, their first taste of a brave new world.

But a new immigration law was passed in 1917 that specified thirty-three classes of foreigners who could not be admitted to the United States, and it also demanded that the immigrants take a literacy test. This law greatly reduced the number of immigrants for some time, but by 1921 the number of arrivals had increased once again to 500,000 a year. New, stricter laws were passed in that year and again in 1924. A final revision went into effect in 1929. Every immigrant was now to be inspected at the American consular office in the immigrant's country of origin, rather than on arrival in America. This changed the United States' immigration system forever.

For Italians, the next two most appealing options were clear: Canada or Australia. The former was showing signs of a cracking economy slightly earlier than Australia; besides, all reports back from earlier departed family members spoke of an exotic, rewarding life on the other side of the planet — precisely the tonic for a downtrodden, often fearful people.

Still, the Australians soon began to mirror their American counterparts, if not entirely shutting their doors then at least closing them slightly. In 1924 Australian authorities introduced measures to control the flow of immigrants, who were now required to have a sponsorship agreement or £40 in cash on arrival, or to hold landing permits issued as a result of having their maintenance or employment guaranteed by relatives or friends in Australia. Essentially, they were sponsored to come to Australia.

It is worth noting that women were seldom included in initial immigration plans. The bulk of the *Re d'Italia*'s passenger list is comprised of single men; others, like Luigi Tagliaferri, made the passage to Australia to lay a foundation for a family to follow them there.

Of the 108 passengers who disembarked in Melbourne, ninety listed 'farm labourer' as their occupation. There were some better-educated passengers amongst them, however. Domenico Caffaro (number twenty-two), for example, was an accomplished musician. Others, like my grandfather, were qualified tradesmen. But Australia was looking for manual labourers at the time and the passengers were willing to reciprocate. In fact, my grandfather did not revert to his trade of cabinetmaking until after the Second World War.

During the 1920s the favoured destination was Queensland, where the sugar industry attracted the majority of the newcomers. It also bred an institutionalised form of racism: Italian cane cutters were discriminated against by the official policy of 'British preference' in employment. A Royal Commission into the influx of Italian migrants did little to assist their cause; in fact, it simply reinforced some of the stereotypes that distinguished northern and southern Italians.

Victoria's share of new immigrants was smaller, and work was found in the rural areas, cutting wood, working on construction projects such as the building of dams and bridges, or in farm work. Tobacco growing at Myrtleford and in the Ovens Valley area attracted Italian immigrants, as did the coal-mining industry at Wonthaggi. Other Italian settlements included areas around Shepparton, Mildura and in Gippsland, and closer to Melbourne, at Werribee, Ferntree Gully, Lilydale and Dandenong. But the promise of riches in the 'lucky country' was seldom fulfilled.

For those who chose to stay in the city of Melbourne, the inner northern suburbs of Carlton, North Melbourne and Fitzroy drew them like a magnet. These areas were close to the markets, where some found work, and more to the point they provided cheap housing and a rich cultural mix of Chinese, Greeks and Jews that established the area as the melting pot it remains today ... despite being a little less affordable than back then.

Some men found work in cement and terrazzo. Francesco Benvenuti's grandson, Paul, recalls the toughness of being a first-generation immigrant: 'He was a concreter and terrazzo worker, and he had hard hands. I remember as a kid he'd squeeze me just above the knee and I'd scream. He didn't mean anything by it, he just didn't know his own strength.'

And they all faced similar challenges, not the least of which was simply getting by from day to day as they carved the rudiments of a new language into something usable.

While immigration was strong, there was little infrastructure to support it — no special services, few mutual aid societies — and citizenship and identity were constructed as British. Little wonder the Italians gravitated to the clubs their community formed, such as the Cavour Club at South Melbourne, founded in 1917, which was the main social institution of the community; the Aeolian Islands Mutual Assistance Association, which served those with origins in the Aeolian Islands; the anti-Fascist Matteotti Club (of which my grandfather was a member); and later the Casa d'Italia (House of Italy) in Carlton.

Assimilation was the challenge, but at every turn there lay a barrier. Australia's isolation provided appeal — it was far from the torment of Mussolini, and the financial and emotional wake of the First World War — but, equally, it was poorly prepared to receive Europeans, especially outside the cities. In Swifts Creek, East Gippsland, for instance — where passenger sixty-six, Antonio Italia, spent time burning off — local Steven O'Brien recalls people giving up on trying to pronounce the newcomers' names. 'The Australians didn't know how to pronounce their names up here so they gave them nicknames: "Pat", "Mick" and "Mustard", different names for different Italians,' O'Brien said to me.

The need for fellowship with other Italians was strong. The De Bortoli family, who first arrived in the country in 1924, are now renowned as the owners of one of Australia's biggest wine producing and exporting businesses. It was customary for groups of Italian cane cutters to head south to the family's New South Wales properties for picking season, so they could drink wine and exchange news of the mother country.

Australian officials were wary of the 'enclaves', as gathering groups of migrants were known. The Italians were seen to gather on the canefields of the north, in fishing ports in New South Wales, South Australia or Fremantle in Western Australia, among the outer or inner suburbs of Melbourne and Sydney, and in scattered farming communities in various parts of the country. In a nation with little sense of its own identity — it was just a quarter of a century since Federation, and the first course in Australian history was not taught until 1927 (by Ernest Scott at the University of Melbourne) — the Italians' proud flaunting of their origins made some uneasy.

It was a cultural ingredient that, in truth, Australia did not overcome until after the second major wave of European immigration in the 1950s.

More Italians had been interned in Australia during the Second World War than members of any other 'alien' race. Italians in New South Wales were watched with particular attention due to the activities of the Fascist Party in Sydney. Australia also held more than 18,000 Italian prisoners of war, transported from the European theatres of war. The irony was that many Italians living in Australia had fought for their new country in the First World War.

Most Italians knew their motherland would enter the Second World War on the side of Germany, which meant that their status in Australia was liable to be jeopardised. Many were not surprised when Australian police and security officers came to arrest them. The methods of identification, arrest and internment had been formulated in August 1939.

In most areas Italian blood was considered reason enough for arrest, regardless of one's political persuasion. Even naturalised British subjects were arrested. In 1942 the number of Italians interned in Australia reached a wartime high of 3651. But as the danger of Japanese invasion subsided, they were gradually released, and by September 1944, only 135 hard-core Fascists remained in the internment camps.

Again, the irony of the following years cannot be escaped: the end of the Second World War triggered a large-scale migration program, and about one million migrants arrived in each of the four decades following 1950. Their path had been made so much easier by their forebears, some of whom travelled to this country on the *Re d'Italia*.

Cane cutters, Innisfail, northern Queensland, circa 1930. Valerio Bianchi (*passenger 46*) is resting his hat and his machete on a piece of cane, back row, third from the right.

PHOTOGRAPH COURTESY CARLA BIANCHI, ELANORA HEIGHTS, NEW SOUTH WALES.

CHAPTER SIX

The Search

THE PASSENGER LIST of the *Re d'Italia* is a fairly innocuous-looking document. Written in consistent, looping handwriting, it provides a mere taste of the immigration experience of those who endured forty-six days traversing the globe in the hope of something new, and something more rewarding.

I could relate to their sense of anticipation every time I crossed another name off the list, and set the search alight again.

As a journalist on a daily newspaper for many years, the discipline of investigating facts tended to come as second nature, even if I had never had the opportunity to exercise it as much as I would have liked. There was always the thrill of the hunt for the breaking story, or the less glamorous slog researching the background of a potential feature. Nothing, however, could have prepared me for the path down which the *Re d'Italia* steered me. The search developed a pulse of its own, becoming a five-year epic that never failed to provide a suspenseful twist, or often to reveal a link with my own past that further entrenched my sympathies with those passengers and my understanding of their descendants.

Some of it was easy, like the case of Ernesto Lago, already mentioned. His daughter, Lina Cecchin, lived only a thirty-minute drive away from my Preston home. The local *White Pages* had sent me directly to her front door in Werribee South.

Had I known how difficult some of the other passengers would be to source, perhaps I would never have moved on to numbers two, three, four and so on with as much enthusiasm. But the encounter with Lina only fed my curiosity, and after a handful of successful searches my obsession was in full swing.

The names located in the *White Pages* were the easy ones. Likewise, Telecom Italia was a boon for me, saving much time and frustration as I sought families out in the homeland. Yet nothing was as valuable as the *Atti di Chiamata*, the nomination forms for the passengers, copies of which I had obtained from the Melbourne office of the Australian Archives. These forms proved essential to my quest, in that they carried the birthdates, birthplaces and parents of both the passengers and their respective sponsors, details of which I could then convey to the respective *comuni* (municipal offices) of the Italian towns to obtain either marriage or death certificates for the passengers, and begin the search for living descendants.

This is where Maria Monaco also proved a wonderful ally. In mid-1999, Maria phoned me in the wake of viewing the A.B.C.'s 'Australian Story' documentary 'In Search of Kings', about my search, to congratulate me on my efforts. Although I had never previously spoken to Maria, I had met her mother and father in the western Victorian town of Colac during my research into the life of another passenger, Giuseppe (Uncle Joe) Violi.

During that phone conversation, I offered Maria the opportunity to peruse the library of passenger photographs and documents I had accumulated over the previous two years. A week or so later, she arrived on the doorstep. Her enthusiasm rubbed off to such an extent that I couldn't help but ask if she was interested in putting her Italian language skills to good use on my behalf.

Maria kindly agreed, and it has only been through her people skills that the life stories of many of the passengers can now be told. It helped that many of the *comuni* were located in small towns, and the staff were not only excited to lend their assistance but, as in many small villages, actually knew the passenger's descendants.

The telephone took me to many other places, destinations such as Belgium, Philadelphia and Gig Harbor in Washington State. Naturally, it took me all around Australia, and into the homes of families whose first representatives in this country had once strolled the *Re d'Italia*'s decks alongside my grandfather and great-uncles.

Each and every passenger offered me a challenge. To best illustrate the sort of methods employed, I offer the following example of my search for the late Ampelio Acquasaliente (Salent).

In October 1997 I obtained information from the Melbourne office of the National Archives of Australia, which revealed that:

- Ampelio Acquasaliente was born in Santulderico di Tretto in the province of Vicenza on the fourth day of April, 1904, to an Italian mother and a father named Emilio, and following his arrival on the *Re d'Italia*, he resided in Koondrook for seven months, Melbourne for five months, Innisfail for four years and Mareeba for six months.

- In his statutory declaration dated 26 July 1933, endorsed by character referees James William Duncan of Innisfail and Thomas Armstrong Day and Oliver Langley Croker of Mareeba, Ampelio stated that he was five feet eight and a half inches (174 centimetres) tall, with brown hair and grey eyes, and listed his occupation as tobacco grower.

- On 5 April 1934, he renounced his nationality and took the oath of allegiance to King George V, before Acting Police Magistrate Andrew Anderson.

My subsequent search of telephone listings for Acquasaliente in the Mareeba and Innisfail areas proved fruitless, as indeed it was in Melbourne and all of the other capital cities. I did, however, manage to locate a G. Acquasaliente in the Gippsland region of Victoria, dialled the number and left a message on the person's answering machine. Later, a man of

African background returned my call to strongly suggest that Acquasaliente was not his surname, and I realised then that the telephone operator had keyed in the wrong spelling.

I then turned my attentions to Ampelio's character referees. I obtained a telephone listing for a Mr B. Day of the Mareeba area and dialled the number. Mr Day told me he was of Aboriginal extraction and was no relation to Thomas Armstrong Day, 'but good luck on your journey'.

I then telephoned a Mrs Day, also listed in the Mareeba district, but she referred me, for some unknown reason, to Miss Lorrie Wilson, who had no idea who Thomas Armstrong Day was.

In desperation I contacted Telecom Italia to determine whether there might just be a listing for the name Acquasaliente in Santulderico di Tretto, the town from which Ampelio hailed. The operator unearthed one listing for an Angelo Acquasaliente.

As the time difference was some ten hours, my friend and interpreter Paolo Coniglio made a call from the kitchen table of my Preston home at midnight on 2 March 1998. It was then that Angelo's wife confirmed that Ampelio Acquasaliente was alive and well and living under the surname of 'Salent' in the Sydney suburb of Rockdale.

At 9.35 that morning, I made the call to Sydney, and heard Ampelio's voice for the first time.

TOWARDS THE END of 1999 I managed to spend my honeymoon with my long-suffering wife Kate seeking out passengers' relatives in Italy. When in Rome ... or Treviso, or Milan, or wherever, we had a mixed bag of success, including meeting two daughters of passengers — the daughter of GioBatta Bellò, who sent me on my way with a lump of beef and a freshly plucked chook, and the daughter of Massimo Girardi.

Lucia Girardi laughed heartily at the story I had gleaned in Australia of how her father would scare off potential theatregoers in the small Queensland town of Caboolture. It seems Girardi senior had a habit of sitting in the front row of the balcony and disposing of his chewing tobacco the only way he knew how — spitting it over the edge. The fact that I could contribute something new to her memories of a father who had passed away twenty-five years earlier gave me an indescribable thrill.

Yet nothing compared with the rare honour of meeting two surviving passengers (apart, of course, from having known and loved my own grandfather Silvio, and great-uncles Igino and Frank). Ampelio Acquasaliente, who was living under the name Salent in Sydney, and Annunziata Faralla.

Twice I confronted mistaken identities, eagerly pursuing Vincenzo DiGregorio and Paulo Corridore when in fact they proved to be men of the same name and era, but no relation. Likewise, Frank Curcio proved highly elusive until my mother stumbled across the fact that his surname was actually spelled 'Cursio'.

Meeting relatives was always a thrill. In the search for Luigi Giarracca, I spoke to his son, Angelo, whose stepson, Corrado, was able to converse in English. When Corrado had a holiday in Australia not long afterwards, we met at the Fawkner home of his acquaintance, Lina Regali. At the kitchen table, over shot glasses filled to the brim with Lina's home-made, ice-cold *limoncello*, we traded stories about Luigi, Vincenzo and all those who made up the *Re d'Italia*'s human cargo.

The fact is, the interaction with passengers' families was as satisfying as tracing them in the first place. At one stage I sent Santo Lanteri's son, Dr Ray Lanteri, several photos of his father. He replied with the following letter, one that perhaps sums up the good wishes I took with me throughout the search:

Dear Tony,

You have given us a lot of pleasure with your research into the passengers from the *Re d'Italia*.

The photo of my father with Mary Musco (the daughter of Sebastiano Musco, who originally supplied the photo to me) was wonderful. His pose and attitude reveal him as a cocky young man and he mirrors the image I have of my own son.

We have not very much to add to your story at this stage ... Mum seems to recall little of his whereabouts prior to their marriage in the late 1930s. She is showing the photographs to those few old friends from that time who are still with us.

This Christmas we will drink a toast to my father, and to all his fellow passengers who, 70 years ago, cast their bread upon the waters. I know you will be doing the same.

Regards,

Ray.

The note was sitting with a parcel at my front door when I found it. I opened the parcel to reveal a bottle of Asti — and, sure enough, my family and I toasted the memory of Santo Lanteri, the De Bolfo brothers and all fellow passengers of the *Re d'Italia* that Christmas.

ATTO DI CHIAMATA
(Nomination)

61 Atto Chiamata
Aprile 1927

Io Sottoscritto **Cernotta Ermenegildo**, figlio di **Ermacora**
I the Undersigned / son of

e di **Tomasetig Luigia**, nato a **Cosizza(S:Leonardo)**
and of / born in

Provincia di **Udine**, il **13 Aprile 1898**
Province of / on the

attualmente residente a **(C/o Roche Bros.) Buangor. Victoria**
at present residing in

Australia,
Australia

dichiaro solennemente con l'Atto presente essere mio desiderio che
do hereby solemnly declare it to be my desire that

Simaz Luigi di Andrea e di Vogrig Teresa nato in Cosizza (San

Leonardo) il 21 Maggio 1901/ ‒ ‒ ‒ ‒ ‒ ‒ ‒ ‒ ‒ ‒ ‒ ‒

‒ ‒

venga non appena sia possibile a raggiungermi in Australia.
come / as soon as possible to join me in Australia.

Ed affinche' non venga posto ostacolo alla **sua** partenza dall'Italia
And with a view that no obstacle be put to / leaving Italy

ed al **suo** sbarco in Australia io sottoscritto **Cernotta Ermenegildo**
and / landing in Australia I the undersigned

faccio noto con l'Atto presente di essere perfettamente in condizione di sopperire
do hereby make known to be perfectly in a condition to provide

ai **suoi** bisogni qui in Australia e mi obbligo di conseguenza sia di recarmi a
for / needs here in Australia and therefore bind myself to go and

riceverl **o** al **suo** arrivo, sia di provvedere—una volta arrivat **o** alle necessita'
meet / on / arrival, to provide—once arrived—for the necessities

della **sua** vita, alla cura della **sua** salute in caso di malattia,
of / life, for the care of / health in case of illness,

in proporzione ai miei mezzi ma in modo e misura tali che ess **o** non avra
in proportion with my means but in such a way that will never

mai a rimanere a carico di alcuna istituzione caritatevole o di beneficenza di questo
become a charge on any charitable institution of this

paese.
country.

Melbourne 8 Aprile 1927 ANNO V

Cernotta Ermenegildo

Firmato del predetto Sig. **Cernotta Ermenegildo** in mia presenza a
Signed by the aforesaid Mr. / in my presence at

Melbourne in questo **8** giorno di **Aprile**
this / day of

1927 ANNO V

R. P. No. **1124 I**
Art. **37** T.C.
satte **₤ 0.14.8**
(Lire Oro 18)

IL R. CONSOLE GENERALE

Grossardi

The *atto di chiamata* (nomination form) for Luigi Simaz (*passenger 28*). This form, submitted to the
Consolato Generale d'Italia in Melbourne, also carries the name of guarantor Ermenegildo Cernotta,
who was already residing in the country and was prepared to act as guardian to Luigi.
The Melbourne office of the National Archives of Australia was able to provide all but two of the 110 nomination
forms for the passengers of the *Re d'Italia*. These forms carried crucial details relating to each passenger's date and
place of birth and parents' names, which enabled the author to follow the information up with the relevant archival
agencies, either in Australia, or in Italy through the *comuni* (municipalities) from which the passengers
originally hailed. The N.A.A.'s two 'missing' nomination forms related to Giacomo Sartori and Patroche
Basile — the two passengers whose fate remains a mystery.

FORM COURTESY NATIONAL ARCHIVES OF AUSTRALIA, MELBOURNE OFFICE.

CHAPTER SEVEN

The Passengers

1. GioBatta Da Vinchie

BORN DOMEGGE DI CADORE, PROVINCIA DI BELLUNO, 6 MAY 1899.
DIED DAW PARK, SOUTH AUSTRALIA, 22 JULY 1968.

Da Vinchie GioBatta, farm labourer, male, 28, single, Italian.

THESE FEW WORDS, penned into the manifest of the passenger ship *Re d'Italia*, were at first all that was known of the first-named of the Melbourne disembarkees, GioBatta Da Vinchie.

Most helpful in the search for GioBatta was his niece, Bruna Valmassoi, who lives with her husband, Giacomo Moras, in Conegliano in the province of Treviso, and whom I found through Telecom Italia. Bruna outlined the family's incredible flight from Mussolini: how the eldest brother, Giorgio (1889–1982), headed to Detroit in the U.S.A.; how the second-born, Iginio (1893–1930), migrated to Lipsia in Germany and became a professor; and how the third brother, Ettore Giovanni (1895–1981), ventured to Chile, South America. There were also two sisters: Giovanna (1893–1936) and Annetta (1897–1989).

GioBatta served in the First World War at the tender age of seventeen. He was a private with the 7th Alpine Troop, and was decorated; the medals were sent to him later in Australia. The War affected all the family, and the Fascist regime persecuted them to such a point that it made life in Italy impossible. For this reason, GioBatta felt compelled to embark for Australia, at that time not a well-known destination for emigrants, but suitable because of his farming origins.

On arrival, he immediately took up residence at 163 Nicholson Street, Carlton — the premises of local bootmaker Signor Villanova. He then spent four years in Beech Forest, a further year in Bairnsdale and another three in Nungurner, near Lakes Entrance. While recorded as a lens maker by profession, GioBatta was a carpenter and gardener to boot, and also spent time woodcutting in the surrounds of Adelaide and then Brisbane. He never married.

Incredibly, GioBatta also served in the Second World War. Naturalised on 4 January 1936, he volunteered for the Australian Military Forces, where he served as a member of the 35th Employment Company from 1 July 1942 until his discharge on 25 October 1943.

As information recently obtained through the South Australian office of Veterans' Affairs suggests, the legacy of war probably took its toll. A social worker wrote the following in May 1967 — the year before GioBatta died:

> GioBatta Da Vinchie is a sixty-seven year old Italian who came to Australia forty years ago to escape Mussolini. He said he fought in the First World War, was wounded [and] recalled the circumstances of this incident quite vividly. It appears that he was shot by a wounded German, and that once he recovered from the shot he then fired and killed the German.
>
> Giombattista says that he is a lens maker by trade, but has not done this work in Australia. In World War II he joined the Australian Army, but his account of this was not so clear. He evidently did not get past Cairns, where he felt ill and spent a considerable time in hospital.

Bruna Valmassoi recalled the excitement of receiving parcels from the other side of the world when her family exchanged gifts. 'GioBatta used to get Aunty [Annetta] to send him these Ciabatte Cadorine slippers, handmade for the long winter nights. I remember that after the [Second World] War he sent me a parcel of raw Australian wool. The wool was valuable to us, as was a purse of kangaroo hide that I was proud to carry for many years with my schoolbooks.'

R.S.L. records reveal that GioBatta Da Vinchie, who had suffered from pneumonia and heart disease, died peacefully in Adelaide's Repatriation General Hospital at ten o'clock on the night of Monday, 22 July 1968. He is buried in that city, in Centennial Park Cemetery.

2. Valentino Beltrame

BORN CANUSSIO, PROVINCIA DI UDINE, 1 JANUARY 1888.
DIED WERRIBEE, VICTORIA, 28 MAY 1957.

WHEN VALENTINO BELTRAME signed on the dotted line on behalf of his business partners in Canussio, he could not have known that this simple act would result in his leaving Italy forever.

It happened because his associates later pulled out of a deal to build a bell tower for the church of San Michele in the local village, and Valentino, as sole signatory, was left to bear the brunt of the costs. Faced with the loss of his own farming property, Valentino soon realised that his only option was to leave behind his wife Veneranda (née Vio) and five young children to try his luck in 'the lucky country'. Valentino disembarked from the *Re d'Italia* in Melbourne with one clear objective: to find enough work and earn enough money to pay off his mortgages, save his land and be reunited with his family. But with the world on the verge of the Great Depression, the opportunities Valentino had so desperately sought were sadly not forthcoming. As such, Veneranda was forced to sell off the property bit by bit, and in the end the Beltrame family lost everything.

In 1929, Valentino sent for Giovanni, the first of his four sons (born 1912). Together they spent those early years working the farms of Koo-Wee-Rup, digging potatoes, although Valentino also spent a brief period cutting cane in northern Queensland.

Eight years later, another son, Mario (born 1920), arrived in Melbourne, with Veneranda, sons Remigio (born 1921) and Onorino (born 1923) and daughter Maria (born 1925) completing the Italian exodus in March 1939.

Reunited at last, the Beltrames settled in Werribee. There, at neighbouring Corpus Christi College (now Werribee Park Mansion), Valentino leased a small area of land upon which he grew cauliflower, lettuce, beans, peas and cabbage. 'Dad's was just one of a number of little farms run by the Italians in Werribee ... most of the farms were run by families from Sicily like the Armaos and Portogallos,' Maria Silvestro (née Beltrame) recalled when I spoke to her in November 1997. 'Everyone worked on our farm — my father, mother, my four brothers and myself.'

The family would be together for only two months before Italy went to war with Australia, and Valentino and his sons were interned at Tatura as suspected Fascists. After they had spent so long apart, this latest turn of events seemed particularly cruel. But Maria, then only a girl of fourteen, remembered, 'It wasn't too bad for us. We had friends help us with the vegetables and take cauliflowers to the market for the six weeks my father and brothers were in the camp.'

'I used to help a man from the same region of Italy, Giovanni Del Zotto, on the farm, while another friend from Melbourne, Ruggero Vinco, would drive the truck to market. Sometimes I'd stay overnight with the Gobbo family in Victoria Street, North Melbourne. Sir James Gobbo (later the Governor of Victoria) was only a six- or seven-year-old boy then.'

In later years the Beltrame sons (with the exception of Mario, who died young) and daughter moved away from the Werribee district. But Mr and Mrs Beltrame remained there for the rest of their lives. Veneranda, born in the same month and year as her husband, died in October 1956, while Valentino's life ended tragically only a few months later.

'He had to go to the dentist in Melbourne and I said, "I'll meet you there" ... I went there and waited for him, but we never found each other,' Maria remembered. Near Werribee Station, Valentino had been hit by the Melbourne-bound train from Geelong, and was killed instantly.

Today, more than forty years after Valentino Beltrame's death, there remain strong visible reminders of the man in the different places where he lived. At Corpus Christi by the river are two water tanks, beneath which can be found two giant cellars. Italian pea pickers sometimes used to sleep there, and it was where Valentino stored his supplies for the farm horses and his barrels of home-made wine.

And by the old church of San Michele, in the tiny northern Italian village of Canussio where Valentino Beltrame was born, stands the bell tower, finally erected in 1929, two years after the man had left forever.

3. Pietro Agostino Formentini

BORN LICCIANA, PROVINCIA DI MASSA CARRARA, 23 APRIL 1899.
DIED LICCIANA, PROVINCIA DI MASSA CARRARA, 15 APRIL 1981.

PIETRO FORMENTINI WAS a simple man who wanted nothing more than a better quality of life for his wife Gesualda (née Bianchi) and their daughters, Armida and Edvige. He made this clear in his application for naturalisation in March 1933, when he succinctly stated that his sole objective was ultimately to gain passage for his wife and family because he '[liked] Australia better than Italy'.

Although he had served Italy in its artillery division, Pietro resolved to seek his fortune in a foreign land. He was twenty-eight when he set foot on Australian soil, having bid a painful farewell to his family almost seven weeks before. Not long after his arrival, Pietro settled in the north central Victorian town of Picola before heading further northwest, in the late 1920s, to Iron Knob in South Australia. From Iron Knob, Pietro ventured southeast to Adelaide where, in the 1930s, he settled at 73 Angas Street. The Angas Street premises also doubled as a workshop, where Pietro plied his craft as a plaster of Paris statue maker for his own business, Nardini and Co.

In his application for naturalisation in 1933, Pietro emphasised that he intended to return to Italy to bring back his wife and two children as soon as his papers came through. Pietro also stated that he had made arrangements for a friend, Giuseppe Porta, to take care of his business during his absence in Italy. This was to reassure the Immigration Department that he intended to return to Australia.

Although his application was successful, it appears that Pietro left Australia forever. His fate remained unknown until the *comune* in his home town of Licciana revealed that he had died there, and was survived by his two daughters, grandchildren and great-grandchildren.

One of the grandchildren, Edvige's son Angelo Onesti, forwarded the following information (written in Italian) from the Italian town of Lecco, in September 1999:

... Pietro Agostino Formentini attended the elementary school of Licciana and later married Gesualda Bianchi. They had two daughters: Armida, born in August 1922, and Edvige, born in April 1924.

Pietro worked the earth in the region of Ripola and in 1927 left for Australia in search of fortune. In Australia he worked the iron mines, but when the advent of machinery put paid to his job he found another — building statues in chalk [*sic* — plaster of Paris], two of which are preserved in Ripola.

When work with the figurines dropped off, Pietro decided to repatriate, and he took his job back in the fields of Ripola. During the Second World War he was deployed for fifteen months in Germany, leaving his darlings deprived of news. Following the war, Pietro returned to Ripola, where he continued to work the earth and practise as a cobbler until the time of his death. He worked solely to guarantee that his family lived life in a dignified way.

Pietro was a good and generous person, always available to all who needed him. He was particularly thoughtful to his daughters and nephews, whom he loved very much, and his goodness extended beyond people, to his relationships with animals, particularly his dogs ...

4. Eugenio Basso

BORN PREMARIACCO, PROVINCIA DI UDINE, 16 FEBRUARY 1903.
DIED CIVIDALE, PROVINCIA DI UDINE, 1 FEBRUARY 1986.

Come sa di sale lo pane altrui.
(How bitter the bread belonging to somebody else.)

THESE WORDS WERE penned by the Italian Renaissance writer Dante Alighieri and included in the text for the funeral service of the late Eugenio Basso.

In 1985, Eugenio returned to the Friulian town of Cividale to spend his final days there. For fifty-seven years, the son of Giovanni Maria and Annunziata Maria Basso (née Taboga) had called Australia home — since late 1927, when Eugenio's sponsor, Attilio Moschioni, helped secure his passage.

The story of Eugenio's life could only be told through the assistance of Mrs Elba Piazza (née Borgnolo) of Griffith, New South Wales. Elba's father, Vittorio Borgnolo, accompanied Eugenio on the *Re d'Italia* all those years ago, and it was Eugenio who acted as best man at Vittorio's proxy marriage in Melbourne in 1932.

In October 1998, Elba phoned to advise that she had just returned from a six-week holiday in Italy, and had compiled a profile of the man following her conversation with one of Eugenio's nephews, Giovanni Maria Basso.

Eugenio spent his early years in Australia as a potato grower in the Koo-Wee-Rup area of Victoria. He would later work in a tannery and, following his retirement, as a gardener. Through it all, Eugenio indulged in his hobby of playing the violin, and was also a keen follower of Australian Rules football.

Following the Second World War, Eugenio left Koo-Wee-Rup for the relative hustle and bustle of suburban Glenferrie, where he took up residence at 41 Haines Street. On 16 June 1951, at 8 Moore Street in neighbouring Hawthorn, Eugenio, then forty-eight, married forty-two year old spinster Beatrice Butcher. Beatrice, the daughter of a railway employee, Charles William Butcher, and Rosa Woodrow, was born on the Isle of Wight.

The November before his marriage, Eugenio made his first trip back to Italy aboard the *Toscana*, and returned on the *Vivaldi* in January 1951. In September 1978, Eugenio completed another return trip to his homeland, this time by air, and on 11 April 1984 went back for the last time, following the death of Beatrice in Kew in 1983, aged seventy-five.

Eugenio died in his homeland a little less than two years later.

5. Vittorio Borgnolo

BORN PREMARIACCO, PROVINCIA DI UDINE, 28 OCTOBER 1901.
DIED GRIFFITH, NEW SOUTH WALES, 14 MARCH 1983.

'PAPÀ, I'M GOING to the other side of the world ... if I move from here there's one less to worry about.'

These were the parting words of Vittorio Borgnolo to his father, Giuseppe, as he prepared to embark on the journey of a lifetime seventy-five years ago. Vittorio was twenty-six when he farewelled his parents and eight brothers and sisters, and boarded the *Re d'Italia* with his lifelong friend Eugenio Basso.

On 12 January 1932, Vittorio married Iolanda Basso — a distant cousin of Eugenio — who was born in Vittorio's home town of Premariacco and was nine years her husband's junior. As the marriage was arranged by proxy, the newlyweds did not meet until 22 May of that year, when Iolanda arrived in Melbourne aboard the *Esquilino*. They always considered that as their wedding day. The Borgnolos would raise two children: a daughter, Elba Ines, born on 9 April 1933, and a son, Edone Luciano, born on 6 January 1938.

Though a carpenter by trade, Vittorio had difficulty finding employment after his arrival in Melbourne, and had to be content with quarry work in Koo-Wee-Rup. He always lamented the fact that his hands bled from labouring in the quarry.

Vittorio spent the first seven months in Koo-Wee-Rup, before receiving word that work was available in the New South Wales township of Griffith. With a friend, and a total of seventeen shillings between them, Vittorio made the train trip to Griffith — or so he thought. For whatever reason, the two men mistakenly alighted from the carriage in Moss Vale and, as they had neither money nor command of the English language, caught a train back to Melbourne and went through the process all over again.

Upon his eventual arrival in Griffith, Vittorio immediately found work with an Australian farmer, Mr Moriarty, at a property eight miles from the centre of town. There he would slog from sunrise to sunset, and venture to Griffith at six-monthly intervals by horse and sulky to bank his wages.

'Dad was made to feel at home by Mr Moriarty and they used to eat their meals together, although the dripping wasn't what he was used to,' Vittorio's daughter Elba Piazza (née Borgnolo) said. 'A piece of *polenta* and *formaggio* and Dad would have been very happy.'

As Vittorio worked diligently and enjoyed a healthy relationship with the property owner, Mr Moriarty was naturally devastated when his worker revealed that he had bought a farm of his own from another

Australian, Mr Vauhan. Purchased for £700 in January 1934, Vittorio's twenty-four acre farm was situated at number 111 Hanwood, three kilometres from the Griffith Post Office.

Vittorio worked the farm at Hanwood as an orchardist for almost fifty years, until his death at age eighty-one. In the ensuing years, his son Edone continued to run the orchard, before selling the property in 1994. But number 111 has remained indelibly etched in the memory of Elba, who still lives nearby. As she says, 'Every time I drive past the farm, I think, "This is where I grew up." You do leave part of yourself behind.'

'In all those years there we never knew hunger,' she continues. 'We were all self-sufficient; we always had a cow providing milk, butter and cheese, chickens galore, and beautiful gardens full of carrots and *radicchio*.'

In 1953, after more than twenty years in Australia, Vittorio made his first trip back to Premariacco. In the ensuing years, locals from that village kept telling him, 'Sell what you've got, come to your *terra* and die here in Italy.'

But Vittorio Borgnolo, who took the Oath of Allegiance to become a citizen of Australia in February 1938, would never go back.

6. Ettore Bonanni

Born Raveo, Provincia di Udine, 7 November 1897.
Died Udine, Provincia di Udine, 22 December 1979.

15. Vittorio Bonanni

Born Raveo, Provincia di Udine, 16 November 1893.
Died Tarcento, Provincia di Udine, 11 February 1964.

The life of Ettore Bonanni ended as it had begun, in the second largest city of Italy's Friulian region. But for four years — from 1927, when he and his brother Vittorio disembarked from the Re d'Italia, through to their departure in 1931 — Australia was Ettore's home.

Four years Vittorio's junior, Ettore was born to Domenico and Margherita Bonanni (née Romano) in the town of Raveo. He was sponsored to come to this country by his old friend Guido Rovere, whose sister Clelia he had married some years before his departure. At that time Guido was living in Queanbeyan, New South Wales.

After an unsuccessful search through the Melbourne *White Pages*, and little luck among the ten Bonanni families listed in Sydney — all hailing, apparently, from the Abruzzo region — I decided to take another tack. Maybe I could track down the descendants of Guido Rovere.

I discovered three listings for the name Rovere in Sydney, and unearthed a vital clue with the second call, to a man named Renzo Rovere. Renzo's wife answered the phone, and said that Albino Rovere, of Gooloogong in New South Wales, was the man I should be talking to — Albino having sponsored Vittorio Bonanni to this country. Unfortunately I soon learned that Albino had died a few years earlier.

In the meantime I pursued the name Rovere with Directory Assistance in the remaining capital cities, and came up with two numbers in the A.C.T. My efforts were rewarded when a Mr Lino Rovere said that he originally hailed from the Italian village of Tarcento and knew the Bonannis. 'I'm familiar with them. They lived at the same end of the street in Mawson,' Lino said. He added that a number of Italian migrants had worked for a Mr Norman Pengilly in the Queensland town of Caloundra in those days; Albino Rovere had been the first of the migrants to arrive.

Lino then put me on to Mrs Lydia Rovere (née Paolini), who in turn referred me to Mrs Mabel Bianchi (née Rovere), of Cabarita in New South Wales. This was the breakthrough I had been looking for: Mabel was the daughter of Guido Rovere, the man who had sponsored Ettore Bonanni to Australia.

Mabel told me that Ettore had married her aunt Clelia Rovere, and that he 'would have returned to Italy at the same time as my father, in about 1935'.

'Dad went back because he hadn't seen my mother for nine years, and during that time I was conceived,' Mabel explained. 'In 1936 he returned to Australia and I came out with my mother in November of that year. We later went to New Guinea, where Dad got a job propping up gold-mining shafts before he was interned.'

Mabel then forwarded me a contact address in the town of Remanzacco in Udine for the daughter of Ettore Bonanni, Signora Ivana Ghilardi. I wrote to her seeking information on 8 January 1999. Three months later I received a letter from Ivana, her husband Amos Ghilardi and her brother Mario Bonanni. The letter said in part:

Dear Mr Tony,

Ettore Bonanni was born in Raveo (Carnia) and died in Udine. He was married to Clelia Rovere, 1901 class, and she is still alive.

Our father lived in Australia from 1927 until 1931 and there, together with his brother Vittorio, built a cow house and worked on a farm.

From 1934 until 1937 he lived in Eritrea, Africa, for the manufacturing of roadworks and during the 1940s he was in Germany. From 1949 until 1951 he was employed in Cameroon, Africa, for the manufacturing of a hydraulic dyke ...

The letter also revealed that Vittorio returned to Italy a few months before his younger brother, Ettore, in 1931, and that he spent the rest of his working life, including some years in Germany, in the building sector. He died in Tarcento in 1964.

7. Luigi Dozzi

Born Pozzo di Codroipo, Provincia di Udine, 19 February 1902.
Died Emu Plains, New South Wales, 23 December 1988.

By the time he took the Oath of Allegiance in October 1946, almost twenty years after his arrival, Luigi Dozzi had seen more of Australia than most Australians see in a lifetime. Like so many of his countrymen, Luigi went where the work was, invariably to far-flung parts of this vast and often inhospitable land.

Luigi's life story was compiled in August 1999 by his eldest son Giovanni (John) Dozzi, now living in retirement in Buddina, Queensland. I located John after gleaning from Luigi's naturalisation papers (obtained through the National Archives) that his eldest son had attended Toowoomba's Downlands College from 1944 to 1948. A quick call to Downlands resulted in confirmation of John's attendance in those years, and the college was able to confirm his whereabouts via its database. The following are John's recollections of his father's life. John's brother Enzo and sister Elsa assisted him in telling this story.

Luigi was the first-born of Giovanni and Oliva Dozzi (née Serafini) and was followed by four brothers and four sisters of which three, one brother and two sisters, died in infancy. Of all the brothers and sisters, Valentina, who resides in Argentina, is now the only one living.

Luigi grew up in a rural community depending entirely on output from the land. As a teenager he went through the difficult times of the First World War of 1914 to 1918, and as a result he grew to dislike war and its futility.

In January 1927, Luigi married Lavinia Cominotto of the town of Grions, five kilometres from his home town of Pozzo. Following the custom of the day the bride moved into Luigi's parents' home, which meant sharing the divided house between them.

In that same year, mainly due to the pressures of having increased numbers living in the one house combined with difficult economic times, it was decided that Luigi should emigrate alone, obtain work and save enough to bring out his wife, who was at this time expecting their first child. The options were Canada or Australia, and from limited information as to the conditions in these countries he decided to try for Australia — a decision based mainly on the reports of a cousin who resided in Melbourne and would act as sponsor.

During his early years in Australia, living with his cousin in Melbourne, he worked and learned skills as a concrete finisher and carpenter, mainly on road construction. In 1933, he received word that tobacco was being grown in the Texas region of Queensland. He moved to that area to learn this form of farming and the following year he took up tobacco growing with two associates near Yelarbon in Queensland. By 1935 he was farming on his own.

In that same year his family back in Italy offered to pay for his return. But Luigi was determined to stay in Australia, and in the following year, with financial help from his family, his wife Lavinia and son Giovanni arrived.

At first the transition from life in a closely knit Italian community to the Australian bush and a galvanised iron hut was devastating for Lavinia. But for Giovanni, who had lived a sickly life in Italy, it meant renewed health, vitality and the marvels of the bush. And slowly, almost imperceptibly, the land grew upon Lavinia. Luigi found that his wife grew strong, resilient, tough-spirited and hard-working.

A second son, Enzo, was born to them on 1 September 1937. Two significant events happened in 1939. Their third child, Elsa, was born on 4 June at Texas Hospital, and that year also brought the happy arrival from Italy of Lavinia's younger brother, Angelo Cominotto. He stayed with them for the remainder of the 1939 season and then left them to take up sharefarming himself.

During these years of hard work, and good seasons tempered by bad, the Italians in Texas had an active social life — according to a descendant's words of many years later, 'You should have been here in those days, the place was alive.' As was common at the time, people shared the good and bad times and helped each other out when they could.

One of the many stories Luigi was fond of telling about this period concerned an evening get-together that dragged on into the small hours of the morning. The men decided to play *bocce* at two o'clock in the morning using a kerosene lantern to light the end of the rink, and it fell to Luigi, as host, to carry the lantern.

Due to the poor light and the copious amounts of beer and wine consumed, the bowlers relied on the lantern carrier to indicate the position of the kitty (the ball at which the bowlers aimed). Every time he told this story, Luigi used to chuckle as he recalled pocketing the kitty, then directing the bowlers here and there, and at the end of the game placing the kitty where it would cause the most consternation.

Lasting friendships were formed during the 'tobacco days'.

In 1946 the family decided to move to Melbourne, hoping that a change in lifestyle might bring better financial security. But although Luigi had already spent several years in Melbourne before Lavinia's arrival, they decided that the venture would not succeed for them — possibly due to the experiences of the intervening years, as well as the fact that they now had a family to support. So some twelve months after arriving in Melbourne they returned to the activity they knew best, cultivating tobacco.

They settled on a farm near the town of Inglewood in Queensland. After the 1949 tobacco crop was harvested there, they began looking for a farm of their own. A property that drew Luigi's interest was located near a farm called 'The Brook', in the Yelarbon district, where he and the family had spent many years sharefarming. So he knew the conditions of the weather, soil and water first-hand. But because he refused to borrow the paltry extra amount to cover the price of the farm, the purchase was passed up.

In the meantime, brother-in-law Angelo Cominotto had moved to the Richmond–Windsor area of New South Wales and successfully established himself as a vegetable grower. Luigi and Lavinia, after passing up the farm near Yelarbon, decided to look around the area where Angelo was farming.

In September 1950 they settled for a small, forty-acre [sixteen hectare] poultry farm in the small town of Llandilo, west of the suburb of St Marys in Sydney. At Llandilo they established a group of friends and soon became renowned for their hospitality. Lavinia began caring for the children of friends who were establishing themselves and needed help. The care she gave to these children created a bond that stood the passage of many years. She came to be respected for her wisdom and her readiness to assist others in need. And as for dressmaking — well, no-one could whip up a garment from a few scraps of material like Lavinia.

In addition to working the small farm of free-range chickens, Luigi took up growing tobacco on a farm near Penrith. The crop grew to exceed his greatest expectations. Experts assessed the crop as magnificent, and he could see that here lay the culmination of his potential as a farmer.

But as the crop neared harvesting in the summer of 1951, disaster struck in the form of a violent storm. The crop was devastated and completely lost. He never recovered from this blow and never grew tobacco again.

However, Luigi was a man of physical strength and resilience. He looked elsewhere for a livelihood whilst Lavinia tended the farm. There was construction work in the vicinity of St Marys, so he took up employment as a concrete finisher. When the construction work finished he found work with a gravel company in the Castlereagh district of New South Wales.

In 1959 the farm at Llandilo was sold and the family moved into a new home at Kingswood near Penrith. Luigi continued his work for the gravel company for several years and then took up a job at a nearby hospital until he retired in 1968.

In 1973, with all three children married, Luigi and Lavinia moved to Woodriffe Street in Penrith, Sydney, where they remained until the frailty that comes with advancing years overtook them. Due to ill health they moved to Edinglassie retirement village in Emu Plains, where Luigi died on 23 December 1988 and Lavinia on 7 May 1999.

They left behind them thirty-six descendants — three children, eleven grandchildren and twenty-two great-grandchildren.

Luigi loved his adopted country of Australia and was constant in his praise and admiration of her. His greatest regret in life was that he had not managed to see his much-loved mother, Oliva, before she died. She passed away in the late 1940s before he had established himself and could afford to visit her.

8. Domenico Campara

BORN ROVERE VERONESE, PROVINCIA DI VERONA, 14 JANUARY 1899.
DIED BOVOLONE, PROVINCIA DI VERONA, 28 NOVEMBER 1995.

WHILE DOMENICO CAMPARA was in Australia only until the mid-1930s, his extended family had a profound influence on those living around Koyuga and Tongala, southeast of Echuca in Victoria's north.

Domenico fathered seven children, some of whom still live in Italy, including Maria, a nun, and Don Giuseppe, the parish priest of Bovolone. Maria explained that she was with her father in Australia for the seven years he was here, but her ill health forced the immediate family back to Italy.

There is little more to the Domenico Campara tale, other than to say he lived his years out surrounded by his family. But the Campara name survived in the area — through a relative, Angelo Campara. He came to Australia in 1911 aboard the *Sidley*. As it happened, Domenico's forwarding address and nominee on the Fremantle passenger list were given as 'Koyuga, Victoria ... Campara, Angelo'. Angelo brought out many of his family members.

Angelo's ten children and extended family were well known in the region, as long-time Tongala resident Ivy Vistarini explained to me. 'I came here in 1947 from Kyabram and they were here then,' she said of the Camparas. 'I think they were farmers. I don't know that they had a dairy farm, but they must have been farmers. And their mother lived to a great old age too. I can just remember her.

'Frank was the eldest boy ... They were all in a band. They'd play in old-time dance bands all round the area — balls and dances at Kyabram, Tongala and Echuca. Joe played the saxophone, Frank played the flat bass, Anne played the guitar. Then there was Nita, now living in Western Australia, Betty, living in Echuca, and the youngest one, Lou, who was world-famous for his piano accordion playing — he was a whiz.'

There is some confusion about the exact relationship between Domenico and Angelo. Some suggest they were cousins. Others recall that Domenico was often called Tony — that name certainly rang a bell with many. 'Tony was Dad's cousin. I've got an idea he went back to Italy,' said Angelo's daughter Betty.

'A Man in a Million'

Giuseppe Zammarchi, during wartime. The photo was developed by
Wolfgang Sievers Photography, 9 Collins Street Melbourne.
PHOTOGRAPH COURTESY WILLIAM AND BERYL JONES AND FAMILY, DRYSDALE, VICTORIA.

9. Giuseppe Alfonso Maria Zammarchi

BORN RIANA DI MONCHIO, PROVINCIA DI PARMA, 14 MARCH 1901.
DIED GEELONG, VICTORIA, 1 FEBRUARY 1987.

THERE ARE FEW more colourful tales of Italian immigration during the era of
the *Re d'Italia* than that of Giuseppe Zammarchi. A close friend described
him as 'a man in a million' — an exaggeration, perhaps, but Zammarchi's
patience and understanding of those around him, in the face of troubles,
typified the resolve that makes for successful immigration.

That close friend, the late Charles D'Aprano, recalled Zammarchi's early
years. 'He was an Italian Communist. He was very active politically and
came from a region in Italy that has been anti-clerical and anti-
establishment for centuries; where democracy is the order of the day, but
with a shade of anarchism. He was anti-clerical, for instance, yet he was
able to work with people of all opinions.'

The advent of Fascism drove Zammarchi to France, and in the years
leading up to his departure on the *Re d'Italia* he worked as a builder, miner
and timber sawmiller, and even on fortifications along the German border

as a concreter. He eventually returned to Italy before setting off for Australia.

Morag Loh's book *With Courage in Their Cases*, which quotes from Wendy Lowenstein's *Weevils in the Flour*, has proved a valuable source of Zammarchi's recollections of his arrival in Australia. Reproduced with the publisher's permission, the following interview with Zammarchi, conducted during the 1970s, gives full weight to the trials facing these new Australians — the financial difficulties, the onset of war and assimilation into society:

On Gaining Work:

When I came to Australia in 1927 it was terrible. When I got in Fremantle I went along the warehouses and it was hundreds of people sitting there and no work. I came to Adelaide, it was worse. When I came to Melbourne you couldn't get a job for anything at all. It was no good to go to the Italian consul for help, it was hundreds of people there and they didn't want to see them.

I was lucky that I was speaking French very good, so I said, "I'll go and see the French consul". He got me a job in Tasmania but I didn't go because at the same time I got another job in a timber mill at Erica. I made up the money I had borrowed from my uncle to come here, I sent them a hundred and some pounds, fifty for the trip and fifty for home. Then I was caught in the timber strike in 1929. It lasted for months and there wasn't much work around after it finished. I had very little money left and a fellow advised me to go to Orbost. "It's good country". By now I could speak English not too bad so I went to Orbost by myself.

At Orbost I met two chaps, two Australians, looking for timber to make a wharf, long beams, twenty-two feet by eleven inches and eighteen feet by nine and you had to have good timber. I went with them, we had two teams of bullocks, a heap of wedges, a saw, axes, hammers. We went all over the mountains, living in the bush, coming from one tree to another, testing to see if they were good. We worked for a while at Cann River and went to Gipsy Point. There the contractor went broke and he didn't pay us.

I came back to Melbourne and picked up a job shifting wheat on a farm on the Wacool River in New South Wales. But the farmer went broke and couldn't pay us either. This time I was really in a bad way. I had just enough money to come back to Melbourne. I had not much money but I had friends, two or three that I had known in Italy. I didn't ask very much, you know, very seldom I asked for money. So I lived with them and I managed.

Then I was very lucky, I met an Italian from the south of Italy. He said to me, "You like to make a few bob?". "You kidding?". "Come on". We went to Neil brothers that had transports. They're in Heidelberg Road now but then they were in South Melbourne. They were cleaning the ashes from the gas works and on the ashes it was lumps of coal and blacksmiths were using it on the forge.

They were giving us a shilling a bag to get this coal out of a great heap of ashes, bigger than a house. This Italian knew everyone around South Melbourne and he said, "We go and we don't say too much and we can't work too hard or they cut us the price. So we make twenty bags, no more, not even if we finish at ten o'clock". We get twenty bags each a day, nobody to look at us, a fellow come and count the bags and pay us every two to three days, no taxes, anything. It was a good job.

Then some friends were up at a place past Myrtleford on the Ovens putting down tobacco. They had written to go up so I went with another chap and worked there from Christmas 1930 to June 1931. There was plenty of work but those days they didn't have much money to pay much wages so we left to come back to Melbourne. That's how it was. We travelled for work all the time. We lived single men, but we didn't get much money. It was no security at all.

In 1937, I'd been nearly ten years in Australia and worked around a lot. My first long steady job it was in St. Arnaud, with a mate, in the bush cutting wood. It was plenty of wood there, good wood, good work and fair money. We did alright. I got the licence for driving in 1932 and we paid off a truck. After another year or so we buy a brand new one for six hundred and fifty pounds and we work until 1937 with that, all the time in the St. Arnaud district. We got to know all the people around there and made a lot of friends.

Then my mate left. He had been wounded in the First World War, shrapnel on the back, and he couldn't take any more. I was left on my own and it was very hard work, and I was getting a bit in a rut. Then they found gold in Tennant Creek so I decided to go. I had just bought another new truck so I drove there. That was June, 1937.

This run of alluvial gold it was nothing at all, a misery. I hung around Tennant Creek and tried prospecting. It was no good at first then I got some gold. Just when I was a bit successful Italy joined the war, June 1940, and they arrested me as an enemy alien, seized the gold in the bank, about five hundred pound's worth, and took me back to Victoria. I had to leave my truck there in Tennant Creek and I didn't see it again until after the war. There was myself and two other Italian boys arrested, one was from an anti-fascist family and the other knew nothing of politics. There were two Germans picked up too. After this I did sixteen months in the iron.

On Internment and the Army:

An enemy alien. They were nuts. I hadn't committed nothing. I was an active anti-fascist, a militant. When I arrived here in '27 it was already clubs, fascist and anti-fascist. The anti-fascists, we had the Matteotti Club in Spring Street near Little Lonsdale Street. I remember there was a plate of glass over the door and a fascist went and broke it so they caught him and belted him. A policeman came to intervene and there was a court case. We won.

During the waterside workers' strike in 1928 the Club would buy sides of beef and were making meals to support the strikers. We left Spring Street because the place was too small and went to the Horticultural Society Hall opposite the Trades Hall, but during the Depression 1931–32 the Club had to close down. The most active members had to leave for work. Many became canecutters in Queensland.

It was a fascist club in Russell Street and the Italian community, the consulate included, had a club in South Melbourne, the Cavour Club. The fascists and their sympathisers took over that. During the war the fascist insignia was pulled out of the Cavour Club, otherwise the authorities didn't bother them. In the 1940s, during the war, the left formed the Italia Libera. After the war we should have gone down and kicked the pro-fascists out of the Cavour Club but a lot of anti-fascists didn't want trouble. So I was a militant since I land in Australia and I still am too but I have never broken any law at all, not now and not then.

They took me from the Northern Territory to Adelaide, then to Melbourne, then to a camp at Tatura near Shepparton. We were with the Germans, it was only about a hundred and ten Italians and the other 900 or 1000 were Germans. Sometimes it was brawling between themselves, the Germans, fascists and anti-fascists and sometimes between the fascists themselves. There was a sect there among the Germans, Jehovah's Witness, and they never have anything to do with the fascists, and one of them, one small chap, he didn't stint, he insulted them. I was frightened some of them will knock him off or treat him badly.

On Hitler's birthday the fascists had a big turn out and they put out a table with some money on it they said Hitler sent to them and anyone that went there they were giving a few shillings. This Jehovah's Witness, he pass there and they call him over and he went and spit on the money. "They are Hitler's money, they are blood money". He had guts.

Then they sent us to Hay. There were 1100 of us Italians there from Queensland, New South Wales and Victoria including about a hundred fascists. There you were like a military man, treated with rations, if you didn't want to work you didn't have to. Only the camp duty was compulsory, every week or a fortnight it was peeling potatoes or cleaning, everyone was doing it. There Tom S. [sic] and I started a school teaching boys English. We had the grammar by an Italian professor that was in England. We had two language classes, one in the evening for advanced students and an afternoon class for beginners. There were about a hundred students.

The school had a left policy, all our references were against fascism, so the fascists organised against us. They told me I would be the first to be found on the top of the barbed wire but when I was going to school at night I had four or five boys with me for protection. There were sailors from two Italian boats and six or seven of them were very bad fascists. But amongst them was some young kids and they came to the school, stuck with it and defended it.

Then one day, one fellow got killed, an anarchist from the north of Italy. It was three or four of them always going to argue the point with the fascists. We warned them not to go but they persisted. The anarchist had an argument then went to the tap to get a drink. They hit him on the head and killed him. There were witnesses but nobody could get the real story. Whoever has done it has gone scot-free.

Many fascists believed the war would finish quickly and they would get compensation. Fascist supporters were taken in by this talk of compensation in the beginning, but as the war drag on they got bad disillusion, because they had family, wife, children outside. Some come to me. "What can we do?". "The best is to see if you can help your family. The war will not be over in 24 hours and fascism will never succeed".

Then it was put around a circular that everyone had the right to apply to be released from the camp. Some fascists would not apply, they wanted to be there, they were sure fascism would win, they thought of themselves like prisoners of war. But most people applied and in the end most were released, even the most rabid supporters. They made a statutory declaration that they would never engage in political activities. Before your release you had to go through a kind of investigation, a kind of court, to satisfy the authorities that you hadn't done anything wrong, hadn't broken the laws of Australia. Most people from the camp went to Sydney to get their cases heard.

I had friends in Melbourne, they used to come to see me at the camp in Hay nearly every month, and they arranged for my case to be heard in Melbourne because I came originally from Victoria.

There was a panel of judges, five or six, and two from Military Intelligence who cross-examined me. I was questioned for more than two hours non-stop. Was I a Communist? A Labor Party member? What did I have against Australia? All sorts of questions.

I had witnesses ready to speak for me, who knew me personally, from Melbourne and St. Arnaud. The judge said to the prosecution, "What have you got to say gentlemen?". "We arrested this man for the security of the state". "I strongly recommend his release". I was released in September.

I worked around as a driver for a while but I knew that at the time the fight was against fascism. We were getting here in Australia a pamphlet from France, *The Republican* I think it was called. And so we knew that in Italy it was people fighting against war. And so I enlisted and went in the army. My company, it was the Fourth Employment Company and we were mostly Greeks and Italians, a sprinkling of Jews, a Finnish fellow, a couple of Dutch, a couple of French. Corporals and officers, it was Australians.

They put us on the wharf, it was three companies altogether. The ships were frightened to be bottled up by

Japanese submarines in the Port of Melbourne and they tried to get out fast. The crane took the goods from the ship and piled them on the wharf, higher than houses, sewing machines, bales of wool, timber. We were loading into trucks and it had been put wherever there was a space, in church halls for instance, until we cleared the wharf. It wasn't only us, it was all the Melbourne waterside workers and parsons and priests at the receiving places as clerks.

When this was finished, as I was a driver, they sent me to Tocumwal and I was there for a long time. We were taking the vehicles off the trains that came from Victoria mostly and driving them to the New South Wales trains and tying them on. It was eight of us on our team and we were there practically 24 hours a day on call. We put American and Australian divisions through. One American division had eighty trains, every three or four hours a train was passing through. The captain had been a country architect and he was a very nice chap, he trusted us, we load day or night it doesn't matter, take charge, sign the paper, off they go. One morning, just past midnight, another captain came in, in charge of young kids. "Go down", I said, "they will have a hot meal ready for you". When they came back, two hours later, the train was ready. He could not believe it, it took him much longer in Melbourne to get that train to go. They said they had given him drivers but not one kid was a driver. Before they left we managed to show them how to tie a truck on quick, two soldiers to do one truck.

At Tocumwal we lived in tents, but for the mess, there was no proper accommodation. We had a kitchen in the open and one day I went down to have a meal and turned the soup. It was maggots, black and white, hundreds of them. I told the boys, "Don't you eat this soup. Look here". The meat was walking. We've got a strike committee together, myself and three or four others and even the Greeks, who were hostile to the Italians because of the fascist invasion of Greece, they understood the situation. From the kitchen the cooks brought something special. "Leave it. Tell the cook to eat it himself". Even the sick people joined the strike, unanimous it was.

We didn't eat anything from the mess but we were still going to the station to unload the trains. First came two fellows with corporals' stripes to investigate and when they saw the situation, everyone solid, they got frightened. Next came a major, then someone from Intelligence. We told them what it was, we simply refused to eat. They saw the situation and immediately put in the carpenters and built a fairly decent mess.

Five or six of us, most of us militants on the strike, were shifted out of Tocumwal after the struggle. Unexpectedly one morning they put us on a truck and take us to Albury, to the Sixth Employment Company. An officer there told me, "You will never drive for me". "Don't you think I am pining for driving. I have done all I want to in my life on those damn trucks, up to twenty hours a day sometimes. So you can imagine how much it worries me".

I was loading at the station for three days then a sergeant put me on a truck again. I drove more and more and soon I even got to take that officer around.

The unit was mixed and it was Yugoslavs. They resented the war terribly, they were very, very bitter. Sometimes you had to calm them down they were so left militant. Yugoslavia was invaded and they felt they had lost almost all. When there was a film show at the camp, before the main film they would show Churchill, Roosevelt, Stalin. When Churchill came they don't say nothing, when Roosevelt came, nothing, but when they see Stalin the house was coming down.

After the War:

At the end of the war I was a couple of months as a driver at Royal Park. It was full of tents then, in front of the zoo and along Flemington Road. Then when I left the army I went back to the Northern Territory to fix up my truck. I found kids had played with it, it needed new tyres. My friend could get them but not immediately so I was there for a while, I met friends I had known from before — the publican, the doctor — and I got work as a miner on the Eldorado Mine. I got tyres on the truck and came back to Melbourne and work on the construction work, a builder's labourer. I got naturalised. I got married too, to an Australian [Florence Ligas], I settled down. I haven't gone back to Italy, I didn't want to. I regard myself as an Australian now. I've spent more time here than anywhere else in the world.

While Zammarchi had served with the Italian Air Forces for six months in the First World War, there was little doubt where his allegiances lay for the remainder of his life. It is fitting, then, that the man who gave his eulogy almost eighty-six years after his birth was another immigrant, Welshman William 'Taffy' Jones O.A.M., who died in March 2001. This excerpt from the eulogy says much about Joe Zammarchi:

My life seems to have started like Joe's when I came to Australia because Joe was one of the first who befriended me. Joe respected this land, its beauty, its hardships, its animals, its birds and above all its trees because as many of you know he earned his living in the bush. From cutting its timber and eating its fruits to digging its gold made Joe glad that he had come to a rather wonderful country.

'She's a good place, Taff,' he used to say. I can pay no higher tribute than that of my own children, who called him 'our Uncle Joe'.

10. Luigi (Louis) Tagliaferri

BORN PEZZOLO, VILMINORE, PROVINCIA DI BERGAMO, 15 MAY 1906.
DIED EAST FREMANTLE, WESTERN AUSTRALIA, 21 MARCH 1971.

IT WAS ALWAYS Luigi Tagliaferri's intention to board a passenger ship bound for America. Driven by a desire to be reunited with his brothers, Giovanni and Antonio, Luigi made the trek to the port of Genoa with that sole intention. Regrettably, he discovered that the quotas for 'the home of the brave' had been filled, and so he boarded the *Re d'Italia*, bound for Australia.

As the days and weeks passed, and the old steamer drew closer and closer to its destination, Luigi tried to come to terms with what fate had decreed. Alone and without the English language, he would somehow have to secure work, food and shelter in a land he knew little about — a land devoid of the friends, family and way of life he knew.

Luigi was one of a family of twenty-one children (twenty boys and one girl) born to Bortolo and Petina Tagliaferri (née Tagliaferri). Thirteen of them survived infancy, and later left Pezzolo for faraway places such as America, Spain, France and, in Luigi's case, Australia. 'Dad originally went to France to work as a builder's labourer as a very young boy of twelve, but he left because there was a virtual famine in that country,' Luigi's son Giulio told me.

Luigi's disembarkation paper carried a forwarding address of a boarding house at 104 Drummond Street, Carlton, the premises of Maria Armanasco. He also had an ally in his cousin, Elia Tagliaferri, at that time living in Gormanston, Tasmania. Elia had left Italy specifically to work in the Mount Lyell copper mine, but later went back to his homeland, where he married and settled permanently.

After a three-month period in Tasmania, where he combined his mining work with timber cutting, Luigi returned to the mainland to take up lodgings in Maria's boarding house. Soon afterwards, he and about eight fellow Italian lodgers were contracted to work in the mine at Yallourn, and were transported there by truck.

But the toil was only temporary, and through a boarding house contact Luigi was advised that more permanent employment could be provided by the Mosconi family, who operated a boarding house outside Kalgoorlie.

Travelling by train and then hitchhiking, Luigi made his way from Melbourne through Victoria to the fruit-growing regions of South Australia. He later boarded a Fremantle-bound vessel from Port Adelaide. But after arriving in Fremantle, he only got as far as the goldfields town of Merredin before he ran out of money, which prompted him to turn his hand to anything and everything to raise some badly needed capital.

Following a brief stay in Merredin, Luigi travelled across some of the most inhospitable country in Australia, to Leonora, about 340 kilometres northeast of Kalgoorlie. There he cut timber on the Wood Line, a seventy-five kilometre stretch of eucalypts, mulgas and lakes bordering the desert. From Leonora, he ventured to Gwalia, completing what had been a six-month pilgrimage from Fremantle. Luigi laboured there for two years, and by 1933 had made enough money to fund his return to Italy. The same year, on his arrival, he married Giulia Pierina, who was from the same town. Pezzolo was only a tiny village, and as was the case with most villages dotted throughout the northern Italian region, its inhabitants were all either directly or distantly related.

Not long afterwards, Luigi returned to Australia and headed to Gwalia to work in the mines, this time with his wife. 'Mum came from the ice and snow and sub-zero temperatures of Pezzolo [in the foothills of the Alps] to the 130 degrees of Gwalia, and the tin shacks with the hessian linings,' Giulio said. 'And there the family remained until 1953, when the mine closed down and we all moved to Fremantle.' Aside from Melbourne, Mount Lyell and Gwalia, Luigi also spent twelve months each in the Western Australian towns of Quairading and Meekatharra.

In March 1938, when he applied for the admission of his brother-in-law, Giuseppe Tagliaferri, Luigi declared that he had no bank account, owing to the recent purchase of a house at Gwalia for £80. But he stressed that he was employed at an average wage of £10 per week by the Sons of Gwalia mine as a machine miner, and had already been naturalised.

In 1937 the Tagliaferris' first child, Lucia, was born, and four years later came their son Giulio. Both children now reside in Western Australia, as does their mother. But the years down the mine eventually took their toll on Luigi Tagliaferri. As Giulio explained, 'Dad died in 1971 from a miners' complaint ... he went downhill quickly of a leukaemia-related condition.'

11. Girolamo Deppi

BORN DOMEGGE, PROVINCIA DI BELLUNO, 30 SEPTEMBER 1893.
DIED FAIRFIELD, NEW SOUTH WALES, 27 FEBRUARY 1964.

GIROLAMO DEPPI WAS born to Lucio and Giovanna Maria Deppi (née Fedon) in the northern Italian town of Domegge, where he later served his country as a member of the Alpini during the First World War. Hostilities later took him to Turkey, where at one point he was captured as a prisoner of war.

But the emergence of Benito Mussolini and the Fascist regime ensured that Girolamo's time in Italy would be all too brief. Although he was one of the first workers assigned to the construction of the *seggiovia*, or chairlift, in Cortina d'Ampezzo, the increasingly unstable political environment forced his exodus to Australia by way of the *Re d'Italia*. Thus, in October 1927, Girolamo said *addio* to his wife Caterina De Bernardo (herself a native of Domegge, born in 1900), and their two daughters Venilde Lucilla, aged five, and Licia Silvia, aged two, planning to save enough money to bring them over later.

Girolamo made it safely to Melbourne on the *Re d'Italia*, but as has already been described, the *Principessa Mafalda*, at that time en route to Rio de Janeiro, failed to reach her destination — leading to a terrible bureaucratic mix-up that impacted on the Deppi family in Italy. 'My mother eventually received a telegram from the authorities to say the ship had sunk and Girolamo had died along with everyone on board,' Licia told me. 'It took the local postman to inform my mother that my father had made it safely to Australia on the *Re d'Italia*, and that the ship that had sunk was not his ship.'

On arrival in Australia Girolamo went where the work was, landing odd jobs on farms around Victoria, including Ballarat, where he picked onions. He settled briefly in Adelaide in 1931, then lived in Brisbane until June 1932 and from then on lived in Sydney.

'At some point he met a man from Tuscany who was making statues in Melbourne,' Licia said. 'My father appreciated that sort of work, and started helping him make the statues. In time he learned the craft and relocated to Sydney, where he began making his own figurines ... religious figurines of Our Lady, along with various animals such as horses, dogs and lions, as well as nudes.'

By the time he was reunited with his wife and two daughters in Sydney, Girolamo had established his statue-making workshop at 236 Riley Street, in the Sydney suburb of Surry Hills. Girolamo worked on the ground floor of what had previously been a hotel, and the family lived upstairs. The size of the family soon increased, with the birth of another daughter, Sidnea (after the city of Sydney), in 1935, and a son, John, in 1940.

The success of the business of G. Deppi Statue Manufacturer enabled Girolamo to secure a block of land for a house in the Sydney suburb of Fairfield, just prior to the outbreak of the Second World War. It also enabled him to afford luxuries like motor cars — first a Buick, then an Essex, a Morris after the War, and later a Ford Prefect.

Girolamo was never interned during the War because he had become a naturalised Australian in 1935. But the War effort demanded that he assist at the Goodyear tyre factory, and he worked there by night while producing his figurines by day. He finally died of a stroke aged seventy, in 1964.

12. Angelo Brotto

BORN GALLIERA, VENETA, PROVINCIA DI PADOVA, 14 DECEMBER 1898.
DIED UPPER FERNTREE GULLY, VICTORIA, 20 JULY 1967.

ANGELO BROTTO ACCOMPANIED his cousin, Ernesto Lago, passenger thirteen, on the voyage to Australia. Angelo, along with another passenger, Angelo Menegazzo (passenger nineteen), was sponsored to this country by Menegazzo's older brother, Giovanni, who declared himself their guardian.

After their arrival, Giovanni lived at 230 Lygon Street, Carlton, a premises listed in the 1928 Sands and McDougall Directory (a directory of residents in all streets of Victoria, which was available from 1912 to 1974) as frequented by Italians. Angelo spent the early years in Melbourne concreting, and for some time also worked on the railways. Following the arrival from Italy of his wife, Caterina Cecchin, whom he married by proxy in 1934, the Brottos relocated to Echuca, where their only child, John, was born in 1937.

Angelo took up market gardening, but unfortunately his farm was hit by severe flooding. This forced the family to relocate to Werribee for a six-year period before they finally settled in Ferntree Gully. It was there that he died in 1967, and his wife passed away there more than a decade later.

'They were just market gardeners and that was it,' their son John said to me. 'They came from Padua, the both of them, and they were lovers then. But they never went back ... too many bad memories.'

13. Ernesto Lago

BORN FONTANIVA, PROVINCIA DI PADOVA, 4 MAY 1899.
DIED LAVERTON, VICTORIA, 27 MAY 1980.

THE MARKET GARDENS of Werribee are visible reminders of the years of toil endured by early Italian migrants like Ernesto Lago. The son of Antonio and Luigia Lago (née Perin), Ernesto was sponsored to Australia by Silvio Lago, presumably a relative from his home town of Fontaniva. It was Silvio who also sponsored the arrival of another of the *Re d'Italia*'s passengers, Attilio GioBatta Bellò (number twenty-seven).

Ernesto was one of four children, three of whom sought fortune in faraway places. While Ernesto's eldest brother Angelo remained in Italy, another brother, Piero, and sister Maria searched for prosperity in Belgium.

Ernesto's time at sea was made somewhat easier by the presence of another passenger, Angelo Brotto. Ernesto and Angelo were cousins, and almost certainly resolved to make the Australian pilgrimage together. 'He had no food, nothing ... he was very poor,' Ernesto's daughter Lina Cecchin (née Lago) said to me. 'I know that in the beginning he cut sugar cane in northern Queensland, before travelling down to Echuca to grow tomatoes and cut trees ... but in the end Dad settled in Werribee.'

The Depression years in Werribee took a heavy toll on Ernesto, who at one stage sought financial assistance from a friend, Antonio Agostino, to buy a pair of shoes. But Ernesto's happy-go-lucky nature got him through, as did his love of dancing which, in the early 1930s, could have secured him an Australian championship had he been naturalised.

By 1935, after he had settled at a property at Farrants Road, Werribee South, Ernesto sent for his wife, Giannina (née Toniolo), whom he had married in Italy in 1923, and their two Italian-born daughters Josephine and Elda. Completing the family was a third daughter, Lina, who was born in Werribee in 1941. There the Lagos lived out the next forty years, until Ernesto's death at age eighty-one.

'Though the years went on we never left Werribee. We always remained within three kilometres of each other,' Lina said. 'I'm still living now, more than fifty-six years later, on the same road where I was born, Farrants Road.'

14. Giovanni Cusinato

BORN SAN MARTINO DI LUPARI, PROVINCIA DI TREVISO, 15 AUGUST 1890.
DIED WERRIBEE, VICTORIA, 14 OCTOBER 1971.

IT IS REASONABLE to assume that when Giovanni Cusinato set foot on number 19 North Wharf, Augusto Goegan was there to greet him. Augusto, at that time living at a house owned by a Signor Santo De Rizzo at 69 Barkly Street in Carlton, had only just turned twenty, and it was he who had pledged written support for his 'Uncle John'.

At that time Giovanni was thirty-six years old, married to Maria Cusinato (née Fratin) and father to four children — Livio, Zaira, Rosina and Luigina. But desperate times call for desperate measures, and Giovanni was forced to extricate himself temporarily from his own flesh and blood to be with his nephew in the new country.

By the time the remaining Cusinato family members came to Melbourne, Giovanni was toiling in Echuca, in northeastern Victoria by the Murray River. There, he and another of the *Re d'Italia*'s passengers, Angelo Brotto (passenger twelve), grew tomatoes and watermelons, which they subsequently transported to Victoria Market by rail.

'But my father didn't do much good at Echuca,' Livio remembers. 'He and Antonio Brotto had to pay freight for all of their work, and they were working for virtually nothing. So I got my father down to Werribee in 1938 and we were reunited in farming ... I worked on a farm day and night, and my father worked for a cousin on land surrounding Werribee College.'

Giovanni lived the life of a farmer until sickness overcame him. By then he had spent more than half his years in Australia, and virtually all of them in Werribee.

15. Vittorio Bonanni

(see Ettore Bonanni)

16. Valentino Fogliato

BORN MOLVENA, PROVINCIA DI VICENZA, 3 OCTOBER 1899.
DIED MOLVENA, PROVINCIA DI VICENZA, 4 JUNE 1972.

LIKE OTHERS WHO disembarked from the *Re d'Italia* that day in 1927, Valentino Fogliato spent many of his years on Australian soil seeking work on farms in rural Victoria. Valentino lived at Leongatha for a year before spending the same amount of time at Yarram; then three years in Myrtleford were followed by seven more in Wangaratta, where he put down more substantial roots than anywhere else.

A document from A.C.T. archives dated 8 December 1939, reveals that Valentino was a tobacco grower in Wangaratta at that time. It also reveals that he had arranged to be married by proxy in March 1939 to Terafina Dalla Valle, thirty-four, who hailed from Salcedo. Although Valentino had completed the necessary proxy papers before the local church authorities of Melbourne's St Patricks Cathedral the year before, he heard nothing from Terafina. Accordingly, he wrote to the clergyman in Italy refusing to go ahead, and there is no record of his ever marrying.

In Wangaratta he was employed by Duncan Martell, whose son Grant recollects that there were often Italian labourers on the property. 'I was about five at the time and they got me drunk on plonk,' he recalls.

Marj Taylor, Grant's sister, is several years older, and remembers the man they called 'Val'. 'He had a habit of getting the eggs, sticking a hole in them and eating them raw,' she said to me.

Another Italian family in the area at the time was that of passenger forty-one, Gaetano Lazzarotto, whose son, Danny, remembers Valentino well. 'We used to call him Val, and he wore very strong glasses. Poor old

Val was a bachelor and he ended up at Mount Buffalo during the War washing pots and pans. He was a good worker, and anybody who wasn't in those days didn't survive. As a person he was a lost soul. He was part of the gang and they were all from the same area in Italy — there was Joe Bosa, Angelo Menegazzo, Valentino Fogliato and the old man.'

Danny believes Valentino may have returned to Italy shortly before or after the Second World War ended. What became of him in his later years remains a mystery.

17. Ermenegildo Ponta

Born Treppo Grande, Provincia di Udine, 22 July 1898.
Died Treppo Grande, Provincia di Udine, 7 November 1964.

It is more than 100 years now since this 'man of the world' was born, and thirty-eight since he died. But the memory of Ermenegildo Ponta, like so many of the *Re d'Italia*'s passengers, lives on in his children and his children's children.

As he had spent precious little of his life in Australia, Ermenegildo left few traces, and it took some time for me to locate his next of kin. I was unable to find any listing for the name Ponta in the Melbourne *White Pages*, although a Telstra operator confirmed a listing in Maylands, Western Australia.

So, in late October 1998, I phoned Gino Ponta, who believed he knew of Ermenegildo Ponta. He said the Pontas hailed from a place twenty kilometres north of Udine called Treppo Grande. 'I remember my father, when we were in France, talking about the old days, and mentioning Ermenegildo, or "Gildo", as he called him,' said Gino, who migrated to Australia in 1952. 'I believe he might have been my grandfather's brother. He was a sculptor, as I recall, who spent a brief period in the United States, and he had a good name.'

I turned to a man named Paolo Coniglio, a teacher at Carlton's Amici Language Centre — yours truly was a student there. Although I have to admit Paolo's patience was sorely tested in his dealings with me on that level, we developed an important alliance through the research for this book. Paolo was extremely interested in the subject matter and, given his fluency in both Italian and English, enthusiastically agreed to make the necessary phone calls to Italy on my behalf, to the families of men like Gildo Ponta.

Coincidentally, Paolo's father held an important position within the Italian Registry of Births, Deaths and Marriages, and was able to unearth the following information:

Ermenegildo Ponta was the son of Giovanni Battista and Romana Ponta, and in September 1925 he married Paolina Ermacora. Ermenegildo's wife gave birth to three children: Irma, born in February 1926, Marina, born in December 1927, and Rino, born in August 1934. Paolo confirmed that all were still alive and residing in Treppo Grande.

Over the phone, Irma confirmed that Ermenegildo was her father, and briefly explained that he lived in Australia for just seven years before returning to Italy. Irma said that Ermenegildo later went to Germany and on to Cameroon before eventually coming home to Italy, where he finally died.

On 29 December 1998, I received the following letter from Treppo Grande, written by Gilda Ponta, the daughter of Mario Ponta and granddaughter of Gildo:

> ...Ermenegildo Ponta was born in Treppo Grande, Udine, on 22 July 1898 and his mother died giving birth to him. He had two brothers older than him, but only he was an emigrant during his life.
>
> His very special life began when he was only seventeen years old and he volunteered for the First World War. He was taken prisoner in Brunico, Bolzano, and moved to a captivity camp in Russia. He said it was very cold and the prisoners were dressed in 'paper'. On his return, I don't know when, he worked as a carpenter and joiner.
>
> My grandfather emigrated for the first time to Germany, but not for a long period. In these years he married, and after my Aunt Irma was born, and with my grandmother pregnant again, he decided to leave for Australia. It was 1927.

He said that during the long journey he learnt the modern dances, unknown in Italy, on the ship's decks. When he arrived in Australia it was a very hard period for him because there was a very long strike and for surviving he went and worked in a restaurant's kitchen as a 'potato peeler'. Here he learnt to cook and in the second part of his life cooking became his new job. Maybe he also worked on the construction of a new road, because on the back of a photo he mailed to Italy in July 1928 he wrote that he was in a 'wood', 245 miles [390 kilometres] from Melbourne ... After this first difficult time he started to work as a carpenter, and when the situation was good for him his father called him back to Italy.

He left Melbourne in September 1931 on the ship *Remo*, which docked in Napoli on 24 October 1931. In 1935 he worked in Addis Ababa, Eritrea, for seven months. Eritrea was an Italian colony, but at that time it became a base for the military campaign against Ethiopia.

My grandfather went back home and then left for Stuttgart, Germany. He stayed there from 1936 to 1942 to work as a cook. During the Second World War he was home and worked in the peat fields near our village. In 1947 he went and worked in Switzerland as a seasonal employee.

He worked as a carpenter and joiner until 1949, when he got a job contract with a French firm — he became house cook for the workers in Edea, Cameroon. The weather there was terrible and he was tired and thin in the few photos of that period. He worked with local workers and hid some food for them in the oven of the kitchen. He stayed in Cameroon until 1952 and had the possibility of going home for two months every two years.

In the final years of his working life he went to Italy again and worked as a cook in the American Military Base of Aviano, Pordenone, until 1958, when he retired. Sadly, he died of cancer in 1964 ...

18. Antonio Cengia

BORN SAN DONATO, LAMON, PROVINCIA DI BELLUNO, 2 JUNE 1904.
DIED WONTHAGGI, VICTORIA, 18 MAY 1984.

A FRIENDSHIP FIRST forged in his home town of San Donato contributed to Antonio Cengia's decision to cross the globe. He was a close confidante of Giovanni Bottegal, who had made the long and arduous pilgrimage to Australia not long beforehand. It was Giovanni — after finding mining work in the Victorian town of Wonthaggi, about 180 kilometres southwest of Melbourne — who signed the *atto di chiamata* form pledging to act as Antonio's Australian guardian.

'Antonio Cengia was a great friend of my father's from the old days, and they worked together in the mines in both Kilcunda and Wonthaggi,' Giovanni's son Lou said to me. 'Tony's forwarding address on his arrival, Dudley Street Wonthaggi, was probably the only address, because Kilcunda had no streets and they couldn't afford a post box.'

But Antonio was accustomed to hardship, having left behind a country that had afforded him few favours. As the eldest of the numerous children of Pietro and Teresa Cengia (née Bottegal) of San Donato, Antonio had been forced to drift from town to town in search of work to help his parents somehow make ends meet. So desperate was Antonio's plight that by the end of 1927 — little more than a year after marrying local girl Anna Tiziani — he was forced to leave her for a new country.

By late November 1927, Antonio was reunited in Australia with his good friend Giovanni, as well as his two uncles, who had secured jobs in the Wonthaggi district. But Wonthaggi was soon caught in the grip of the Great Depression, and Antonio again found himself a pawn in a dreadful game of life. 'No-one was being employed, and even when he found a day or two's work on a farm, the farmers were unable to afford to pay him in money,' explained Antonio Cengia's daughter, Teresa, when I spoke to her. 'At least Antonio got a feed of rabbit stew, which was the staple diet in those days.'

By 1934, Antonio was again forced to look somewhere else to better his livelihood, and Tasmania was that somewhere. The copper mines of Queenstown proved to be Antonio's salvation, and for the next five years he toiled long and hard below the ground. But after returning to the mainland in 1939, he again secured employment at Wonthaggi, having fronted at the local mine office on a daily basis.

Not until the end of the Second World War — more than twenty years after they had exchanged marriage vows — were Antonio and Anna reunited. It was 1947 by the time Anna made the flight aboard one of the first passenger aircraft to Australia. Hers was a five-day sojourn that took almost six weeks off Antonio's forty-six day voyage across the seas. Three years later, in October 1950, Anna gave birth to a daughter, Teresa, 'which, after all that time, was a great joy to them. And I was their only child,' Teresa told me. 'There was a baby who died straightaway, but you just didn't speak about those things.'

Antonio retired before the Wonthaggi mines closed down in 1964, and was able to afford a sentimental journey home to San Donato to spend six months with his beloved mother. There were other little luxuries along the way too: spending time fishing, enjoying a well-earned beer with Giovanni Bottegal, or riding his push-bike ten kilometres to the beach. Not until 1960 did Antonio purchase his first car and learn to drive.

In later years Antonio found enjoyment in the precious time spent with his grandchildren, after Teresa married. But when he lost Anna after a long illness in April 1974, although he lived another ten years, Antonio Cengia lost interest in his own life.

19. Angelo Menegazzo

Born Cittadella, Provincia di Padova, 21 October 1905.
Died Werribee, Victoria, 28 May 1978.

Although they lost their first-born, Mario, after just seven months, Antonio and Domenica Menegazzo (née Zen) would in time rear six more sons — all of whom were destined to leave Italy by the time they had grown into men.

The sons were Giuseppe, Giovanni, Mario, Guido, Virginio and Angelo. With the exception of Giuseppe (who migrated to Argentina, where he would become known as 'Don Giuseppe' in recognition of his charity work), Australia was the country in which they all settled.

Giovanni was the first of the five Menegazzo brothers to arrive in Melbourne, on an earlier voyage in 1927. He settled in Swanston Street before finding accommodation in Lester Street and later Drummond Street, Carlton, where he ran a boarding house with his wife, Maria. She had arrived with their two daughters, Savina and Irma, from Italy in July 1929. Maria maintained the boarding house and prepared the meals, while Giovanni, a qualified cabinetmaker, plied his craft for Sunshine Cabinets.

Giovanni was living at 230 Lygon Street, Carlton, at the time when he nominated both his brother Angelo and another passenger, Angelo Brotto (passenger number twelve), to come to this country. The two Angelos arrived in Melbourne on the *Re d'Italia* in November 1927. Guido joined them two years later, Virginio in 1938 and Mario in 1954.

Soon after Guido's arrival, the three Menegazzos ventured to the northern Victorian town of Kerang, as employment had dried up in the city. There they would work during the week, returning at weekends to the Carlton boarding house managed by Maria and the two girls.

Six months later, with her children by her side, Maria made the move to Kerang to be with her husband. By then, the Menegazzo brothers had found steady work building roads, and while tip trucks did assist them in this cause, the lack of modern-day equipment meant most of what they did was done by hand. 'They went working on the roads when the Depression came along, and things were pretty bad,' Angelo's son Ray said. 'They were building roads for the local government up in Kerang, but wherever there was work they went ... and they lived in tents.'

During the mid-1930s, Giovanni and Angelo purchased a farm in Duncan's Road, Werribee South. The two brothers toiled diligently on that property, where almost everything had to be done manually. The men worked with horses and sowed lettuce seeds by hand, marking the lines on the farrows with sticks. Together they helped one another through a drought, while Guido — who had remained in Kerang — forwarded money to keep them going. Guido later joined his brothers in Werribee South, after purchasing another farm, in Farrants Road.

Angelo went back to Italy in 1937 and married Luigina (Gina) Rebellato. Antonio Gobbo, the father of former Victorian Governor Sir

James Gobbo, was best man, and Angelo, in time, would be Sir James's godfather.

Upon their return to Melbourne in 1938, the newly wed Menegazzos purchased a fruit shop in Sydney Road, Brunswick, where their first child, Ray, was born. Following Ray's birth the family was again on the move, this time to Mount Donna Buang, in northeastern Victoria. There Angelo cut timber by day and slept in a tent by night. Soon after, the family relocated to Werribee South, where Angelo worked on a sharefarm owned by Amedeo Lago.

In 1941 Mr and Mrs Angelo Menegazzo purchased their own farm at O'Connors Road, Werribee South, where they remained until they died. There a second son, Gerald, was born in 1942, then Peter in 1943 and finally Julian in 1947.

Not content with life on the farm, and interested in diversifying his business interests, Angelo took control of the Tattersall's Hotel on the corner of Little Lonsdale and Russell Streets, Melbourne. For four years, from 1952 to 1956, Angelo ran the hotel, before returning to Werribee to spend his final years.

Angelo Menegazzo's hard life was typical of most of those who made the voyage from Italy. As his son Ray said to me, 'Dad never spoke much about his very early days ... I think it was so hard for the early migrants that he preferred not to remember.'

20. Antonio Querin

Born Cordenons, Provincia di Udine, 26 August 1899.
Died Mont Park, Victoria, 23 October 1964.

Although he came to this country as a tailor by profession, Antonio Querin never had the chance to attain the quality of life he so desperately sought. The son of Angelo and Luigia Querin (née Venarus), he was sponsored to Australia by Cesare De Zan, who hailed from the same home town, Cordenons. Immediately following his arrival, Antonio settled at 67 Drummond Street, Carlton, before making the short move to 169 Cardigan Street in 1928. And that would be his home until 1943.

Little is known of Antonio's achievements in those first fifteen years. What is known is that throughout this time he somehow had to cope with a terrible illness, later diagnosed as Parkinson's Disease.

By 1943, the illness had taken such a toll on Antonio that he was admitted to St Joseph's Home of the Little Sisters of the Poor in Northcote. In August 1951, the Little Sisters lodged an application for naturalisation on Antonio's behalf, at the reduced fee of ten shillings. The Little Sisters informed the Commonwealth in the application that Antonio 'reads and speaks English very poorly [but] has an adequate knowledge of the responsibilities and privileges of Australian citizenship'. The Little Sisters also noted, 'Applicant has no income or property and has applied for an invalid pension.'

On 27 November 1952 — just over twenty-five years to the day since his arrival on the *Re d'Italia* — Antonio renounced his Italian nationality, took the Oath of Allegiance to His Majesty King George VI, and was granted his Australian naturalisation.

Antonio Querin, Australian citizen, never married, and would spend the final twelve years of his life (making a total of twenty-one) with the Little Sisters of the Poor. He was hospitalised a month before his death and was survived in Italy by his brother Veriglio. He is buried in an unmarked grave owned by the Little Sisters in Fawkner Cemetery.

21. Gaetano (Jim) Sartori

BORN MALO, PROVINCIA DI VICENZA, 16 FEBRUARY 1902.
DIED BENDIGO, VICTORIA, 8 FEBRUARY 1964.

HANGING ON A wall in the foyer of the Central Deborah Gold Mine's gift shop in Bendigo is a large black and white reproduction of a fifty-five year old photograph. The photo, which is included in this book, depicts a group of blackened workers who had gathered after a long day's digging deep down in the darkness of the northern Victorian earth.

At the rear of the group, three in from the left, is a man known to his mates simply as 'Jim'. He wears a woollen suit coat, rolled back to his elbows to reveal powerful forearms dirtied by the mine dust. And he stands proudly with the Central Deborah's true characters — men such as 'Aspro'

White, 'Deafy' Cameron and Bill 'Pop' Spooner — with whom he worked between March 1943 and December 1947.

This is Gaetano Sartori, who in 1927 boarded the *Re d'Italia* bound for Australia.

In September 1998, I obtained a copy of Gaetano's death certificate, which stated that he had died in Bendigo more than thirty-five years ago. As was often the case with this sort of breakthrough, I informed my father, who wisely bounced the name off a friend from Bendigo, Gabe Scinetti. Gabe then contacted his mother and father, Irma and Laurie Scinetti, who, as it happened, fondly remembered Gaetano.

'We knew him from quite a few years ago. He was a good man, a hard worker, and worked in the mine most of the time,' Irma said. Laurie, who was well aware of the photograph at the Central Deborah, also regarded Gaetano as 'a lovely man':

> We met Gaetano in Bendigo in 1949. He had just finished in the mine and had started work for Mr Svanosio, delivering sand and screenings in a truck. We kept in contact with him until his death from the miner's complaint [tuberculosis] in 1964, and everyone working in the mine at that time died for the same reason.
>
> During the 1940s Gaetano lived with a family by the name of Panozzo. At the Panozzos' they played cards during the day — *presetta*, or twenty-seven, and *briscola* — Italian card games. And he liked a drink too. I remember his brother Francesco had just arrived [he came to Australia in 1950], and on this particular night Gaetano said to him, 'Go and get a carton of beer.' His brother replied, 'It's too late, it's six o'clock closing,' and Gaetano said, 'Don't worry, the bloke at the pub will look after you.' As his brother walked out the door, Gaetano turned to me and quipped, 'Bloody new Australian!'

Armida Trenti, Gaetano Sartori's niece, recalled many details of her uncle's life:

> He was a real gentleman. He could name all the gold reefs in the area like the Central Deborah, and where they started and where

they went. When I was in the mood I'd sit there talking to him
— maybe if I'd been a boy I might have been more interested.

In the early years Zio Jimmy cut tobacco in Myrtleford,
until he met someone who said there was plenty of work in
the mines in Bendigo. He came to Bendigo and worked the
mines for a long time. Later, he worked on the Country Roads
Board, patching roads, and working the flags that told you
when to stop and go. But he eventually retired from that,
because the cold was too much. He was in his late fifties by
then, and he was just short of sixty-two when he died.

I was only fourteen when Zio Jimmy died of miner's
complaint. Just before he died, all the poor fellow did was go
from the chair in the kitchen to the armchair in the lounge
and onto the bench in the verandah. At night you could hear
him breathe and he sounded like a cement mixer.

Keepers of the Flame

We are warmed by the flame that, through the centuries,
we have been able to keep alight, at all times,
and on any foreign soil.

— Maria Carbonetto, internment camp, Tatura, Victoria, 1943

| Maestro Domenico Caffaro, 1932. | Maria Carbonetto, on the eve of her departure to Australia from Italy, 1927. | Giovanni Giuseppe Costella, 1927. |

Photographs courtesy Antonietta (Toni) and Ernest Koller, Frankston, Victoria.

22. Domenico Giovanni Mario Caffaro

Born Ivrea, Provincia di Aosta, 29 November 1904.
Died Aosta, Provincia di Aosta, 16 May 1986.

23. Maria Maddalena Costella (née Carbonetto)

Born San Remo, Provincia di Porto Maurizio, 19 April 1899.
Died Frankston, Victoria, 3 February 1989.

24. Giovanni Giuseppe (John Joseph) Costella

Born Torino, Provincia di Porto Maurizio, 21 March 1923.
Died Kew, Victoria, 9 October 1979.

ON THE AFTERNOON of 1 May 1998, at a house in suburban Boronia, a sixty-nine year old woman named Antonietta (Toni) Koller finally brought to an end what had been a long and frustrating family search. At the request of her nephew, Robert De Marinis, she agreed to shed light on the lives of three of the *Re d'Italia*'s disembarkees — Domenico Caffaro, Maria Carbonetto and Giovanni Costella.

It was after I joined Robert in the family room of his residence that Toni recounted each life and its impact upon hers. In doing so, she brought to an end months of personal disappointment for me as I attempted to fit together the pieces of this intricate family jigsaw.

My search for Domenico, Maria and Giovanni had begun in late 1997, with the customary scouring of the telephone books. I was unable to find any listings for either Carbonetto or Caffaro, while the three or four listed Costellas contacted said they bore no connection with the man who was just a boy of four when he disembarked from the steamship. The Melbourne office of the Australian Archives did, however, yield invaluable material. I learned there that Domenico Giovanni Mario Caffaro was born in Ivrea, Aosta, on 29 November 1904, and as of 1931 was married and living in Melbourne with one dependant child aged two and a half. At this time, Domenico applied to the Department of Home Affairs for the admission from Italy of his brother, Alfieri. In doing so, Domenico's spectacular business success was outlined by the department's officer:

> The applicant is a native of Italy and he arrived in Melbourne from that country per the *Re d'Italia* in November 1927 ... he states that his capital on arrival was a little over 200 pounds.
>
> Since his arrival he has resided almost continuously in Melbourne. His first employment in this country was an engagement with Messrs. J.C. Williamson Ltd., theatrical people, as a stage assistant. This engagement, however, only lasted a few months.
>
> After leaving this position, Caffaro was employed by Messrs. Fairley Bros., cake manufacturers of Liddiard Street, Hawthorn. He states that he had experience in this particular line in Italy, as his father was in that line of business at home. He continued in

the employ of this firm for about 18 months, and while employed there received a wage of five pounds per week.

In December last, Caffaro commenced in business on his own account as a block cake manufacturer at 38 Johnston Street, Collingwood. The applicant manufactures for the wholesale and retail trade block, fruit and plain cake, also sponges etc. He supplies city and suburban cake shops, and states that he has a large connection with country storekeepers in such towns as Bendigo, Mildura, Rochester, Echuca, Elmore, Shepparton and Albury. In addition, he conducts three rented shops at Prahran, South Melbourne and a stall at Victoria Market.

At the present time, the applicant states that his fortnightly output of cake is 7000 pounds of block cake (made up in six pound blocks) and one and a half tons of sponge. During the same period his consumption of raw materials is as follows:

- three tons of flour purchased direct from the millers,
- two tons of 1A sugar,
- three quarters of a ton of margarine,
- 10,000 eggs and two tons of assorted dry fruits.

All his purchases, he states, are on a strictly cash basis. The above turnover of products would, at first sight, appear to be somewhat amazing, but an examination of the applicant's passbook seems to verify the volume of his business transactions. He states that he has already been offered through an old established firm about six months ago a figure approximating two thousand pounds for his business. There appears to be little doubt that the applicant is a keen businessman at this particular line of trade.

Domenico was also an extremely gifted musician. His proficiency at the piano earned him a place in Giovanni Cera's Tango Orchestra, whose sweet sounds won the favour of regular listeners to popular Melbourne radio station 3LO.

In the early 1930s he formed the Toti Opera Company, named after a popular Italian singer of the day, Toti Dal Monte (Antonietta Meneghel — 1895–1975). As musical director and producer, Maestro Caffaro oversaw the company's productions at Melbourne's Princess Theatre, with the support of art director Giuseppe Federici (formely of the Colon Theatre, Buenos Aires) and managing director Mario Massa. In the Toti Grand Opera Season of June 1932, Domenico conducted the Princess Theatre orchestra in a performance of Verdi's *La Traviata*. A photograph of a distinguished-looking Domenico, resplendent in tuxedo and white bow tie, appeared in a souvenir program available to the public on opening night. The caption beneath the photograph read: 'Maestro Cav. uff. Domenico Caffaro, from the Royal Conservatorium of Milan, Regio Theatre of Turin and Coliseo Theatre of Buenos Aires.' Domenico's love affair with the tango stemmed from his time in Buenos Aires. He was hypnotised by the sultry Latin rhythms and subsequently composed several musical pieces, which he played on the South American accordion, known as a *bandoneón*.

But the music could not hide the gravity of Domenico's gambling problems, which impacted disastrously on his thriving bakery concern. In 1938, information was received by the Commonwealth Investigation Branch that he had become a bankrupt who, while working as a stage assistant with J.C. Williamson, was in trouble during the production of *Balalaika* for owing money to the conductor, Carlo Briglia. Commonwealth Investigation Branch inspector Roland S. Browne then learned that 'Domenico had a wife in Melbourne whom he deserted for Maria Carbonetto, who is alleged to be a married woman living apart from her husband'.

MARIA MADDALENA CARBONETTO was born in San Remo on 19 April 1899, one of five children of Giovanni Battista Carbonetto and Vincenza Rondelli. In 1916, Maria married a man named Paolo De Marinis. The marriage ended in tragic circumstances less than two years later, when Paolo died of pneumonia during the First World War, but in April 1918, two months after her husband's death, Maria gave birth to their son,

Francesco. Francesco De Marinis lived with his mother until he was six years of age, when he was taken in by the Salesian College in Turin as a war orphan (this was a custom in Italy to help all widowed mothers educate their children).

At some point in the early 1920s, Maria married a man named Agostino Costella, of Borgota. In March 1923, she gave birth to another son, Giovanni Giuseppe Costella. Two years later, Agostino bade farewell to his wife and child and set sail for Melbourne aboard the SS *Caprera*. They were never officially divorced, but Agostino never saw his wife and child again (although their paths crossed intermittently via correspondence). He is understood to have died years later in Queensland.

In October 1927, Maria boarded the Melbourne-bound *Re d'Italia* with Giovanni. As Agostino refused to pay for the passage of Maria and Giovanni, Maria was forced to scrimp and save to cover their fares. But she couldn't afford to take Francesco with her and the boy was left in the care of the Salesians. It wasn't until July 1934, after she had saved enough money to finance the reunion, that Maria greeted Francesco in Melbourne when he arrived on the SS *Esquilino*.

Maria's motivation in making the trip had nothing to do with Agostino Costella and everything to do with Tersilla Scala, a girlhood friend from the old days in Turin. Maria and Tersilla were both accomplished seamstresses, who used to take their handmade dresses to the mountains and sell them to the poor wives of the *contadini* (farmers). Tersilla left for Australia with her family in the early 1920s, but kept in constant written contact with her old friend. Eventually, Tersilla persuaded Maria to make the move, and Maria and Giovanni spent their first days after arrival at the South Melbourne home of the Scalas.

ALTHOUGH I WAS unable to make phone contact with anyone bearing the name Carbonetto, Caffaro or Costella, my prayers were answered in December 1997, when I located Robert De Marinis, the son of Maria's child by her first marriage, to the fallen soldier, Paolo.

Coincidentally, I had met Robert for the first time in vastly different circumstances some weeks before, at the Punt Road football ground in Richmond, of all places. I had gone there to cover a Richmond Football Club training session for the *Herald Sun* and had actually bought a hot dog from Robert, who had set up his van at the ground to accommodate the hungry onlookers. On that occasion Robert and I started to talk about football, not realising we would soon be waxing lyrical on more sensitive, personal matters.

When I called Robert just after Christmas in 1997, he immediately reminded me of our chance meeting at his hot-dog van and the conversation quickly turned to footy and how 'Richo' (enigmatic Richmond forward Matthew Richardson) would fare in the ensuing season for the Tigers. When both of us had got that out of our systems, Robert confirmed his links with the three passengers, whom he said had all since died. A wonderfully upbeat and positive individual, Robert talked fondly of his forebears, not least of his late father, Francesco.

Robert told me that Francesco De Marinis, after being brought out to Australia, lived in Fitzroy with his mother, brother and a sister named Antonietta from 1934 to May 1941, and spent the ensuing four years at internment camps as an Italian prisoner of war. In December 1949, Francesco married Anna Centonze, who gave birth to three children — Robert, Sandro and Marisa. He then became a self-employed radio and electrical sales and service man of De Mar Electrics in Lygon Street, Carlton, and his love of radios was such that the family dubbed him 'Marconi' (after Guglielmo Marconi (1874–1937), inventor of the radio telegraph). Francesco later ran a demolition yard known as De Mar Demolitions and in 1982 built a shack by the Red Bank Weir, about sixty kilometres out of Balranald, New South Wales, where he and his wife lived out their final days.

While the archival material substantiated Robert's revelation that Francesco and Giovanni had a younger sister, I wasn't exactly sure where the mysterious Antonietta fitted into the frame. Robert confirmed that Antonietta, or Toni, was alive and well and living in Frankston. He also suggested that it would be best to talk to Toni about Domenico, Maria and Giovanni. And so in May 1998, at Robert De Marinis's Boronia home, I

met Toni Koller for the first time. There, in the company of her husband
Ernest, together with Robert's brother Sandro and their respective spouses,
Toni told me her incredible tale.

Toni revealed that not only was she Maria Carbonetto's daughter, but
fellow passenger Domenico Caffaro was her father and she was conceived
aboard the *Re d'Italia*. Which meant that she was, at least in the embryonic
sense, a surviving passenger!

'Domenico Caffaro met my mother on the *Re d'Italia* ... my mother
loved him very much ... that is all I know,' said Toni.

The family know Toni as 'Aunt Toti' — a nickname derived from the
same source as the name of her father's opera company, the singer Toti Dal
Monte, who also happened to be Toni Koller's godmother. 'The Italian
Opera Company came out in the early 1930s. Toni's father was one of the
conductors and got Mum in as a dresser of the sopranos, one of whom was
Toti,' Robert De Marinis told me.

Toni told me that she was born in Carlton on 25 July 1928, and that her
mother had settled down with Domenico after abandoning what she said
was 'an ill-fated arranged marriage' to her second husband Agostino.

'At that time Agostino Costella was already in Melbourne and established
in a fruit shop in Bourke Street, which I remember as early as 1934 or '35,'
Toni said. 'I recall him once sending a basket of fruit to our home to butter
us up, but Mum offered it to the delivery man. In the end, Agostino retired
and died in Queensland.'

Six years after Toni's birth, Domenico Caffaro set sail for South America
aboard the SS *Ormonde*. Upon his return, he secured work with
Melbourne's Myer Emporium as musical director on a salary of £9 a week.
In 1934, Domenico, then thirty, abandoned Maria and Toni for an
eighteen-year-old woman named Amelita Iorio, whom he married in
Melbourne in April of the following year. In 1936, in East Melbourne,
Amelita bore him a son, Alfieri (the name of Domenico's brother), but what
became of the boy remains unknown.

By 1939, the financially ruined Domenico had severed ties with Amelita
and Alfieri, and again sailed solo — this time for his homeland of Italy,
never to return. He settled in his old home town of Ivrea and twenty years
later married again, this time to Teresa Minuzzo, in Chatillion, Valle

d'Aosta, in October 1959, according to Italian municipal records. Ten years later, Domenico and Teresa moved to Maria Carbonetto's home town of San Remo, before settling in neighbouring Donnas in 1971. On 16 May 1986, Domenico Caffaro died in Aosta.

FOLLOWING ARE TONI Koller's own personal reminiscences of the lives of Domenico Caffaro, Maria Carbonetto and Giovanni Costella.

Domenico Caffaro:

Though I don't know a lot about my father, here are some of the things I do know. He was a great composer and musician, and while I haven't got any music that my father composed, I have a medal upon which are inscribed the words 'Al Professore Domenico Caffaro. Conservatorio Paganini, Genoa.' I also have from Argentina a memento inscribed 'Asociación Argentina De Autores Compositores de Musica Buenos Aires'. My father was once on the same ship as the then Prince of Wales (later Edward XVIII) and was asked by him to play the piano, which he did until the wee hours of the morning.

Mum said to me that the difference between Domenico and Costella was that Costella never once picked up his son or even spoke to him. She said that whereas Costella collected her pay and doled out barely enough to buy food, which at times forced her virtually to beg for anything extra, my father was affectionate, never took any of her money and would share any extra money with her.

My first memories of my father go back to when I was a three- or four-year-old in Fitzroy. At that time my father worked for J.C. Williamson's as a musical conductor, while Mum worked in the wardrobe department at the Princess

Theatre making costumes. And that is where I remember the music.

I also remember Domenico backstage in the clothing room of the Princess Theatre and hearing the music of *La Traviata*, especially the moment where the gypsies dance with the tambourines. My father also used to practise playing the piano in the front room of our home at 17 King William Street, Fitzroy, and I used to dance to the music. He'd watch me dancing in the shine of the piano, and he'd change the rhythm in the middle of a song to see what I would do.

Two nuns from the school I attended would often come to the front door to hear him play. He was a wonderful pianist, and he was very much influenced by Latin American music, from his time in Argentina. Domenico was also a conductor for J.C. Williamson and worked for radio station 3AW [as well as performing with the Tango Orchestra for 3LO]. In 1932, he formed his own opera company, but it didn't last very long because at the end of 1933 he went to Italy and Argentina, having previously been to Argentina in 1925.

In 1934, he returned to Australia with presents from his mother to my mother — a pearl necklace and silver bracelet. He also brought back Argentine costumes covered with sequins and stones. I remember him and Mum making maracas at home because none were available here. They'd put beans inside halves of a hollow ball, sew the halves together, attach handles and paint them gold.

When the Myer Mural Hall opened, Domenico led the orchestra. But he also baked cakes, a craft learned from his father, a pastry cook in Aosta.

We remained together at King William Street for a little while longer. Domenico used to give piano lessons to people like Antonietta Triaca — whose father was one of the heads of the Italian community and who later taught me Italian — as well as Amelita Iorio, Domenico's future wife.

Domenico left King William Street and we didn't see him again until the morning he married. My father never drank, but he was drunk when he came to see us on the morning of his marriage and said he'd been roped into it. My mother and I didn't see him again for a long time.

My father lived in Nicholson Street opposite the Academy School where I went and sometimes he would wait for me out the front. He used to ask me up for a drink, which happened two or three times, then one day he said, "Would you come and live with me and Amelita?" I loved my father, but I adored my mother and there was no way I was going to do that.

My father had big ideas, but things always went wrong. Perhaps he wasn't a good businessman — and he was a gambler too. The last time I saw my father was early in 1938. I never heard from him again, other than a letter he sent me almost forty years later. That was when he revealed that he had composed a version of the 'Our Father' for the Pope. He sent us the record and a music sheet (which I still have) and asked us to forward it to Mr Giovanni Cera, a musician he knew here, but who had retired by that stage. I don't remember any other details of that letter, but I do know there was no emotion. Mum and I wrote back, but we never got a response.

I am happy to think that for a time my father loved us very much. For a few years I kept dreaming that he would come back because I loved him very much, but by the time I married I'd forgotten about him. As for Mum, I came to realise how much she must have loved him, for in the last few days of her life she addressed my husband Ernest by the name 'Domenico' several times.

Maria Carbonetto:

My mother's father had a carnation and rose farm in San Remo. The family also ran a little *osteria* with a pergola covered in grapevines. My mother had three sisters and a brother. Her father made the wine and her mother cooked the rabbits, and nobody in the whole of San Remo cooked rabbits like her.

In 1917 Maria met a handsome young soldier, Paolo De Marinis, in San Remo. A love affair ensued, but in February 1918 he was killed in the War. He got caught in an avalanche with the Alpini, and though he survived the avalanche he developed pneumonia and died in hospital, not long after Mum had made it there to visit him.

Maria subsequently joined De Marinis's brothers and sisters in Torino, which is where she gave birth to Francesco, two months after his father died. The De Marinis family introduced Maria to Agostino Costella and talked her into marrying him. They subsequently had a son, Giovanni, or 'Nino', who was born in Torino, and Maria worked right up until the birth. Agostino was a security officer in a clothing factory and searched staff members as they came out. He got Mum work there as a machinist, and together they toiled at the clothing factory for four or five years until Agostino left for Australia aboard the *Caprera*, in October 1925. Two years later, Mum left for Australia on the *Re d'Italia*, which is where she met my father, Domenico Caffaro.

Maria's two best friends in Italy were the Scala sisters, one of whom was Tersilla. On her arrival in Australia, Mum gave her forwarding address as 'c/o the Griffith G.P.O.' The Scalas were presumably living in Griffith, but I don't think Mum ever made it there.

My happiest recollections are of the days at 17 King William Street, of my father playing the piano and Mum helping to cook the cakes. I know he had a bakery, because of what Mum told me, as well as a stall at South Melbourne market. At the bakery, friends helped them cook biscuits in the big oven, and they also had two cars, which they used to drive around to sell cakes. In the end Herbert Adams put them out of business by undercutting the prices.

Names and Description of Passengers—*continued*

Port where embarked.	Name. Separate line to be used for each Passenger.	Class or Berth.	Profession, Occupation, or Calling.	Sex (M. or F.)	Age last Birthday.	Married, Single, Widowed	Country of Last Permanent Residence.	Nationality. British or Alien.	Race specifying Country.	Country of Intended Future Permanent Residence.	Remarks
ples	Carrieri Antonio	3ᵉ	joiner	m	35	m	ITALY	A	Italian	Australia	
	Curcio Francesco	"	farm lab.	m	26	m	"	A	"	"	
ina	Italia Antonio	"	"	m	44	s	"	A	"	"	
"	Spadaro Carmelo	"	"	m	31	m	"	A	"	"	
"	Giordano Paolo	"	"	m	29	m	"	A	"	"	
"	Pisa Michele	"	"	m	30	s	"	A	"	"	
"	Guida Annunziato	"	"	m	33	m	"	A	"	"	
"	Benavoli Giuseppe	"	"	m	49	m	"	A	"	"	
"	Lanza Salvatore	"	"	m	36	m	"	A	"	"	
"	Italia Michelangelo	"	"	m	23	m	"	A	"	"	
"	Musco Sebastiano	"	"	m	28	m	"	A	"	"	
"	Mineo Luigi	"	"	m	29	m	"	A	"	"	
"	Romano Gaetano	"	"	m	30	m	"	A	"	"	
"	Lanza Francesco	"	"	m	24	s	"	A	"	"	
"	Corridore Paolo	"	"	m	35	m	"	A	"	"	
"	Di Giglio Domenico	"	"	m	42	m	"	A	"	"	
"	Vinci Bruno	"	"	m	41	m	"	A	"	"	
"	Pileggi Francesco	"	"	m	37	m	"	A	"	"	
"	Gattuso Carmelo	"	"	m	43	m	"	A	"	"	
"	Scutti Michele	"	"	m	33	m	"	A	"	"	
"	Violi Paolo	"	"	m	30	m	"	A	"	"	
"	Covelli Carmine	"	"	m	34	m	"	A	"	"	
"	Taranto Francesco	"	"	m	57	m	"	A	"	"	
"	Taranto Giuseppe	"	"	m	24	s	"	A	"	"	
"	Di Gregorio Vincenzo	"	"	m	51	m	"	A	"	"	
"	Giarracca Luigi	"	"	m	45	m	"	A	"	"	
"	Casomento Giacomo	"	"	m	17	s	"	A	"	"	
"	Taranto Giovanni	"	"	m	13	s	"	A	"	"	
"	Segreto Michele	"	"	m	18	s	"	A	"	"	
"	Virgona Felice	"	"	m	16	s	"	A	"	"	
"	Virgona Angelo	"	"	m	14	s	"	A	"	"	
"	Pisone Annunciata		domestic	f	19	s	"	A	"	"	
"	Speranza Sebastiano		fisherman	m	18	s	"	A	"	"	
"	Chiera Domenico		farm lab.	m	55	m	"	A	"	"	
"	Zappia Giuseppe	"	"	m	44	m	"	A	"	"	
"	Lotorto Giuseppe		mason	m	32	m	"	A	"	"	
"	Violi Giuseppe		farm lab.	m	40	m	"	A	"	"	

A page from the list of incoming passengers who disembarked from the steamship *Re d'Italia* at 19 North Wharf, Victoria Dock, Melbourne, on Thursday, 24 November 1927.

The steamship *Re d'Italia*, approaching Station Pier, Port Melbourne, circa 1925.
PHOTOGRAPH COURTESY POLLY WOODSIDE MELBOURNE MARITIME MUSEUM, SOUTHBANK, VICTORIA.

A postcard image of the *Re d'Italia*, mailed to Cogollo del Cengio, northeast of Schio, in Italy. It was marked for the attention of the family of Giovanni Massacavallo, who had disembarked from the *Re d'Italia* at Port Adelaide in November 1927. It carries the signature of Vicenza shipping agency representative Luigi Fantinelli. The back of the card reads (in Italian): 'With pleasure I announce to you that the ship *Re d'Italia* safely arrived in Adelaide on 19 November. Distinguished regards, Fantinelli Luigi.'
POSTCARD COURTESY RAY MASSACAVALLO, SAFETY BEACH, VICTORIA.

An aerial view of Victoria Dock, Melbourne, circa 1927.

The gates of Victoria Dock, through which the passengers of the *Re d'Italia* emerged, 1927.

Domenico Caffaro (*passenger 22*) photographed in Italy, circa 1933, following his return from Buenos Aires. The musical instrument featured is a South American bandoneon that Caffaro learned to play. Caffaro loved Latin rhythms and composed several pieces that boasted a South American feel.

PHOTOGRAPH COURTESY ANTONIETTA (TONI) AND ERNEST KOLLER, FRANKSTON, VICTORIA.

The Tango Orchestro in the studio of Melbourne's 3LO radio station, 1930. Front row, left to right: Domenico Caffaro, Giovanni Cera, Pietro Piccini. Back row: Angelo Candela, Ezio Giannaccini. The musical instruments in this photo include a grand piano, mandolin, Spanish guitar, piano accordion and violins.

PHOTOGRAPH COURTESY ITALIAN HISTORICAL SOCIETY PHOTOGRAPHIC COLLECTION, MELBOURNE, VICTORIA.

Maria Carbonetto (*passenger 23*), Italian
internee, Tatura internment camp.

John Joseph Costella (*passenger 24*),
Executive Officer of Melbourne's Mercy
Maternity Hospital, circa 1970s.

Maria Carbonetto, wardrobe mistress with the Borovansky Ballet, backstage with Australia's first
prima ballerina, Kathleen Gorham, in the late 1950s. Gorham, who danced with the legendary
Dame Margot Fonteyn and Rudolph Nureyev, was at the pinnacle of her career at this time.

The tiny town of San Nicolò di Comelico, nestled beneath the majestic Dolomites in northern Italy, from which Igino (*passenger 32*), Francesco (*passenger 33*) and Silvio De Bolfo (*passenger 34*) departed in late 1927, to be reunited with their elder brother Benedetto in Melbourne. Each of the brothers was baptised in the church of San Nicolò and attended the local school, but none of them ever returned there after coming to Australia.

PHOTOGRAPH COURTESY OF THE AUTHOR.

The ice-chest manufacturing business of Silvio De Bolfo and Francesco Coluzzi in Bari, southern Italy, circa 1923 or 1924. Standing, from left to right, are Gino Cevo (the accountant); Francesco Coluzzi (from the town of Campolungo, near Campitello di Cadore); a relative of Francesco Coluzzi; and Silvio De Bolfo. Seated are Igino De Bolfo; Francesco Coluzzi's son (name unknown); and a local Bari boy (name also unknown). Another accountant employed in the business, Gino Rene, from Genoa, is not in the picture.

PHOTOGRAPH COURTESY RITA COSTAN, SAN NICOLÒ DI COMELICO, PROVINCIA DI BELLUNO, ITALY.

Silvio De Bolfo's preliminary passport, stamped in Belluno, which granted him rail access from Calalzo to Genoa, where his passport to Australia would have been issued prior to embarkation on the *Re d'Italia*.

Silvio De Bolfo's Certificate of Naturalization, dated 17 December 1934 and signed by the Governor-General of Australia, Sir Isaac Isaacs.

Igino De Bolfo (at right) with fellow soldiers Bob Dyer (left) and Vic Richardson (centre), Labuan Island, North West Borneo, 1945.

Silvio De Bolfo (far right), taking part in gymnastics training during his time with the Guardie Granatieri, circa 1919.

The wedding portrait of Silvio and Maria De Bolfo (née Cincotta), Kerang, Victoria, 1935.

Mum continued to make biscuits at King William Street with a man named Rosario Ruggiero. They later sold the biscuits at market, and Rosario continued to make them right through until the late 1970s. Mum worked as an assistant cook at the Masonic Club in Flinders Street prior to the outbreak of the Second World War, then as a cook at St Vincent's Hospital during the War years, until her internment in 1942.

During her time at the Masonic Club, she would get up at five in the morning and wake me to plait my hair. She would go to work an hour later, cook breakfast and lunch until 2.30, then come home to wash for the boarders who lived with us. She would then return to the lodge to cook the evening meals until 10.30, and that was her day.

Mum didn't pull any punches when it came to politics either. She was pro-Fascist and pro-Mussolini. She had a ham radio from which she used to obtain bulletins directly from Italy and distribute them amongst the Italians. Her catch cry over the airwaves used to be 'Zio Roberto's doing well', and what the authorities didn't know was that 'Roberto' stood for Rome, Berlin and Tokyo. She was a member of the Cavour Club, a prominent Italian community club, before the War. There they used to teach all of us to recite the words 'I love Australia, my native land; I love Italy, my motherland.' We had to be faithful to both.

The fierce Italian patriotism that burned brightly in Maria's belly was fuelled by the fact that her first husband, Francesco De Marinis, had died fighting for England in the First World War. Consequently, she and her children 'wanted nothing to do with anything that helped England', according to the report of investigations officers who in 1941 found her in illegal possession of a wireless.

The Victorian Security Service officers discovered the wireless during a search of her new house at 75 King William Street on the night of Saturday, 10 May. Her sons and daughter were in the house with Maria at the time of the search. Also present were a concreter, Carmelo Conte, and a St Kilda waiter, Angelo Rigoni, both of whom boarded in rooms sublet by Maria, as well as Gustav Radda, another boarder, and committed Fascist Domenico Pellizzoni, both of whom lived next door with the Triaca family. Gustav was a member of the touring Vienna Boys' Choir, while Domenico was married to the Triacas' eldest daughter, Flora.

According to the officers' report, the inspection of the house revealed 'a considerable number of items of Fascist and Nazi ideology'. Further, they wrote:

> In the room occupied by one Carmelo Giuseppe Conte, who has since been interned, were, inter alia, fascist party badges, a Mussolini medal, tessera, etc.
>
> In the room occupied by Francesco De Marinis, who has since been interned, and Giovanni Costella, the following material was confiscated for evidence:
>
> - Four photos of Francesco in uniform of young fascist;
> - One tunic of uniform;
> - One small picture of Mussolini;
> - One Italian bankbook showing credit of L.500;
> - Quantity of miscellaneous Italian papers and literature;
> - Notebook of names and addresses of radio customers;
> - A recess under the stairs, which was fitted up as a workshop, containing much wireless equipment and two sets under repair.
>
> In the sitting room was found a bronze bust of Mussolini, Italian flag, fascist symbol, portrait of the King of Italy, photograph of Hitler to which was pinned a swastika emblem. There can be no doubt as to the pro-fascist atmosphere and sympathies of the occupants of this house, nor that it was used as a meeting place for Italians.

Officers also observed that during the course of the search, several persons visited the home, at least two of whom were children of internees, 'one of whom admitted to being a member of the Melbourne *fascio* [community of Fascist sympathisers]'. The officers further reported:

> Mrs Costella has conducted an active correspondence with Italian prisoners of war interned in Australia. On 20 Jan. 42, a letter received by her from No. 11010, Paolo Magi, said, inter alia, "your pride of race and attachment to the land that gave you birth were well-known even before the war. But to express it in times like today! Bravo!".

One officer, Fitzroy's Constable Carter, wrote that in an interrogation of Maria the following June, 'she stated that Mussolini is a great man, and when Mussolini appealed for gold, she forwarded her wedding ring to Italy and in exchange received a wedding ring in metal which she now wears'.

Constable Carter concluded that Maria made no secret of her love of Fascism, regularly associated with known Fascist sympathisers, showed little regard for national security and was a potential danger in harbouring either escapees from internment camps or persons of Fascist leanings. And he believed that a restriction order would not be adequate, 'in view of the fact that the subject appears to be a determined woman who is apparently oblivious to any punishment meted out to her'.

The upshot of it all was that, in June 1941, Maria was fined £5 at Fitzroy Court for being in possession of the wireless without the permission of the Postmaster-General's Department. Then, seventeen months later, on the afternoon of Saturday, 7 November 1942, Maria was detained as an unnaturalised Australian and transported to an internment camp in the Victorian rural area of Tatura. In December, Maria's request on compassionate grounds to be reunited at the camp with her daughter were granted by the Federal Attorney-General, Herbert Vere (Doc) Evatt.

Toni Koller again takes up the story:

> When the authorities came to arrest her at the house they asked her questions like, 'Would you let your daughter marry a Japanese?' and 'Would you blow up a bridge', to which she responded, 'Who do you think I am, Mata Hari?'

I was fourteen and had just got home from the pictures with my girlfriend when I discovered that Mum was gone. My brother Nino (Giovanni) was there, along with an Australian friend, to pacify me, and they said to me, 'Don't worry.'

About three days later, Father Ugo Modotti helped Nino put me on the train to Tatura to be with Mum in the internment camp, and I stayed with her there for sixteen months. Although there was barbed wire, the food was better than it was outside, and Mum always said it was the best holiday she had in her life. In the mornings we used to stand to attention for inspection and then go to breakfast, where the women and men used to take turns cooking. We lived in a family compound and played music, danced and played *bocce*. I also learned to play tennis at the compound and continued with my piano lessons, and I celebrated my fifteenth birthday there.

Having been reunited with Toni at Tatura, Maria turned her attentions to the welfare of Francesco and Giovanni — the former having been interned at Barmera camp in South Australia, the latter in a Victorian labour battalion, chopping wood. From the sanctity of her hut in Camp 3D, Maria wrote a series of letters to them, all of which were screened before they were mailed to the two boys.

One such letter to Francesco, dated 16 December 1942 and marked 'SECRET', reads in part:

Do you think I mind being here? Quite the reverse. It is good luck and an honour for me, luck because I felt really tired and this holiday is exactly what I wanted, and honour because being Italian is not dishonourable and I shall never deny the faith that comes to us from our fathers ...

In another letter, dated 21 May 1943, Maria conveyed the following sentiments to her friend, Flora Pellizzoni:

...if everybody knew how happy I am to be here perhaps they would all want to come. Do not think that I am sad or anything else; quite otherwise. It is a small sacrifice that even I offer to the mother country, to that blessed land, to that faith that makes us worthy children of a glorious race. What would I be if I grumbled about my lot? If I were to refuse to suffer that little bit which my poor life can offer for a held idea? Take heart, Signora Flora. The sun shines even for the poor people. I know you are very sad. Why? The Lord said to San Pietro, 'Man of little faith, we should not think about drowning in the stormy tempest, but have faith in the one in whom we have reposed it'. For this reason I hope and I am happy, and I desire nothing and lack nothing ...

And in another, to Signor Tannucci, she wrote:

We are all united in the same faith — the faith that makes us worthy sons of Rome. We are all illuminated by the same light, the light that makes visible to the world the doctrines of our faith. We are warmed by the flame that, through the centuries, we have been able to keep alight, at all times, and on any foreign soil. Exiles in foreign lands, our thoughts are always for Italy.[1]

By the beginning of 1944, the Allies had already invaded Italy and Mussolini had been overthrown. Accordingly, Maria's commitment to the fading Italian ideology began to waver, but her commitment to the welfare of her three children, particularly Toni, only intensified. Maria longed to be released from the Tatura camp and, together with her daughter, return to Melbourne to be reunited with Francesco and Giovanni.

'I was a Fascist when the Fascist Party was in power, but the Fascist Party is now finished,' she told Lieutenant Horwood, the investigations officer at Tatura camp, during an interview on 19 January 1944. 'I love Italy, my country, better than myself, but I would not do anything to harm this country where I live. Yes, Fascist books and papers were found in my house because I was Fascist then, but not since the Fascist Party was made illegal when the War came. I never did any harm to Australia. I have never made propaganda against Australia.'

Maria's sentiments left Lieutenant Horwood in no doubt of her character:

> Honest and industrious, it is felt that this woman would keep
> to any undertaking she gave, and that she is at present more
> concerned with the upbringing of her daughter than in the
> progress of Italy's politics.

Maria and Toni were released from Tatura camp on 29 February 1944, on the condition that they didn't return to 75 King William Street, the reason being, as Toni suggests, 'that so many Italians were in the place that the authorities were probably fearful of espionage!' Accordingly, mother and daughter moved into a shop at 500 Lygon Street, East Brunswick, and were there for a few months, during which time Maria returned to St Vincent's to cook for the night nurses.

In 1946, when members of the Italian Opera Company toured Australia, Maria applied for a job as a dresser. Maria's experience as a dressmaker ensured that she got the job, 'which turned her life around', as Tony explains:

> Maria toured with the company to New Zealand, and later
> worked for Mr Henry at J.C. Williamson until she retired in
> 1962, completing a sixteen-year association. She met them all
> through J.C. Williamson, from [actress] Vivien Leigh to
> Kathleen Gorham.[2] She used to make tutus for Kathleen, and
> Kathleen wouldn't have anything else. She also did the
> beading for the costumes worn in *My Fair Lady* and she
> toured New Zealand twice with the Borovansky Ballet
> Company.
>
> Following Mum's retirement she lived with my brother in
> Rockingham Street, Kew, until he got married in 1964. She
> then came to live with Ernest and me the following year and

in 1969 joined the De Marinis family, where she remained until 1973. She then returned to live with us, and grew vegetables, cooked and knitted.

Mum underwent her first operation aged eighty-nine for cataracts, and in October 1988 complained of a pain in her side. She underwent surgery in January the following year, when it was discovered that she had cancer, and she died in hospital three weeks later. She died on 3 February 1989 at 6.30 in the morning, and at that precise time at home I suddenly awoke. I had heard my mother call my name.

Mum was very religious, always went to church and always had time to listen to people. She had a hard life, but you wouldn't get a bad word out of her. John and I were very attached to Mum because we knew how hard she worked to put us through school.

John Joseph Costella:

My mother once told me that John, known as 'Nino' to all his family and friends, would wander all over the *Re d'Italia* wanting to meet people. She told me that she went looking for Nino one day and actually found him in the captain's cabin eating grapes. When she picked him up to take him out, Mum was embarrassed to find that the captain had just walked in. But the captain smiled and said, 'Nino and I are old friends, he visits me every day.'

Nino was a good brother. Being five years older, he often looked after me while Mum was at work. Sometimes on Saturdays we'd walk to the Fitzroy Regent Theatre in Johnston Street to see the matinée. On one particular occasion it was raining when we left the theatre, and Nino was worried that I was going to get wet. So he decided that we would catch the tram, even though we had no money for the fare. I was scared, but fortunately the tram was crowded and we made the four stops without a problem. Even at eleven years of age, he was thoughtful and caring.

With Mum working, Nino used to take me to places like the cinema.[3] He also used to take me to Vespers at St Patrick's, quite a walk from King William Street. John was very religious. He started serving at mass at a young age, and eventually became head altar boy at St Patrick's Cathedral. Archbishop Mannix liked him very much, except once when Nino put his hand under the hot incense burner and, with a naughty word, sent the burner flying. We all laughed over this for a long, long time.

Into his teens, Nino had three passions: bike riding, the Richmond Football Club and playing a friendly card game, known as *bestia*, with the gang. On Saturdays he would go to watch the Tigers, and if they won, great, but if they lost he'd be off to bed without tea. Some Sundays he would go for very long bike rides with his good friend Franco Spada. On one of these trips, at a place called 'The Devil's Elbow' at Ferntree Gully, he had a bad accident, suffering a very bad head wound, which left him with a distinctive scar.

Nino went to Parade College in East Melbourne and was dux, and then on to St Kevin's to complete his matriculation. He later went to night school to become a qualified accountant, and in 1941 obtained his first job as a clerk for a factory that manufactured sausage skins.

During the War, and Mum's time in internment, Nino went woodchopping at Broadford for the Allied Works Council. I remember him visiting us regularly at the camp at Tatura, and because the railway station was a fair way from the camp he'd take his bike and ride from the station.

Nino used to do bookkeeping at night, and his best customer was Rosario Ruggiero, who used to make biscuits with Mum. Rosario would always give Nino a big block cake and a box of biscuits for his troubles.

Soon after the War, Nino gained a position with a firm that made Kelvinator refrigerators, where he remained for several years. He then accepted a position with a large manufacturing company, but after three years the company started to fail, and Nino was asked to falsify the books. He resigned immediately. This was an incident that affected him greatly, and it was some time before he started to look for work again. Nino then secured the position of head accountant of St Vincent's Hospital under the director, Mr Grace, who later became one of his very good friends. From there he went to the Mercy Maternity Hospital and became its first chief executive officer.

Throughout his life Nino was a very heavy smoker. His heart problems began at age thirty-five, and at fifty-four he underwent a heart bypass operation. But even that did not stop him smoking, nor did the pleas of his family, doctors and friends to end the habit. In the early hours of 9 October 1979, while drinking his first cup of coffee for the morning, my dear brother died.

Nino's funeral at St Patrick's Cathedral was packed, with a guard of honour on both sides of Clarendon Street, for he had wonderful people skills and was truly gentle. It was clear from the very outset that Nino would be well liked throughout his life, because he had a cheerful smile for everyone. This was the very quality the staff of the Mercy Maternity Hospital said they would miss the most.

John Joseph Costella, J.P., A.A.S.A., A.C.I.S., A.H.A., was survived by his wife, Helen, son John Paul and daughter Maria Helen, when he died at just fifty-six years of age. Later that year, the Sisters of Mercy included the following tribute in their annual report:

Tuesday, October 9, 1979 was certainly a day which will be remembered by all at the Mercy Maternity Hospital, for early on that day we received the news that John J. Costella, our Chief Executive Officer, had died suddenly at his home. As the news spread around the Hospital the grief and concern expressed by all was certainly a tribute to the high regard in which he was held.

Mr Costella came to work for the Sisters of Mercy on April 6, 1970, some ten months before the Hospital was officially opened. Prior to this appointment he had spent 15 years in general administration at St Vincent's Hospital. It was this experience that enabled him to commission this Hospital and provide a leadership by means of which he made an outstanding personal contribution. His service was given with great devotion, marked by calmness and courtesy.

The Sisters of Mercy will long remember him for all he did to uphold and perpetuate our particular charism of "Mercy Unto All".

John Joseph Costella, the first chief executive officer of Melbourne's Mercy Hospital, was only a boy of four when he clasped his pregnant mother's hand and followed her down the gangway in 1927. Fifty-two years later, Maria followed her son's coffin out of St Pat's.

Once again, Maria's immense strength saw her through — as it had done through two World Wars, the Great Depression, two marriages and a long-term relationship with the prodigiously gifted, if emotionally flawed musician Domenico Caffaro. Each of the three relationships yielded a child, and all of them she dearly loved.

Perhaps Toni Koller put the lives of the three passengers in the proper context when she said:

Mum and Dad lived through the worst of a depression and a war, and we lived with them in a strange little place called Fitzroy, where everyone knew everyone. We all wanted the War to end, and while we didn't realise it then, looking back now the children of my generation were the lucky ones, for we were young, things got better and it was a beneficial time for us.

25. Francesco Benvenuti

BORN ROMANS, PROVINCIA DI UDINE, 30 OCTOBER 1891.
DIED FITZROY, VICTORIA, 29 JUNE 1966.

THE TWENTY-FIFTH of the *Re d'Italia*'s Melbourne disembarkees was incorrectly listed as 'Benvenuto, Francesco'; Francesco *Benvenuti* was the man who completed the journey. Francesco, the son of furnace foreman Giuseppe and Appollonia Maria Benvenuti (née Amabile), came to Australia with his good friend from the Friuli region, Luigi Segat (passenger twenty-six), quite probably for political reasons. Francesco's grandson, Laurie Sartori, takes up the story:

> Francesco Benvenuti and Luigi Segat may have come out together. This is real family gossip, but Francesco probably came out because he wasn't a Fascist. There was a middle group, the people who sided with Matteotti, and he was one of those.
>
> My grandfather tried to go to America first, but didn't make a go of it and went back to Italy. On 30 September 1920, in the town of Rivolto, he married my grandmother, Nicolina Cengarle, from Codroipo, not far from Romans. They had three children, Enrica, Jack and Maria, who was only a teenager when she died of pneumonia in November 1941. My grandfather came out in 1927 and my grandmother followed him in '35 with the kids.
>
> Francesco lived in a boarding house somewhere in the Carlton area and he always worked in concrete. In the early years he worked for Negri, then he worked for Mardigan. When Mum first came here they lived in Collingwood, but they later moved to a house at 783 Drummond Street, Carlton. Dad lived there until he died in 1966, and my grandmother died in 1990. They are buried with Maria in Fawkner Cemetery.

26. Luigi Segat

BORN ROMANS, PROVINCIA DI UDINE, 30 MAY 1887.
DIED NORTH FITZROY, VICTORIA, 10 AUGUST 1959.

IN OCTOBER 1997, in the lounge room of her home in the northern Melbourne suburb of Reservoir, a kindly lady named Maria Reginato — the daughter of Luigi Segat — told me the following story:

My father originally left the small town of Romans in 1925, but my mother, Angela De Appolonia, died a couple of months after he left and so he returned to be with us five kids. Mum died about three months after I was born.

My father remarried, returned to Australia in 1927, and completed another return trip in 1934. My older brothers, Jack and Dante, came out in 1937 and 1938, and they paid for the rest of us to join them. But the War broke out, and my stepmother, Angelina Magrin, stepbrother Mario, natural brother Oreste and I had to stay behind.

The rest of us finally arrived in Australia in August 1948 by aeroplane — the very first plane — which took five days. My father and my brothers were so scared to lose us on that plane, and it cost a lot of money, but they didn't care how much they paid, they wanted us out here. Dad paid for all of us to come out, but Oreste, who had learned his trade as a tailor in Milan, developed an illness and Dad had to sell the house to pay the hospital. Dad lost it all.

My older sister, Vilma, married in Venice, and never wanted to come to Australia. Later she came here with her husband and loved it so much that she returned three times before she died.

Dad used to work in Carlton as a concreter. During the War he brought a little potato farm in Gippsland, but he started to get unhealthy, so my brothers got him out of there and back into the concrete business. He was a big man, but he collapsed in the street from a heart attack on his way to bank the day's proceeds. He was seventy-two when he died. After that my stepmother lived with my tailor brother and her stepson until she died, about twenty years ago. My stepbrother Mario and I are the only ones still here.

27. Attilio GioBatta Bellò

BORN ONÈ DI FONTE, PROVINCIA DI TREVISO, 11 OCTOBER 1901.
DIED ONÈ DI FONTE, PROVINCIA DI TREVISO, 14 MARCH 1959.

THE SON OF Giovanni and Angela Bellò (née Vauzo), GioBatta came to Australia as an unmarried man. He worked on a potato farm, as well as in the sugarcane industry, although the whereabouts of this employment is unclear. In fact, he remained in Australia only a short time, probably until 1934, as it just did not work out financially. He returned to Italy on a cargo ship, was married, and his wife gave birth to a son and a daughter. He died in Fonte in 1959 of a paralysis.

Forty years later, fate brought me to the home of GioBatta's daughter, Antonia Dasin (née Bellò), in Via Castellana, Fonte. Accompanied by my Italian cousins, Giada and Edy De Bolfo, I took the liberty of visiting the Dasin sharefarm as part of a memorable four-week extended honeymoon with my wife Kate, in December 1999. Our honeymoon took in the glorious locales of Florence, Milan, Lake Como and, of course, the De Bolfo brothers' home town of San Nicolò.

Antonia welcomed me into her home and was totally supportive of my endeavours to chronicle her father's life. But as she was only a child when she lost her father, Antonia's recollections of GioBatta's life were sadly all too few.

28. Luigi Simaz

BORN COSIZZA, SAN LEONARDO, PROVINCIA DI UDINE, 21 MAY 1901.
DIED CLODIG, PROVINCIA DI UDINE, 29 SEPTEMBER 1935.

IN OCTOBER 1927, twenty-six year old Luigi Simaz said goodbye to his family and friends in Cosizza, just a few kilometres from the Slovenian border in northeastern Italy. Like most of his fellow voyagers who packed their meagre belongings and boarded the old steamship, Luigi's farewells were tinged with sadness. Would he ever see his people again?

Luigi was the son of Andrea and Teresa Simaz (née Vogrig), who reared three other children: Antonio, Emilio and Maria. He grew up in a township whose inhabitants had been heavily embroiled in the Battle of Caporetto on 24 October 1917. This was an Italian military disaster during the First World War in which 600,000 war-wearied and demoralised soldiers either deserted or surrendered before an Austro–German offensive on the Isonzo front, northwest of Trieste.

The ravages of war made it hard for the Cosizza people to forge a normal living. One of them, Ermenegildo Cernotta, left for Australia and new beginnings in 1925. In April of 1927, he put his signature to the nomination form endorsing Luigi's admission to this country. Seven months later, Luigi disembarked from the *Re d'Italia* in Melbourne. His movements in the ensuing years are uncertain. At some point in the late 1920s or early 1930s, Luigi returned to Cosizza, where, on 4 March 1935, he married a local girl, Elisabetta Cernotta. She had given birth to his son, Natalino, two years beforehand.

But just six months later the Simaz family was devastated by the death of Luigi in shocking circumstances. Ermenegildo Cernotta's niece, Liliana, now living in the outer Melbourne suburb of Dandenong, takes up the story:

> Luigi went on a drinking spree into a *paese* three or four kilometres north of Cosizza, called Clodig, and got into an argument with a man from Brida Superiore, Vittorio Vogrig. Vogrig hit him on the head with a piece of wood and killed him. Vogrig presented himself to the authorities and served twelve years in Sicily. He later met and married a Sicilian girl and they both moved to England.

Liliana Cernotta herself was born in Liessa, Grimacco, three kilometres from Cosizza, a year after Luigi's death, but told me, 'This was one of the most shocking events in the valley. These things just don't happen. I was born in 1936 and I remember the story being told. It was a big event. I was a little girl then, and in those days, with no T.V. or radio, people talked a lot, and this story has been told over and over again.'

My initial conversation with Liliana took place on the evening of 24 January 1999. Three days later, Liliana contacted me to say she had discovered in her home a photograph of four men, one of whom was Luigi, taken in Italy some years before his voyage to Australia. She subsequently forwarded me a copy of this photo.

A few weeks later, Liliana again contacted me to advise that she had located an address for Natalino Simaz, Luigi's son, now living with his wife and family in Sambreville, Auvelais, in Belgium. I promptly forwarded an introductory letter to Natalino, which was accompanied by a copy of his father's photograph, the passenger list, his father's nomination form and an image of the *Re d Italia*. Later I forwarded him a copy of the 'Australian Story' video, with accompanying French script.

Natalino clearly suffered and was teased for his illegitimate birth, and he also felt sad for his mum because of it. On 4 October 1999, I received the following letter from him, penned in French and later translated for me by George Gimel, a family friend who came to Australia from postwar Europe as a teenager with his parents:

Dear Mr De Bolfo,

I hope that you will forgive me for not replying sooner but I thought about it at length, not just to refuse your request but for sentimental reasons. To express those very personal memories, the beginning of my life in very difficult circumstances, is still very painful for me today.

I sincerely thank you for my father's photograph. It gave me great pleasure. It is in fact the only one I have ever seen of him ... How did he spend those years in Australia? The date of his return to Italy, all this is still unknown to me. I also cannot tell you much of the period between his return and his brutal disappearance, of his activities or his personal problems, because I just don't know.

I, Natalino Simaz, was born on 1 January 1933. I was therefore an illegitimate child until the marriage of my parents on 4 March 1935. On 29 September 1935 my father died. My parents therefore only had six months together as a married couple.

To give you an idea of this period, you should be aware that it was a poor area. There were more illiterates than educated people and the moral code of the Catholic clergy was the law. I was therefore a child of sin.

In those days even men who were married and fathers with children were assumed to have the right and freedom to go out with other men to places of entertainment (local fairs, drinking establishments), the perfect environment for futile arguments amongst men affected by excesses of alcohol. However, I will not allow that to taint my father's memory.

How would we have behaved under the same circumstances?

Following this sad event, my mother and I were in some way rejected by the family, particularly that of my father. It was a long and difficult period. My mother went back to work, while I lived with my maternal grandfather Faustino Cernotta — my only protection in my mother's absence and the only one who showed some affection to me . . .

In 1942 my mother remarried, to Giuseppe Obit, who returned from France following the War. He was a good man, also a widower, with three children — Lorenzo, Angelo and Maria, from two to three years older than me. Of their union came a boy, Giacomo, in 1943.

My stepfather left for Belgium on 11 November 1946, to work in the coal mines like so many of his compatriots did at the time. The Italian state and the Belgian government had in fact passed some treaties. Coal for manpower. Necessity and poverty dictated our migration to Belgium.

We had settled in Belgium barely two months when my stepfather was struck with pleurisy. The state of his health was such that it became impossible for him to continue his work. We, the boys, found small jobs, while our sister started to work for a doctor. In 1949, the situation became intolerable and it was therefore decided that our parents would return to Italy.

With the agreement of the local authorities, the children (all minors) could remain in Belgium so that they need not be dumped again into the social misery that afflicted Italy at the time. Imagine the despair in which my mother found herself. Giacomo was five years old.

In October 1949, when my parents returned to Italy, I was sixteen years old. I was sent to a boarding house and once again separated from my mother. I was earning little money, just enough to pay my board. I therefore applied to work in the deep underground shafts of a coal mine, which paid a higher salary.

It was difficult to keep going , but a learning experience in life, because it is impossible to explain what you feel when you find yourself in a mine shaft in the bowels of the earth when you are so young. That period lasted four years, before I finally found work in the open air.

At the age of twenty-one I had the chance of my life. I met a young Belgian girl, Eliane Tondu, and we married on 24 September 1954. Between the two of us we achieved miracles . . . I found in marriage a certain stability and I thank my wife with all my heart. From our union were born two children — Elizabeth in 1957 and Philippe in 1958.

I overcame the enormous handicap of my lack of education and tried to fill this void as quickly as possible. I undertook evening classes at a technical school. My command of the French language did not come easily due to my age. The major difficulty with the other topics was my lack of education during childhood.

But by the grace of God, I did not lack intelligence or courage. After eight years of evening classes, as well as a regular day job, I obtained a diploma in foundry technology and I could hold the position of foreman in that area.

Giuseppe Obit died in 1984, aged seventy-nine, and Elisabetta Cernotta died in 1993 at the age of eighty-one. Towards the end of their lives they received a small pension, which eased their final days.

I hold close to my heart my mother's saying, which I now offer to you. 'When we had teeth, we did not have bread. Now that we have bread, we do not have the teeth.' This phrase epitomises the life of poor people. It's all to their credit that they remained good, honest and courageous.

In closing, dear Mr De Bolfo, I have tried to give you as much information as I can. The life of my father was very short and my mother and I were separated practically all of our lives. I felt the need to fully explain myself as homage to her. In view of my age during these events, not many things were explained to me.

I am very touched by your project to invite the descendants of the passengers of the *Re d'Italia* to the launch of your book. I will permit myself to express some reservations on the topic of this trip. Following a recent health problem (thrombosis, without serious complications), I try to manage. We could look at this problem again when the time comes.

Concerning yourself, permit me to offer you my congratulations for the work you have undertaken. One must have courage to show life in its positive and negative aspects, so that present generations do not forget that the better living conditions they are enjoying are due to the sacrifices of previous generations.

The noble profession of journalism that you practise means that you wield a double-edged sword. Publicly relating sporting or other events can bring either enormous joy or bitterness and disappointment for those who lived them.

I conclude by saying that it is possible to tell still much more about this slice of life that was ours.

Dear Mr De Bolfo, I trust that this letter will find you as well as your near ones in good health.

My wife and I offer you our sincere salutations.

Natalino Simaz.

Natalino Simaz knew little of his father's life. But this brave man knew everything about the impact his father's death had on the life he subsequently led.

On the evening of Friday, 26 July 2002, my friend and Italian interpreter Maria Monaco made a phone call to Natalino from my home in Preston. The purpose of the call was to inform Natalino and his wife, Eliane, of the November release of the book, in the hope that they might be able to make plans to attend the launch in Carlton. Natalino's wife, Eliane, answered the phone, and though she could only converse in her native French language, the tone of her voice made it obvious to Maria that something terrible had happened.

It sounded as though Eliane was tring to tell Maria that her beloved husband Natalino had died a few days earlier. Seeking confirmation, I telephoned Liliana Cernotta in Dandenong. Liliana promised to seek confirmation through an acquaintance in Cosizza. The following morning, Liliana rang me to confirm the worst.

29. Giuseppe Conforti

BORN DUBINO, PROVINCIA DI SONDRIO, 28 MARCH 1883.
DIED BENDIGO, VICTORIA, 28 JUNE 1943.

HAILING FROM THE Swiss region in Italy's northwest, Giuseppe Conforti spent his early years in America, prior to his marriage to Maria Torri. But Maria did not want to settle there, prompting Giuseppe's return to his homeland. Soon afterwards Giuseppe purchased a tract of land. Regrettably, he was unable to meet the necessary repayments, which resulted in his lone departure to Australia, leaving behind Maria and two children, Peter (born in 1915) and Maria (born in 1917).

Upon arrival in Melbourne, Giuseppe made the trek to the northern Victorian town of Bendigo, where he was put up by the Svanosio family at 9 Condon Street. Giuseppe was a good friend of Andrea (Andy) Barri, who had acted as his sponsor. Andy spent most of his life in the Bendigo area, with the exception of a brief sojourn to Heathcote, where he cut wood.

Giuseppe also worked in the Bendigo district, as a dairy farmer. He worked to repay his debts, and repay his debts he did, but he would never be reunited with all family members. His wife died after the Second World War, in 1959, and his daughter is still living in Italy. Neither of them ever came to Australia. Only his son Peter ever saw him again, when he arrived in Australia just prior to the outbreak of the War.

'In 1939, before the War, he asked me to come out, and I had four years with him before he died,' said Peter, now living in Bendigo. 'He got sick, went to Bendigo Hospital and died there. He could have gone back, but the War stopped everything, and now he is buried in Bendigo.'

30. Angelo Valentino Benetti (Andrew Benett)

BORN RECOARO, PROVINCIA DI VICENZA, 1 MARCH 1909.
DIED HEIDELBERG, VICTORIA, 6 MAY 1979.

THROUGH THE REGISTRY at Recoaro it was discovered that Angelo Benetti returned to Italy, and resided at Contrada Cornaletti 2, Recoaro — his last confirmed address — in or around 1936, before apparently migrating to Belgium with brother Luigi and sister Margherita. Their whereabouts would have remained unknown but for a family tragedy that brought Angelo back to Australia a handful of years later.

Angelo's brother, Vittorio, came to Australia in 1925. Indeed, it was he who nominated Angelo. He moved to Streatham, near Lake Boga, just outside Ararat in country Victoria. He then worked the mine at Kilcunda, near Phillip Island, but sadly died in 1937 of osteomyelitis of the jaw and asthenia, aged just thirty-four. It seems the younger brother saw fit to leave his siblings in Belgium and return to Australia to secure Vittorio's final resting place in Fawkner Cemetery.

Although it is known from achival records that he spent time in the Yarra Valley township of Silvan in the 1950s, during which time he anglicised his name via deed poll, Angelo's movements in later years become vague. However, it is known that at some point he married Nellie Smith, who already had a son from a previous marriage. The couple settled in The Broadway, West Rosebud, and they remained together for thirty-nine years, until Angelo's death in 1979 in the northern Melbourne suburb of Heidelberg. His ashes were scattered at Springvale Crematorium.

31. Antonio Dal Sasso

BORN LUSIANA, PROVINCIA DI VICENZA, 24 APRIL 1895.
DIED LUGO, PROVINCIA DI TREVISO, 24 SEPTEMBER 1959.

TONY DAL SASSO, Antonio's nephew, who lives in the western Melbourne suburb of Newport, recalls Antonio as the second of seven children. He had two brothers, Giacomo and Giovanni (Tony's father), and four sisters, Maddalena, Caterina, Alice and Lucia. It was Maddalena's husband, Giovanni Maddalon, who sponsored Antonio to Australia. 'I think he worked in a quarry in Victoria somewhere, and he went up to Gippsland to work on the roads. He and his wife, Antonia Martinaggia ('Zia Ninella', as Tony remembers her), had two sons. Pietro was born in 1920 and went missing in action on the island of Crete, on 4 November 1951. The other, Domenico, was born in 1924. He had left the factory on his way home one day, but they found him dead on the side of the road in Verona, on 15 October 1971.'

Antonio lasted just four years in Australia, but as things were tough for his family back in Italy he returned to his homeland. 'He never came back, and he never talked about Australia,' said Tony.

SONS OF THE DOLOMITES

Igino De Bolfo, Melbourne, circa 1930.

Francesco De Bolfo, Melbourne, circa 1930.

Silvio De Bolfo, Melbourne, circa 1930.

IMAGES COURTESY JOHN AND MAUREEN DE BOLFO, HEIDELBERG, VICTORIA.

32. Igino (Jim) De Bolfo

BORN SAN NICOLÒ DI COMELICO, PROVINCIA DI BELLUNO, 10 JANUARY 1911.
DIED GLENHUNTLY, VICTORIA, 24 DECEMBER 2001.

33. Francesco (Frank) De Bolfo

BORN SAN NICOLÒ DI COMELICO, PROVINCIA DI BELLUNO, 14 SEPTEMBER 1903.
DIED BRUNSWICK, VICTORIA, 10 AUGUST 1987.

34. Silvio De Bolfo

BORN SAN NICOLÒ DI COMELICO, PROVINCIA DI BELLUNO, 18 JUNE 1902.
DIED HEIDELBERG, VICTORIA, 29 APRIL 1981.

THE FOLLOWING DETAILS of Igino De Bolfo's life were lovingly prepared by his eldest daughter, Joan Miskin (née De Bolfo):

Igino De Bolfo, affectionately called 'Nino' — or 'Jim', as he was known in Australia — was the tenth child of Giovanni Battista and Giovanna De Bolfo (née Zandonella). He was named after the patron saint of the day of his birth, and was christened, according to custom, the following day.

Nino's earliest memory was of seeing the family house on fire, and for a short while the family moved out of home while the damage was repaired. As a young child he sang for the Italian soldiers who had taken over the family's front room for an officers' mess, and he remembered seeing soldiers returning injured from the front in horse-drawn ambulances or on mules. His mother would often stop the injured and give them a bowl of soup and bread to eat.

In the last year of the First World War the town was occupied by the Austrians, and Nino remembered how food would be hidden. In fact, the family tried to leave the valley, but after travelling for twenty miles [thirty-two kilometres] it was obvious there was no way out of the area and the family returned home. Most of the food in the house had been found by the Austrians, but they had missed the large supply of potatoes cleverly hidden by Nino's father under the boards in the floor of the cellar.

Nino completed four years of schooling at San Nicolò. His fourth grade report, for the school year 1921 to 1922, shows that he was a very strong student in all subjects, with the exception of design. He topped the class despite being the youngest in the grade, with students up to four years older than him. His teacher's comment was *'Ha sempre fatto bene, con diligenza e volontà'* — 'He has always performed well, with diligence and willingness'.

Nino and his first cousin Ottavio completed another year of schooling sitting at the back of the grade three and four composite class. Nino enjoyed learning, but unfortunately the size of the family made it impossible for him to undertake further schooling. Throughout his years of schooling, Nino joined his brothers in delivering the bread baked by his mother before going to school each day, and also helped his father.

With Benedetto in the army, Silvio working in Bologna, Francesco learning his trade of upholstery and Gilberto attending college and living with his mother's parents, Nino was the eldest child still at home. He worked with his father after completing his schooling. He then found employment for a few months with a local carpenter, before joining his brother Silvio in Bari making ice chests. For two years he spent nine months of the year in Bari, returning home to work alongside his father or brothers for the other three months.

Nino, Frank and Silvio migrated to Australia with the sponsorship of eldest brother Ben. Just before they left, Aunty Rosina, his mother's sister, who worked in Milan, visited Nino and brought him some tea. She advised the young boy that he would have to get used to the taste of tea, but the cup that she gave him tasted terrible. It was a great relief to Nino that his first cup of tea in Australia tasted much better, thanks to milk and sugar!

Nino's memories of the voyage have already been documented in earlier pages. Following his arrival, Nino worked briefly at Uncle Andy Mattea's fish shop. Then, with the assistance of a hiring agency, Nino obtained farm labouring work picking tomatoes in rural Victoria, leaving his three older brothers in Melbourne. Late one night he was taken by carrier to the seaside town of Rosebud. It became quite a frightening trip when the lights failed, and he had to walk a further three miles [five kilometres] to get to the farm. He was supposed to be given ten shillings a week for his efforts, but he was never paid.

Nino then worked on a Moran & Cato asparagus farm managed by a man named Don Haigh, and he remembers the kindness extended to him by Don and his wife. It was here that Nino learned all about the Australian sun. He worked all day out in the sun and actually thought he was going to die, but he was in fact suffering from sunstroke.

During this time, Nino taught himself to speak, read and write English. Still in Rosebud, he worked as a farmer for a Mr Ralph for three years and by that stage had earned enough money to put a deposit on a farm. But sadly, in his second year of farming, just before he was about to pick a very good crop of early tomatoes, Rosebud was flooded and he lost the farm. During this time Nino had also taken up cricket, and in order to keep him in the team, work was found for him nearby at Cape Schank.

In 1937, he went to work for his brother Silvio, then Ben, in a fish shop in Carnegie, a suburb of Melbourne, where he served in the shop and cooked the fish and chips. Two years later, Nino became an Australian citizen.

With the outbreak of the Second World War, Nino volunteered for service. He organised for his rostered day off to be on a Friday so that he could help his brothers in the fish shop. After he completed his military training at Fisherman's Bend, Nino remained at the depot as a temporary corporal, and by the time he served in New Guinea he was a sergeant. Just out of Port Moresby, his foot was injured by falling timber and he spent six weeks in hospital. He returned to Australia, then served in North Borneo. At the end of the War, Nino underwent further surgery on his foot at the Repatriation Hospital in Heidelberg, and returned to work in the fish shop in Carnegie in 1946.

It had always been agreed that Nino would be the first to return to Italy for a visit, but unfortunately he contracted malaria during his army service and could not even travel on a train, let alone make the journey by sea to Italy. For many years he suffered bouts of malaria and also underwent a number of operations on his feet. He always had to wear specially made surgical shoes provided by the Department of Veterans' Affairs — even to play lawn bowls.

Nino married Armida (Amelia) Masocco at St John's Church in Carlton in 1949. Initially Nino and Amelia lived behind the fish shop along with Nino's brothers Ben and Gilberto (who had come to Australia in 1937), because there was a housing shortage. They later moved to their own house in Tranmere Avenue, Carnegie, and in 1952 the fish shop was sold. But even thirty years later, Nino could not walk into the local shopping centre without somebody recognising him as 'Mr Fish and Chips' and stopping for a chat.

Nino soon found work with the Department of Works and stayed there for two years. With the assistance of his neighbour, Ted Ambrose, he joined Noel Searle Glass and worked there until he retired in 1977.

Just before he retired, Nino took up lawn bowls and played competition bowls for his club, and over the years he worked his way up to playing for the A-grade team. Nino and his partner, Roe Fletcher, won the Victorian Metropolitan Group 14 Bowls Pairs — the first bowlers in their club to win such a competition.

Nino and Amelia had three children — Joan, Peter and Susan. The children enjoyed the legacy of their father's days working in the fish shop — fresh and beautifully cooked fish, chips and potato cakes. The family house in Carnegie had numerous fruit trees and a large vegetable garden, with tomatoes always ripe before Christmas.

If there was something to fix or someone needing assistance in the neighbourhood, Nino was always ready to help. It was rare for Nino to show anger, except in one area. He was a true-blue, one-eyed Carlton supporter, and whether at football matches or in front of the television, he always made his feelings known to that 'biased' umpire.

His children, grandchildren, nephews and nieces all have memories of him as a man who loved children. He would play and make a fuss of any child. How many young children did he convince to ask their teacher if he could come to school? Nino was keen to give his children the educational opportunities that he never had. Always keen on sport, he supported his children's efforts in that area too. In one of Susan's netball matches the umpire threatened to penalise her team, because Nino was complaining that the umpire was unduly favouring the opposition!

More than seventy years on, Nino could speak for all his brothers when he looked back with pride on what he had achieved for himself and his descendants.

'Not going back after the war to see Mum and Dad was the only setback, but I wouldn't have gone back for anything else,' Nino said at the time. 'So many things have happened in that time, good things and bad things, but I'm still alive. And I couldn't be happier. I wouldn't have changed my family or my way of life for anything that's happened.'

EARLY IN 1997, Frank De Bolfo's daughter, Anne, penned the following story of her father's life:

Frank was the third son of Giovanni Battista De Bolfo and his wife Giovanna Zandonella, who produced thirteen children in all. The surviving eight children helped with the family bakery business, which operated from the basement of their home.

Frank attended the elementary school in San Nicolò di Comelico and, as was common for the time and the region, left after completing six years' education. He then took up an apprenticeship in upholstery at Cortina D'Ampezzo — a trade he was never to practise professionally in Australia, but would dabble in as a hobby, even in his later years. Cortina is about eighty kilometres from the family home and is now a world-class ski resort in the heart of the Dolomites. It is a far cry from the town Frank knew as an apprentice.

After his apprenticeship, Frank did a period of National Service in the Alpini Regiment of the Italian Army. But the country was caught in the grip of the Great Depression, and in 1927 Frank and his brothers left Italy forever.

For a time after his arrival in Australia, Frank worked in the Mildura area and also on the building of a reservoir in the bush. He also worked on a road-building gang around Trafalgar, and in the Gippsland–Walhalla area cutting railway sleepers with a work gang. Frank used to delight in telling the story of going out into the scrub alone one day and being confronted by an enormous goanna. Naturally he'd never seen or heard of one before, and believed he was being set upon by some huge carnivorous (and probably man-eating) monster! He was relieved to find out after his escape that goannas are easily appeased by a few slices of bread.

For the majority of his working life in Australia, Frank worked on the Melbourne wharves. During the Second World War his job was deemed an essential service and, as such, Frank was not interned, as were many other Italian immigrants. But it was necessary at this time for him to renounce allegiance to the King of Italy.

In the late 1940s Frank took up residence in a boarding house in Moor Street, Fitzroy, which was run by Albina Dal Brun (née Menara). Albina, her husband Francesco and her children Alvise, Elvira and Aurora had migrated to Australia from the town of Schio in the Veneto region of Italy. Their youngest daughter, Alba, had been born in Australia on 29 July 1926. Alba worked as a cashier in restaurants owned by the Codognotto family, but was also her mother's main help in running the boarding house.

It was while Frank was helping Alba to get her mother walking again after a bout of ill health that romance blossomed, and they were married in 1949. Frank was a late starter at forty-six, and his bride was twenty-three. They stayed on with Alba's mother until they bought their own home in West Brunswick.

The property at West Brunswick was bought for cash, as was everything else both major and minor purchases. Tough times during the Depression and a hard life back in Italy had contributed to Frank's frugal nature, and in his mind mortgages and loans were strictly out of the question.

Frank's and Alba's first child, Benedict John (Ben), was born on 27 June 1950. A daughter, Frances, born on 4 June 1951, was the next addition. Two more daughters completed the family: Anne Marie (the writer of this), born on 4 April 1957, and Gina Theresa, born on 19 April 1961.

Before Anne and Gina were born, Alba's mother's health had started to fail and, by then widowed, she moved in to live with Frank, Alba and their two children. Frank was compassionate and caring towards his mother-in-law, as he had been whilst living at the boarding house, and continued to help nurse her, even building a hospital-style bed hoist so that she was able to move about in bed. She stayed with Frank and Alba until her death in 1984.

Frank worked hard to provide a good Catholic education for his children. He delayed his retirement until after the age of sixty-five so he could continue to provide for his children's educational needs. He was compulsorily retired at the age of sixty-seven, but he still wanted to continue working. He was extremely proud of his children's educational and working achievements, and he was later to be a devoted and loving grandfather.

Frank's main, if not only, form of transport was his trusty bicycle. Although he had learned to drive, and held a driver's licence for many years, Frank was most comfortable on his bike. It was no impediment to his day-to-day routine, or to his ability to transport various household goods. It was not unusual for him to come home from a timber mill balancing huge sacks of sawdust for the garden on the handlebars (forty or fifty kilograms each, and sometimes two at a time), or to do the same with bags of wheat or pollard for the chickens, not to mention the weekly grocery shopping, boxes of live chickens, or fruit and vegetables from the Victoria Market.

He was knocked off his bike a couple of times, thus beginning a spate of operations and periods of ill health, which would dog his later years. But Frank rode his bike for many years, stopping only in his late seventies after a hip replacement operation.

Frank always maintained a large and productive garden. The front garden was always a mass of flowers, but the back garden was the working garden. The beautiful roses and hydrangeas at the front of the house gave way to a kitchen garden that supplied a myriad of the family's needs, and grapevines and fruit trees abounded too. Visitors were always given the grand tour by a proud Frank.

As a child in the bakery Frank watched his mother cook, and he later put much of what he had observed to good use. He loved to cook, and despite the fact that Alba was a very good cook in her own right, Frank did much of the cooking for his family. He would make huge pots of soup every Sunday morning, and *pasta* sauce every week. The special treats were home-made *ravioli* and *gnocchi*, which he and Alba would always make together. Frank also made *canederli* (Tyrolean dumplings) which are peculiar to the Austrian border areas of Italy, and every now and then we'd also be treated to his home-made cakes and scones. He also made light-as-a-feather *crostoli* (pastry strips lightly fried in oil and dusted with sugar) every Easter and Christmas.

Frank never returned to Italy and the village of his birth. Despite that, he was always Italian at heart. He had a deep love of the language and was proud to speak 'pure' Italian, rather than dialect. When he brought the first family stereo, the first records purchased with it were Italian operas. He played them loudly as he attended to his garden.

Though not a churchgoer, Frank had a strong faith and deeply religious beliefs. He taught his children to pray (in Italian) and he said his prayers without fail every day.

Alba passed away suddenly on 21 September 1984 at the age of just fifty-eight. Frank died at home three years later and was buried at Fawkner Cemetery with his wife.

In October 1997, Silvio De Bolfo's only son, John (the author's father), penned the following story:

Silvio, the second child of Giovanni and Giovanna De Bolfo (née Zandonella), was born in San Nicolò, Provincia di Belluno, northern Italy, on 18 June 1902. By the time he took those first few steps down the gangway at Victoria Dock, Silvio was twenty-five years old, a member of the local *guardie granatieri* (grenadier guards), and a cabinetmaker by profession. He had come to this country with his certificate of apprenticeship, obtained in his early years at Santo Stefano, near his home town San Nicolò, along with the practical experience of running an ice-chest manufacturing business in the warmer environs of Bari in southern Italy. A photograph of Igino ('Uncle Nino') and him standing by an ice chest, as well as Silvio's certificate of apprenticeship, are treasured possessions of the De Bolfo family.

Following the brothers' arrival in Melbourne, Silvio and his younger brother Frank bought a fish shop at 64 Koornang Road, Carnegie. It was around 1934 or '35, and by then Silvio had gained the necessary piscatorial knowledge, having worked part-time in the neighbouring fish shops for a few Spaniards, one of whom operated out of Glenhuntly Road, Caulfield. Although he was a qualified cabinetmaker, I cannot recall my father plying his craft in those early years in Melbourne.

In 1935, my father met a young girl named Maria Cincotta. She was about eighteen at the time, and although living with her sister in Elsternwick, she regularly caught the tram to Carnegie to her job, serving customers in the local fruit shop. This fruit shop was right next door to the De Bolfos' fish shop in Koornang Road.

One particular day Silvio walked in and suggested to the lady running the shop that he would like to visit Maria. The lady relayed the message to Maria with the words, 'De Bolfo's coming to see you tonight.'

Maria would normally sleep at the shop on Thursday and Friday night and head home on Saturday morning. On the Saturday morning after they first met, she was preparing to catch the tram home, only to find Silvio waiting outside in his ute. And although he graciously offered her a lift home, young Maria politely declined. 'I'm not allowed to go home with strangers,' she reminded the fishmonger, to which Silvio promptly replied, 'Come on, I'm not going to hurt you.'

Mum later rejected Dad's offer of a wristwatch, again saying, 'I can't accept that, I don't know you well enough.' But she took the watch eventually, and when her mother quizzed her about the item, Maria insisted, 'I found it in the shop.'

Mum and Dad married in that very year, 1935, in Kerang, as Mum's mother and father were sharefarmers up there. In May of the following year, not long after the newlyweds moved into a new fish shop and dwelling at 477 Glenhuntly Road, South Caulfield, I was born.

With Silvio gone, and Frank having gained work as a stevedore on the Melbourne waterfront, Ben, Nino and another brother Gilberto (Bert) continued to run the shop in Koornang Road. Bert had arrived in Australia on the passenger ship *Esquilino* on 5 July 1937, and would return to his homeland twice: once to visit his mother five days before she died, and again, for good, in 1952. Bert later married a local girl, Rita Costan, and with her reared four children —

Cornelio, Giuliana, Andreina and Benedetta. Bert and Rita lived their lives in the De Bolfo family home in San Nicolò, and spent forty-two years together as devoted husband and wife before Bert's death at eighty-five, on 17 March 1994.

At some point during the Great Depression, Silvio and Uncle Ben turned their hands to concreting for the De Marco brothers, who were at that time big names in the business. With the Depression biting hard and the pair of them desperate for work, they heard that the De Marcos were sponsors of an Italian tug-of-war team. Since Silvio and Ben — and indeed Frank and Igino — all boasted sturdy physiques, they reasoned that if they could crack it for the De Marco tug-of-war team they could ultimately crack it for concreting work.

The De Bolfos ventured to the site of what later became known as the St Moritz ice-skating rink, to participate in the tug-of-war trials. My father did very well as anchorman, Frank was the knot-man and Uncle Ben just about pulled them out onto The Esplanade adjoining. Carlton footballer Sergio Silvagni's father, Giacomo, was also a member of that team, which ultimately competed in the Victorian championships, and, more importantly, landed that badly needed concreting work with the De Marcos!

Dad was also politically active, was a member of Melbourne's Club Matteotti and was a welcome participant in many of the local anti-Fascist rallies. He was never one to back off from a stoush either, especially when it came to racial abuse. He and Frank once happened to be in a pub in South Melbourne when three or four local wharfies gave a little Sicilian bloke a good going-over. Frank and Silvio told the wharfies to cut it out, and when they replied, 'You want some too?', it was on for young and old. But that was the wharfies' mistake, as Silvio whacked each one of them in the breadbasket and Frank booted them in the backside and out the door just as quickly.

On those rare occasions when he wasn't working, Silvio's weekends were taken up playing poker, and for big money too. Uncle Ben, who would remain a bachelor all his life, happened to be a member of a card club in what was the old Eastern Market — now the site of the soon-to-be-demolished Southern Cross Hotel on Exhibition Street. Before Ben became a member there, the pair of them would play cards in an upstairs room behind Florentino's.

I remember, at the appointed time on Sunday nights, leaving my aunt's place in Smith Street with Mum after our regular visit to go and fetch Silvio. Mum used to send me up the flight of stairs and into the room to get him, only to be told, 'One more round, one more round!' As a result, I'd be backwards and forwards relaying messages between Mum and Dad.

Dad used to get his wine from Alexander and Patterson wine merchants, rather handily located beneath the Eastern Market, where the card playing occurred. He would extract the wine from the huge vats, fill his demijohns, take them home and bottle the wine — always chablis, no red. And he'd drink a glass with every meal.

Towards the end of the Second World War, Silvio developed bad arthritis. The illness prompted his admission to St Vincent's Hospital, where he was to spend some time, and later forced him to sell the shop. Then, following a twelve-month stay at my maternal aunt Teresa Zagame's place at 98 Smith Street, Collingwood (now Caffè Figaro Ristorante), Silvio purchased a double-fronted Victorian dwelling at 84 Raglan Street, Preston, and settled there with his family in 1947.

In later years, my father again took up the cabinetmaking trade he had learned back in another lifetime in Santo Stefano. Dad worked for T.S. Gill and Sons, glaziers and shopfitters, in Preston, and for A.V. Jennings on prefabricated houses. At the time of his retirement, he was working at the Royal Children's Hospital as a carpenter.

My father died on 29 April 1981, aged seventy-eight — one year and one day after his older brother Ben. They are buried within close proximity of each other at Springvale Cemetery, which, as Mum once explained, allows them that chance late at night to cut the cards and play just one more round!

THE OCCUPANT,
31 SHOWERS STREET,
PRESTON

Giuseppe Destro's passport photograph, 1927.
PHOTOGRAPH COURTESY MARISA NEGRELLI (NÉE ANDREATTA), BULLEEN, VICTORIA.

35. Giuseppe Destro

BORN MALO, PROVINCIA DI VICENZA, 19 MARCH 1899.
DIED PRESTON, VICTORIA, 28 DECEMBER 1974.

THE TOUCHING TALE of the potter Giuseppe Destro might never have been told were it not for the unswerving support of a kindly lady at the Melbourne Registry of Births, Deaths and Marriages.

Frances Marino had already unearthed numerous certificates relevant to the *Re d'Italia*'s passengers. Furthermore, she had gone to the trouble of exploring variations of the names supplied to her — a case in point, the passenger Gaetano Sartori, whose death certificate she discovered was actually registered under the name 'James Sartori'.

Some information on Giuseppe Destro had already come from the A.C.T.'s Archives in Deakin as far back as November 1997. In a naturalisation document dated 28 April 1937, Giuseppe gave his father's name as 'Santo' and his mother's as 'Maria Schizzaroto'. He also revealed that he had served with the Italian Army during the First World War, and that since his arrival had lived in the Queensland towns of Ingham and Innisfail for three and a half years, Adelaide for one year (where he worked for Bennett Pottery Works), and the remainder in Melbourne. Indeed, his address was listed as 410 St Georges Road, Thornbury, a northern suburb of Melbourne.

I located only one listing for Destro in the Melbourne *White Pages*. A chain of phone calls then led to 'Nat' Destro, in Adelaide.

'Giuseppe was my father's cousin,' Nat explained. 'I only met him a couple of times — when I first came to Australia in 1949, and on one other occasion. I remember my mum saying he married late, when he was between sixty and seventy. He used to have a nephew in Melbourne, who I think died, and a niece living there too.' Nat suggested I call his sister, Narcisa Martini, in South Australia, but Narcisa could shed little light on Giuseppe's life.

Meanwhile, I discovered that a Signora Angela Piazza, who sponsored Giuseppe to Australia all those years ago, was still alive at age 100. Regrettably, a relative of the old woman explained that Angela was now under constant care in a Myrtleford nursing home and unable to assist.

I then turned to Frances Marino at the registry for help. I supplied her with details of Giuseppe's birth, which were enough for her to locate the relevant death certificate. According to the certificate, Giuseppe Destro died of a heart attack three days after Christmas Day, 1974. Nat Destro's belief that Giuseppe had married late in life was also confirmed by the certificate, which revealed that Giuseppe had exchanged vows at age fifty-six with Evelina Guadagnini. Crucially, the certificate also carried Giuseppe's last known place of residence: 31 Showers Street, Preston.

As I lived in the Preston area, I thought, 'Why not go round to the house?' Through the tenant's real estate agent, I sourced the owner: Marisa Negrelli (née Andreatta), Giuseppe Destro's great-niece.

At two o'clock on the afternoon of Monday, 30 March 1998, I met Marisa for the first time. We sat at the kitchen table of the Negrelli family home, where Marisa painted a glorious picture of her late great-uncle. Here is Marisa's story:

Giuseppe always spoke about how there wasn't enough money in Italy, and how he came to Australia alone. I remember him saying that he came out on a cargo ship with bunks everywhere, and that people basically lived on top of each other.

Someone met him down at the dock, possibly Angela Piazza, and he went with her. He didn't know anybody else. Soon afterwards he went to Ingham in northern Queensland. Maybe he knew someone there; I'm not sure.

He was a very quiet, unassuming man. He was a solitary person who did his own thing most of the time. He wasn't from the same mould as anyone else and he didn't seem to have many close friends. The fact that he was a potter when everyone else was a farmer made him different. We used to love to watch him when he had the pottery wheel turning. We used to ask if we could touch the clay. He'd spin the wheel around and in no time there'd be a vase. It was like magic. He made ducks too, and painted them all red. He must only have had red dye.

This was around about 1955, when he was living at our place at 80 Plenty Road. It was a very long block, but not terribly wide, and all I can remember him having was one bedroom, a kitchenette and a bathroom. You then walked out onto a verandah, which took you to his workshop, his kiln and his potter's wheel. By then he was making pottery for his own pleasure, just because he liked working with clay. Giuseppe had chickens and things, and he didn't seem to be working anywhere else at that time. He did a lot of odd jobs now and again, like helping out at the brickworks in Showers Street, where he last lived.

At some point my mother mentioned to Giuseppe that she had a maiden aunt, Evelina Guadagnini, in Italy. Soon after that they began writing to each other, and before too long they married by proxy. It was 14 March 1955 when he stood before a priest in Melbourne and she before a priest in Italy.

He was fifty-six and she was fifty-four. Evelina arrived in Australia aboard the *Surriento* on 17 October of that year, and together she and Giuseppe settled at 80 Plenty Road. From Plenty Road they moved around the corner to a little two-bedroom place in Raglan Street, and then to the premises at 31 Showers Street.

Giuseppe and Evelina were so different it was unbelievable. She was meticulous to the point where she drove you insane, while he was so easy-going it didn't worry him. But to us they were the grandparents we never had. We were their family and they really felt a part of the household. As neither had a licence to drive, they always walked around. They used to come to our place every single day at one o'clock and they'd stay until half past four, after Giuseppe had checked his fobwatch. They'd always leave at that time to beat the peak-hour traffic crossing Plenty Road and High Street.

When I got my driver's licence I took them to places they had never seen, like St Kilda Beach. When Giuseppe died I found an old piece of paper in the garage with a date on it, which was the date of the last time I took him for a drive. When I saw that I felt so horrible, because in later years I wasn't able to take him out as often. As you get older and bring up a family of your own, suddenly there are other priorities.

Giuseppe always seemed to be very happy. In fact I never saw him unhappy. Even in his years in Ingham he never mentioned that he was struck with hardship, or at least his stories never sounded that way. And how he loved to tell us stories!

36. Giovanni Pizzato

BORN ASIAGO, PROVINCIA DI VICENZA, 16 JUNE 1903.
DIED ASIAGO, PROVINCIA DI VICENZA, 9 DECEMBER 1986.

GIOVANNI PIZZATO WAS the younger of two sons — the elder being Vittorio — born to Giovanni Battista and Santina Pizzato (née Dalle Ave). Giovanni left Italy for economic reasons and, following his arrival in Melbourne, made for the country, possibly Myrtleford, to cultivate tobacco.

But after seven or eight years he returned to Italy, having received a letter from Vittorio in Chicago, requesting that he tend to the needs of his parents. Giovanni went home with all his savings just prior to the outbreak of the Second World War, but unfortunately, as the *lira* was devalued at the time, he lost everything. After the War Giovanni became a carpenter. He married Giovanna De Michiel, who bore a son, Vittorio, to him in 1952. He died in Asiago, where his wife and son remain to this day.

Giovanni's brother, Vittorio, who spent his entire life in the United States with the exception of a few return trips to Italy, died in Chicago. He has a daughter, Lilian, living in Tennessee and a son, Giovanni, living in Chicago, employed as an executive with the Coca-Cola Company.

37. Angelo Rigoni

BORN ASIAGO, PROVINCIA DI VICENZA, 6 SEPTEMBER 1905.
DIED ASIAGO, PROVINCIA DI VICENZA, 9 DECEMBER 1968.

ANGELO RIGONI WAS the son of Domenico and Domenica Rigoni (née Besavento). He boarded the *Re d'Italia* in Genoa with a cousin, Cristiano Rigoni, and was sponsored by Giacomo Rigoni, presumably another relative, who at that time lived in Adelaide.

Cristiano Rigoni's son, the late Chris Rigoni, knew of Angelo, but knew very little. Angelo, he said, returned to Italy very early in the piece. But Chris kindly referred me to his cousin, Cristina Costa, for more information. Cristina, who lives in one of Melbourne's eastern suburbs, Lower Templestowe, then referred me to her brother, Tarcisio Rigoni, who resides in the northern Italian town of Asiago, Angelo's birthplace.

In early 1999, on Cristina's advice, I forwarded a letter to Tarcisio. A few weeks later Tarcisio wrote to inform me that Angelo, who was known to his friends as 'Gino', had died more than thirty years earlier. But he did reveal that Angelo's widow, Nicolina Stella, then aged eighty-seven, was alive and well and living in Asiago. Not long afterwards, my good friend and translator Maria Monaco put in a long-distance call to Nicolina on my behalf. Maria explained the purpose of her call and Nicolina responded with a few welcome details.

Angelo, it seems, remained in Australia for just a few short years. He cut timber in the Seymour district of Victoria before returning to his homeland around 1931. In 1932 he and Nicolina married and subsequently became proud parents to three daughters. Angelo later took up the profession of accountancy, which resulted in his gaining employment with a cheese and butter factory in Asiago for what would be a twenty-year stint. On retirement, Angelo worked the land as a farmer, but cancer cruelly cut his life short at the age of sixty-three.

In late 2001, Yvonne Mogorovich (née Stella), a friend who was indirectly linked with the lives of the passengers Luigi Stella and Sebastiano Speranza, told me that she was heading back to her home town of Asiago for three months and would be happy to meet with Nicolina.

On her return to Melbourne in January 2001, Yvonne called to inform me that she had brought back a glorious photograph of Angelo Rigoni, taken in a studio in Smith Street, Collingwood, around 1928. Incredibly, Yvonne also discovered that she and Nicolina were related, in that Nicolina's father and Yvonne's maternal grandmother were brother and sister.

'Nicolina was my mother's first cousin. I knew we were related as soon as I saw her face,' said Yvonne.

38. Tiziano Luciano Paganin (Paganini)

BORN LAVARONE, PROVINCIA DI VICENZA, 26 APRIL 1890.
DIED TEXAS, QUEENSLAND, 29 JUNE 1969.

BY THE DUMARESQ River on the Queensland–New South Wales border is a town fifty-five kilometres southeast of Inglewood. The town is called Texas (also a home to passenger seven, Luigi Dozzi), and it is where Tiziano Paganin finally settled more than fifty years ago.

Perhaps the very name of the place struck a chord with the man from Lavarone, who had previously spent eight years in the United States and was actually a naturalised American. In fact, Tiziano also spent eight years in Germany and five more in France before his arrival in this country.

The son of Antonio and Angela Paganin (née Marsari), Tiziano married twenty-nine year-old Teresa Gusparetto in April 1921 in Fara, Vicenza. Teresa presented her husband with three children: Gasperino, who was born in Clinton, America, in 1922; Romeo, born in Breganze, Italy, in 1925; and Caterina, also born in Breganze, the following year.

Following Tiziano's arrival aboard the *Re d'Italia*, he spent the first year moving between Melbourne and the mining town of Wonthaggi, then relocated to Wollongong in New South Wales, where he stayed for the next five years. Two years at Scone were followed by a six-year stint in Tamworth before he moved to Texas during the War — 'less the three years in internment in South Australia', according to the archives. Tiziano was interned in February 1942 in Gaythorne, Brisbane, transferred to the South Australian camp at Loveday the following month, and finally released on 22 June 1945. Tiziano's naturalisation applications were rejected during the War, on the basis that the 'applicant is an enemy alien who has not resided 20 years in Australia'.

Tiziano's grandson, Ron, still lives in the Texas area. 'Nonno went back to Wollongong during the mid-1950s, came back to Queensland in 1959 for two or three years and then went to Texas and bought a house. He was there for a couple of years, went to Stanthorpe for a couple more, and then came back here to Texas, to Goondarin. I live straight across the road from Goondarin and I stayed on the old dunghill,' Ron said.

'Nonno started to get ill when he returned from Stanthorpe. He died around 1969 and is buried in Texas. Gasperino, my dad, died a few years ago, "Rina" (Caterina) died in the mid-1970s, and Romeo was drowned up at a property called Gunyan when the river was in flood, around the 1930s.'

39. Luigi Tomaso Groppi

BORN COMANO, PROVINCIA DI MASSA CARRARA, 1 SEPTEMBER 1905.
DIED SHEPPARTON, VICTORIA, 26 OCTOBER 1994.

THE TOWNS OF Massa and Carrara, in the northern part of Toscana (Tuscany), are best known for their marble quarries. In fact, the white marble of Carrara is unrivalled for both texture and purity, and Michelangelo himself sought it for many of his sculptural masterpieces.

It was from this region that Luigi Groppi hailed. The son of Alfonso and Palmira Groppi (née Maffei), Luigi came to this country with the support of his *paesano* (fellow townsman) Angelo Benedetti, who had previously settled in the town of Wattle Vale in Victoria's north central region. He travelled on the *Re d'Italia* with a friend from the same region, Ridolfo Pasquali (passenger number forty).

In October 1997, I tracked down Luigi's son, Alf Groppi, in Shepparton. Alf was happy to oblige with the following recollections of his father's life:

> 'Louey' didn't talk that much about where he came from and he only went home once. I know he's got a brother and sister still living over there, and he had another brother in America who passed away.
>
> When Dad came to Australia he met up with two cousins in Seymour. They had a firewood mill and cut timber in the Seymour area. At that time Mum was living in Nagambie, and because Dad had relations in Nagambie, they met by word of mouth and married in 1934. I was born in 1935, my sister Nina was born in 1938, and another sister, Gloria, was born in 1942.
>
> After a while, Dad and the cousins all went up to Oaklands in New South Wales to do the same job: cutting firewood for Melbourne. They opened a mill up there and sent the timber by rail to Melbourne, but a sawing accident cost Dad two fingers. Later, he and the cousins bought trucks and carted petrol from New South Wales to Melbourne and back again.

We all moved to Lemnos in 1942 when Dad bought a farm and started growing tomatoes, peas, beans and things. After the farm at Lemnos was sold, we shifted to a bigger farm at Shepparton East. There we continued to grow vegetables, but we employed a lot more people. Then, when the soil couldn't stand it any more, we got into dairying.

Dad retired in Shepparton about thirty years ago, but he still kept occupied. He did a bit of work in town for a real estate agent, Dalgety's, and because there were a lot of Italians in the area and he had both languages, he was handy.

I was also heartened to learn from Alf that his mother, Elizabeth Mary Groppi (née Comi), was in good health and happy to assist with her own recollections of Luigi's life:

Louey had cousins in Nagambie, which is where he went after a stint in Seymour. One of those cousins is an aunt to me, and that's how I came to meet him. It's funny how things happen, and looking back I have no complaints with my life and how it all worked out.

He and the cousins started on the woodmill and he did a few years on the wood. He later bought 120 acres (forty-eight acres) and went into dairying. I was used to working from when I was a child, but he was very, very good and very helpful, and he'd try anything before he'd say, 'You can't do it, it's not worth it.'

The Australians weren't friendly like they are today, but there was a little bit of that on both sides. I can remember when I was young there'd be groups of Australians on their own and groups of Italians on their own, and as time went by they mixed. But in the early days it was hard to mix when they couldn't understand each other, and they were happy as Larry on their own.

Louey went back to Italy in 1963. He wanted me to go with him, but to leave the place and the kids was too hard. I said, 'It's better for you to go alone; you know them all.' He went back to see his folks. He saw his mum and dad and said they were pleased to see him. It was hard for him to leave Italy, but he had a lovely time. And when you stop and think what he did, it's a great thing to be able to leave your own country and set up in a foreign land.

Later, in January 1999, I made the trek to Alf Groppi's home in Shepparton. Alf, Gloria and Elizabeth were all there to greet me, and they wouldn't let me leave without a bag full of Alf's homegrown tomatoes and more wonderful memories of a kind father and loving husband.

40. Ridolfo Giuseppe Pasquali

BORN PROTA, PROVINCIA DI MASSA CARRARA, 20 JANUARY 1904.
DIED PROTA, PROVINCIA DI MASSA CARRARA, 22 APRIL 1990.

THE FOLLOWING LETTER was penned (in Italian) by Angiolino Pasquali, the son of Ridolfo Pasquali, with whom I had earlier made telephone contact (with the assistance of Telecom Italia):

Dear Tony,

...Ridolfo was a member of a large family of twelve. The economic conditions affecting the family were precarious and, like many other young Italians of his epoch, my father decided to make the trip to Australia, where it was said there was plenty of work on offer. The objective wasn't to stay in Australia for the rest of his life, but finally to return to Italy with some money, which would help him begin a better life.

Deciding to join another townsperson [Pietro Maffei] already in Australia, Ridolfo left from Genoa aboard the *Re d'Italia* in October 1927 with a friend, Luigi Groppi, who, unlike my father, remained in Australia for the rest of his life.

My father arrived in Melbourne in November 1927, remaining five years until 1932. In that time he did not work in urban areas, but dedicated himself to cutting down trees in forests where, according to him, human life had never been before. In 1932, as a result of the severe crisis in Australia due to the Depression, and to avoid losing all that he had accumulated in that time, Ridolfo decided to return to Italy. He disembarked at the port of Naples on his return and went home to his town of origin, where he bought a house and land in the country.

In October 1933 he married Emma Boschetti. Their first daughter died a few days after her birth in 1935. I was born on 8 May 1937, with a twin sister who also died three months later.

During the Second World War, my father worked in a factory that produced war goods in Pallerone di Aulla, Massa Carrara. At the same time, with the help of his family, he dedicated himself to cultivating his land. He also took care of his domestic animals to produce supplies necessary for survival, as it was impossible during the War to obtain supplies from anywhere else.

In July 1944, at the height of the War, my father was deported by the German troops to the concentration camp at Mauthausen.[4] He had no involvement with the partisans, nor did he have any political affiliations. He and a handful of fellow workers in an Italian factory were simply rounded up by the German officers and transported there. For the first three months or so my father was treated very badly, but he was very fortunate in being appointed attendant to a German officer who treated him well. He managed to survive there until the end of the War in 1945, and returned to Italy in better health than ever before. On top of that, he was outfitted with an entire wardrobe of new clothing by that same German officer, who drove him home. From that time until he was eligible for the pension at age sixty, my father worked at various local factories and basically led a normal, simple but honest life. In 1983 he and my mother celebrated their golden wedding anniversary.

Throughout his old age my father lived happily, without any particular health problems, in the house he bought on his return from Australia — the house where I still live with my family. He died as a result of some cardiac problems on 22 April 1990 at the age of eighty-six ...

41. Gaetano Lazzarotto

BORN VALSTAGNA, PROVINCIA DI VICENZA, 29 MAY 1894.
DIED COBRAM, VICTORIA, 5 JULY 1980.

The modest premises of Mrs Fanny Legovich at 28 Fitzroy Street, Fitzroy, were where Gaetano Lazzarotto spent his first night in his new country. Gaetano, together with another passenger, Giuseppe Bosa (number forty-two), gave that forwarding address on arrival at Victoria Dock in November 1927. It was also the address of Gaetano's older brother Teodoro, who five months earlier had pledged in writing to act as a sponsor to both men.

Gaetano's distinctive surname made it easy for me to make a family connection, for there were just seven Lazzarottos listed in the Melbourne *White Pages*. After a couple of calls, I was referred to the Lazzarotto family in the tranquil northern Victorian township of Cobram. There, in October 1997, I made contact with one of Gaetano's daughters, Julie Hussey (née Lazzarotto), who told the following tale:

Dad came out here from the north of Italy, near Treviso. He was part of a big family and I wouldn't even know their names. My dad went to America as a young man with some of his brothers and made quite a bit of money, which he sent back to Italy. Eventually he came to Australia and later sent for his wife, Agata (née Brolese), and their two children.

Pop and Mum raised five children in all — Romeo, Renato, myself, Gloria and John. The two oldest boys were born overseas and I was born in Carlton, as were Gloria and John.

I have a feeling Dad worked as a contractor in the Carlton area, but in later years moved to Wangaratta, where he grew tobacco as a sharefarmer. Times were hard in those early years, and I remember Mum saying that in Carlton they were giving out food parcels rather than dole payments. But Mum had a cow and chooks and a vegetable garden to keep us going in Wangaratta.

Pop and Mum were healthy people who worked hard. They bought a bit of land in Cobram and grew a bit of fruit and a few olives, but even then they couldn't make much. Before retiring, they bought a dairy farm in Cobram East, now run by my brother John.

42. Giuseppe Bosa

BORN FONTE, PROVINCIA DI TREVISO, 4 JUNE 1892.
DIED ONÈ DI FONTE, PROVINCIA DI VICENZA, 7 MAY 1957.

GIUSEPPE BOSA ACCOMPANIED Gaetano Lazzarotto on the *Re d'Italia*, returning to Italy almost thirty years later to live out the remainder of his life. In between, Giuseppe left an indelible impression on those who knew him.

Prior to his journey to Australia, Giuseppe had spent some time in St Louis, Missouri, which is why he was fortunate enough to be able to converse in English by the time he arrived here. He immediately sought work in places like Horsham, Lake Cargelligo in New South Wales, and also Griffith, and he assisted with the construction of the channel from the Upper Yarra. As a coach builder by trade, he had abilities with carpentry, and was able to construct the channel moulds into which they poured concrete.

Giuseppe met Caterina Brunello in Italy, where they married in 1921 and had five children — Bortolo (or 'Bert') in 1922, Concetta (or 'Connie') in 1923, then Pia (who died at ten months) in 1925, another Pia in 1926 and Aurelia in August 1927. Caterina came out with the children in 1935, and a year later Pio (nicknamed 'Kangaroo') was born.

The Bosas lived in Hanna Street, South Melbourne, until 1939, when they moved to the corner of Lightwood and Colonsay Roads, Springvale, where the Sandown Park dog track was later built. Giuseppe worked for McIntosh and Duff, an engineering factory in Kings Way, and later for a firm of toymakers in Malvern. He also had a brief stint making pumps for the moulders Kelly and Lewis in Springvale.

'Dad was an ingenious man with a very inventive mind, and he used to make Italian bowls, *bocce*,' Pio recalls. 'We were all virtually self-contained in Springvale, because Dad kept a cow, chicken, turkey and ducks on three and a half acres [1.3 hectares] there.

'In the end, Mum and Dad moved to Harrisfield, by the Springvale Cemetery, and in 1956 Dad decided that he wanted to go home to die. He returned to his home town that year and died of peritonitis in 1957, and Mum stayed here and died in Melbourne, a week after suffering a stroke, in 1959. He is buried there and she is buried here.'

43. Marco Giuseppe Rizzolo

BORN CONCO, PROVINCIA DI VICENZA, 26 AUGUST 1910.
DIED HOBART, TASMANIA, 18 JULY 1980.

HIS WAS THE quintessential Italian success story — the tale of a man who came, who saw and who concreted. Marco Rizzolo, the *Re d'Italia*'s only passenger to adopt Tasmania as a permanent place of residence, eked out his early career as a terrazzo worker. Archival records dated September 1939 show that Marco was employed as a stonemason with Murara and Vellar of Liverpool Street, Hobart, having spent his first nine years in the country in Melbourne, before moving to Tasmania in 1936.

By the end of 1939, Marco could read and write and converse fluently in the King's English. He had also secured a home at 20 Glebe Street, North Hobart, which he shared with his Tasmanian-born wife Coral Doreen Rizzolo and their son Peter, to whom she gave birth in December 1937. They would later have four more children — Kayleen in 1940, Gail in 1943, and twins Beverlyn and Gary in 1951.

Although the family's peaceful existence was interrupted with the outbreak of the Second World War, events conspired to assist Marco, by then an internee in Hobart. Because he was an Australian citizen he was never actually interned in a camp, but he had to report regularly to the authorities. 'As part of that internship, Dad worked on the construction of the Royal Hobart Hospital, and it was at that time that he established his own terrazzo business, the Tasmania Terrazzo Flooring Company, out of 3 Digney Street, Dynnyrne, near Sandy Bay,' son Gary said to me. 'He built the business up and employed a lot of men, mostly Italian immigrants who came to Hobart looking for a job.'

Through the War years and into the postwar period, Marco oversaw his thriving terrazzo business. 'For as long as I can remember we lived in Digney Street. We moved there after the War,' Gary said.

Marco loved playing the piano accordion, and around this time he was a member of a band that also included another piano accordion player and a drummer. The trio regularly played in Tasmania's Italian clubs.

Gary continued, 'Some time later Dad established a stonemasonry business called Marco Rizzolo & Sons Monumental Masons, on the corner of Warwick and Elizabeth Streets, which later relocated to Forster Street, Newtown, and finally to Glenorchy. My brother Peter helped manage the business, which is still going. It has since been left to Peter's son, Brad, and is now called Heritage Stone.'

Not long after Marco's retirement in the mid-1960s, Marco and Coral brought their marriage to an end. Marco died in Hobart in 1980. When Coral died in early 1997, the surviving Rizzolo siblings placed her body in Marco's grave at the Cornelian Bay cemetery. That was because, as Gary put it, 'they were together longer than they were apart'.

44. Sebastiano Bonan

Born Crosara, Provincia di Vicenza, 2 June 1905.
Died Sale, Victoria, 13 March 1983.

The day he bid *addio* to his father and mother in 1927 was the last time Sebastiano saw Andrea and Caterina Bonan. But Sebastiano left with his mother's blessing and his father's trade, and both stood him in good stead for the next fifty years.

Sebastiano spent his first night in Melbourne at the Carlton home of one G. Villanova, bootmaker. For the next few months, Sebastiano lived and worked in his trade of concreting in the South Gippsland town of Boolarra before relocating to neighbouring Yarram. There, at St Mary's Church in July 1935, he married Angelina Minotti (born 1914), from Guildford, near Maldon.

'I was only sixteen when I came to Australia aboard the *Toscana* in 1950, and Sebastiano sponsored me out. He paid my fare and slowly I paid him off. He was a very good man,' recalls his nephew, Andy.

The late Ray Bonan, Sebastiano's son, remembered his father's stories of working throughout the Depression.

'It was Depression time when Dad arrived, and he and a lot of Italians set up in the bush. Dad wandered around and ended up in this area when a man named Antonio D'Astoli offered him work at his local café.'

Antonio D'Astoli's son Max reinforced how tough things were in that era: 'At that time Sebastiano was one of three Italians working on the roads at Ryton, in the hills out the back of Yarram. When the work dried up, Sebastiano Bonan, Peter Moresco and Joe Ghino came down and pitched a tent by the road near the Tara River. And that's where they lived until they got themselves on their feet.'

'Dad was a concreter for the local shire, and built up a business in Yarram,' said Ray. 'He got crook after a while and died in 1983. Mum died in 1993.'

45. Cristiano Rigoni

BORN ASIAGO, PROVINCIA DI VICENZA, 2 JULY 1895.
DIED MYRTLEFORD, VICTORIA, 16 DECEMBER 1982.

THE ASIAGO THAT Cristiano Rigoni knew was a place enveloped in adversity. Its people were subjected to economic and political burdens, and for Cristiano there was the added trauma of losing his father, Cristiano senior, in tragic circumstances. His son, the late Cris Rigoni, of Myrtleford, shared with me his memories of his father in October 1997:

Dad lost his father when he was only four. His father was cutting hay with one of those new contraptions, and cut his thigh open. It happened early in the morning and he bled to death before anyone woke up.

Cristiano came to Australia with his cousin, Angelo. Cristiano had a brother, Domenico, but he never came to Australia. He suffered from a gas attack in the First World War and died in the 1940s, but some of his family members are out here.

Things were pretty tough over there. Cristiano and Angelo couldn't make a decent living and so they took a gamble. Angelo eventually went back to Italy and never returned here, but Cris stayed on, and after a year or two in Melbourne, stared work on the Silvan Dam in 1929 or '30. He went up to Koondrook near Kerang and into dairying when I came out with Mum (Cristina, née Longhini) and my sister Maria. Mum was born in America of Italian parents who eventually returned to Italy, which is where she met Dad.

My sister was nine and I was ten when we landed in Melbourne, on 4 May 1931. We all went up to Koondrook and did dairying there. Then we moved around, growing tomatoes. My younger brother Dino was born in 1933 and Angelo in 1935. After a while we went to Melbourne so I could learn the trade of motor mechanic. I did my apprenticeship in 1937 at City Road, South Melbourne, and we all settled at 18 Hotham Street, South Melbourne. Dad worked for De Marco Brothers, the timber workers, not far from dry dock.

In 1940, after the War broke out, he went back to Kerang to milk a few cows for three or four years. Mum and Maria remained in South Melbourne, while I left for Alice Springs, where I did a five-year stint with the Allied Works Council. We all met up again after the War in '45 and built a garage in northern Victoria. But parts were hard to get, and after six years in the garage we bought a block at Gunbower and grew tobacco.

I married a tobacco grower's daughter, Silene (Sally) Rossato, in January 1946, and I stayed in the tobacco industry. My brother Angelo, the youngest bloke, has been chairman of the tobacco cooperative there for years. Dad and Mum stayed in Gunbower for a time, then in 1960 they shifted to Myrtleford. Dad was eighty-seven when he died in December 1982. Mum died in 1993 at eighty-nine.

Although Cristiano saw his old home town once more in the 1960s, he inevitably returned to the country that had taken him in, and enabled him and his wife to rear their four children. And the memory of the man lives on through his great-grandson, Guy Rigoni — now an Australian Rules footballer for the game's oldest club, Melbourne.

46. Valerio Bianchi

BORN ASIAGO, PROVINCIA DI VICENZA, 30 OCTOBER 1905.
DIED WARRIEWOOD, NEW SOUTH WALES, 26 JANUARY 1976.

VALERIO BIANCHI SPENT his first night in Australia at 13 Easey Street, Collingwood. But Australia was anything but 'easy street' for Valerio and his cousin Antonio (passenger forty-seven), who before too long made for sweltering northern Queensland to cut cane.

And it was in the Top End, in Ayr in northern Queensland, that my search for Valerio began. Archives told me that by late 1934, Valerio lived at a place called McDesme, having been anywhere and everywhere from Griffith to Ingham. Valerio's certificate of naturalisation, dated 1934, presented me with a vital clue: the signature of a character referee, Cecil Giddy of Ayr.

After a couple of calls to Directory Assistance, I came up with a number for Cecil's nephew, the late Ray Giddy, in the region. (Ray died on 1 August 1998.) Ray explained that McDesme is a district 'five kilometres from Ayr near the north coast railway line, and one of the best sugarcane communities around'. Ray's wife Jean added that Cecil and her husband's father used to cut cane together on a farm in the district. Jean said she knew Cecil's sister, Daisy Stanbrook, who was now in a nursing home, and would sound her out on Valerio Bianchi.

On the evening of 22 February 1998, Jean rang with news. 'I asked Daisy if she knew Valerio and she said, "Oh yes, I can remember him. He worked for a man named Menso, who had a farm next to the Giddy property." Mr Menso had two boys, and I caught up with one of them, Charlie, the other morning. I said to him, "Did you ever hear of a Valerio Bianchi?" and he said, "Oh, that's Uncle Val." Charlie told me that Valerio married his mother's sister and that they later moved to Sydney. He told me that he is dead, but she is still alive, and living down there.'

Jean then put me on to Charlie's father, Tom Menso, who in turn referred me to Valerio's widow, Carla Bianchi (née Piferi), in Elanora Heights, Sydney. On the morning of 23 February 1998, Carla, then eighty-four, paid the following tribute to her late husband:

> Valerio was the eldest of five children, the others being Dina, Iolanda, Ester and another brother, Pasquale. Before coming to Australia, Valerio spent four years repairing railway lines in France, which explained why he was proficient in French and later English, as well as Italian.
>
> I'm not sure how long Valerio remained in Melbourne following his arrival, but during the Depression he worked everywhere, including Queanbeyan near Canberra. In northern Queensland he was a cane cutter and tobacco grower. He was quite good at growing tobacco, and did his own drying with his own recipe. His tobacco was a beautiful golden colour, which earned him a £10 grant from the government of the day for the best dried tobacco.
>
> On one occasion in northern Queensland he was bitten on the ear by a redback spider. The bite was potentially fatal, particularly with no doctor around in those times, but a very old Australian told him to douse his ear in powdered ammonia, which they used in the tobacco process, and he got better.
>
> Throughout the early 1930s, Valerio was sharefarming opposite my sister Maria's and brother-in-law Tom's farm in

Ayr, fifty miles [eighty kilometres] from Townsville in northern Queensland. I arrived in Australia in 1934 and we married in 1936. Valerio worked on a sugar farm with Andy Clive in Ayr, in McDesme, and I lived with my sister Maria Menso at the farm opposite. That was where he proposed to me, and it all happened very quickly. But we didn't have any children.

In early 1945 we bought a forty-acre [sixteen-hectare] property in Warriewood Valley, in New South Wales. There we set up twelve glasshouses and grew tomatoes until 1960. After Valerio became ill with rheumatoid arthritis and a man bought us out, we bought a nice acre block in Ingleside. We then sold the block and moved to Elanora, where I've been ever since.

While we were in Warriewood, Valerio brought his mother Angela Bianchi (née Carli), father Giovanni and sister Dina out from Italy. His mother died eighteen months later, then his father, and his sister moved to Melbourne to marry. Another sister, Iolanda, died in Italy, and her body was transferred to Warriewood.

When we sold the farm in 1960 we went to France and Italy on a holiday. We went on the *Orontes* and when Valerio got to France he was greeted by his sister Ester. They had not seen each other for twenty-three years and a photograph of this reunion made the French newspapers.

47. Antonio Bianchi

BORN ASIAGO, PROVINCIA DI VICENZA, 6 SEPTEMBER 1906.
DIED ASIAGO, PROVINCIA DI VICENZA, 28 OCTOBER 1993.

GIG HARBOR IS a long way from the port of Melbourne, but it was in this nook of Washington State, in the northwest of the United States, that the life story of Antonio Bianchi finally emerged.

Antonio was aboard the *Re d'Italia* with his cousin Valerio when the old ship set sail from Genoa in October 1927. The cousins had come at the behest of Cristiano Strazzabosco, an old friend from Asiago who lived in Queanbeyan, southeast of Canberra. I knew precious little else about Antonio's life, but in Carla Bianchi, the widow of Valerio Bianchi, I had an able ally. Carla wrote to tell me that although she could shed little light on Antonio's life, other than that he returned to Italy after only a few years, she intended to make contact with distant relatives in Antonio's home town of Asiago, in Italy's Alto Adige region.

True to her word, Carla phoned back to say she had found a contact for one of Antonio's two daughters, Giuseppina 'Pina' Miranda (née Bianchi), in Gig Harbor. Allowing for the seventeen-hour time difference, I put in a call to Pina at 1.15 on the morning of Monday, 21 September 1998. I don't know who was the more excited, she or I, as she related the following story:

> My father had two sisters, Augusta and Vittoria, and three brothers, Angelo, Orelio and Giovanni. He came back to Asiago from Australia in 1934 and a year later married my mother, Maria Cunico. My father and mother always lived in the house they bought in Asiago when they were first married. I was born in August 1940, and my sister Mary was born in March 1945. We lived through the War, had a nice childhood, and though we were not rich, our family was happy.
>
> My father left Australia because he got homesick, but he always told me stories about how he enjoyed working on the cane farms. He said that he and Valerio worked together, and they were happy times. He always talked to me about the things they did. Just the same, it sounded like he and Valerio had a hard time, doing what they did.
>
> Dad had a lumber business and all the brothers worked together in the lumber yard from the mid-1930s to about 1955. They cut the timber and cleaned it, and made boards for floorboards. It was a good business.
>
> My future husband was in the military, stationed in Vicenza, about an hour's drive from Asiago. We married in Vicenza in 1960, then left for the United States in 1964. We

also spent time in Schaffenberg in Germany, Texas, California and finally Washington State.

Dad stayed with me for a year in California, and that's when I really got to know him. He used to drink wine and smoke his pipe, and he always had it in his mouth, lit or unlit. Back home he used to love walks in the hills and picking mushrooms, and he played *bocce* on Sunday afternoons.

Initially I didn't go back to Asiago a lot, but in the last few years I went back almost every year. I was there with Dad for his last birthday, on 10 September 1993. He died that October — on the same date and at the same time of day as my mother, who died when I was just fifteen years old.

Dad was a very strong man, mentally and physically. He was a hard worker, and was a very hard person. They were not warm back then the way we are now in raising children, but that was because of the difficult lifestyle. In those days I really didn't like my Dad very much, but in time we became close.

LAST OF THE KINGS

Ampelio Acquasaliente, circa 1927.
PHOTOGRAPH COURTESY AMALIA AND ROSA SALENT, ROCKDALE, NEW SOUTH WALES.

48. Ampelio Acquasaliente (Salent)

BORN SANTULDERICO DI TRETTO, PROVINCIA DI VICENZA, 4 APRIL 1904.
DIED ROCKDALE, NEW SOUTH WALES, 13 JANUARY 2002.

THE MELBOURNE OFFICE of the Australian Archives provided the first few vital clues about Ampelio Acquasaliente (see chapter six), including the fact that he renounced his Italian nationality. This strongly indicated that Ampelio was committed to remaining in Australia for the long haul, but I had difficulty locating any trace of a phone listing, either in Victoria or interstate, for the distinctive name 'Acquasaliente' (which in English means 'rising water').

Were it not for a vital shred of archival information — Ampelio's birthplace of Santulderico di Tretto in the province of Vicenza — I would never have solved the mystery of his whereabouts. Knowing his birthplace provided me with the chance to return to the source in late 1997, and seek out a contact number in that region for the name Acquasaliente. The operator came back with one: a Signor Angelo Acquasaliente. I asked for a favour from Paolo Coniglio, who was happy to put in a call to the Acquasaliente household from my Preston home at midnight, on 2 March 1998.

Paolo got an answer from a lady and explained — in Italian — that he was calling on my behalf. He explained the purpose of the call, and asked if she had ever heard of a man named Ampelio Acquasaliente, who had migrated to Australia from Santulderico di Tretto in 1927.

There then came a brief pause, as Paolo allowed the lady to answer. During this time, a rapid transformation came over Paolo's face. His jaw suddenly dropped, and his eyes seemed to emerge like saucers from their sockets.

Paolo ended the brief phone conversation, put down the receiver and turned towards me. I grabbed Paolo by the arm and demanded, 'What did she say? What did she say?'

'She said she is a distant relative of Ampelio Acquasaliente. She told me Ampelio has changed his name by deed poll to "Salent". She said he is still alive, living in Sydney, and here's his telephone number!'

I had located a survivor of the *Re d'Italia*, who by my reckoning was a month shy of his ninety-fourth birthday. It was a precious moment, and one I'll never forget. At 9.35 the following morning I made the vital phone call. A lady (whom I later came to know as Ampelio's daughter, Amalia) answered the phone. I asked if Ampelio was there and she went to get him. Moments later he came to the phone. He greeted me with that wonderful booming voice common to northern Italians, and familiar to me through my grandfather and his brothers.

'Is that Mr Ampelio Acquasaliente?' I asked.

'How did you know my real name?' came the response.

I enthusiastically explained the purpose of my call and that I knew of his original surname as listed on the *Re d'Italia*'s passenger list.

'Oh! Oh!' came the reply. 'Well, I'm very pleased and happy to talk to you!'

In meeting Ampelio I can say I was truly blessed. Here was an absolute gentleman who, despite his advanced years, boasted a wonderful memory for the past and just as healthy an outlook on the present and the future. Ampelio was extremely enthusiastic about my efforts to get these individual and collective memories down on paper. His dear wife Rosa and children John and Amalia were equally supportive, and it was an absolute privilege to be welcomed into the Salent fold.

Having made the vital connection with Ampelio and his family, I subsequently sought assistance from Amalia. Would she be prepared to gather details of her father's life on my behalf? 'You know, the family has always known of Dad's wonderful history but we've never got the story down, and here you've come out of the blue ... send me a series of questions you want asked and I'll put them to Dad,' she kindly offered.

The next day I fired my questions off to the Salent household. About three weeks later the following story, accompanied by various news clippings and photographs relating to Ampelio's life, arrived safely in the mail:

> I was the fourth of six children born to Emilio and Amalia Acquasaliente, who married around 1898. My father was thirty years old at the time, my mother twenty. I had four brothers — Giovanni, Alessandro, Romano and Pietro — and one sister, Eliza. I also had a stepbrother, Oresti, from my father's previous marriage.
>
> Until the age of two I lived in my birthplace of Sabarro, a hamlet within Santulderico di Tretto. The family then moved to Le Asti, to a house owned by the grandfather of Giuseppe Raumer, the man who later sponsored me to Australia. My father found life difficult in the mountains, and after five years relocated with the family to San Martino, our home for the next seven years.
>
> I did not undergo any form of schooling during my childhood and instead went to work. My life as a child was a poor one, and my brothers and I were left to fend for ourselves from a young age. At ten I broke stones on the side of the road for the local council. At eleven I needed to arm myself with my older brother's birth certificate, as you had to be at least twelve years of age to work. The only problem there was that they would call me by my brother's name and I wouldn't answer them.
>
> My father worked as a merchant controller for the Rossi Company, which produced clothing, and observed all goods transported to other towns such as Pevi, Torrebelvicino and

Schio. He was a very important person in our town and everyone knew of him, as he spent most of his time at the local bar. The locals kept a corner for him by the window so that he could keep an eye on things and complete his work. Unfortunately, he spent most of his time there and not enough time helping with the upbringing of his family. Eventually he left to live his own life without family. My mother didn't even report him to the police, because if she had he would have been arrested and lost his job — a job handed down to him by my grandfather.

My mother, who used to tend to the sheep singing (and she had a beautiful singing voice), took care of the family, and my older brothers and sisters helped out. We had relatives who were well off, and sometimes we would go there to be fed lots of potatoes and *polenta* to help us grow.

My two younger brothers were also deprived of an education, given that the First World War had begun and the schools were shut down so that they could be used by the soldiers. We were right near the front line, and the bombs were falling near the town centre. While all this was happening, my older brothers, sister and myself went to work ferrying goods from the local railway station to the Rossi factory in Pevi, which was the largest factory in the area. We all worked there to help our mother clothe and feed us, and we also managed to save enough money to buy a house in Poleo, where there were schools for my younger brothers to attend, and that is where I ended up living before I came to this country.

In April 1923, at age eighteen, I entered the military. I completed three years of military service with the Guardia di Finanza (the Financial Police, or 'White Collar Cops'), was later posted to Verona for five months' training and then moved on to Catania in Sicily for a further twelve months. I subsequently sought a transfer to Trieste to complete my service, and was discharged in April 1926.

I then returned to the Rossi factory, where I continued to work until September 1927, when I departed for Australia. My military pay-out, coupled with the money I made from my work, covered the cost of my trip — 1500 *lire*.

Not long after my arrival I got my first job, picking tomatoes in the small Victorian country town of Koondrook, near Barham by the Murray River in the northwest of Victoria. This job lasted about seven months. I returned to Melbourne, but there was no work available, and what made it difficult was that I couldn't speak English and was unable to get a recommendation for any work. So after about six months I decided to go to Sydney to try my luck.

Upon my arrival in Sydney I tracked down some friends from Italy named Tony and Giuseppe Franchin. They had returned to Sydney after working stints in Adelaide and the Northern Territory, and while they could not find work for me, they allowed me to stay with them rent-free. So I cooked and did odd jobs for the Franchins, and lived off the small amount of money that I had. In the end, the Franchins lent me the money to head north to Queensland.

I was told that if I headed to Mossman, northwest of Port Douglas, I might find some work until the cane-cutting season started. My first cane-cutting job came on a farm owned by Charlie Della Vecchia at South Johnstone, southwest of Innisfail. Charlie was a relative on my mother's side. For five years I cut cane on Charlie Della Vecchia's property, and for another three or four years on other properties in the South Johnstone area.

In 1928 two of my brothers, Pietro and Giovanni, arrived in Australia. Late the previous year I had organised for them to come here, through a man who agreed to act as their guarantor. I completed the paperwork and they came out. My brothers joined me on Charlie Della Vecchia's property, but later gained work elsewhere. Pietro ventured south to Tully to work on the property of Mr Zaffonatto, while Giovanni gained work on another property close by.

When Pietro completed his season's cane cutting he told me he wanted to head northwest to Mareeba, where there were reports of excellent tobacco crops. I lent Pietro some money, which he put into a business partnership with two other men on a tobacco farm in Mareeba. Following a successful opening season, Pietro decided to purchase his own property with Giovanni, on the Barron River just out of Mareeba. I lent my signature to the paperwork, as I had become a naturalised Australian and they had not.

Regrettably, things took a turn for the worse with the farm, and after six months cutting cane elsewhere I spent the next six months cutting cane there to help them out. But my brothers lost everything. After the Second World War started, Pietro and Giovanni were rounded up by the police at Mareeba, transported under house arrest to Cairns and shipped to a Western Australian internment camp, where they would remain for three years. By then the farm had become overgrown and damaged by fire, which prompted Giovanni to head to South Australia following his release, and Pietro to return to Queensland to be with his wife Alice.

It was during my time in Queensland that I bought an English book — which I still have — to help me learn the language. Being around Australian friends and talking and listening to them certainly helped, and I am glad to say that I can now read and speak English pretty well — although my writing still poses a lot of trouble.

In 1937, I returned to Sydney and took up employment in the concreting business. I worked for the Melocco brothers, Mick Basanno, Mr Angelotto and Mr Tonitto. The Melocco brothers owned a site in Leichhardt, but I worked with them at different places on and off. Throughout that time I lived alone in a small room in a boarding house in Flinders Street, Darlinghurst.

While living in Sydney I was the victim of a swindle, which subsequently led to a court case. A man had approached me suggesting he could help me find work in the mines of Kalgoorlie, where there was good money to be made. He asked me if I had money, and when I said yes, he suggested it was best for him to forward that money on to Kalgoorlie, so that by the time I arrived there would be work waiting.

I agreed, went to the bank, withdrew all the money I had, £200, and arranged to meet him at a city hotel the next day. When I got to the hotel he took out an envelope and wrote down the address of the place I was to forward the money to prior to my arrival. He put the money in an envelope, sealed it and placed it in his jacket, but unbeknown to me he had another sealed envelope, carrying the same address, but stuffed with pieces of paper. We then walked to the post office to mail what I thought was the envelope to Kalgoorlie.

The man was to see me off the next day as I boarded the train to Kalgoorlie, but he never showed up. I thought something was not right, so I went to the nearest police station and explained what had happened. A policeman decided to accompany me to the post office to see if we could find this letter, and sure enough we found an envelope stuffed with pieces of paper rather than money.

I tried to track the man down, without luck. But a friend of mine, who was with him when we met, told me where I might find him. I informed the police, who caught up with the man and arrested him at Rosehill Racecourse. I was then asked to identify the man in a line-up, which proved very difficult, as he was all dressed up and looked different. But I told the police, 'I think that's him', and the matter went to court.

The lawyer for the man kept saying to me, 'You think this is the man, but you're not sure?' and 'You want to put an innocent man in prison?' And because I could not speak English very well, the court set the man free and I ended up

The Da Vinchie family. Standing, left to right: Ettore (1895–1981), Giovanna (1893–1936), Iginio (1893–1930), Giorgio (1889–1982), Annetta (1897–1989), Toni (1902–1938) and GioBatta (1899–1968) (*passenger 1*). Seated, their parents Teresa and Francesco.

PHOTOGRAPH COURTESY BRUNA VALMASSOI, CONEGLIANO, PROVINCIA DI TREVISO, ITALY.

Gaetano Sartori (*passenger 21*) amongst fellow workers, Central Deborah Gold Mine, Bendigo, Victoria, 1946. Back row, left to right: A. (Tim) Yates, Alf Salter, Gaetano (Jim) Sartori, Doug Ermel, Tom O'Brien, L. 'Poddy' Veal, Ron Hoskins. Second row: 'Aspro' White, Colin Neale, Tom Mason, Charles Ellis, Eric 'Deafy' Cameron, Terry Yanner, Tom Rowe. Third row: Fred 'Bluey' Yates, Harry 'Chick' McQualter, George Lee, 'Snub' Pollard, Frank Gill, Charles Clifford (paymaster), Inez Ermel, Bill Brazier, W. (Bill) Harris, Jim Ross. Front row: Charles White, John (Jack) Teasdale, Harold Roy, Stuart McDonald (mine manager), Jack McQualter, Bill 'Pop' Spooner, John 'Jack' McCracken, unknown contractor.

PALL MALL PHOTOGRAPH, COURTESY CENTRAL DEBORAH GOLD MINE, BENDIGO, WITH THE PERMISSION OF JAMES ANDREW LERK.

A postcard photograph believed to have been taken in Cosizza, San Leonardo, circa 1924. Standing, left to right: Luigi Simaz (*passenger 28*), Antonio Cernotta. Seated: Ernesto Terlicher, Antonio Simaz.

PHOTOGRAPH COURTESY LILIANA AND LAURIE CERNOTTA, DANDENONG, VICTORIA.

The Dal Sasso family on the day of the marriage of Antonio (*passenger 31*) to Antonia Martinaggia, in front of the Dal Sasso home in Laverda di Lusiana. At the back, left to right: Maddalena and her husband Giovanni Maddalon, Caterina, Alice, Giacomo, Antonio, Antonia (née Martinaggia) and Giovanni. In front, left to right: Lucia, parents Maddalena and Pietro, and a cousin, Domenico Dal Sasso.

PHOTOGRAPH COURTESY THE FAMILIES OF MARIA BUSANA (NÉE DAL SASSO), WONTHAGGI, VICTORIA, AND TONY DAL SASSO, NEWPORT, VICTORIA.

Giuseppe Destro (*passenger 35*) (left), with possibly the proprietor and the apprentice, possibly Bennett's Pottery Works, Adelaide, circa 1932.

Luigi Groppi (*passenger 39*) behind the wheel of his timber truck, Seymour, Victoria, circa 1934. A sawing accident had already cost him two fingers. When he developed appendicitis years later, Luigi was forced to sell the truck to cover his medical expenses.

Passport document — Regno d'Italia, Passaporto per l'Interno

Provincia di Vicenza
Circondario di Schio
Comune di Schio

Vale per un anno

CONNOTATI

Età *anni 15*
Statura *media*
Capelli *castani*
Fronte *regolare*
Sopracciglia *cast.*
Ciglia
Occhi *azzurri*
Naso *regolare*
Bocca
Mento
Barba
Viso *regolare*
Colorito *sano*
Corporatura *regolare*
Marche particolari

Firma del richiedente

*Ampelio
Acquasaliente*

N. 1825 d'ordine   Allegato F. Mod. 1916

In carta libera è gratuitamente
per povertà comprovata.

REGNO D'ITALIA

Bollo straordinario
o
Visto per il bollo

PASSAPORTO PER L'INTERNO

IL SINDACO
del Comune di Schio

rilascia il presente passaporto per l'interno del Regno
a *Acquasaliente Ampelio*
figlio di *Emilio*
e di *Bravo Amalia*
nato a *Tretto* Circondario di *Schio*
Provincia di *Vicenza* addì *4-2-1904*
di professione *bracciante*
i cui contrassegni personali sono a fianco indicati.
Rilasciato in seguito a consenso dato dalla R. Prefettura di Vicenza
e dal Padre.
Dato a *Schio*, addì *20-11-18*

IL SINDACO

Visto per l'autenticità della fotografia del richiedente

IL SINDACO   Il Segretario

'At eleven I needed to arm myself with my older brother's birth certificate, as you had to be at least twelve years of age to work. The only problem there was that they would call me by my brother's name and I wouldn't answer them.' Ampelio Acquasaliente (Salent) (*passenger 48*) was issued with a new certificate of employment every year, and this one dates from 1918, when he was fourteen. The birth date given, 4 February 1903, is actually that of his elder brother, and Ampelio later wrote his real date of birth, 4 April 1904, on top of it.

Ampelio Acquasaliente, aged three. The outfit he wears was bought for him by his aunt, who wanted to adopt him at one stage.

PHOTOGRAPH COURTESY AMALIA AND ROSA SALENT, ROCKDALE, NEW SOUTH WALES.

Ampelio with the author and the ABC's Brigid Donovan, following filming for the 'Australian Story' program at the Salent family home, June 1999.

PHOTOGRAPH COURTESY AMALIA AND ROSA SALENT, ROCKDALE, NEW SOUTH WALES.

An informal shot of the Acquasaliente family just prior to the departure of Ampelio (*passenger 48*) in 1927. Standing, from left to right: Pietro, Romano, Eliza, Ampelio, Alessandro and Giovanni. Seated, their mother Amalia. Their father Emilio had abandoned the family when the children were still quite young.

PHOTOGRAPH COURTESY AMALIA AND ROSA SALENT, ROCKDALE, NEW SOUTH WALES.

This glorious document marked Ampelio Acquasaliente's discharge from the Guardia di Finanza on 28 April 1926.

The envelope that contained the suicide note of Antonio Gnata (*passenger 53*), addressed to '*Pappa* [sic] *E Mamma*'.
ENVELOPE COURTESY PUBLIC RECORDS OFFICE, MELBOURNE.

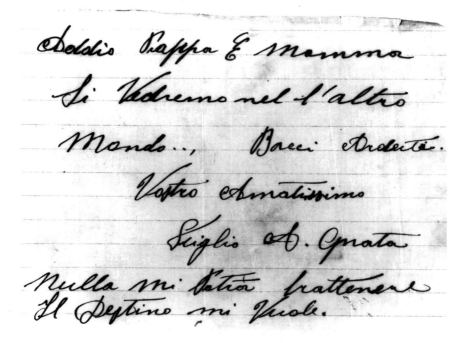

The suicide note itself.
SUICIDE NOTE COURTESY PUBLIC RECORDS OFFICE, MELBOURNE.

The Stawell quarry where Antonio Gnata spent his last days, circa 1930.

The gathering by the grave of Antonio Gnata, Stawell Cemetery, 30 May 1998. From left to right: Tony Busana, Maria Busana (née Dal Sasso), John Dal Sasso, Tony Dal Sasso, Stawell parish priest Father Wally Tudor, the author, Veronica Dal Sasso, Ilda Dal Sasso and Ellenor Musumeci, Secretary of the Stawell Biarri Genealogical Society.

losing everything, including my £200, which was a lot of money in those days.

I then took up a number of jobs. I helped manage boarding houses, three in Paddington and one in Glebe, and also a private nursing home in Kings Cross. I would take care of the maintenance of all these places, which rented rooms to a lot of migrants who came and went. In 1941 I worked for the glass works in Moore Park, and then the sugar works in Pyrmont from 1942 to 1943.

During my time in the boarding houses the Americans were here because of the War, and they paid a lot for rooms. This prompted us to pay our permanent tenants to leave so as to get the Americans in. The Americans would pay £5 a week, whereas the permanent tenants paid only £1 a week.

The Australians did not like the Americans being here during the War, because they were able to get their hands on lots of things, like chocolates, cigarettes and stockings. The Americans had plenty of money to spend, whereas the Australians did not. The Australians were given ration books with coupons that could only be used for scarce items such as meat, petrol, butter, sugar, shoes, furniture, blankets, beer and cigarettes.

The Australians treated Italian migrants very badly in those early days. Whereas the Italians were prepared to take on any kind of work, the Australians would not. Which prompted them to refer to us as 'bloody dago bastards' and say things like, 'You came to take our jobs, you can't even speak English, go back to your own country.' Whenever I went out I always made sure I spoke English so they would not call me names. If ever they heard you speaking in Italian they'd start on you, but I only ever got into a fight with an Australian once.

It happened when I was in a pub with a friend who had just arrived from Italy. He and I were conversing in Italian, when a man said, 'Why don't you speak in English?' I tried to explain to him about my friend, but he didn't want to listen, got angry, and asked me to come outside. I knew what was going to happen, so I followed him out the door, but got the first punch in, knocked him out and left!

The Italians did have a hard time of it here, but that is the case with any newcomers to a strange land — someone is always going to say something bad about them, no matter whether it's 1927 or 1997.

After the War I worked for a short time with the Italian-owned Silk Screen Printers in Rushcutters Bay. The company intended to expand in Sydney but could not, so the owners sold up and moved to Tasmania. After a short while they contacted me, asking that I come down to work for them as watchman for the factory. This was because things were always being stolen and they knew they could trust me. I went down and installed new locks on all the factory doors and windows and nothing was ever taken.

In 1948 I returned to Sydney after two years with Silk Screen Printers. By then I had relinquished ownership of my brothers' farm, which in the end cost us everything.

In Sydney I was tracked down by a man called Vince Giuffre, who had heard I was a good worker and offered me the chance of employment. At that time I had intended to go to Brisbane to join a friend, Tony Franchin, one of the founders there of Nanda Pasta. Vince Giuffre asked when I intended to leave for Brisbane, and I said in two months. He then asked if I wanted to work for him up until that time, 'and we'll see what happens'. I agreed, and ended up working as a storeman and maintenance man with the company, Popolare Metal Stamping Company in Parramatta Road, Camperdown, until my retirement, through ill health, in 1971. I was sixty-seven when I retired, but ended up returning to the company (which had relocated to Marrickville) as a part-time gardener for ten more years.

It was at the Popolare factory in 1954 that I met my future wife, Rosa Murdica, one of a number of Italians working at Popolare. This particular day she walked in carrying a plant of basil for a lady she worked with, and I asked if she had any more. The next day she walked in with another plant and we started to talk, even though she was scared to talk because work regulations did not allow for the men and women of the factory to converse. I started to escort her home, which is when we were able to talk again.

At the time, Rosa was living in Redfern with her sister and brother-in-law, who was particularly strict with her. After finally being introduced to them, Rosa's brother-in-law said, 'If you want to go out with her you have to be married within three months.' And so we were, at St Fiacre's Catholic Church, Leichhardt, on 24 April 1954. I was fifty and she was thirty-four.

I did have a lot of lady friends who wanted to marry me, but I told them I was too young to get married. Besides, I had a very hard life in Australia from the time when I had arrived, and travelling around made it very hard for me to settle down with anyone. But by 1954 I had settled and found a steady job, and marrying Rosa seemed like the right thing to do, which I am happy to say it turned out to be.

My wife and I had two children, both born in Sydney — a son, John, in 1955, and a daughter, Amalia, in 1961. My son is married with five children, who bring a lot of joy and happiness to me in my old age as I watch them grow.

I decided to shorten my name to 'Salent' by deed poll. The name 'Acquasaliente', which has thirteen letters, would have made it very hard on my children, particularly when they started school, so I opted for the change in 1959. I chose 'Salent', as my brother Pietro, who died in Cairns in 2000, aged ninety-three, had already adopted the surname 'Acqua' to make it easier for him. But if you put the two together you still get something close to 'Acquasaliente'. I am happy with my name the way it is, because I've lived with it for the past forty-three years, and see no need to change it back.

It was in 1975 — forty-eight years after I first left — that I made my one and only return trip to Italy. I thought it would be nice to take my family back to where their father and mother were born. The old home town had changed a lot since I had left. It had grown into a very large city, compared with the little country village I remembered.

My sister, two brothers and their families were there at that time. My sister, Eliza, was in a nursing home in Schio, my brother Romano was living with his family in Poleo and the other brother, Alessandro, had moved to Milan with his family. To see them again, and catch up with what they and I had done in the previous forty-eight years was a very emotional time for me, considering that when I first left they had thought they wouldn't see me again. So I am glad I did go back to see them when I did. Sadly, my brothers and sisters in Italy have all passed away now, as have all the old friends I left behind. I only have nieces and nephews left there.

A lot has changed in Australia too, since I first arrived — the cities, the lifestyles of the people and the working conditions. People have so much more now than I had, such as government assistance. And they say unemployment is high, although I think that during the Depression it was much worse. It's a pity some of today's younger people aren't able to experience the conditions people of my time worked under — they were not pleasant.

As for the cities, they have become so much bigger, to cope with the numbers of people who are here and keep coming here. And I think the people are much more friendly, and they mix better with other cultures. In my time, people of different nationalities had trouble mixing. But I never thought I was torn between two countries. I made my decision to come here and Australia became my new home.

In terms of my early years in this country, I would not like to go through it again. I was on my own for a very long time and I couldn't trust anyone. But from the time I settled down, got married and had a family I became more content and happier than I ever was, for family is the most important thing. I now live a quiet and happy life, and take each day as it comes.

I think most people have regrets about something or other. There are a lot of things I did in my early years that I know I would have done differently now. But that is life and that is how life is dealt you.

We as immigrants were pioneers who helped this country to become what it is today. We worked in sugarcane fields, and helped with the construction of small houses and big buildings, dams, bridges, tunnels and roads. Some of the larger Australian companies were founded by Italians who were never scared to do a good, hard day's work.

49. Giacomo Sartori

Born Italy, circa 1893. Died ?

Look Closely at the original, handwritten list of the *Re d'Italia's* Melbourne-bound passengers and you will discover a small 'x' by the name of Giacomo Sartori. The question of what that 'x' represents only adds to the mystery of what became of the forty-ninth disembarkee — if, in fact, he did disembark. According to documents lodged at the time of his arrival, Giacomo Sartori gave the forwarding address of 'S. River Pine Lake, via Horsham'. Sadly, when asked, none of the locals of today's Pine Lake farming community in western Victoria could lay claim to ever having heard of the *Re d'Italia's* passenger — even though the Sartori name is prominent throughout the region, in places such as Maldon, Yandoit and Daylesford.

One man, Jim Sartori of Geelong, said that Giacomo Sartori's name 'does ring a bell. We had a Sartori reunion in Yandoit not so long ago and that name came up.' But he could shed no more light on the matter.

The Melbourne Registry of Births, Deaths and Marriages was able to confirm that a man named Giacomo Sartori, son of Mario Pietro and Maria Sartori (née Costa), died aged seventy-four in the inner Melbourne suburb of Fairfield back in 1975. However, this man's age does not correspond with that of the passenger, who in 1927 was thirty-four years of age, as stated on the disembarkation list. And his widow, Maria, told me 'I'm pretty sure my husband arrived in Melbourne on Christmas Day 1925, and he didn't go to Horsham first.'

Regrettably, the Melbourne office of the Australian Archives did not have in its possession Giacomo Sartori's *atto di chiamata*. The form, which carries details of the relevant passenger's date and place of birth and parents' names, would undoubtedly have brought a swift conclusion to a life story that, at the time of print, remains shrouded in ambiguity.

50. Marco Frigo

Born Cesuna di Roana, Provincia di Vicenza, 21 June 1910.
Died Wangaratta, Victoria, 24 January 1931.

A WHITE MARBLE headstone in Wangaratta Cemetery is the only visible testament to the tragically short life of Marco Frigo. Marco, believed to be a distant cousin of fellow passenger Basilio Frigo (number fifty-one), was the son of Antonio and Domenica Frigo (née Valenti). Antonio, who had himself migrated to Australia some years before, arranged for his sixteen-year-old son to join him at O'Shannassy River in the Upper Yarra area. A new weir was under construction for the storage of nearly a billion gallons of water and the control of stream flows.

But Marco would eventually turn his hand to tobacco cultivation in Myrtleford, where his life would come to an untimely end.

The *Myrtleford Mail* of 28 January 1931 reported as follows:

A young Italian, Marco Freigo [*sic*], died in the Wangaratta
Hospital on Saturday afternoon. He was 20 years of age and

had been three years in Victoria, coming from Cesuna, Italy.

He had been working at tobacco cultivation at Myrtleford but some time ago took ill from appendicitis, and was admitted to the hospital. He was interred at the Wangaratta Cemetery on Monday morning. Father Byrne read the burial service and Irvings Pty Ltd carried out funeral arrangements.

Soon after Marco was laid to rest, Antonio Frigo returned to northern Italy to be reunited with his surviving loved ones — thus bringing to an end the Frigo family's brief link with this country. The *comune* in Vicenza has since confirmed that the Frigo family's Italian lineage has ended.

All that remains in this country is the white marble headstone in Wangaratta Cemetery, upon which is carved the fading inscription:

FRIGO MARCO. N: Cesuna, 21.6.1910, M: 24.1.1931. Il padre desolato. P. RIP.

51. Basilio Frigo

BORN CESUNA DI ROANA, PROVINCIA DI VICENZA, 26 JULY 1911.
DIED CARLTON, VICTORIA, 16 SEPTEMBER 1936.

BASILIO FRIGO'S SENSE of adventure brought him halfway around the world, but it was a headstrong nature that contributed to his untimely death.

Basilio bade his final farewells to his father Giovanni and mother Corona, and the hills of Tresche Cesuna, an area of Cesuna di Roana, in October 1927. Following his odyssey at sea, Basilio was reunited with his older brother, Domenico, then living in Moira, a tiny New South Wales border town about 20 kilometres north of Echuca on the mighty Murray River. Earlier that same year, Domenico had also sent for another brother, Emilio. Once together, the three brothers ventured to the Myrtleford district, where they tilled the land and grew tobacco.

Although his life was short, memories of Basilio remain etched in the minds of those who knew him. His nephew, Tony, described Basilio as 'a well-liked man, and a big man, tall and strong, with a fair complexion'. Some of these observations were reiterated by Mrs Adi Sandri (née Frigo), the goddaughter of Basilio's brother Domenico. 'I have a photograph of him. He was a tall chap, with very curly hair, and a lovely young bloke. He had a girlfriend and I remember her, but they never got the chance to get married.'

Towards the end of 1936 Basilio was living with Adi's father and mother in the Ovens Valley. It was at this time that he was labouring with a bout of influenza, from which he would most likely have recovered had he not made one fatal decision.

'Someone in Melbourne had arranged a party and Basilio left Myrtleford to come down,' Adi recalls. 'My mum and dad said, "Don't go, you've got bronchitis", but try telling that to young people. He went to the party, danced, worked up a temperature and caught pneumonia.'

Basilio Frigo died soon afterwards, at 38 Canning Street, Carlton. He had contracted bronchial pneumonia as a result of the influenza, which placed a strain on his heart he could not overcome. Emilio and Domenico buried their brother at Fawkner Cemetery. Together they commissioned a stonemason to chisel into the marble headstone the words:

The sunset and night won't come for you, Basilio Frigo.

Not long after the funeral, Emilio went back to his native land, never to return, while Domenico lived out his life in the new country.

52. Luigi Andrea (Ludwig Henry) Stella

BORN GALLIO, PROVINCIA DI VICENZA, 23 JULY 1909.
DIED CAMPERDOWN, NEW SOUTH WALES, 17 JULY 1967.

HE LEFT THE port of Genoa with £10 in his pocket and the dream of bettering his life in a faraway place. The dream would take Luigi Stella from his home town of Gallio in Italy's Veneto region to the port of Melbourne, and ultimately on to Sydney, where he served as a painter and docker on the waterfront.

Luigi was the son of Pietro and Maria Anna Stella (née Rigoni). In his youth he worked as a farmer, and it was probably this lifestyle that encouraged him to make the move. After all, his sponsor and relative,

Bortolo Valentino Stella, had already settled in Mirboo, in Victoria's idyllic southern Gippsland region.

Luigi arrived in Melbourne in November 1927 and, together with a fellow passenger, Cristiano Rigoni, took up lodgings at 148 Canning Street, Carlton, the home of a Signor Domenico. There Luigi also shared lodgings with his *paesani* Cristiano Stella and Giacomo (Jack) Silvagni, who was the father and grandfather of Carlton footballers Sergio and Stephen Silvagni respectively.

Although he spent the first thirteen years in Victoria, it is not known whether Luigi ever joined Bortolo Stella in Mirboo. But archives indicate that Luigi lived the life of a bachelor in Sydney, at 136 Foveaux Street, Surry Hills, and was a weaver with Hatbands Pty Ltd of Waterloo.

As Luigi's life from 1949 onwards was something of a mystery, I turned to the Melbourne *White Pages* for assistance in tracking him down. Regrettably there were around 100 listings for the name 'Stella' and I was confronted with the daunting scenario of putting in that number of phone calls.

But someone always knows someone, who knows someone else, and it took me barely a dozen calls before I was referred to the right man: Mr Ray Stella, proprietor of the Dromana Hotel on the Nepean Highway. Ray confirmed that he knew of a number of Stellas hailing from Luigi's home town of Gallio, but suggested I contact his (Ray's) sister, Mrs Yvonne Mogorovich (née Stella), in Thornbury.

Yvonne believed that Luigi died in Sydney of a heart attack years ago and never married. But happily she was able to put me onto Luigi's nephew, Peter Fracaro, in nearby East Brunswick. Peter told me the following story:

> Luigi Stella died a long time ago. He was my mother's brother, and in 1968, when my mother came to Australia, he was already dead. He wasn't married, but he lived with a woman, and we never knew if there were any children — there was just no communication. He died in Sydney, and my mother used to say she'd like to find out which cemetery he's buried in.
>
> My mother, Anna Rigoni, was born in 1907 and passed away several years ago. She knew some English by the time

she came here, because she had been to America. My sister came to Australia in 1956 and I came to Australia with another sister in December 1959.

The only time I ever met Luigi Stella was when he came back to Italy in 1952 or '53, and I was twelve or thirteen at the time. When he went back to Australia that was it. He never wrote and we never saw him again. And he died in Sydney in July or August of 1967.

Luigi Andrea Stella, also known as Ludwig Henry Stella, and a painter and docker by profession, died at age fifty-seven of heart disease at Camperdown's Royal Prince Alfred Hospital. Luigi, formerly of 263 Noble Avenue, Greenacre, was survived by Lilian Faith Stanhope, whom he had married six years earlier. They had no children.

THE QUARRYMAN
FROM SALCEDO

Antonio Gnata, in a photograph believed to have been taken in
Salcedo in 1926, the year before he left for Australia.

PHOTOGRAPH COURTESY MARCELLO DAL SASSO AND VIRGINIA GNATA (NÉE LOVISON),
FARA, VICENZA, ITALY, VIA MARIA BUSANA (NÉE DAL SASSO), WONTHAGGI, VICTORIA.

53. Antonio Gnata

BORN SALCEDO, PROVINCIA DI VICENZA, 30 JUNE 1905.
DIED STAWELL, VICTORIA, 30 MAY 1938.

OF ALL THE life stories of the passengers on the *Re d'Italia*, few are as sad or
as tragic as that of Antonio Gnata.

Antonio was just twenty-two years old when he took his first steps down
the battered gangway and onto North Wharf in November 1927. But he
would be dead barely a decade later, in circumstances so shocking that news
of his untimely demise was never conveyed to his mother in the old country,
for fear it would break her heart.

In fact, Antonio's ultimate fate would remain a mystery to his
descendants for the next six decades. It seemed that the man's life story died
with him, and it wasn't until I had completed three months' research in
early 1998 that I could convey to Antonio's niece and nephew the terrible
tale of what became of the quarryman from Salcedo.

I INADVERTENTLY STUMBLED onto the story of Antonio Gnata in January 1998, at the western suburbs home of a good-natured man named John Dal Sasso. I had found John's name listed in the *White Pages* and called him to ask if he bore any connection with another of the listed passengers, Antonio Dal Sasso (number thirty-one). John confirmed a connection, but said it would be best for me to talk to his father, Tony Dal Sasso. So we all met at John's home on a warm summer's night.

Tony, who turned out to be Antonio Dal Sasso's nephew, is a real character. A post-Second World War migrant with a happy disposition and general love of life, Tony delighted in telling tales of the glorious days of his Italian youth, over an ample glass of his home-made *vino*. During a break in discussion, Tony turned to the list of passengers I had brought with me and pored over the names. To his excitement, he discovered the name of another relative, Antonio Gnata.

Tony told me that his mother, Ida, was the sister of Antonio Gnata and that Ida later married Antonio Dal Sasso's brother, Giovanni, in Italy. In other words, Tony was a nephew to the two Antonios who made the voyage on the *Re d'Italia*.

He could shed little light on what fate befell his maternal uncle, other than that he believed a man by the name of Gnata had been buried in the cemetery in the western Victorian town of Stawell many years ago. He suggested I contact his sister, Maria Busana, in Wonthaggi, for further information.

I called Maria, who was interested to learn of Antonio's given name, 'because he was always known as "Nini", to distinguish him from his father'.

'He served with the Alpini around the time of the First World War, and my mother told me he was a very nice man,' Maria said. 'He worked here with other people from the same town of Salcedo. From what I understand, he had a bit of money saved up which he lent to people, but when he got sick and needed the money the people couldn't repay him. He was good enough to give them his heart, but he wasn't able to get it back.'

ANTONIO GNATA WAS born on 30 June 1905 in Salcedo, in the province of Vicenza in northern Italy. He was one of eight children reared by Antonio Gnata senior and Giovanna Lucia (née crosara). His siblings were Luigi, Maria, Orsola, Erminia, Ida, Caterina and Amedeo.

Upon his arrival in Melbourne, Antonio was reunited with Amedeo, who had himself migrated to Australia three years earlier on the steamship *Regina d'Italia*. Amedeo, who assisted with younger brother Antonio's passage, had settled in the eastern Victorian town of Traralgon, where he split redgum for railway sleepers in and around the Gippsland area.

But the Gnata brothers' time together would be all too brief, for less than a year after Antonio's arrival in Australia, Amedeo set sail for Italy aboard the steamship *Orama*. Eight years later Antonio applied for the readmission of both Amedeo and a close friend and fellow miner from Salcedo, Vittorio Azzolin — but his application was rejected. This disappointment would later have a profound effect on the lonely Italian.

Antonio spent his first six years in Australia as a quarryman at a number of Victorian sites, such as Boorara, Whitfield and Pyramid Hill, and also in Berrigan in New South Wales, in the employ of Charles Snell of Oakleigh. He also worked seasonally as a cane cutter in the northern Queensland town of Giru. In March 1934 he became a naturalised Australian.

Maria's assertions of her uncle's generosity are supported by an immigration memo of August 1937, which reveals that Antonio also attempted to secure passage for his old Italian friend Azzolin. The memo notes that Antonio had lent another fellow countryman, Vittorio Livardo of Myrtleford, £50 to assist him in a tobacco-growing venture, and further states: 'He maintains his people in Italy by periodical remittances and has therefore not accumulated any appreciable assets.'

MARIA, A KINDLY woman who migrated to Australia with her mother in 1953, said that when she first arrived she had endeavoured to learn more of Antonio's death through those who knew him here, 'but nobody said much'. She always believed that Antonio, who never married, had died in the late 1920s, and that his furniture was sold to pay for the burial. 'But no-one would tell us where he was buried, and [his death] was bad for our family, especially my mother's brother Amedeo, who had returned to Italy a few years before.

'When Antonio died the other family members never told his mother, because she was blind and it would have destroyed her. She always said, "When is he going to write to me?" and until the day she died they used to read her letters that they had made up.

'I did hear that he may have been buried in Stawell Cemetery, which I visited more than thirty-five years ago on my honeymoon to Warrnambool and Peterborough. But some chaps working there said they had no idea where the grave was, and I never found that grave.'

Maria suggested I contact a man by the name of Antonio Quaresima, who had known Antonio Gnata and might be able to shed more light on the subject. In April 1998 I paid a visit to Antonio Quaresima at his home in a northern suburb of Melbourne. He told me that Antonio Gnata died in a quarry accident at Stawell between 1930 and 1940, but said he knew nothing else. However, I had the distinct impression that he knew more than he was revealing.

I then turned my attentions to the Stawell Cemetery, as Maria Busana had done thirty-five years before. The cemetery was not listed in the phone book, so I sought assistance from the caretaker at nearby Ballarat Cemetery, who referred me to the Northern Grampians Shire Council in Stawell proper. A man at the council then directed me to Mr Barry Werry, who had in his possession the records of Stawell Cemetery.

On the evening of 24 April, Barry revealed that Antonio Gnata, born in Italy and late of Scallans Hill (or 'Wild Cat Hill') in Stawell, died there on 3 May 1938 (a date which later proved incorrect, as Antonio actually died on the morning of 30 May). Barry confirmed that Antonio's burial was conducted at Stawell Cemetery, at grave number 4863a, although no headstone marked the site.

About a week later I made contact with Ellenor Musumeci of the Stawell Biarri Genealogical Society, in an effort to determine how Antonio had died. Ellenor confirmed that the Society had access to the local newspapers of the day, including the relevant edition of sixty years ago, and told me that she would investigate.

In early May, she called to say that she had discovered what had happened to Antonio, warning, 'Do you really want to know?' I told her that of course I needed to know, and a day or two later Ellenor forwarded me a copy of the following item from the *Stawell News*, dated Wednesday, 1 June 1938:

GRIM TRAGEDY
MAN KILLED AT QUARRY
HEAD BADLY MUTILATED

An awful tragedy occurred at Mr C.S. Snell's quarry at Wild Cat Hill on Monday morning, the victim being an Italian named Antonio Gnato [*sic*], who had been engaged as a "powder monkey" at the works.

At about 10.30 a.m. Mr Charles Holmquest had occasion to go to the quarry, and looking down he noticed the body of a man lying on a ledge about 16 feet from the surface. Holmquest called to the man, and receiving no response, concluded that there had been an accident and went and informed Mr Tilly, the manager of the works. Mr Tilly proceeded to the spot and saw that a tragedy had occurred, and communicated with First Constable T. Hunter and Dr Gibson, who proceeded to the scene.

The body was raised to the surface and the gruesome fact was revealed that the head had been blown to pieces and only a small portion of the chin remained on the trunk. Death had occurred about an hour previously.

An electric battery used in blasting operations was found near the body. From the surrounding circumstances, certain conclusions were reached as to how the man met his death, and the police are collecting evidence to lay before the deputy coroner at the adjourned inquest to be held on a date to be fixed.

There was no one else working at the quarry at the time of the fatality.

Gnato was an Italian, aged about 28 years, and came from Queensland two or three years ago. He resided in a hut near the works, and when the police searched the hut they found a letter written in Italian to his parents, who reside in Italy. The letter was translated into English, and it is understood that when it is presented before the Coroner it will throw some light on the tragedy.

The police enquiries pointed to the conclusion that there was no foul play.

The deputy coroner (Mr C.C. Hunt) visited the scene of the tragedy and viewed the body, and after taking formal evidence of identification gave an order for burial and adjourned the enquiry to a date to be fixed.

The funeral took place yesterday afternoon from Messrs F.J. Crouch and Sons funeral parlours.

The interment took place in the Stawell Cemetery and many of deceased's friends attended to pay their last sad tributes of respect. The coffin bearers were Messrs Leo Savoia, Geo. Trusgnh, Adolfo Sartori, A. Boag, C. W. Holmquest and H. C. Roussac. Rev. Father W. N. Close conducted the service at the graveside. Messrs F. J. Crouch and Son carried out the funeral arrangements.

When blasting operations are in progress and after the face of stone to be brought down has been drilled, a charge of gelignite is inserted in the hole together with a cap attached to the end of a length of wire being connected to an electric battery. When the operator connects the wire to the battery, the charge is fired.

Whether Gnato placed a cap in his mouth and connected it to the battery will be disclosed at the enquiry.

The extent of the injuries can be gauged by the fact that Gnato was not recognisable.

One letter in the possession of the dead man spelt his name Gnato, another Gnatto, and a third Gnata.

The Italian Consul's office was communicated with, and did not seem to have any knowledge of the dead man.

Ellenor also included a further item from the *Stawell News*, dated 27 July 1938, about the Coronial Enquiry into Antonio's death. The Coroner, Mr. C.C. Hunt, determined 'that death was due to the effect of some highly explosive substance which had blown off practically the whole of his head — such injuries having been intentionally self-inflicted'. Mr Hunt had earlier heard statements from Dr Gibson, fellow Stawell labourer Charles William Holmquest and Frederick James Tilley, the manager of Snell's Quarry. The Coroner's report stated in part:

> Tilley gave evidence of Gnata's employment with the Quarry. "He was employed as a powder monkey and had charge of the explosives. At that part of the quarry where the body was found, no blasting had taken place for the previous three or four days." Mr Tilley then gave a demonstration on the floor of the court with the battery and charge. "From inspection of the ledge on which the body was found I could find no evidence that deceased had been engaged in ordinary blasting operations," concluded Mr Tilley. "I don't think that a detonator would have sufficient power to blow his head right off; I think it would have needed a plug of gelignite as well."

KEN SMITH, a local Stawell identity now in his seventies, told me he remembered the day Gnata died. Ken's family lived not far from the quarry at the time.

'It was early in the morning and we were having breakfast at home when the blast went off, and I can remember either my brother or my mother saying, "They're starting early",' Smith said. 'Charlie Snell had the contract and there was quite a team of Italians working for him. I'm not quite sure how many Italians there were all up, but there were a good twenty-five to thirty working there and they lived on the site, most of them. They had huts and tin shacks and they lived pretty rough, the poor buggers, with no electricity or running water. They had no recreation there, and the only recreation they could get would have been in the town, a mile and a half away ... they'd have to walk there to get a drink or a bit of tucker.

'The quarry was at a place called "Wild Cat Hill", and why it was called that I can't really say. An old bloke thought it had something to do with the blokes who put down the main Melbourne to Adelaide rail line through the cutting being known as "wild cats", but I can't be sure. In later years they filled the quarry in with the town's rubbish, and eventually it's been levelled off and the trees have grown back.'

CHARLES SNELL, who died a little over ten years ago aged eighty-nine, operated quarries in a number of locales, including the main depot of Oakleigh, as well as Culcairn, Pyramid Hill, Axedale and of course, Stawell. Snell's nephew, Henri Claude Roussac, was one of his drivers, and a pallbearer at Antonio's funeral. Henri's son, Charles, told me in August 1998 that 'I can remember my father quite liked Tony'.

'I'm trying to think back sixty years ago, and I can only go on what my father told me. He said Tony lived on his own near the quarry and he used to play the accordion. My father told me that Tony had word to go down to the Italian Consulate in Melbourne, which he did a number of times, and always came back worried.' This substantiates archival evidence that Gnata was having difficulty securing safe passage into Australia for his older brother Amedeo and for Vittorio Azzolin. 'He said Tony was one who kept things to himself and who kept things bottled up, and whatever happened in Melbourne set him off.'

Charles said that he used to accompany his father on Saturday mornings to the quarry, 'which we used to call "the black range". They [the Italians] used to bring the bluestone to the crusher, load up the trucks and transport it onto the train carriages. It was bluestone screenings for making roads or for using as ballast between railway lines'.

'The quarry, to my knowledge, operated for about three years, from 1937 to 1940, and my uncle employed a lot of Italians. Tony was well liked at the quarry, and it was a terrible shock for them when it happened, for it's something that doesn't happen every day. I was only about fifteen at the time and these things don't impress you too much.'

THE *STAWELL NEWS* of 1 June 1938 also reported the tabling to the court of Antonio Gnata's suicide note, which was translated by a local truck driver, Adolfo Sartori, who also acted as one of Antonio's pallbearers.

Sixty years later, in a tiny office of the Australian Archives' Melbourne branch, I held this note, which had been wrapped in plastic and lodged somewhere within the Public Records Office's vast depository at Laverton. The folded note was contained in an old white envelope, upon which were written the words '*Pappa* [sic] *E Mamma*' in pen and ink. The sight of these simple words evoked a strong emotional reaction in me and I held my breath as I reached for the envelope's contents.

A few moments later I unfolded the letter and cast my eyes over the last lines penned by a deeply troubled man to his loved ones:

> *Addio Pappa E Mamma*
> *Ci Vedremo nel l'altro Mondo . . ,*
> *Bacci Ardenti.*
> *Vostro Amatissimo Figlio*
> *A. Gnata.*
> *Nulla Mi Potra trattenere*
> *Il destino mi vuole.*

Which translated means:

> Goodbye Father and Mother
> We'll see each other in the next world . . ,
> Ardent kisses.
> From your most beloved son
> A. Gnata.
> Nothing can keep me
> Destiny wants me.

Having discovered the awful fate that befell Antonio, there was now only one duty left to perform: to relay the circumstances to Antonio's surviving niece, Maria, and nephew, Tony.

Tony and Maria were grateful to learn of these developments, as the final chapter had now been closed on a story that had for so many years remained incomplete. But with the anniversary of the death of Antonio Gnata looming, this horrific story at least carried a wonderful postscript.

On the morning of 30 May 1998 — sixty years to the day since Antonio Gnata took his own life — a small group of people made the trek to Stawell Cemetery: Tony Dal Sasso, his son John, daughter Ilda, granddaughter Veronica, and myself. Meeting us at the cemetery were Antonio's niece, Maria Busana, and her husband Tony, who had completed a four and a half hour drive to Stawell that morning from their Wonthaggi home.

Also there were Ellenor Musumeci and the Genealogical Society's Vice-President, Charles Kerr, along with Father Wally Tudor, the parish priest of St Patrick's Church, Stawell.

While I have never kept a diary, the poignancy of this occasion compelled me to record the day's events as follows:

At eleven o'clock on what was a fine and mild autumn day, Father Tudor conducted a short, moving service by the grave — one of three unmarked graves lying side by side. There Maria laid two bouquets made up of yellow-centred white daisies, yellow, orange and white lilies, yellow and red roses and white chrysanthemums — the first flowers ever placed there.

At the completion of the fifteen-minute ceremony, all visitors were introduced to Colin Woodgate, the owner of the site of the now filled-in quarry. On Colin's property was a ramshackle old timber and tin hut, quite possibly that in which Antonio spent his final hours.

The visitors followed Colin in their cars on a short three-kilometre journey to the hut. It adjoined an elongated timber work shed, built beneath a magnificent ghost gum, whose huge limbs jutted out over the dwelling like the timber spokes of a giant umbrella. The living quarters of the hut, the dimensions of which I would compare with those of an old prison cell, comprised graying, weather-beaten, vertical weatherboards, a timber door with a rusty chain lock, and a red-brick chimney.

Inside could be found a few hay bales and the brick fireplace, from which dangled a piece of old rusty chain, presumably for the purpose of supporting the boiling billy. A few pieces of corrugated iron roofing were missing — the legacy of a recent storm, according to Colin.

Colin said people had asked him why he had never demolished the hut, and he always replied that there was something interesting about the old structure. The story involving Antonio Gnata only served to rekindle this interest, and the archival information I presented to Colin was gratefully received.

He then took us on a five-minute walk from the hut up a small incline to the quarry. I say 'up' to the quarry, because where the quarry had once been was now a man-made earthen mound rising thirty metres above its natural surrounds, having been gradually filled in over the past fifty years. From the top of this mound one has an unimpeded view over a pea-green valley to the blue-grey of the majestic Grampians.

Afterwards we returned to the cars. I walked back with Maria, who was clearly moved by the whole experience. In contemplating the reality that this was the place where Antonio met his terrible end, Maria could be heard saying softly to herself, 'Life . . . life.'

Then we all drove a couple of hundred yards to the site of the old cement crusher — or what was left of it. Scattered around the scrub, in loose granite and quartz-encrusted earth, were jagged chunks of bluestone — the stone Antonio Gnata helped extract from the mine during the last eighteen months of his life.

At one point, Colin uncovered an elongated fifty-centimetre by twenty-centimetre bluestone slab, which John Dal Sasso suggested should become the temporary headstone of Antonio Gnata's grave — so it did. In fact, everyone took their little pieces of bluestone to remember their very special time here.

We then gathered at the local Stawell hotel, The Brix, to talk about Gnata and the Italian quarry workers. Father Wally made a pledge to Maria Busana and Tony Dal Sasso that Antonio Gnata's memory would be acknowledged at mass the following day. We then said our goodbyes and went our own ways.

I later learned that on the following morning, at Maria's request, Charles Kerr returned to Antonio's grave and dug holes for the vases that Maria had brought for the flowers. There he found the Bible and bottle of Holy Water mistakenly left behind by Father Tudor at the completion of the service.

On the night of Thursday, 30 July 1998, Maria Busana rang to say that a wonderful photograph of Antonio as a young man, taken prior to his ill-fated departure for Australia, had just arrived from Italy. It had been sent to her by her brother, Marcello Dal Sasso, and by Virginia Gnata (née Lovison), the widow of Antonio's elder brother Amedeo. Maria has since suffered a severe stroke, which has greatly restricted movement in one side of her body. However, with the support of her family, she is making steady progress and her spirit has been buoyed no end by a bronze plaque since placed on the grave of her dear uncle.

Antonio Gnata's difficult life and lonely death brought home to me in the most resounding manner the adversities confronting the migrant — of having to farewell family, friends and home, maybe forever, and of embarking on an uncertain future in some faraway place where differences in culture, lifestyle, language and customs are as vast as the oceans separating the new land from the old.

Perhaps such sentiments will strike a chord with future visitors to Stawell Cemetery, who may care to place a flower at the final resting place of the quarryman from Salcedo.

54. Massimo Girardi

BORN CONCO, PROVINCIA DI VICENZA, 8 JANUARY 1900.
DIED ASIAGO, PROVINCIA DI VICENZA, 23 NOVEMBER 1971.

On 4 April 1927, in the northern Queensland town of Home Hill, Olivo Poli (who later died tragically in a cane fire in Ayr) put pen to paper in the presence of a local J.P. He scrawled his name in pen and ink across the bottom of a document nominating Massimo Girardi 'to join me in Australia'.

Massimo, true to his word, set sail six months later aboard the *Re d'Italia*. Much of this story was recalled by Olivo's widow, Teresa Poli. Massimo came to Australia to cut cane, leaving behind his wife, Anna, and two children. After the War, around 1952, he returned to Italy to be with them.

Massimo's mother's maiden name was Predebon; a distant cousin, Joe Predebon, of Caboolture, Queensland, recalls a slice of Massimo's life:

> Massimo used to chew tobacco and clean out everybody's pipes. He used to be in the picture show upstairs and if you were downstairs you had to watch where you put your feet because he'd spit on the floor from the top deck!
>
> Massimo used to live by himself in the cane barracks, provided by the people for whom he and the others cut cane. They were all in a gang, and in those days there was any number of gangs.
>
> Massimo was there the day my godfather, Marco Poli, died of a snake bite. It happened at Home Hill in 1942. The cane cutters were clearing land by hand and Marco disturbed a female snake that was resting there. The snake swung around and bit him on the leg.
>
> Off-season work was slack, so Massimo and all the others would clear the land by hand. They used to live hard. On

Saturday mornings they'd go into town, sit in the bar from ten o'clock opening and not go home until closing time.

Massimo is believed to have been interned during the War, though he was let out during the day. 'I do know that he returned to Italy with a few dollars,' Joe said. 'When the War finished a lot of them packed up and went home, and never came back. I saw him in Italy in 1967 when he was playing *bocce* in the local town. There was a *bocce* court and a bar there, and when I talked to Massimo he used to enjoy breaking out into the English language.'

In late 1999, on my month-long honeymoon pilgrimage to Italy, I had the good fortune of meeting Massimo Girardi's daughter, Lucia (nicknamed 'Lucilla'), at her home in Ospedaletto Euganeo, Provincia di Padova, in northern Italy. Flanked by her two grandsons, and in the company of my cousins (and interpreters) Ettore and Edy De Bolfo, Lucia delighted in hearing the stories I conveyed of Massimo's time in Australia.

55. Osvaldo Reffo

BORN SAN MARTINO DI LUPARI, PROVINCIA DI PADOVA, 29 JULY 1893.
DIED SAN MARTINO DI LUPARI, PROVINCIA DI PADOVA, 16 MARCH 1972.

OSVALDO REFFO WAS a much-travelled passenger on the *Re d'Italia*, but his life would ultimately end where it had all begun: in the tiny town of San Martino di Lupari.

Osvaldo was the son of Fortunato and Angela Reffo (née Meneghello). In 1920 he married Adelina Tonin, who bore him a daughter and two sons — Angela in 1921, Antonio in 1924 and Sergio Mario in 1935. It was Antonio who, in July 1998, related some details of his father's life to me over the phone from Italy.

A carpenter by trade, Osvaldo came to Australia alone, having been nominated by Mario Conte, a friend from his village and a great-uncle to A.F.L football's Rocca brothers, Saverio and Anthony. Mario had work tending a tomato garden by Merri Creek, near the corner of Strettle Street and Anderson Road in Thornbury, Victoria.

Following his arrival, Osvaldo spent his first days at the Brunswick Street address of Cannizzaro and Santi, the local fishmongers. He later worked in the bush, possibly at Erica, lopping timber for railway sleepers. Osvaldo remained in Australia until 1932, and then travelled to France to be reunited with his wife and her brothers and sisters. He remained there for eighteen months before venturing to eastern Africa searching for employment in March 1935. On the eve of the Second World War he was placed under house arrest by English authorities there, and incarcerated in Kenya as an Italian prisoner of war for five years.

Upon his release on 10 November 1945, Osvaldo's travels came full circle when he returned to Italy stricken with malaria. He worked as a carpenter in his home town of San Martino until his death at age seventy-eight. His beloved wife Adelina survived him by three years and died in Cittadella.

56. Agostino Parlato

BORN RECOARO, PROVINCIA DI VICENZA, 20 FEBRUARY 1881.
DIED LIVERPOOL, NEW SOUTH WALES, 18 AUGUST 1949.

AGOSTINO PARLATO FOUGHT for Italy on the Austrian border for three years of the Great War before the signing of the Armistice in 1918. Between 1905 and 1925, his wife Angelina gave birth to eight children: Virgilio, Carmela, Ugo, Maria, Augusto, Ferdinando, Mario and Alessandro. But when he boarded the *Re d'Italia* in 1927, Agostino could not have known that it would only be Ferdinando he would ever see again.

At some point Angelina had decided not to follow Agostino to Australia, but the circumstances surrounding her decision are unknown.

When he disembarked alone from the old steamship that November, Agostino headed for the Victorian coal-mining town of Morwell, probably to the Brown Street address of his nominator, Antonio Dal Pia. After a brief stay there, Agostino relocated to Nathalia in western Victoria, where he settled for the next five years. He then crossed the border into New South Wales, to The Rock, before relocating three years later to Colo Vale and Braemar via Mittagong.

In Colo Vale, Agostino worked for Griffiths & Co. as a charcoal burner and was, according to his many citizenship applications, generally regarded as a valued member of the community. These applications also revealed that, while he suffered from slight deafness, Agostino learned to converse in the King's English with reasonable fluency. Despite this, for nine years from 1938 on, Agostino's applications for naturalisation were constantly rejected by the Commonwealth, for reasons unknown.

In 1946, Agostino — now a resident of Pine Road in the Sydney suburb of Fairfield — made another citizenship application. He then applied for entry visas for Angelina and two of his sons, Ferdinando and Alessandro, after learning that his wife had changed her mind about coming to Australia. On 18 February 1947, before Liverpool Clerk of Petty Sessions William Carluke Lindsay, Agostino Parlato of Horsley Park, Horsley, in the State of New South Wales, finally took the Oath of Allegiance to His Majesty King George VI.

Despite his best efforts, Agostino was unable to secure passage for Angelina and Alessandro. But Ferdinando did make the journey to Australia to be with his father, who by now was in his late sixties and in extremely poor health. Soon after this reunion, on or about 18 August 1949, Agostino Parlato died.

An old friend, Nina Zovi, who helped with Ferdinando's arrival, remembers Agostino's final hours. 'The night before Agostino died, I took my two kids to see him. That night he said to me, "You know, Nina, I won't be coming back ... I don't know where I'm going, but wherever it is I'll pray for you" ... and he died at about four the next morning. He was a lovely man, a really good man, whom I used to call "Zio". He did a lot for me.'

Ferdinando remained in Sydney, where he died in 1968, and is survived by his wife Tina, sons Agostino and Giovanni, and stepson Angelo.

57. Pasquino Giovanni Bertagna

BORN BACCANA DI LICCIANA NARDI, PROVINCIA DI MASSA CARRARA, 21 JANUARY 1901.
DIED SERAVEZZA, PROVINCIA DI LUCCA, 28 OCTOBER 1976.

PASQUINO BERTAGNA'S YOUNGER brother, Ernesto, nominated him for entry to Australia. He was already married to Annunziata Alessandrini, and their only son, Dante, was born while he was in Australia.

Ernesto had himself been nominated by the Grilli family. Ernesto's wife, Rina, with whom I made contact in February 1998, told me that Joe Grilli sponsored Ernesto, who in turn nominated Pasquino. 'I later came to Australia to marry Ernie, with whom I had been corresponding. I married him in the Victorian town of Heathcote in 1950,' said Rina, now living in the Melbourne suburb of Balwyn.

Rina's daughter, Margaret Belli (née Bertagna), said that Pasquino and her father Ernesto cut timber in the Barmah Forest, where they lived together until Pasquino's return to Italy in April 1935. 'He did not return with many worldly goods, apart from a shotgun, which his son Dante told me later killed a few Germans as well as rabbits,' Margaret said.

Following his return to Seravezza, Pasquino and his wife set up a small bakery. Life was smooth for them until 1941, when the War precipitated Pasquino's involvement with the *carabinieri*. 'He remained in the *carabinieri* until 1944, when he was discharged. He returned home to find Seravezza ravaged by seven months of battle, and hunger became the order of the day for him and his family,' Margaret told me.

'Following the War there was a shortage of work. At one point, Pasquino's son Dante found work (as a bricklayer's apprentice) where Pasquino could not. Which prompted Pasquino to return to Baccana, the place from which his family originally hailed, to find work there. It was in these hard times that Ernesto would send parcels of clothes from Australia to his brother — something Dante never forgot.

'In 1953, Dante finally secured work for his father as a labourer with the *comune* of Seravezza, where Pasquino remained until his retirement in 1966. Pasquino's wife died in 1968 and he died eight years later.'

In late 1999, Margaret herself made the pilgrimage to Seravezza, armed with a photograph of the *Re d'Italia* to show Dante. Dante, who died in Seravezza in April 2001, had the photograph copied, enlarged and framed.

The photo took pride of place on his mantelpiece and was the subject of his constant attention.

58. Anselmo Giovanni Sist

BORN VALLENONCELLO, PROVINCIA DI PORDENONE, 29 OCTOBER 1886.
DIED PORDENONE, PROVINCIA DI PORDENONE, 31 OCTOBER 1970.

ANSELMO SIST'S LIFE story took me the best part of two years to uncover, and all because of a simple oversight on my behalf. I had mistakenly believed that the ornately handwritten name on the passenger list was 'Sisti'. (Intriguingly, Anselmo's was also one of two names ruled out in red pencil, which must have contributed to my error.)

I wrote to the *comune* of Pordenone requesting information on families named 'Sisti', but drew a blank. However, a kindly employee suggested that perhaps the name was in fact 'Sist', pointing out that I may have mistaken the crossed 't' in Anselmo's surname for a dotted 'i'. This was no random guess on his part. Incredibly, that very employee turned out to be Anselmo's grandson, Sergio, and it was he who sent me the following letter:

> ...It is with great pleasure that I answer your request for information regarding Anselmo Giovanni Sist, who was my grandfather. I always heard him talk of his experience as an emigrant to Australia, which he happily recalled because it was certainly his most fortunate time. In fact, previous experiences in North America did not end very well, mainly due to his health.
>
> We descendants — children and grandchildren — have good memories of him, above all because of the life he told us about ...
>
> Anselmo Giovanni Sist married Angela Del Ben. Their children were: Teodolinda, born 10 August 1908, died 18 November 1985, who married Sigisfredo Taiariol; Albina, born 10 August 1910, died 1911; Giordan, born 22 June 1913, who married Olga Caratti and lives in Pordenone; and Ernesto, born 7 March 1922, who married Costantina Sist and lives in Pordenone.
>
> Anselmo's grandchildren are Gastone, Armando and Luigia (to Teodolinda), Dilvo (to Giordano) and Sergio and Gianpaolo (to Ernesto). Anselmo died in Pordenone on 31 October 1970. His wife died on 27 February 1971.

I later discovered that the red line was scrawled through Anselmo's name because he had disembarked from the *Re d'Italia* in Port Adelaide five days before it reached Melbourne. It is clear that Anselmo spent his first few days in South Australia, but exactly where and for how long will probably never be known.

59. Giovanni Battista Mantovan

BORN SAN SERAN, COMUNE DI RONCADE, PROVINCIA DI TREVISO, 17 MARCH 1895.
DIED MAREEBA, QUEENSLAND, 16 AUGUST 1974.

GIOVANNI MANTOVAN WAS married with three children in 1927, when an argument with his wife saw him sever ties with all of them. Together with his friend Beniamino De Bortoli (passenger sixty), Giovanni boarded the *Re d'Italia* bound for Melbourne.

From there he made for the far north, to the cane fields of Mareeba, about fifty kilometres southwest of Cairns. Although his early days in Mareeba are sketchy, Giovanni's later years took him to the nearby town of Innisfail, where he worked as a cook and as a cane cutter until his internment as Italian prisoner of war in late 1942.

In June the following year, Giovanni was one of twenty internees released from the Wayville Detention Barracks. A week later he went to Port Augusta, where he got a job working for the Commonwealth Railways through the Allied Works Council. Three months prior to his release, in a statement to Mr G.S. Reed K.C. and Captain J. Paterson, at Loveday, Giovanni spoke of his divided loyalties:

> I applied for naturalisation in 1938, but it was too late. I do not know whether I will bring my family out after the War. It is understood that everyone wants his country to win the War.
>
> If I were in Italy I would want Italy to win, and if I were in the army I would fight. I would not like to be shot if I helped my country. I would not put dope in the soldiers' food.
>
> I am not a Fascist. I give the Fascist salute when I am with the others and I have to do it. My son is nineteen — I do not think he is in the Italian Army.

In November 1997 I located Giovanni's son Artemio, who years ago was reunited with his father in Mareeba, and lived there until recently, when he moved to Brisbane to be with his daughters. This is what he told me:

> I wasn't very close to my father because he left the family, but I think there was also a political situation. In any case, I was three years old when he left Italy. My older sister, Anna Maria, was born in 1922, and my younger sister, Teresina, was born in 1926, and both are still alive in Italy.
>
> In those days it was hard for everybody, and the majority of people suffered, but my father got five acres of land and a house after he married, and wasn't too badly off. He had a fight for sure with my mother, Maria (neé Bosco), and after the last child was born he left.
>
> After he arrived in Melbourne, my father went to Sydney, but moved on after a week. He then stayed in Brisbane for a few days, but went on to northern Queensland because he had a friend on the sugarcane plantations. Finally he came up here, to a place just outside Mareeba, where he planted tobacco. And he bought a little place just outside Barron Bridge, on the Barron River.
>
> I met up with him again when I came out in 1954, but he never said much about the early days. I came out after the War because there wasn't much work around, my father was here, and I thought, 'Bugger this, I'm coming out.' I asked my father to write the ticket to Australia, which he did, and I came out with my mother. She got back together with him for a few years, but returned to Italy in 1959 or 1960. And that was the last time they saw each other.
>
> My father remained single until he died in 1974, aged seventy-nine, and he's buried in Mareeba. He was a farmer all his life.

60. Beniamino De Bortoli

BORN ASOLO, PROVINCIA DI TREVISO, 16 FEBRUARY 1885.
DIED CAVARZERE, PROVINCIA DI VENEZIA, 18 FEBRUARY 1957.

BENIAMINO DE BORTOLI'S story is an immigrant's tale of eroded hope and sadness. Born in 1885, he married Virginia Carraro and left for Australia in 1927 with his friend Giovanni Mantovan when his wife was pregnant with their seventh child. Arriving in Australia, he found work as a carpenter on a vineyard in Griffith, making wooden barrels.

In May 2000, Beniamino's grandson, Marino, whom I had tracked down in the town of Bollate, near Milan, sent me the following letter:

Dear Signor Anthony,

These notes, as promised, trace the course of Beniamino's life in Australia. To tell you the truth, these recollections are a bit sad, but represent the reality that many people of the period, like my grandfather, faced when they left for places unknown in search of a bit of luck.

Without a family at their side to offer reassurance and comfort in their most difficult moments, Beniamino and many like him experienced the misfortune of not knowing how to face these realities.

Beniamino wrote to his family for the first two and a half years then, disturbingly, his correspondence ceased. Twenty-three years later, on his wife's insistence, his children agreed that one of them should go to Australia to find news of their father. So my father, Olivo De Bortoli, left on 19 March 1953, boarding the emigrant ship *Surriento*.

Olivo arrived in Sydney and caught a train to Griffith to discover, remarkably, that Beniamino was still there. He found Beniamino, almost seventy, living like a pauper and surviving through minimal work. Alcohol had driven him to silence.

To pay for their return to Italy, Olivo worked in Australia for two years. In November 1955, he and Beniamino went home, and Beniamino was finally reunited with his wife

Virginia after a separation of almost thirty years. A family agreement saw few mention Beniamino's 'missing years', but they had taken their toll and he died barely more than a year later . . .

61. Nicola Nicolazzo

BORN CONFLENTI, PROVINCIA DI CATANZARO, 5 MAY 1904.
DIED FITZROY, VICTORIA, 16 NOVEMBER 1954.

NICOLA NICOLAZZO CAME to Australia on the recommendation of a friend, Nicola Mastroianni, who ran a fruit shop at 453 High Street, Northcote, a northern suburb of Melbourne. He left behind his wife Katerina (née Butera) and their daughter Maria, who had been born in Sunbana two years before his departure.

Nicola's early years were spent in the eastern New South Wales town of Forbes, followed by stints in Victoria, in Echuca and then Swan Hill on the river Murray. He later returned to Melbourne, and during the Second World War he found work at Western and Murray butchery in Footscray. It was at this time that Nicola was sentenced to fourteen days' imprisonment for changing his address without the written permission of an Alien Registration Officer — an offence for which he had previously been fined in Forbes.

When the War ended, Nicola was finally reunited in Melbourne with his wife Katerina. In May 1998, in the presence of her daughter Pina at the family home in the northern Melbourne suburb of Thomastown, Katerina (who died on her ninety-first birthday in May 2000), told me the following story:

> We eloped when I was fourteen, after Nicola and his friends formed a gang and basically kidnapped me. I had gone out into the field to get sticks for the fire and when I turned around I saw all the men encircling me. I got upset, but Nicola took me to an abandoned farmhouse, where we stayed for eighteen days.

When the parish priest of our place said I had to be fifteen years and six months old before we married, Nicola went off to war to serve as a soldier for a year and we married in Conflenti when he returned. When I was sixteen we had our first child, a boy, Bruno — Nicola's father's name. But he died of severe burns at four years old. He fell into the boiling liquid of a cheesemaker, and although they tried to save him he fell victim to infection. On 14 November 1925 a set of twins was born. The boy, whom we would have called Pasquale, was born dead, but the girl, Maria, survived.

Maria was almost two years old when Nicola left for Australia. I remained in Italy to tend to my mother and my daughter. The intention was for Nicola to bring us out to Australia later, but the difficulty was that he couldn't read or write, and when the Second World War started, everything was shelved.

We never heard from him from that time on, and presumed he was dead. But after the War we found out from the Red Cross that he was alive, and once contact was made, plans were again put in place for us to go out. My mum said to me, 'Don't go, you don't know what he's done or what you're going to', but I said, 'He's my husband, I want to go.' So I said goodbye to my daughter, Maria, who by now was married and settled in Italy, and I came to Australia.

When I arrived in Melbourne it felt funny. The place seemed strange. My husband was out of action at the time too. He had hurt his leg while working in a Smith Street biscuit factory. Nicola had been a factory worker for the whole of his time in Melbourne, but he never worked again. I worked for two years after my arrival, packing *pasta* in boxes at a factory in Collingwood, and for five months at a place where they made slippers, in Johnston Street, Fitzroy. At the *pasta* factory an Australian lady used to converse with us in Italian.

At that time we were renting a house in Brunswick, but we later bought a place at 634 Station Street, North Carlton. We had a friend whom we'd visit near Our Lady Help of Christians Church in Brunswick, but we rarely went out to socialise. In those early days in Fitzroy I saw a lot of people getting drunk, which left a bad impression, and I got homesick. Nicola wanted to go back too, but he got sick with an ulcer and that's what ended his life.

Pina was born in 1952, two years before Nicola's death, but I was alone with him in the hospital when he died and I caught the tram home on my own. Nicola was buried in Melbourne Cemetery. I never married again . . .

62. Domenico Salce

BORN ROCCA CASALE, PROVINCIA DI AQUILA, 5 NOVEMBER 1902.
DIED DROUIN SOUTH, VICTORIA, 2 FEBRUARY 1986.

63. Quintino (Queeny) Salce

BORN ROCCA CASALE, PROVINCIA DI AQUILA, 3 JULY 1898.
DIED DROUIN SOUTH, VICTORIA, 20 SEPTEMBER 1980.

THE SALCE BROTHERS were inseparable from the moment they boarded the *Re d'Italia* through to their final days in Victoria's beautiful Gippsland region.

Today the Salce legacy lives on in the Gippsland town of Drouin South, where Domenico's son Tony lives with his wife and family. It was there, over a cuppa and a bikkie at the kitchen table, that Tony passed on his recollections of the brothers' lives:

Domenico was my father, and 'Queeny' his brother, and they were from Rocca Casale in the Abruzzo area. There were eight or nine in their family, and as there wasn't much work in Italy they thought they would migrate here. They nominated a friend of Dad's here, but unfortunately when they got here the fellow wasn't around. He'd promised them work, but the Depression was on, the work wasn't there and he didn't turn up.

One bloke had a lot of land in Strzelecki country, so Domenico and his brother went up there and cut ferns between Warragul and Korumburra. They then got a job milking cows for ten shillings a week, and worked for that boss for a long, long time. They later hired a bit of land around Poowong, between Korumburra and Drouin, and planted a few peas. But in the first year on that property they bought implements and horses and I believe they went broke. They then came across a fellow who had a lot of land at East Poowong. The fellow wanted someone to milk cows, so the brothers took on that task once more and actually took up shares in the farm. And they milked 100 cows a day, working from morning till night.

The brothers stayed at that farm for about four years, until 1938 — the year my mother Angelina (née Carnivale) and I came out. I was about eight or nine at the time. Dad and Mum had married in Italy a few months before he left for Australia, and I had not yet been born when he left. I also have a brother fifteen years younger named Rino, born after we arrived here, who is now living up towards Sale.

About a year after we arrived the two brothers decided to buy a farm for themselves, but then the War broke out. Although my uncle wasn't naturalised and couldn't buy land, my father was naturalised and in 1944 he bought a block near Drouin, which is where I am today. The Abletts were our neighbours, and [Australian Rules football legend] Gary Ablett's grandfather, Arthur Ablett, built this house.

We cultivated the land and grew vegetables for a few years, and slowly we got cattle and started milking by hand. As we continued to clear the block we increased our cattle, and ended up with about forty or fifty cows. After a while my uncle, who was a bachelor, decided to go out on his own. He leased a bit of ground, grew peas and potatoes and did all right. Meanwhile my father kept on milking on the farm and I was there to give him a hand.

Time marched on and Dad bought another property and cleared that. Queeny started milking on that property, and decided to sell his property to my brother because he was getting on in years.

My father then decided to go to America for a while, to meet up with his brothers and nephews. He was there in California a couple of months, and reckoned he had a great time.

Dad was pretty healthy for most of his life. In the end he had a leg off, but got an artificial leg and got over it. He passed away in 1986 at the age of eighty-three. Mum died four years before Dad, in 1982. She wasn't as old, seventy-seven, but her heart was pretty crook.

Queeny bought a little place on his own and continued to milk, but he got crook too, sold out and finished up. He was nearly eighty and had nobody to look after him, so he asked if he could live with me, which he did. He stayed with me for the last five or six years. He had a stroke, and though he lived until he was eighty-two, he never got over it.

Queeny used to say he wasn't married, but he was. Unfortunately she didn't do the right thing by him when he was away, so he neglected her. He had a daughter too, and we used to say to him, 'Bring the daughter out here.' He was pretty hard to convince, but he finally convinced himself. He sent some money over and promised the daughter he would bring her out, but the daughter didn't tell him she had a boyfriend and the money was put towards their marriage.

The son-in-law was a pen pusher. He came out to the property for two weeks. Queeny put him in the shed to push spuds instead, but the son-in-law said, 'I didn't come out here to work, I came out to see what you've got', which made my uncle mad and prompted him to say, 'I'll pay for him to go back!' And he never saw his daughter again.

The brothers were always very close, even when they were separated. Together they had been through the hard times and the good times and they never did things by halves.

The brothers are still together, reunited in Warragul Cemetery.

64. Antonio Carrieri

BORN GIOVINAZZO, PROVINCIA DI BARI, 30 NOVEMBER 1892.
DIED PORT PIRIE, SOUTH AUSTRALIA, 3 SEPTEMBER 1950.

FOR SEVEN AND a half years of his early adult life, as a sergeant major in the Italian army, Antonio Carrieri served his country in war. A radio telegraphist, he transmitted messages in Morse code from the battlefields surrounding the Piave River.

Antonio farewelled his pregnant wife, Giuseppina (Josie) Scuo, and boarded the old ship bound for Melbourne. Although he came with qualifications as a draughtsman, Antonio was forced to take work as a farmhand in Sydney, for these were Depression times. But the experience proved invaluable to Antonio, because the farm was owned by an Australian, with whom he had to learn to converse in English. One of Antonio's five brothers, Michele, had arrived in Port Adelaide on the *Orsova* in February 1924. Michele had returned to Italy by the time Antonio arrived in Melbourne three years later, but their reunion took place at last when Michele came back in 1930. They were reunited in the South Australian industrial town of Port Pirie, 227 kilometres north of Adelaide on the Spencer Gulf. But the reunion was cut short by Antonio's return to Italy to be with his wife Josie, who in 1931 gave birth to their only son, Paolo.

Now living in Adelaide, Paolo recently celebrated fifty years in Australia. In 1949, after the Carrieri family had weathered the worst of the Second World War, he accompanied his father back to Australia. Once again Antonio farewelled Josie, on this occasion for the last time.

'Dad came back after the War and I came with him. We left Italy on the *Toscana* in December 1949 and arrived at Port Adelaide on 27 January 1950,' said Paolo. 'My father was a draughtsman by trade back home and he took up the occupation in Adelaide. Again he was reunited with his older brother, Michele, who by now was working for the railways. But Michele died not long afterwards, and Antonio went back to Port Pirie, having found a job in the newspaper.'

The move would prove tragic for Antonio and the Carrieri family. 'My father was working as a subcontractor in an acid plant near a smelter. He was working on the ground floor when a piece of timber fell from the second floor and hit him right across the head,' Paolo told me. 'They should have taken him to hospital when it happened, but they didn't. A week later he had a stroke, and he spent the last three months of his life in Port Pirie Hospital.'

In 1951 Josie came to Australia, where she remained until her death in Adelaide almost thirty years later. On her request she was buried with Antonio in the cemetery at Port Pirie.

THE BLIND MAN
FROM NOCERA

Francesco Curcio's name on the passenger list. No picture of him exists.
LIST COURTESY NATIONAL ARCHIVES OF AUSTRALIA, MELBOURNE OFFICE.

65. Francesco Curcio (Cursio)

BORN NOCERA TERINESE, PROVINCIA DI CATANZARO, 12 MAY 1901.
DIED PRAHRAN, VICTORIA, 14 NOVEMBER 1977.

FRANCESCO CURCIO WAS a loner. He never talked about his life. Even the recollections of those who knew him in his later years give contradictory impressions of this unfathomable man. The dark secrets of his past remained with him until he died, almost fifty years to the day since he first set foot on Australian soil. Secrecy was a credo 'Frank' took with him to the grave, and even then, finding the final location of his mortal remains took some digging — metaphorically speaking.

What would prove an on-again, off-again, three-year search for the story of Francesco Curcio began with a check of the *atto di chiamata* of 1927, which offered the first vital clues: the time and place of Francesco's birth, and the names of his father and mother (Angelo and Giovanna Ferlaino).

In August 1999, the *comune* of Francesco's home town of Nocera

Terinese confirmed the date of his birth. Moreover, it provided vital details of the family Francesco farewelled in 1927. According to the *comune*'s documentation, Francesco was married to Maria Guzzo, three years his junior, who died on 23 December 1984. They had three children: Angelo, who was born on 29 February 1924; Giovanna, born on 9 December 1925; and Teresa, born 25 November 1927 — just hours after her father had disembarked from the *Re d'Italia* in Melbourne. Although Angelo was recorded as having died in Nocera Terinese on 27 October 1951 — hit and killed by a train, as I later learned — Francesco's death was not recorded. However, both Giovanna and Teresa were listed as still living in Nocera Terinese, so I sought them out via Telecom Italia's Directory Assistance.

On the evening of 17 August 1999, my friend and interpreter Maria Monaco made a phone call to the town of Nocera Terinese and the home of Signor Pasquale Parise. Pasquale is the son of Teresa Parise (née Curcio), Francesco's daughter. Pasquale answered the phone and was happy to convey the essence of Maria's message to his mother, who also happened to be at home at the time. Teresa was somewhat vague in her responses to Maria's questions about Francesco, and so it was left to her son to convey what little he knew. It seems that Francesco never made contact with the family again after he left in 1927. In fact, all they knew was that he had died a blind man somewhere in Australia, possibly Sydney, in the early 1980s.

I later made contact with the New South Wales Registry of Births, Deaths and Marriages, to be told that the death certificate could only be made available to next of kin. So, to the telephone book. There were dozens of listings for the name 'Curcio'. I made many calls, pursued many leads and was told many tales, but none related to the man whose life I was trying to unravel.

Over the ensuing weeks, months and indeed years, as I pursued the many and varied sources of information pertaining to other passengers, I put the search for Francesco Curcio on hold. In fact, by August 2001, I had accounted for all of the 108 Melbourne disembarkees with the exception of Giacomo Sartori (passenger forty-nine), Patroche Basile (Passenger 105), and of course, Frank.

THE VITAL BREAKTHROUGH came from a most unexpected source: Maureen De Bolfo, my mother. Mum had been conducting research into the history of her own family. To that end, she had become quite adept in her methods of research, and they included making her own luck. On the night of Saturday, 25 August 2001, Mum rang to say that she had been on the hunt for Francesco Curcio. She told me that earlier in the day she had been using the extensive database of the Family Research Centre in Fairfield and, for the hell of it, had keyed in a variation of the spelling of the surname. Lo and behold, the database offered death registration certificate number 27679 for a Francesco (Frank) *Cursio*, who died at Prahran in 1977 aged seventy-four, and whose father and mother were listed as unknown.

Mum explained that while this man's age would have placed his birth in 1903 rather than 1901 as stated on the nomination form, it was plausible he died alone and as such might never have divulged the exact date of his birth. Whatever the case, Mum's lead was definitely worth pursuing at the Collins Street premises of Melbourne's Registry of Births, Deaths and Marriages. There I obtained the relevant death certificate for Francesco Cursio. The certificate revealed that Francesco's last known residence at the time of his death was 1 Donald Street, Prahran, that he was buried in Fawkner Cemetery and, significantly, that he was born in Nocera — the birthplace stated on the passenger's nomination form of 1927.

I now knew that one single letter in Frank's surname had probably cost me two years of research, and would have remained a mystery were it not for the foresight of my dear mum.

ARMED WITH THE death certificate, I returned to my office, telephoned Mum and excitedly conveyed the news. I then put in a call to the administration block at Fawkner Cemetery, lodged my request and was promptly told that Francesco was buried in a grave laid at the expense of the Villa Maria Society for the Aged. I was also informed that Francesco shared the grave with two women — Evelyn Prior, who died in September 1984, and Mary Elizabeth Carroll, who died in October 1995 — and that a slab had been placed over the grave a year after Mary's death.

I drove out to Fawkner on the afternoon of 30 August 2001 and after some searching discovered the grave in the Roman Catholic section, compartment U, grave 16220. A greying marble slab placed over the grave carried the word 'Carroll', along with the following inscription:

> In loving memory of Mary Elizabeth Carroll
> Born 4th June 1912
> Died 12th October 1995

There was no acknowledgement of either Evelyn Prior or Francesco Cursio. It then dawned on me that Francesco's last known address — 1 Donald Street, Prahran — might well be that of one of the Villa Maria's centres. And so it transpired.

I dialled the number for Villa Maria at 1 Donald Street and introduced myself to a man named Ray Whiting. Ray, a worker at Villa Maria, told me that the name Francesco Cursio did indeed mean something to him, but I'd be better off speaking to one of the centre's former residents, Ruben Ryan. Ray added that Ruben, now seventy-four and blind from birth, had been transferred earlier in the year to the Villa Maria centre in Bundoora after thirty-seven years at Prahran, and that he would surely have known Francesco.

ON THE AFTERNOON of 27 August 2001, I put in a call to Ruben, who confirmed that he remembered Francesco Cursio, who, like him, had been totally blind. This is what Ruben told me:

> I knew Frank Cursio, all right. I was in the Prahran hostel from 1963 until June this year and he was there at Prahran from the early 1970s until he died. He lost his sight, I believe, in an accident. Before he came to the hostel he was at Villa Madonna on the corner of The Avenue and High Street, Windsor. It's an apartment block now.
>
> He was an extremely volatile person. If you crossed him he could get a bit nasty. It happened to me once. I actually

collided with him in a hallway and he tried to throw me down the stairs. I was totally blind, so was he, but he thought that what I had done was deliberate.

He never talked about the past. It was a part of his life no-one knew about. He was a bit of a recluse, and I didn't know all that much about him. He went to a craft centre somewhere and he used to make cane baskets.

He actually died of a heart attack at the College Lawn Hotel on the corner of Greville and Perth streets, Prahran, not far from Villa Maria. He was having a few drinks in the bar and he just toppled over. That is all I can tell you.

Ruben then referred me to the Royal Victorian Institute for the Blind and to the Vision Australia Foundation. He suggested the institute would be able to confirm when Francesco was actually admitted to Villa Maria and suggested that it might have a photograph of Francesco in an old annual report. Regrettably, the institute carried no photographs, but Vision Australia promised to ring me back.

It was at this point that I rechecked my notes of the conversation I had had with Frank's grandson, Pasquale Parise, in August 1999. Pasquale had told me then that he thought his grandfather had died a blind man — a revelation I had forgotten about which, in hindsight, I could have immediately acted upon had I thought to contact the Institute for the Blind.

On 29 August I contacted Antonio Frigo, a retired funeral director who was listed on Frank's death certificate as having handled the funeral arrangements. Coincidentally Antonio, as I later learned, was a nephew of another passenger, Basilio Frigo (passenger fifty-one) and, somewhere down the line, was probably related to another, Marco Frigo (passenger fifty). Antonio agreed to chase up the records on Cursio, but later called to say that he was unfortunately unable to provide any fresh information.

Later that evening, Ruben Ryan rang back to say that he had been speaking to a man named Dick Teague, who knew Frank Cursio when they were together at Villa Madonna throughout the 1950s. Dick told him that Frank was very upset at not being able to get the pension, and that his solace came through the playing of a piano accordion. Ruben told me that he believed Frank lost his sight in some industrial accident, possibly in a quarry. He gave me a contact number for Dick and also suggested I try to locate Vince Raffa, now living in retirement in Murrumbeena. Vince, he said, was a barber in Commercial Road, not far from the Braille library, and cut Frank's hair for years.

AFTER ENDING THE call to Ruben, I promptly rang Dick Teague. Dick, himself blind since the age of nine, told me the following about Frank:

> I first met him back in 1956, when I arrived at Villa Madonna in The Avenue in Windsor. I asked him a few times why he wasn't working and he was very disgruntled because he wasn't receiving any pensions from the government, no public transport allowances, etc. He didn't seem to worry about work. He was a very angry fellow.
>
> When I first came across him in '56 it was two-storey where the men were living. We had single rooms up there and he came at me wielding his walking stick like a bayonet. I told him I wasn't going up there again unless I took the walking stick away from him, so he backed off. I don't know if he had too many friends, even of his own nationality.
>
> I've got an idea he was a 'muso' of some kind and I vaguely remember hearing a piano accordion once or twice in '57. He was also interested in keeping fit by working weights and he had dumbbells in his room.

ON 30 AUGUST 2001, I scoured the telephone book, seeking a listing for a V. Raffa in Murrumbeena. As there was no such listing, I put in a call to an R. Raffa of Mulgrave, which is reasonably close to Murrumbeena, in the hope he had heard of Vince.

Rob Raffa of Mulgrave had indeed heard of Vince — Vince was his father. As Rob said of his dad, 'He'd be nudging eighty and he's been out of the shop for seven years now, but he would definitely remember Frank.' Rob took my phone number and agreed to put in a call to Vince on my behalf. A few moments later, he rang back to say his father would be happy to talk and volunteered Vince's number (which was silent).

Vince Raffa told me, in his broken English, that he had spent half his life at his barber shop, at 68 Commercial Road, Prahran:

> I was there forty years and I cut hair at another place ten years before that, so I was cutting hair for fifty years. When I had my barber shop in Commercial Road all these blind men came from Villa Maria down the street. Frank Curcio used to come to the shop and I cut his hair. He spoke little English.
>
> Frank I knew a good six to eight years. I knew him very well. He used to come to the shop and he enjoyed speaking Italian. He was a short man, very stout, with a big face, and always used to walk with a stick because he was blind. He wore glasses and he had a lot of hair.
>
> I would have described him as a very good man, but very easy to upset. He had a lot of fight in him. One thing I can tell you is that at Villa Maria he was not a very pleasant man. Ruben Ryan used to tell me all the stories about Frank from Villa Maria. Because he was Italian he thought they were against him, but they weren't. They looked after him. I used to say to him, 'Frank, behave yourself' and he'd say, 'Vince, I'm Italian, they're Australian and they're all over me.'
>
> There was a cook at Villa Maria, Anastasia, who used to help him a lot. He also used to know a very nice family somewhere in Carlton. Each Easter they used to take him to their place and he was very proud of them, but I don't know their names.
>
> Frank normally came in every two weeks for a haircut, but sometimes he came in just to talk. One day he came in with a

cane basket he had made at the craft workshop and he gave it to me. I said, 'I'd like to pay you for this' and he said, 'Vince, you are a friend of mine so you don't pay, but I tell you what — give me a free haircut.' That's what I did — and I still have that basket with me today.

ON THE MORNING of 6 September, a man named Maurice Greene called from Vision Australia, to volunteer a phone number for Mrs Betty Grainger in Toorak. Betty, he told me, was a driver for Vision Australia, and used to chauffeur Frank Cursio from his home in Fitzroy to Vision Australia's workshop in Kooyong in the early 1950s.

It quickly became clear that Betty, now eighty-three, and still making sandwiches for the people under the care of Vision Australia, is one of those compassionate people who are so rare in this day and age. Such compassion undoubtedly helped Frank Cursio out of his terrible plight fifty years ago, as I learned from hearing Betty's recollections:

> I was born in Australia, but my husband happened to be English. In January 1953 I came back to Australia from England as a widow, with my sons, Robin and David. Not long after my arrival, my mother, Hilda Stephenson, saw an advertisement in the *Herald* for voluntary drivers to help the blind people. At the time I had a blue Bentley and my boys were at school, so I decided to volunteer.
>
> I remember Frank very well. I drove him around for many years. He was a very nice man and I never saw a temper in him at all. I don't know much about his early years. He never mentioned family and I never cared to ask.
>
> From what I remember Frank lost his sight in a workplace accident — something to do with dynamite in a mine — and he had no sight at all. He lived in terrible conditions in Brunswick Street when I started driving for him in 1953. He lived in a bungalow at the back of an old bank. There was one

room, with no sanitation and a water tap in the yard, and he never even had a proper bed. I actually got a bed for him.

I used to take Frank and three other passengers to and from the Kooyong Centre for the Blind once a week. All of them used to love to listen to the purr of the Bentley's engine. On the way back from Kooyong Frank used to say to me, 'Could you take the other people home first? I like to sit with you while you drive around. It helps fill in the day.' Frank was always the last one home.

When my second husband took ill I was forced to stop driving Frank to Kooyong. I was very glad to later learn that he had been taken to Villa Madonna and then Villa Maria, where he could be looked after properly.

Frank was a loner. He always led me to believe he didn't have a soul in the world. I used to say to him, 'You should mix with other people' and he'd say, 'People drive me quite mad — I'm terribly independent and I prefer to live alone.' He was a very nice, decent man.

A FEW DAYS later I visited Vince Raffa's house in Murrumbeena. He and his wife Teresa, both happy people, greeted me at the door. We had a wonderful talk about old times over a cup of Teresa's flavoursome *espresso* coffee. Before we bade each other farewell, Vince left the room, returning a few moments later with the wicker basket Frank once crafted.

Vince handed me the basket, which now takes pride of place in my study and serves as a constant reminder of the blind man from Nocera.

On the night of Friday, 21 July 2002, Maria Monaco placed a phone call on my behalf to Francesco's daughter, Teresa Parisi (née Curcio), now seventy-four and still living in Nocera Terinese.

Maria told Teresa everything: of how Francesco had spent many years in a nursing home, how he had died in Melbourne a quarter of a century ago and how he had been laid to rest in a shared grave whose headstone carried the name of another person.

Teresa's initial response was to ask whether Francesco had fathered any children in Australia, which he did not. Teresa then told Maria that she was truly grateful to learn what became of her father, who disembarked from the *Re d'Italia* only hours before she was born in Nocera Terinese.

66. Antonio (Tony) Italia

BORN CASSARO, PROVINCIA DI SIRACUSA, 26 AUGUST 1883.
DIED PARKVILLE, VICTORIA, 11 AUGUST 1949.

IN THE DAYS, weeks and months that it took the *Re d'Italia* to meander across the globe, Antonio Italia had ample opportunity to contemplate what fate might hold in store for him in the new land for which he was headed. How comforted Antonio must have felt by the prospect of finally being reunited with his sponsor and younger brother Angelo.

Angelo Italia was at that time employed by a man called William Boucher on a property known quaintly as 'Walnut' in the East Gippsland town of Swifts Creek. 'I don't know what came first — the people or the walnut trees,' said local historian Helen Clothier of the Walnut property. 'In the 1860s there was a settlement where they planted walnut trees, built a Methodist church behind it and, to give it an address, called it Walnut ... it was near Boucher town, four kilometres from Swifts Creek.'

Italians were certainly prevalent at Walnut at the time, according to one of William Boucher's distant relatives, the eighty-six year old Russ Boucher. 'William Boucher, as I always say, was a forty-second cousin, and he did a lot of road contracting at Walnut. The names of the Italians don't ring a bell, but there used to be a lot of them working on a property owned by a chap named Bill O'Brien. He had them picking up sticks and burning off, and a lot of them were there two or three years.'

But what of Antonio Italia, who was more than likely reunited with Angelo in this most unusual Victorian rural community? My cause was initially helped by a stroke of good fortune: a chance conversation with Michael Mineo — the son of another passenger, Luigi Mineo (number seventy-five) — proved the catalyst for unravelling the Italia tale.

On the night of 5 May 1998, after I had contacted Michael in search of a photograph of his father, I asked if he had ever heard of any of the other passengers who hailed from Luigi's home town of Cassaro. Antonio Italia's was the first name I volunteered, to which Michael replied, 'Italia?... My wife's maiden name is Italia.'

In fact, Michael's wife Giovanna (Joan) was the daughter of Angelo Italia and therefore Antonio Italia's niece. 'Antonio died when we were at Langwarrin, roughly fifty years ago,' Joan said. 'I think he ended up dying of pneumonia. I was just a child then, and all I ever knew was that he and my father came here for a better life.' But Joan's elder sister Mary remembered more, and helped to flesh out the tale:

Antonio died of pneumonia and was sixty-five when he died. When I came to Australia in 1938 my Uncle Tony was already with my dad, and he lived with us in Langwarrin for several years. Angelo and Uncle Tony also had a sister, Paola Garro (née Italia), whom Angelo also brought out, and she also died in Victoria.

Uncle Tony couldn't read, but Dad went to school until grade three, the equivalent of year eight. Dad had been to America beforehand, too. He left home at seventeen and a half, went to America, and stayed there for about ten years before he returned to Cassaro to marry Mum. My first brother, Salvatore, was born in 1923, and my second brother, Giuseppe, in 1925. Then Dad left for Australia. All up he came to Australia three times, returning to Italy for the first time during the Great Depression in about 1930 — I was born in November of that year. Eventually the whole family moved to Australia.

Uncle Tony was ten years older than my father and he never had the privilege of going to school, because his father died when he was very young. He wasn't the educated one of the family and he could only sign his name with a cross. He didn't really have a profession, and he worked for us as a labourer on a market garden when we lived at Langwarrin. He never married either.

I remember going to see Uncle Tony in St Vincent's Hospital. He might have been there for about a month before he died. He's buried in Melbourne, but I really don't know where.

I later discovered that Antonio Italia is buried in an unmarked grave, 8501, in U section of Fawkner Cemetery's Roman Catholic section. The grave was paid for by his brother Angelo. As Mary said, 'Dad was Uncle Tony's only real connection.'

67. Carmelo Spadaro

Born Motta Camastra, Provincia di Messina, 10 January 1896.
Died Babinda, Queensland, 29 July 1957.

A THIN RED line was pencilled through the name of Carmelo Spadaro on the list of incoming passengers at 19 North Wharf, Victoria Dock. This was because Carmelo had listed his forwarding address as 'Babinda No. 2, Queensland' and did not disembark from the *Re d'Italia* until the old steamer reached its final port of call, Sydney, in early December 1927.

Carmelo had bade farewell to his father Michele, mother Venera (née Strazzeri), wife Domenica (née Galiana) — whom he had married just two years earlier in Motta Camastra — and daughter Carmela. He would never see them again.

Babinda, about 50 kilometres southeast of Cairns, was where Carmelo's nephew, Biagio Scarpignato, had settled. It was Biagio who first nominated Carmelo in a written application to the Italian Consulate in Melbourne, dated 10 July 1926. Carmelo finally made it to northern Queensland and in the summer of 1928 took up lodgings in Aloomba, halfway between Babinda and Cairns. Two years later he joined Biagio at Babinda, and there he remained until he died.

The years in Australia were not kind to Carmelo. At some point in 1942 he was interned, and remained a prisoner of war until 21 March 1943. By the time of his release, Carmelo had developed the symptoms of Parkinson's disease, which would ultimately incapacitate him totally, and even render him unable to speak.

A letter dated 4 April 1950, from Babinda public accountant G.I. Burnell to the Commonwealth Immigration Officer in Brisbane, stated that because of his illness, Carmelo was 'unable to meet your requirements with regard to taking the oath'. Commonwealth Migration Officer E.A. Bird, in a memorandum to the Department of Immigration Secretary dated 17 May 1951, also noted:

> Spadaro is at the present time stricken with Parkinson's disease and is unable to speak the English language sufficiently well to discuss matters of general interest. However, he can understand the language slightly when spoken to him and is able to speak falteringly in his native tongue. He has an adequate knowledge of the responsibilities and privileges of Australian citizenship [and] the Officer-in-Charge, ASIO, Brisbane has advised there is no security objection to this application.

The A.C.T. archives reveal that on 26 September 1951, Carmelo Spadaro appeared before Stipendiary Magistrate Edward Darius Smart to renounce his Italian nationality. Carmelo's application for naturalisation was endorsed by Salvatore Contarino of Babinda Creek Road, Babinda, who had known him for thirteen years, Salvatore Gangemi of Babinda, who had known him for twenty years, and Babinda Justice of the Peace Charles Matthew Barrett.

In an earlier application for naturalisation, dated 12 December 1950, Carmelo said that he was living at Jackson's Farm, Babinda, and was currently unemployed. He explained that he had formerly followed the occupation of a farm labourer, but had 'not been able to work for five years'.

Carmelo was only sixty-one when he died of senility on 29 July 1957. Two days later he was laid to rest in Babinda Cemetery, where the Reverend T. Burkitt presided. Though cemetery records reveal that Carmelo was buried in grave 38, row R of the Catholic section, a Cairns council worker recently advised me that there is no headstone, 'because nobody bothered to place one there'.

Biagio's widow, Antonina Scarpignato, still lives in Babinda, but is the only remaining link between Carmelo Spadaro, the town of Motta Camastra, and the Cairns region. 'I remember that when I came to Australia a lot of Italians came from that area, but there's no-one left now,' Antonina said. 'Carmelo never went back to Italy and he has no relatives either here or over there. His wife and daughter, who remained single, have both passed away.'

68. Paolo Giordano

Born Rometta, Provincia di Messina, 17 August 1898.
Died Rometta, Provincia di Messina, 17 January 1994.

Once again, a passenger of the *Re d'Italia* was drawn inexorably to the land — Paolo Giordano, the son of Francesco and Caterina Giordano (née Armò), was nominated by a friend, Giuseppe Saÿa (who came out on the *Palermo* in January 1927). When he arrived in Australia Paolo joined his friend in the Victorian Town of Bunyip to farm. They were accompanied there by Michele (Mick) Pisa (passenger sixty-nine), another native of Rometta, and his brother Antonino.

Paolo and Giuseppe purchased a 300-acre (120-hectare) farm, but regrettably the Great Depression sent them broke. The pair returned to their homeland in 1932.

Giuseppe came back with his daughter in 1938 and continued farming in the Bunyip area. There he died in late 1952, about a month after Michele Pisa.

Paolo and his wife Caterina had three children: Caterina, Angela and Francesco. Paolo lived out the last sixty-two years of his life with them, back in his home town.

69. Michele (Mick) Pisa

Born Rometta, Provincia di Messina, 3 December 1897.
Died Narracan East, Victoria, 26 July 1952.

Michele Pisa and his *paesano*, Paolo Giordano, were reunited in the Gippsland farming town of Bunyip with Michele's brother Antonino and their good friend Giuseppe Saÿa. In mid-1927, Antonino and Giuseppe pledged their sponsorships of Michele and Paolo respectively, just months before the pair took their leave for Australia aboard the *Re d'Italia*.

Although Paolo ultimately returned to his home town of Rometta, Michele remained in Bunyip until his death, some fifty years ago. The name 'Pisa' endures in Bunyip. 'My father Antonino was Mick's brother, and there were about nine of them in the family,' nephew Frank Pisa explained. 'Some of them ended up in America, but my father was the first to come here and brought Mick out a year later. Together they cleared some land and planted potatoes.'

The brothers were temporarily separated when Mick made for Murchison in Victoria's Goulburn Valley, where he grew tobacco and grafted vines. 'But he came back here in 1945, to a farm at Thorpedale, near Narracan East,' Frank said.

'Around 1948 he married a widower, Rosaria Barravecchio, who had a daughter, Lina, from a previous marriage. They later moved to East Gippsland, but Mick suffered heart problems and died young, because in those days they couldn't help him.'

Josephine Nardone was only a girl of six when her father, Salvatore Pisa, was reunited in Bunyip with his brothers, Antonino and Michele. 'We all came out after the War in 1951 — myself, my older brother and Dad,' Josephine said. 'We hadn't lived in Bunyip for a year when Mick asked us to move to Narracan to help him, and he died soon afterwards. To this day I live on the property that we later bought from Mick's wife, and the old house where he used to live still stands on the farm.'

Although she had little more than a year to get to know her uncle, Josephine has one wonderful memory of Michele Pisa. 'He used to sing in the old halls of the area, and he used to sing the songs performed by Beniamino Gigli — popular songs like "*O Sole Mio*" and "*Torna a Surriento*",' Josephine said. 'I remember his singing, and he truly did sing beautifully.'

70. Annunziato Guida

BORN BRANCALEONE, PROVINCIA DI REGGIO CALABRIA, 7 SEPTEMBER 1894.
DIED BRANCALEONE, PROVINCIA DI REGGIO CALABRIA, 12 JANUARY 1970.

ANNUNZIATO GUIDA, TOGETHER with his friend and cousin Giuseppe Benavoli (passenger seventy-one), boarded the *Re d'Italia* at the port of

Messina in October 1927. Following their arrival in Melbourne, Annunziato and Giuseppe shared lodgings with their friend and sponsor, Antonino Pratico, at the Franklin Street premises of Angelo Bagnato.

The trail of Annunziato appeared to end there. It was not until 1998, when a kindly Strathmore-based fruiterer named John Sculli — whom I had got to know through his relationship to another passenger, Paolo Violi (number eighty-four) — told me that he would soon be heading for Brancaleone with his brother, and promised to seek out the surviving relatives of Annunziato there on my behalf. At some point in September of that year, John made contact with the Guida family and unearthed the following information.

Annunziato Guida was the son of Fortunato and Maria Francesca Guida (née Gallieri). In 1922, he married Anna Battaglia, a seventeen-year-old local girl. It was a marriage that would endure for almost fifty years.

Anna gave birth to two children — a son, Fortunato, in November 1923, and a daughter, Francesca Maria, in February 1927, eight months before Annunziato's departure for Australia. Fortunato died in Calabria in 1990, but Francesca was there to greet the Sculli brothers when they arrived in Brancaleone.

Some time later, I made phone contact with Francesca Maria Surace (née Guida), who could relate little of her father's life, other than the following: 'Annunziato was a farmer. He came to Australia for work, as there were no jobs in Italy. He went there by himself, and he returned to be reunited with his family in 1958, a year after I married.'

At age seventy-five, Annunziato Guida died after falling off a donkey. His wife Anna survived him by eighteen years, and died in Brancaleone on 23 January 1988.

71. Giuseppe Benavoli

Born Brancaleone, Provincia di Reggio Calabria, 21 March 1878.
Died Brancaleone, Provincia di Reggio Calabria, 20 May 1962.

WHILE THERE IS much to tell in the life and story of Giuseppe Benavoli, precious little is known of his time in Australia. He came out to Australia with a cousin of his, Annunziato Guida.

Incredibly, Giuseppe Benavoli had eleven children (one of whom, Giuseppe, was adopted) who survived into adulthood in Italy. One of them, Vincenzo, who died in Cesano Boscone, Provincia di Milano, in June 2002, recalled that his father wasn't pleased with his farm job in Italy and wanted something different. 'Giuseppe came to Australia, but he only stayed a while because life was hard here and he had little money — he went back after a couple of years', Vincenzo told me in April 1999.

Giuseppe Benavoli had married Girolama Borrello in 1914. Girolama was born in Brancaleone on 30 January 1900 and died there on 1 December 1983. Their children were Anna Maria, who died at eight months in 1916; Domenico Giuseppe, born in 1917, who married Margherita Domenica; Pasquale, born in 1920, who died in Libya in 1942 during the Second World War; Anna Maria, born in 1922 and now living in Alcamo, Provincia di Trapani; Antonio, born in 1924, and now living in Santa Caterina dello Ionio; Fortunato, born in 1926; Mariana, born in 1931; Francesco, born in 1933, and now living in France; Vincenzo, born in 1936; Stella, born in 1938; and Pasqualina, born in 1938.

In August 2002 I made telephone contact in Santa Caterina with Antonio, or 'Toto', as he is known to his surviving siblings. Antonio, now seventy-eight, remembered that Giuseppe worked as a farmhand for a wealthy landowner (possibly J.P. Morrissy, J.P., in Colac) but returned to Italy after suffering an arm injury while working a horse.

'He returned to Italy, sold off the land he owned and basically led a leisurely life. He left the running of the family to my mother,' Antonio said.

72. Salvatore (Sammy) Lanza

BORN CASSARO, PROVINCIA DI SIRACUSA, 7 OCTOBER 1891.
DIED PARKVILLE, VICTORIA, 3 JUNE 1979.

IN NOVEMBER 1927, Salvatore Lanza and his younger brother Francesco (passenger seventy-seven) were reunited with a third brother, Giuseppe, who had arrived in Melbourne the previous year. Their parents, Paolo and Grazia (née Costanzo), remained in Italy.

Seventy years later, following a simple flick of the pages of the

Melbourne phone book, I made contact with Giuseppe's son, Frank, living in the northern Melbourne suburb of Glenroy. The following are his recollections of the brothers' lives:

> My father Giuseppe originally sent for his two brothers, before returning to Italy in 1931, where my mother, Maria (née Sortino), gave birth to me the following year. I came to Australia on the *Napoli* in May 1949, but my father somehow lost his passport and never came back.
>
> In those early years the brothers used to travel all over Victoria by push-bike or by horse to get work because jobs weren't easy to find, and they all worked very hard. They worked in the bush cutting timber and for many years they lived in a tent. They all stuck together.
>
> Uncle Sammy had three sons — Paul, the oldest son, who has died; another, Sebastiano, who has had a stroke; and Angelo, who lives close by. Uncle Frank had three daughters — Lina, now living in Queensland, Francesca, now living in South Australia, and Grace, now living in Victoria — while my father Giuseppe had two sons, Paulo and Francesco (me), and two daughters, Grace and Giuseppina (or Pippa).

73. Michelangelo (Mick) Italia

Born Cassaro, Provincia di Siracusa, 15 July 1904.
Died Tatura, Victoria, 23 October 1991.

I WAS GIVEN an important lead in locating the descendants of Michelangelo (Mick) Italia while researching the life of a fellow passenger, Sebastiano Musco (passenger seventy-four). A relative of Sebastiano's named Tony Musco, on hearing me mention Michelangelo's name during a brief conversation, suggested I scour the area between Shepparton and Murchison, where most of the Italias had congregated.

Tony referred me to a man named Sebastiano Italia, whose wife believed a Michelangelo Italia once lived in Tatura. She was right — in

January 1999 I made contact with Mick's widow, Giovannina (Jean) Italia (née Licciardo).

On 22 January, I made the 180-kilometre trek to Jean's house in the Goulburn Valley town of Tatura, west of Shepparton. Jean was at the doctor's when I arrived, but her son Joseph was there to greet me. Joseph, who is disabled, has an extremely friendly disposition and poured his heart out to me.

He was happy to talk to me about a lot of things — but particularly his love for his father, Mick. When I asked Joseph what he remembered most about his father, he replied, 'He always looked after me. I miss him a lot.'

Jean arrived ten minutes or so later and told me that today was her seventy-fourth birthday. I wished her many happy returns of the day. She said she hadn't been too well, but gladly agreed to talk to me about Mick and the old days. She kindly lent me Mick's naturalisation certificate and promised to forward me a photo of Mick at a later date. In the kitchen over a cuppa, Jean started to talk about her dear husband:

> I was born out here and met Mick in Shepparton. He never mentioned to me whether he had already been married in Italy, and he could have been, but I never asked questions. He was also older than I thought he was. I found out that he was eighty-one when he died, but he didn't look his age.
>
> He came from Cassaro in Siracusa, his mother's name was Lucia Gallo and his father's was Sebastiano, and he was a cousin of the Lanza brothers, Salvatore and Francesco [passengers seventy-two and seventy-seven]. He had a sister named Lucia who died very young, and two brothers, Sebastiano and Salvatore, who never came out here.
>
> Mick, who originally looked after sheep in Siracusa, wanted to come out here to try his luck, and his uncle, Luigi Gervasi, got him out. He found a job at the coalmines in Dandenong, but after a while he was put in the internment camp in Dhurringile. When the War finished, he went to Paracoota Station, near Echuca on the New South Wales border, where they grow oranges. The boss, Mr Watson, used

to give Mick £3 a week to pick them, and Mick always took the kids and me over there to get oranges.

I was twenty when I met Mick on the farm of my brother-in-law, Dominic Macaroni. At the time Mick was picking peas in Shepparton. He also grew tomatoes after the War. I married him in Tatura on 18 June 1944, after we'd been going out for about twelve months, and Tatura was where we eventually settled. Mick was naturalised in 1946.

Mick and I had seven children — Sebastiano, in 1946, then Maria (Mary) in 1948, Mariano (my dad's name) in 1949, Bernadette, who died at birth in 1950, Joseph in 1953, Joanne in 1955 and Michelle Angela in 1965. He was marvellous with his children, especially Joe, who was crippled. He often took Joe to the market, where they knew him well.

In later years Mick suffered from Alzheimer's disease and he began to forget things. He kept working, but after three or four years his problem became so bad that he had to retire. The last five years of his life were spent in a nursing home in Mooroopna. Over the course of those five years he couldn't remember me as his wife, and thought I was his mother. But he could remember Joseph, Michelle and Mary.

Mick was a great man. He looked after his family, worked hard for them and gave them everything he could give. He was a terrific father, terrific worker and wonderful husband. We were very close, and when I lost him it was very, very hard.

74. Sebastiano Musco

BORN CASSARO, PROVINCIA DI SIRACUSA, 3 OCTOBER 1899.
DIED FOOTSCRAY, VICTORIA, 4 JULY 1970.

THE SEARCH FOR the life story of Sebastiano Musco began with a quick flick to page 1966 of the second volume of the Melbourne *White Pages*, where seventeen listings for his surname appear. Several phone calls later, I was in contact with a Mrs Musco of Keilor, who revealed that Sebastiano was her father-in-law's brother. She explained that Sebastiano had been dead for some time, but referred me to Maria Quaranta in Melbourne's eastern suburbs.

Maria is Sebastiano's only daughter. In October 1997, I phoned Maria and outlined my search. Like most of the descendants, Maria was totally supportive of my cause and arranged for a meeting a couple of days later. Beside the kitchen table, with her husband Guido by her side, Maria related the following story:

> My mother and I came to Australia in 1935, but I was only ten months old when Dad left Cassaro for Melbourne in 1927. Dad had married my mother, Sebastiana Di Pietro, in 1922, and I was their only child.
>
> The story I heard from him years later was that he had to get away from Fascism, which he didn't like. The other one was that he was a gambler who had to come out to get work to pay his debts. In any case, he left behind his father Francesco, mother Maria, brother and sister Giuseppe and Rosina, and Mum and me.
>
> He came out with Santo Lanteri [passenger 109], a great friend of his, and though he was a stonemason he couldn't get a job anywhere. He told me he did a bit of gardening and eventually went to Sydney to get work. He said to the person up there that he would be happy to work for food and bed, but the fellow said, 'I can't even give you that.' As a result, my father was forced into the country and went to a place called Barham.
>
> Dad was leasing land for tomato and bean growing there. He told me that in those days the food stores would advance you meat, bread, groceries and money, maybe six months in advance of the crop. He said that after six months' work he had paid all his bills and made threepence, which he used to buy an ice cream ... and then he started all over again!
>
> After Barham, Dad went to Balranald in the Riverina, which is where he was when we arrived. He worked on

different farms and continued to grow tomatoes, beans and peas. In the end we all moved to Melbourne, at the beginning of 1948. In those days you couldn't get a house, so we rented rooms in O'Grady Street, North Carlton.

Later that same year I married my first husband, Carlo Musco, an Italian prisoner of war. Carlo and I had met during the war through a newspaper called *Il Risveglio* (*The Awakening*) — a slightly socialist or Communist paper available in Balranald. At the time when I was living in Balranald I had organised a benefit concert as a means of raising money for clothes to be sent overseas. *Il Risveglio* ran my photograph, the paper was forwarded to the prisoners of war in the camps, and Carlo Musco saw my photograph. He found out my address from the paper and wrote me a letter.

We're not relatives at all, but we got into regular correspondance partly becuase of having the same surname — and fell in love, prompting his escape from the camp. We were married in Melbourne very quietly. After about a month, my husband started helping my father, selling produce in a fruit market, but someone spied on him, the police had him arrested and he was deported. I was pregnant at the time.

He came back in 1949, forty days after my son was born, but he was from a different social structure and we eventually went our separate ways. In the meantime I ran a milk bar in Newmarket for two years and later bought a house in Flemington. In 1978 I married Guido Quaranta.

My dad worked in the market, but in the end he was threatened — it could have been the Mafia. Dad was too honest with the growers, but there were people there who didn't like him sending the growers the right money. He later went to work in a wool processing mill in Footscray, while my mother, a very good dressmaker, plied her craft in a factory. Together they bought a house in Sunshine.

Dad was a very sociable man. He was a bit of a philanderer — a bit of a gambler, a bit of a lover. He was always well dressed and he loved the good things in life — the operas and the concerts — and the only time I ever saw operas and concerts was when I was with him. Even though he couldn't sing a note he always loved music. I remember while we were picking or growing tomatoes he'd say 'Maria, sing me a song' and in my soprano voice I'd sing 'Io de' Sospiri' from *Tosca*.

Dad was seventy-one when he died. He wasn't ill, but not long before he died Mum suffered a stroke, which prompted Dad to leave his job to look after her. He wasn't used to this restricted lifestyle and became exhausted from caring for Mum, and he was also suffering from the early symptoms of Parkinson's disease. He went to hospital to have a rest, but he never came out. He died in 1970 and Mum died in 1974.

75. Luigi Mineo

BORN CASSARO, PROVINCIA DI SIRACUSA, 4 JULY 1898.
DIED MERLYNSTON, VICTORIA, 30 AUGUST 1959.

LUIGI MINEO WAS the eldest of three children and, as such, shouldered the greatest responsibilities. In the early days of the First World War, these responsibilities assumed huge proportions, as Luigi's two surviving sons Sam and Michael readily attest.

Towards the end of 1998 — more than 100 years since Luigi Mineo's birth, and almost forty years since his death — Michael answered my phone call and confirmed the family connection. Michael kindly referred me to his older brother, 'as I was born in Australia and anything I know is a little vague'. So it was that Sam — or Salvatore, as he was christened — revealed the following details:

Dad's father was called Carmelo Mineo, but I'm not sure of his mother's name,[5] as she died giving birth to her third child. He had a brother and a sister, and he was the oldest. He served in the First World War in northern Italy. He used to talk about the

River Piave (the main line of Italian defence), the War, and what he used to go through. One thing he never forgot was climbing the mountains with donkeys carrying armaments, and hanging on to the donkeys' tails. But he came out of the War quite OK.

Things were pretty tight back then, but there was enough income for him. Like his father, he was a shepherd, and he also used to make ricotta. He'd buy ricotta from neighbouring shepherds as well, and take it all off to market.

Dad married my mother, Sebastiana Gallo, in 1922 — she was only sixteen at the time. My elder brother, Carmelo, was born in 1923 and died a few years back, and I was born in 1925. My younger brother, Michael, was born in 1935.

Dad came out to Australia on his own, and I was only two when he left. The rest of us came out in 1933, before which time he had worked on road construction gangs in Gippsland. He never talked much about that, other than to say he had to keep busy otherwise he would have got the sack. They worked like slaves.

We later lived in Koondrook on the Murray, where Dad did dairy farming and grew tomatoes on a few acres he had leased. He later grew just tomatoes, and he picked up six or seven acres when we moved to Barham on the border of Victoria and New South Wales.

The War came and we were severely restricted. We were growing vegetables and the Australians needed food, so we weren't interned, but our Ford utility was taken from our garage, as was our shortwave radio, which we used to listen to the Italian news. So we basically had nothing at that stage, and on top of that my father had to present himself to the local police station each week. This was despite the fact that the police used to come to the house regularly to interrogate him about his views on Fascism. I think my father was a socialist, but he certainly wasn't Fascist.

As soon as the War finished, things returned to normal, and we were allowed to buy a farm for dairying, sheep and a few tomatoes. I left for Melbourne in 1952 of 1953, because I wasn't for the farming life. My younger brother Michael left at about the same time and got a job, while my elder brother Carmelo stayed on the farm with my parents.

Dad was a very genuine fellow. He was a very social, friendly sort of person, a very hard worker and a good father to us. He used to smoke a fair bit and his main hobby was to see his friends and enjoy a beer and a chat. I would say he was very helpful person to anybody. He would go out of his way to help anyone if he could.

My father died in 1959 aged sixty-one. Mum was about seventy-eight when she died in 1984, and they're both buried in Fawkner Cemetery. There was never any talk about going back, or any inclination ... things were different then.

76. Gaetano Romano

BORN CASSARO, PROVINCIA DI SIRACUSA, 2 APRIL 1897.
DIED CASSARO, PROVINCIA DI SIRACUSA, 18 JULY 1968.

THE SEARCH FOR Gaetano Romano took me full circle around the world, from the Sicilian town of Cassaro where he was born more than 100 years ago, to the Melbourne suburb of Airport West, right near my home.

I had already exhausted all avenues of inquiry among the Romanos listed in the Melbourne phone book, none of whom had ever heard of the man who came to this city more than seven decades ago. I concluded that Gaetano must have returned to Italy after only a few short years, and was quite possibly remembered only by old-timers within the Cassaro community.

In August 1999, my friend Maria Monaco contacted the Cassaro *comune* on my behalf. Maria was able to confirm with a gentleman at the *comune* that Gaetano had in fact died there, and was survived by a daughter, Sebastiana, in neighbouring Rossitto. Maria found a phone number for Sebastiana through Telecom Italia and dialled it up. Moments later Sebastiana answered, and not only confirmed her family connection, but also revealed that she was one of three daughters and two sons of Gaetano and his wife, Grazia (née Gallo).

Further, Sebastiana explained that one of her sisters, Rosina, had married a man named Emanuele Mirabella and was living in Airport West — about a fifteen-minute drive from my home in Melbourne's northern suburbs! I could hardly contain my excitement when Rosina's son Elio answered my call and confirmed the connection with Gaetano Romano.

A week later, I visited the Mirabella family home, having armed myself with my four ring-bound folders full of passenger stories and photos. Rosina and her family quickly warmed to what I was doing and Rosina proceeded to reflect on the life of Gaetano Romano, as follows:

> My father had two sisters and one brother. His brother's name was Santo, the older sister was Carmela and I can't remember the younger sister's name. I don't know what happened to any of them. He served in the War from 1915 to 1918, and at one point was captured as a prisoner of war in Croatia. For a long time he was presumed dead, and the authorities sent letters to his family informing them that he had in fact died. But he survived the War, and when it ended he returned to Cassaro. His family were astonished at his return, and held a *festa* to celebrate.
>
> My father came to Australia to make his fortune. He always intended to send the money back for purchasing land in Cassaro. In the meantime, my mother, Grazia, ran a little grocer's shop in Cassaro, and at the same time looked after my older brother Salvatore and my two older sisters, Teresa and Sebastiana.
>
> Barely a year after his arrival, my father thought about going back. He had spent time in Bairnsdale, making roads in a gang. He had worked with two horses in very remote areas, and the work was very hard. At the same time, he and all the other men had to look after their own washing and cooking. All they had was tinned food.
>
> But he often used to come to Melbourne, and he fondly told us of how he went to Luna Park and remembered the big

Antonio Gobbo (second from right), his wife Regina Gobbo (née Tosetto) and son Flavio entertain friends in the back yard of their house in Newry Street, Carlton, Melbourne. Also pictured: Beniamino Mardegan (back, centre), Osvaldo Reffo (*passenger 55*) (back, right), Angelo Menegazzo (*passenger 19*) (with bow tie), his brothers Giovanni and Virginio, and Domenico Negri (with moustache, lying at the front). The Gobbo house was a place for lodgers, and on Sundays many terrazzo workers dressed up for lunch. (Coincidentally, *passenger 25*, Francesco Benvenuti, did concreting work for both Negri and Mardegan in his early days in this country.)

PHOTOGRAPH COURTESY ITALIAN HISTORICAL SOCIETY PHOTOGRAPHIC COLLECTION, MELBOURNE, VICTORIA.

Agostino Parlato (*passenger 56*), time and place unknown.

PHOTOGRAPH COURTESY TINA PELLEGRINO, FAIRFIELD WEST, NEW SOUTH WALES.

Pasquino Bertagna (*passenger 57*), time and place unknown.

PHOTOGRAPH COURTESY MARGARET BELLI, BALWYN, VICTORIA, AND DANTE BERTAGNA, SERAVEZZA, PROVINCIA DI LUCCA, ITALY.

Beniamino De Bortoli (*passenger 60*) and his son, Olivo, on a bridge, possibly in Griffith, New South Wales, circa 1955.

PHOTOGRAPH COURTESY OLIVO AND MARINO DE BORTOLI, CAVARZERE, PROVINCIA DI VENEZIA, ITALY.

Cavarzere, Italy, 1956. Beniamino De Bortoli is reunited with his wife, Virginia (far right), after almost thirty years. Daughter-in-law Elsa and son Olivo stand between the pair.

PHOTOGRAPH COURTESY OLIVO AND MARINO DE BORTOLI, CAVARZERE, PROVINCIA DI VENEZIA, ITALY.

A studio photograph of Nicola Nicolazzo (*passenger 61*), Melbourne, circa 1940s.

PHOTOGRAPH COURTESY KATERINA NICOLAZZO (NÉE BUTERA) AND PINA NIGRO (NÉE NICOLAZZO), THOMASTOWN, VICTORIA.

The photograph accompanying the alien registration application of Antonio Italia (*passenger 66*), dated 2 October 1939.

PHOTOGRAPH COURTESY NATIONAL ARCHIVES OF AUSTRALIA, MELBOURNE OFFICE.

Francesco Lanza (*passenger 77*), aged between twenty and twenty-one, as a member of the National Service's 157th Regiment, officiating at Zara, 1924 to 1925.

PHOTOGRAPH COURTESY GRACE O'HALLORAN (NÉE LANZA), DANDENONG, VICTORIA.

Domenico De Giglio (*passenger 79*) and his wife Maria Giuseppa, time and place unknown.

PHOTOGRAPH COURTESY CONCETTA GIOVINAZZO (NÉE DE GIGLIO), VILLA TESEI, BUENOS AIRES, ARGENTINA.

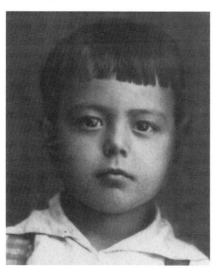

Passport photograph of Giovanni Giuseppe Costella (*passenger 24*), 1927. At four years, eight months and three days, Giovanni was the youngest of the *Re d'Italia*'s Melbourne disembarkees.

PHOTOGRAPH COURTESY ANTONIETTA (TONI) AND ERNEST KOLLER, FRANKSTON, VICTORIA.

Vincenzo Di Gregorio (*passenger 88*) — at fifty-one years, one month and three days, the oldest of the *Re d'Italia*'s Melbourne disembarkees.

PHOTOGRAPH COURTESY SEBASTIANO FALCONE, GRAVINA DI CATANIA, ITALY.

The 'man of honour', Francesco Pileggi (*passenger 81*), at eighty-seven, 1977.

Giacomino Casamento (*passenger 90*) in the classic prizefighter's stance.

Giacomino Casamento in his fruit shop in Lava Street, Warrnambool, Victoria, in later years.

The five Virgona brothers, circa 1937. Left to right: Giuseppe, Angelo (*passenger 94*), Francesco, Bartolo and Onofrio. This photo was taken not long after Francesco's arrival, but all is not what it seems. Francesco arranged for Angelo and Bartolo (who were already in Australia) to be photographed with him in a Melbourne studio, but wrote home to be sent photographs of Giuseppe and Onofrio, who were at that time still in Italy. He then had the images superimposed to form the quintet. Onofrio arrived in Australia not long after this photograph was completed, but the Second World War claimed the life of Giuseppe before he could migrate.

PHOTOGRAPH COURTESY FRANCESCO VIRGONA, MORNINGTON, VICTORIA.

'The little bird of Lipari', Annunziata Picone (*passenger 95*), aged nineteen, 1927.

PHOTOGRAPH COURTESY TONY AND MARIA ZIINO, MILL PARK, VICTORIA.

Annunziata Faralla (née Picone), seventy years later.

PHOTOGRAPH COURTESY KATE DE BOLFO, PRESTON, VICTORIA.

Jack Taranto (*passenger 91*) (left) in the back yard of his landlord and employer Arch De Losa, with Arch's uncle Felix, Gardenvale, Victoria, circa 1938.

PHOTOGRAPH COURTESY JOHN LOPES, FOOTSCRAY, VICTORIA.

Sebastiano Speranza (*passenger 96*) with his daughter Carmelina, and granddaughters Nancy and Angelina, a week before his death, in May 1972.

PHOTOGRAPH COURTESY VINCENZA MARMORA (NÉE SPERANZA), CASTLE HILL, NEW SOUTH WALES.

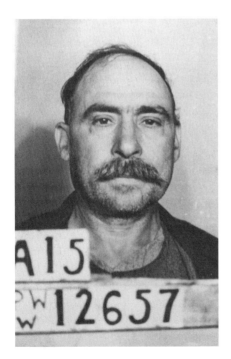

Giuseppe Zappia (*passenger 98*), Australian prisoner of war number 12657. He was interned first at Wayville and later at Loveday camp, from 1942 to 1943. During his internment, Zappia was a member of the 'True Italian' Movement. He was released on 23 December 1943.

PHOTOGRAPH COURTESY NATIONAL ARCHIVES OF AUSTRALIA, CANBERRA OFFICE.

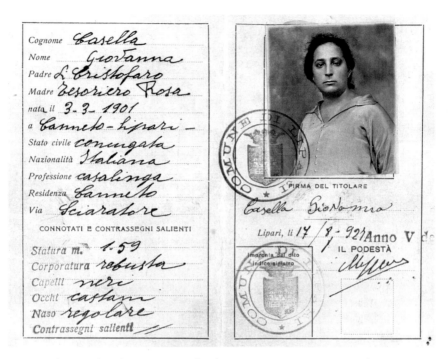

Passport photograph and accompanying details pertaining to Giovannina Famularo (née Casella) (*passenger 101*), then twenty-six years of age, August 1927.

PHOTOGRAPH COURTESY MARY LUPIS (NÉE FAMULARO), GREENSBOROUGH, VICTORIA.

Giuseppe Sanzaro (*passenger 104*), having just acquired his evening edition of the *Herald*, Melbourne, circa 1960.

PHOTOGRAPH COURTESY MARIAROSA SANZARO, FRANCOFONTE, PROVINCIA DI SIRACUSA, ITALY.

Giuseppe Sanzaro, circa 1929, by the since-demolished inner-city Methodist Mission in
Brunswick Street, between King William and Hanover Streets, Fitzroy, Melbourne.
The three-storey building to the right of the photograph is Cox Bros Furniture Emporium.
PHOTOGRAPH COURTESY MARIAROSA SANZARO, FRANCOFONTE, PROVINCIA DI SIRACUSA, ITALY.

Brunswick Street, Fitzroy, 1999, and the author stands in the exact place where Giuseppe
Sanzaro was photographed seven decades before.
PHOTOGRAPH COURTESY KATE DE BOLFO, PRESTON, VICTORIA.

face. He used to relate the story of how he and his friend boarded the second carriage on the Scenic Railway, and of how the two girls sitting in front turned around and laughed at the sight of two grown men throwing up!

As the years went on, my father thought about remaining in Australia and sending for his wife and family. But when my mother decided she didn't want to leave, he didn't want to force the issue, so he returned. He came home to Cassaro just prior to Christmas 1930. I was born in 1931, and another brother, Giuseppe, was born in 1936.

My father bought the land he had wanted in Cassaro, worked as a wholesaler and made good money. He then went to Argentina to work while my mother kept running the shop, but he didn't like the place and lasted only a couple of years there before returning to Cassaro again.

My first vivid memory of my father is of him teaching me how to count from one to ten in English. My father and mother looked after our family and we had a good life. We were never short of anything. During the Second World War everyone else was starving, but our family were never short.

I came to Australia to be with Emanuele Mirabella, my future husband, whom I had met through a photo. He had a truck, which he used to deliver groceries to farms throughout Victoria. One day he went to the house of my cousin Lina, and her husband, Michele Italia, who had come to Australia after the war and were living in Tatura. Emanuele saw my photo on the mantelpiece there and asked, 'Who's this?' My cousin told him who I was, gave him my address, and he started writing. It just went from there.

I left Italy to meet my future husband in Australia in June 1963. That was the last time I saw my father. When I left, he gave me an English–Italian dictionary, which he had bought in the Leonardo Art Shop in Little Collins Street all those years before. 'Keep this as a memento of my time in Australia,' he said as he handed me the book, 'because without this I would have been ruined.'

For me, my father was a great man. He was respected by everyone, including my husband, to whom he'd write every two weeks. He never got to meet my husband, and both men were really upset about that. My father died in 1968, and my mother in 1986. Though I never had the chance to see my father again, my husband, daughter Angela and myself got back to see my mother before she passed away.

77. Francesco Lanza

BORN CASSARO, PROVINCIA DI SIRACUSA, 12 APRIL 1904.
DIED GLADSTONE PARK, VICTORIA, 11 OCTOBER 1997.

Friends aren't for a day, they're for life.

— Francesco Lanza

ON 10 OCTOBER 1997, after locating a telephone listing for a Mr F. Lanza of Gladstone Park, I picked up the phone, dialled the number and waited. After a couple of moments the call was answered by an old man. I then introduced myself and asked if he had ever heard of anyone called Francesco Lanza, who disembarked from the *Re d'Italia* in Melbourne almost seventy years earlier.

To my great astonishment, the old man replied, 'It's me!'

The realisation that I had finally located a surviving passenger of the *Re d'Italia* brought me great joy — a joy that seemed to be shared by Francesco himself. In broken English, he told me he was ninety-three and still going strong, and was happy to talk about the old days. He then suggested I contact his daughter, Grace O'Halloran, to assist with interpreting. I dialled the number Francesco had given me and left a message on Grace's answering machine.

Not long afterwards, Grace called back and kindly agreed to interpret. When I asked her what her father's memory was like, she proudly stated, 'My father's ninety-three going on twenty-one — he'll tell you what time he

boarded the ship and the colour of the shirt he was wearing.' I asked Grace
if we could all meet at his Gladstone Park home within the next day or so.
Grace, who lives in Dandenong, suggested a get-together the following
Sunday week. I happily agreed to this, and advised her that my girlfriend
Kate (now my wife) would accompany me armed with her trusty camera.

Four days later, Kate called me from the secondary school where she
taught. She said that she had been flicking through the newspaper and had
seen Francesco Lanza's name in the death notices. She thought the name
was familiar and had rung me to ask if this could be *my* Francesco Lanza.
It was. The notice, which carried a photograph of the old man, stated that
Francesco had, at age ninety-three, died suddenly the previous Saturday —
the day after I had contacted him!

My delight at finding this man had turned all too suddenly to shock,
sorrow and, of course, disappointment. That evening I left a message of
condolence on Grace's answering machine. Later that night, Grace's
husband, Michael, rang back to acknowledge the call and to ask if I would
come to the funeral. The following morning, at the Church of the Good
Shepherd in Gladstone Park, I paid my last respects to Francesco Lanza —
a man I had never met, but to whom I nevertheless felt strongly connected.

Outside the church I introduced myself to Michael and to Francesco's
grandson Peter, but did not approach Grace, who was consoling
Francesco's wife, Carmela. About two months later, Grace paid a visit to
my home and reminisced about her father's life:

> Francesco was the fifth and last child in his family. Francesco's
> father's name was Paolo and his mother was Grazia (née
> Costanzo). His father, a farmer by profession, died in 1915 at
> age fifty-six, which forced the then eleven-year-old Francesco
> to leave school to help support the family. Francesco's mother
> lived until she was eighty-four — she died during the Second
> World War, but Dad didn't find out for twelve months, as the
> mail from Italy came via the United States because of the
> restrictions.
>
> From 1924 to 1925, Francesco completed two years'
> military service in the 157th Regiment at Zara [now Zadar,

Croatia]. He then resumed his education, because he was sharp at arithmetic and his family realised he had a very quick mind, along with an amazing ability to recall times, dates, people and places.

Francesco's older brother, Joe, who was already married in Italy, came to Australia in or around 1925, for economic reasons. Two years later, Salvatore [passenger seventy-two] and Francesco came together on the *Re d'Italia*, and spent their first night in a little house in North Melbourne, opposite St Mary's Church in Howard Street. Later, whenever he came through the city, Francesco would board at 'The 100-room House' in nearby Victoria Street [a classic Victorian boarding house, still standing].

The day after their arrival, the brothers went looking for work, which was difficult to find in those early years. Salvatore would walk many miles — often twenty a day — only to be rejected for work because of his European background. 'Bloody Iti, go home or I'll set the dogs onto you' was quite often the reception, but he always managed to find something in the end.

Francesco went up north to Charlton looking for work, and found a job in Inglewood stripping gum leaves to make eucalyptus oil for a couple of weeks. Four men cut one cart's worth per day, he recalled. He then found work at Wedderburn, where a new reservoir was being built. He spent three months there working on the dam, which is when he finally repaid his fare on the *Re d'Italia* to his elder sister. It had taken him fourteen months to do so and it prevented his sister from having to sell her house.

Francesco also worked his way through Moe and either walked down or caught the train to Bairnsdale, where he laboured as a fruit picker. In 1930 he worked briefly at Omeo clearing timber, as one of the original pioneers in the building of the Omeo Highway through the high country of Gippsland. Here he was reunited with his brothers Salvatore and Joe.

Throughout this period they lived out of tents and made only ten shillings a week.

Once a fortnight the construction authority would supply the brothers with their payment as well as with food supplies, and if there was a delay the brothers would eat rabbits. At one stage, Joe, Salvatore and Francesco made a pot of soup to eat, and everybody put salt in it. A huge row ensued, and Salvatore and Joe returned to Italy ... though it probably had a bit to do with the work situation as well, and no doubt this was the straw that broke the camel's back.

For about two years Francesco worked for a Mr Kerrigan, who owned a lot of land in the Yarram area. Up until the weeks before he died, Francesco always spoke highly of Mr Kerrigan, who headed a wealthy Irish family and gave him many responsibilities of his own. The securing of full-time work was envied in those days, and the only stipulation for Francesco's full-time employment was that he travel with the family in their horse and jinker to mass every Sunday.

In 1932, Francesco bought a property at nearby Mack's Creek consisting of 212 acres at fifteen shillings an acre, and on it he put twelve cows, twelve chickens and twelve roosters. Francesco built his own little hut on the property, but high water near Yarram a few months later destroyed everything, and the cows died in the snow. He then went back to fruit picking and sharefarming dairy and vegetables at Toora.

After that he decided it was time to go ahead with a proxy marriage to Carmela Di Giorgio. He knew Carmela from his home town, although she did not remember him, as she would only have been eleven when he left. Carmela was a seamstress and had made a special dress for the engagement photo, so she was photographed sitting in position to show the dress off. But when the photograph arrived, Francesco returned it with the express wish that he wanted a photo of her standing up. For all he knew, he could have been marrying a cripple!

The engagement photo carried the date 1 June 1936. He formally stood in the church at Yarram, while Mum stood in a church with two bridesmaids — and Salvatore as a stand-in — in her home town in Italy. So began a happy marriage of more than sixty-one years.

Carmela came to Melbourne aboard the *Esquilino* in March 1937 and Francesco was there to meet her. They spent their first night together at 'The 100-room House', and the next day set off for Yarram — where Francesco had bought a new property in nearby Binginwarri. A year later, I was born in Yarram Hospital.

At Binginwarri, Francesco and Carmela cleared the land of bracken fern and blackberries, and milked cows by hand, separating the cream, morning and night. They went to Yarram once a month to shop, and Mum made her own bread. The Kerrigans would look after me for the day while my parents did the shopping. When the war started, Francesco escaped internment beacause of the dairy farm, although he still had to report to the local police once a week.

Six years passed, and Carmela got rheumatism pretty badly, which prompted the doctor to recommend that the family seek a warmer climate. Hence a move to Murchison for two years (1943 to 1945), where they leased some land and grew peas and beans picked by Italian prisoners of war stationed at Dhurringile. These men were brought out daily on trucks and supervised by the military as they harvested the vegetable crops, before they returned to the camp at night. Carmela would also cook for the prisoners.

It was at Murchison that my sister, Lina, was born in 1944. A year later, the family moved to another vegetable farm at Robinvale, where Francesco and Carmela became naturalised. Then, in 1946, Carmela gave birth to Frances, the last of the sisters.

For a couple of years, Francesco worked as a market gardener in Robinvale, then he bought a thirty-six acre (fourteen-hectare) vineyard in the district. It was at the time of the immigration boom, and Dad sponsored a lot of people to come out and work for him at the vineyard. He set up a 'pickers' hut', which would provide them with accommodation for nothing, and he arranged work for them until they could establish themselves in their new country as he had.

The Lanza family lived in Robinvale for thirty years, and grew dry fruit, mainly sultanas and grapes, for the wineries. In 1975, at the age of seventy-one, Francesco retired. Later that year the family moved to Melbourne, to a house in Gladstone Park, where he continued to grow vegetables, in the back yard.

Soon after his retirement, Francesco went back to Italy for the first time after almost fifty years, and saw his brother Joseph and sister Paola. He felt that his home town of Cassaro hadn't changed that much, but found that the younger people were lazy and wouldn't do anything, and that they 'didn't stop for red lights'. He was glad to come back to Australia and said that he wouldn't go back again.

Francesco brought back with him three seeds from the carob tree that his great-grandfather had once planted in Cassaro on the land that they owned. He had them hidden in the top pocket of his coat on the flight home. They all struck, and he planted one in his front yard. For twenty years the carob tree bore minimal fruit, and finally he pulled it out because it wasn't bearing enough.

Francesco was a great one for education, having received a decent education himself, and ensured that his children all got a good schooling. He always said, 'Knowledge is no load to carry.' Another favourite expression was 'Friends aren't for a day, they're for life.'

Although my time with him was cruelly confined to an all too brief, if memorable, telephone conversation, to me Francesco Lanza will always be more than just a voice. In later learning of his life story, so lovingly told by his daughter Grace, I came to understand that this was a man who weathered the hardships of life in the twentieth century, who embraced his new country and all the people in it, and who lived all of his ninety-three years to the fullest.

78. Paolo (Paul) Corridore

BORN CASSARO, PROVINCIA DI SIRACUSA, 5 MAY 1892.
DIED SILVAN, VICTORIA, 22 FEBRUARY 1960.

'HE WAS A good father, a good family man and the interests of his family were his first priority.' These were the words of Paolo Corridore's only surviving daughter, Carmela, now in her seventies and living quietly with her husband Tony Augello in the Yarra Valley township of Silvan, Victoria.

In our initial phone conversation, Carmela preferred not to say any more about her father's life. But Paolo's naturalisation application of June 1944, which I obtained from the Australian Archives' head office in the A.C.T., did go some way towards filling in the gaps.

The archives revealed that Paolo Corridore was the son of Salvatore and Grazia Corridore (née Gallo), and that in April 1915 he married Sebastiana Gervasi in his home town of Cassaro. During this time, and as the First World War raged, he served in the sixth infantry regiment of the Italian Army. Following the War, Paolo settled into married life with Sebastiana, and together they raised two children: Grazia, who was born in May 1920, and Carmela, born in March 1924.

On his arrival in Melbourne in 1927, Paolo sought the support of his relative and sponsor, Sebastiano Di Pietro, of Bairnsdale, and a friend, Salvatore Lanteri, of 15 Howard Street, West Melbourne. Although he could only sign his name at the time, Paolo later taught himself to read and write in English.

Paolo secured work at Omeo, where he remained until the end of 1929. He then worked at Yarram for four years, Wangaratta for another four and Woori Yallock for one more, before eventually settling in Silvan in 1938. Seven years later, Paolo's naturalisation application was approved, as was his request to be known as Paul.

After some persistence on my part, Carmela kindly agreed to share some precious memories of her beloved father:

Dad fought in the army for four years, but got nothing for it. There was no food and he used to scavenge for discarded potato peelings, which he ate raw. He survived the War, but returned with a bad back, which for a time prevented him from working. And as he got no money from the government he really struggled.

Later he discovered a way of coming out to Australia and got help from his uncle Sebastiano Di Pietro, who had migrated in 1922. When Dad left Italy he said, 'I'm never coming back.'

I was only two years old when Dad left, but I always felt as if he were around me. I remember when I was naughty, Mum would point to a photograph of my father on the wall and say, 'Don't be naughty — your father's watching.'

He wrote letters to us all the time. He'd never miss. You couldn't find a better person. He had a heart of gold. He wouldn't tell us everything he went through, but he'd correspond regularly and Mum would send him back cigarettes in the envelope.

He knew [fellow passengers and Cassaro natives] Santo Lanteri [109], Sebastiano Musco [seventy-four], Michelangelo Italia [seventy-three], Luigi Mineo [seventy-five] and Carmelo Menta [110]. They all came out here, but they didn't stay together. They found their own way. Santo Lanteri was at Barham for a long time, Musco used to carry loads in a truck. Some we saw again, some we didn't.

We left for Australia at the end of April 1937 on the *Oronsay*, and arrived here twenty-six days later. I came out with my mother and my sister. We arrived at Victoria Dock and he was waiting there for us. It was a great joy, I can tell you. He had nothing to give, though, because he had spent all his money on the passenger ship.

But through years of hard work, clearing land by hand and growing produce, the Corridores carved an honest living out of the land, and Carmela speaks with great affection of both her parents.

79. Domenico De Giglio

Born Serrata, Provincia di Reggio Calabria, 20 October 1887.
Died Serrata, Provincia di Reggio Calabria, 22 February 1980.

Seventy years after his great-uncle Francesco Cotela secured safe passage for him, Mario Cotela helped solved the mystery of what became of passenger number seventy-nine.

Mario was one of those many wonderful people who, like me, seemed irresistibly drawn into the search. He also happened to be well connected with Melbourne's Italian community, and was adamant that he would secure an address or phone number for one of Domenico's descendants or relatives.

A day or two later Mario called with the vital lead. He had discovered that Domenico's wife, Maria Giuseppa (née Motorro), had borne three daughters — Rosaria (Rosa), Giuseppina (Peppina) and Concetta — and that Concetta married Rocco Giovinazzo and was living in Argentina. Mario had also learned that Rocco's brother Vincenzo happened to be living in nearby Glenroy in the northern suburbs of Melbourne, only a local phone call away. I located Vincenzo's number in the *White Pages* and dialled it up. Vincenzo answered and happily confirmed this story, adding that his brother sadly had recently died in Argentina, but his sister-in-law was still living there.

I put in a call to International Directory Assistance, requesting a listing for a Concetta Giovinazzo or De Giglio. The operator came up with a number for a C. De Giglio in Buenos Aires which I jotted down for safekeeping. A day or two later I called my friend Maria Monaco with the news. Maria agreed to phone Concetta on my behalf, and convey my motives to her. This she did — to Concetta's great excitement.

Maria took down Concetta's address so I could mail her everything I had, including copies of the passenger list, a photo of the *Re d'Italia* and the relevant *atto di chiamata*. (These mail-outs were posted to the descendants of all the passengers as soon as I had established the connection.) About a month later, in October 1999, Concetta Giovinazzo (née De Giglio) wrote me the following letter:

Dear Tony,

I received your letter with great pleasure. I would like to talk to you first about the nomination form, which I read. The man who nominated my father is my uncle Francesco (Cotela), my father's sister's husband, and he was a saintly, hard-working person. The aunty's name was Caterina.

Many of these things I don't remember, because at that time I was only six years old, having been born in 1921. But our family was composed of my father, mother and three daughters — one older than me, born in 1914, named Rosa, me the second, and a younger one called Giuseppina. My two sisters still live in Italy.

My mother worked at home and out in the field, where my father had a small olive farm and vines that he worked on — the job of a peasant. He said that in Australia they used to work on a farm in which they planted potatoes and picked peas. My father was a happy and good person who occupied himself with his family, and it was in the interests of the family that he migrated to Australia to progress a little bit.

My father came back, but I had to emigrate to Argentina, because my husband left Italy in 1950. I joined him in 1954. I've got three children — one son and two daughters. The son and one of the daughters are Italian and the youngest was born in Argentina. I love Italy so much, because it was the country I was born in.

Three times my husband and I came to Australia, the land that my father cared about. My husband died five months ago, but he has a brother in Glenroy and a sister in Adelaide and we all love each other.

Excuse me for being late, but my sister thought that she would remember other things. My father died at the age of ninety-two and I know that he had conviction in Australia. He believed in Australia.

Thank you,

Concetta.

80. Bruno Vinci

Born Serrata, Provincia di Reggio Calabria, 26 December 1886.
Died West Brunswick, Victoria, 23 August 1969.

A Queen Street boarding house run by a Mrs Jenny Peasley was the address Bruno Vinci volunteered on his arrival in Melbourne in November 1927. Vinci and his good friend Domenico De Giglio (passenger seventy-nine) disembarked from the *Re d'Italia* together, but while Domenico eventually returned to Italy, Bruno made the inner Melbourne suburb of Brunswick his permanent home. A quick search of the *White Pages* gave me a Brunswick listing for Giuseppe Vinci, Bruno's son, and in November 1997 Giuseppe kindly told me his father's story:

My father came out in 1927, one year before I was born. He left behind his father, Francesco Vinci, his mother, Angela (née Fiumara), and some of his sisters. He and Domenico De Giglio were friends in the small Calabrian village of Serrata, and it just so happened that he and De Giglio came out together. Dad was very happy here. He worked hard in the bush, was a sawmiller in the forest, and also dug potatoes and picked peas on farms throughout the Gippsland area.

Dad went back to Italy, I think to be with his family, in 1931. De Giglio had some oranges and olives on his property over in Serrata and went back after the War, in 1947 or '48. By then his family had grown up and there was no need for him to come back.

After the War I came here with my brother and sisters, and we later brought Mum (Maria Rosa) and Dad back out to live. The oldest of Bruno's children was my sister Angela, born in 1920, then came another sister, Filomena, born in 1922, Carmelo, born in 1923 and me, Giuseppe, born in 1928. Carmelo and I came to Australia on separate voyages in 1951. Angela came out around 1960, Mum and Dad came here in 1962 and Filomena in about 1963 or '64. I originally lived in

Fitzroy after I arrived, but when I married we all lived together in Brunswick, at 7 Grantham Street.

Dad died seven years after he arrived here, aged eighty-two and a bit. My father was seven years older than my mother, and Mum died seven years later. She died in 1976 and was eighty-two and a bit also. My father liked his garden, glasses of beer and a smoke of his pipe. He was an active person, and dug the garden until he was over eighty.

'MAN OF HONOUR'

Who knows how many tears he shed, how much anger and pain
he suffered, poor man! All his dreams, made with excessive
assuredness, all of a sudden were suffocated in a great bitterness,
in an infinite disillusion, in an indescribable distress.

— Nicola Pileggi, with Ugo Mollica, on his father, Francesco Pileggi,
from the family memoirs, *Frammenti di Sofferenza* (*Fragments of Suffering*)
(Arti Grafiche Edizioni, Ardore Marina, Calabria, 1997)

Francesco Antonio Maria Pileggi, at age thirty-seven, 1927.
PHOTOGRAPH COURTESY ADRIANO PILEGGI, CAMINI, PROVINCIA DI REGGIO CALABRIA, ITALY.

81. Francesco Antonio Maria Pileggi

BORN CAMINI, PROVINCIA DI REGGIO CALABRIA, 30 SEPTEMBER 1890.
DIED CAMINI, PROVINCIA DI REGGIO CALABRIA, 19 AUGUST 1980.

OF ALL THE paths trodden by those who disembarked at Victoria Dock that
1927 day, none so graphically depicted the standards of southern Italian
morality — and its sharp contrast with the values of Australian society —
as that of the Calabrian hailed by the inhabitants of his home town as a
'man of honour'.

Francesco Antonio Maria Pileggi was listed as a married man of thirty-seven when he stepped off the *Re d'Italia*. His nomination form was signed by his guarantor, Nicola Bombardieri, care of the Morgan Mill in Gould, Victoria. Nicola's fruit shop, at 411 Flemington Road in the centre of Melbourne, was another forwarding address volunteered by a fellow Calabrian disembarkee, Domenico Chiera.

Archival material relating to Francesco's life was non-existent, which suggested that his time in Australia was only brief — he had either died or left the country, never to return. Experience had taught me that disembarkees who settled long-term in the new country ultimately sought Australian naturalisation, but there was no evidence to suggest that Francesco had pursued this course of action.

The handful of Pileggis listed in the various local phone books revealed little; I also pursued descendants of Francesco's sponsor, Nicola Bombardieri, again to no avail. I even considered contacting the American screenwriter Nicholas Pileggi, whom I had seen interviewed for a television documentary on the life of the acclaimed film director Martin Scorsese. Pileggi wrote the screenplay for *Goodfellas*, which was directed by Scorsese and based on Pileggi's book, *Wiseguy*, about life in the Mafia. Although I didn't pursue this line of inquiry, I have no doubt that Francesco Pileggi's life story would strike a chord with Scorsese's collaborator.

In mid-July 1999, I sought the assistance of my Italian-speaking friend Maria Monaco, whom I had first met just a week or two earlier. Maria contacted Telecom Italia's Directory Assistance for a phone number for the Camini *comune*, in the quest to locate descendants of Francesco.

We discovered that Francesco had in fact returned to the town of Camini, where he died on 19 August 1980. The *comune* revealed that Francesco had a brother, Nicola, and had been married and fathered eight sons and a daughter — Attilio, Giovanni, Aldo, Vincenzo, Antonio, Raffaele, Pietro, Nicola and Marietta. (I was soon to discover that he had also had four children by an earlier marriage, not recorded in the *comune* archives.) Maria was also supplied with the following family address: Contrato Travaura, 89040, Camini, Reggio Calabria, Italy.

A day or two later, I posted a letter to that address. The letter contained photocopied images of the passenger list and the relevant nomination form,

a photograph of the *Re d'Italia* and a short accompanying note —
addressed 'To whom it may concern' — penned in Italian with Maria's
assistance. On Monday, 11 October I received a handwritten letter in
Italian from a member of the Pileggi family in Camini, which, translated,
read as follows:

Honourable Mr Tony De Bolfo,

I am sixteen years old and my name is Adriano Pileggi, and I
am the grandson of Francesco Antonio Maria Pileggi.

I am very pleased because you seem to be an honest and
good person . . . I am happy to have received, in the name of
the whole Pileggi family, dates and documents that concern
my grandfather and also all the other Italian emigrants who
went to Australia in search of a better life and a better social
standing back in 1927.

I have tried to provide you with all the material you will
need for the writing of your book. We all look forward to
reading the stories of those 110 passengers. I have sent
photographs of my grandfather when he was young at thirty-
seven and when he was old at eighty-seven, as well as his
whole story from birth to death. I have also sent you the book
Frammenti di Sofferenza [*Fragments of Suffering*], written by
my uncle, Nicola Pileggi — the first son of Francesco from his
first marriage, to Concetta Immacolata Micelotta.

Anyway, I thank you from my heart and wish you great
success with your book in Australia, as well as in Italy. I close
my letter by telling you that I personally have tried to help
you because I believe that I am involved with a really good
person. I invite you, on behalf of the entire Pileggi family, to
come and stay as our guest, so you can visit the beautiful land
of Calabria . . .

Best wishes,

Adriano Pileggi.

I was deeply touched by the sentiments in Adriano's letter and fascinated by the small, eighty-seven page paperback *Fragments of Suffering*. The book, published in Calabria in 1997, was written by Ugo Mollica with the cooperation of Nicola Pileggi. Adriano also included a summary of his grandfathers' life, closely based on this book.

Desperate to learn of the book's contents, but unable to decipher the Italian text, I asked Maria if she was willing to translate the sections pertinent to Francesco's life, which she happily agreed to do. A week later, Maria called to say, 'You know, I haven't been able to put this book down.'

The tale began with Nicola's preface, entitled 'Why These Pages', which said in part:

> I have only tried to collect from my memory the fragments of suffering, variously scattered through many years of life, offering them for your consideration, in the hope that the hardship of my experience might serve as a warning and an admonition to those who often worry and despair over commonplace mishaps or trifles.

Mindful of these words, I went on to read Adriano's summary of the life of Francesco Maria Pileggi, drawn from his uncle's autobiography:

> 30 September 1890, Camini, Calabria. In this economically depressed land, where a feudal order is still in force and the peasants can hardly provide for the maintenance of their families, a great worker takes his first steps. A man who, in the course of his life, gave prestige and dignity to the family of the Pileggis. His father is a poor peasant and his mother brings a precarious balance to the family. In this little town at the margins of the world, in this land of Calabria on the Ionian coast, is born Francesco Antonio Maria Pileggi.
>
> At the young age of sixteen Francesco chose the only road he knew to escape the frightening misery of his land, emigrating in 1906 to the United States of America. After establishing himself in the famous city of New York, he called

for his brother Giuseppe, who was also very young, and they started working there together. Francesco's time in the United States lasted nine years, until 1915, and everything was going well for the two brothers. But one day some bad news reached them from Italy regarding their father, who had been injured at work and was nearing the end of his life.

So it was that Francesco left his brother Giuseppe in New York to join his dying father in Camini. After he had spent a few weeks with his parents in Camini, Francesco and the entire Pileggi family again received dreadful news, this time from New York. The terrible news was that Francesco's brother Giuseppe, who had remained in New York, had been, for reasons still unclear today, brutally murdered.

In the meantime, the First World War had erupted in Europe and Francesco was called up for the army to defend his country. He fought on the Piave front, where terrible battles took place, and in 1972, at eighty-two years of age, he received from the President of the Republic the Onorificenza di Cavaliere [Knight's Decoration] of the Order of Vittorio Veneto, in recognition of his service in battle.

When the War ended with victory to Italy and her allies against the Austro–Hungarian Empire, Francesco returned safe and sound, and not long afterwards, in 1919, he married Concetta Immacolata Micelotta. From that marriage four children were born — first Nicola (born 12 September 1921), then Giuseppe (born 3 March 1923, died 2 April 1996), Stella (born 1 August 1925, died 4 August 1953) and finally Carmelo (born 20 August 1927, died 15 May 1953).

In Francesco's family peace and serenity ruled, but the economic side remained disastrous. Because of this, Francesco took to the sea, to emigrate, this time not to America but to Australia, having been called out by his fellow townsman, Nicola Bombardieri, in the hope of providing a more fitting livelihood for his family. He set sail from the port of Messina, and reached Australia on 24 November 1927. As soon as he arrived in the new world he got straight to business, working hard and sending money every month back to Italy, to his impoverished family.

But about a year after Francesco's departure, dark clouds descended over the household, which in a short time would ruin a family with four innocent children. Francesco's wife, Concetta Immacolata, started to neglect her duties as a wife and mother. In fact, she began to lead a loose and thoughtless life, casting a blot on the honour of the entire family, attracting the hatred and scorn of her relatives and neighbours. Concetta Immacolata took more and more lovers, holding parties, letting her children practically die of hunger, and entirely forgetting her poor husband Francesco, who had gone to Australia in search of prosperity, for the good of his family.

So Francesco's mother wrote a letter to her son, telling him everything that had happened. I leave you to imagine his state of mind when he received that terrible letter.

After he had received the letter, nothing was known of Francesco for about three years. There was no more money, no more news, only an absolute silence. Who knows how much the poor man must have suffered, seeing all his dreams suffocated by a great bitterness, in an infinite disillusion.

But one day, towards the end of November 1933, Francesco, after years of absolute silence, returned to Italy unannounced (otherwise no-one would have known what became of him). Within a few days of his arrival, he was quickly surrounded by all his friends and relatives. He had come back with the intention of divorcing Concetta Immacolata, taking his four children and returning to Australia to start afresh.

In the meantime Concetta Immacolata's lovers, knowing they had offended Francesco, and also knowing Francesco had Mafia friends who would back him, out of fear conspired with Concetta Immacolata to kill her husband, to close once and for all the chapter of his life.

So, on Christmas night, 1933, while Francesco was at home with his wife, there was suddenly a knock at the door. It was one of Concetta Immacolata's lovers, and he invited Francesco outside for a talk. (In fact, all of her lovers were waiting outside, with rifles in their hands ready to shoot him.) Francesco refused to go out, and the man who had invited him to do so arrogantly came into the house, threatening Francesco.

Francesco realised that on the wall near his shoulders hung a bundle of sticks with an axe inside it. He quickly grabbed the axe and, with the strength of desperation, cut the man's head off with two blows. Seeing this, Concetta Immacolata, in tears, stood up and started hurling abuse at Francesco. He, having now lost control and imagining that his wife had organised his murder, threw himself at Concetta Immacolata and struck her with two blows, cutting off her head as well.

Christmas night 1933 will always remain a part of Camini history.

Francesco, convinced that the other lovers who had been outside would have gone, went out of the house, but when he went out, the lovers, who had remained there, started firing at him in total darkness. They hit him in the shoulder, but without inflicting mortal injuries. So he started running, pursued by those assassins.

In a downhill lane one of them slipped and fell in front of him. Francesco, by now at the height of exasperation, tried to kill a third person. But the others following began shooting, forcing him to keep running, to his sister's house.

Having reached her house, help arrived, and in the meantime the house filled with people and the news of the incident spread rapidly around the region. Justice then intervened, and the *carabinieri*, accompanied by the local Fascists, after a major anti-criminal operation that took less than an hour, arrested all the brutes who had played a part in the ambush. Francesco was arrested last, and treated with great respect by the forces of the law.

So Francesco remained in jail for fourteen months before the trial was held. When the great day of the trial arrived the judges acquitted Francesco Pileggi and set him free, since it was recognised that he had been legitimately defending his honour. But those who tried to kill him were sentenced to years of imprisonment.

Having arrived back in Camini, Francesco was hailed by the entire population as a hero. He found himself at the centre of the throng, which escorted him like a conqueror, with music and banners. The most frequent cry that could be heard was 'Viva Francesco Pileggi, man of honour!'

So, having returned home in this way, Francesco was welcomed with great respect by his family and friends, and resolved to put everything behind him and rebuild his life, staying in Camini and ending his days as a migrant.

A short time later he became engaged to a twenty-one year old woman half his age, and on 25 August 1934, at the age of forty-four, Francesco Antonio Maria Pileggi was married for the second time, to Maria Caterina Galeota.

With this marriage Francesco rediscovered the happiness he had lost, and from this second marriage nine children were born: Maria (born 4 June 1936), Attilio Gaetano (born 21 August 1937), Vincenzo (born 8 December 1938), Antonio (born 4 November 1941), twins Pietro (born 28 June 1944) and Rosina (born 28 June 1944, died 20 February 1951), Raffaele (born 23 October 1947), Giovanni (born 25 June 1951) and lastly, Edoardo Salvatore (born 14 June 1953).

All these children, together with the four children from Francesco's first marriage to Concetta Immacolata, brought life to the big family. In all the subsequent years of his life, in all the years of his old age, Francesco dedicated himself to his family, educating his children and enjoying a happy life. His great passion in his final years was the countryside, and he also spent precious time with his young grandchildren.

Francesco died on 19 August 1980, marking a tragic loss for Camini of the honest and benevolent person that he was. He now rests with his second wife, Maria Caterina, in the Camini cemetery. But he leaves behind his heirs, and today there are nine children living — one, Nicola, from his first marriage, and the remaining eight from his second — each one with their own work, their own families and their dignity.

Having spoken of the living children of Francesco, it is important to mention the other members of the family who are no longer here. So, we remember Giuseppe, who died at seventy-three, Stella, who died at twenty-eight, Carmelo, who died at thirty-three, and finally Rosina, who died at seventeen.

Today the Pileggi family are one of the largest and noblest families of the town, living honestly and happily, and always in the midst of the tragedies that enveloped them, in the Calabrian town of Camini.

Adriano Pileggi
(Grandson of Francesco Antonio Maria Pileggi and son of Giovanni Pileggi).

Francesco Pileggi's shocking story, revealed in graphic detail by his grandson, definitely bears out the old adage that truth is stranger than fiction. In unearthing this terrible tale, I felt convinced that nothing in life could surprise me any more.

82. Carmelo Giovanni Gattuso

Born Biscani, Provincia di Catania, 9 March 1884.
Died Hawthorn, Victoria, 4 May 1964.

He was happy with his lot when he died in 1964,
and he never talked about the past. When you talked
to him about the past he started to cry.

— Ignatius Gattuso, on his father, Carmelo

Carmelo Gattuso's death certificate revealed that he had died at his home in Currajong Road, Hawthorn. There, more than thirty-four years later, I introduced myself to his surviving son, Ignatius. From the table by the kitchen window, through which could be seen the little vegetable garden Carmelo once worked, Ignatius told his story:

> My father had one sister, Maria, in Italy and another, whose name we do not know, who went to Argentina. He was only six years old when his father Ignazio and mother Giuseppa Gattuso (née Leopardi) passed away, so he never really knew his parents. And it was never known what actually happened to the sister who left for Argentina, because Carmelo kept in touch with Maria, but not the other sister.
>
> Upon Ignazio's death the family vineyard was divided, and my father obtained much of the property before he married. But after my father met and married my mother, Maria Dell'Universita, in 1923, he moved to her home town of Licodia Eubea. Then, when their first child Giuseppina was born in 1924, and myself in 1926, he saw the need to come to Australia for the benefit of the family's future.
>
> Times were tough in Italy, but they were every bit as tough here — no idea of the language, no jobs. He found it hard to find work, and he used to pick potatoes for five shillings a day. He lived in a shed in Werribee which was home base, but in those early years he still moved around all the time. In spring he went to Gippsland picking peas, and occasionally he went to Portland. But he always returned to Werribee.
>
> I came to Australia in 1948 and my mother Maria Anna and sister Giuseppina came eighteen months later in 1949. We were all reunited and went to live with him in Werribee. When I came here the first thing I said was, 'This is Australia? I want to go back.'
>
> For me, Werribee wasn't a home town. It was just vacant land with five or six houses at the most. The family lived in a little shed that my father rented in Church Street, Werribee

South, for four years from the time of our arrival. My father then bought a house in Bulleen Avenue, not far away, and the house is still there as it was. We lived there for the next five years.

In 1949 my father began work in a foundry in Williamstown. He used to work the metal grinder, and he lost a finger too. But he worked there until his retirement in 1956, and the following year the entire family moved to this place, at 33 Currajong Road, Auburn, a suburb of Melbourne.

My sister had married Frank Vaccaro in Australia in 1952, but in 1956 he died, leaving her with a young child and another baby on the way. This prompted my sister and my father and mother to vacate their home in Werribee and join my wife and me in Auburn. We had to talk my father into making the move. He said, 'If I come to Melbourne I want a big garden and a chook house, otherwise I won't come.' So I purchased the house and when he saw it for the first time, he said to me, 'Not bad.'

In the end, my father spent every day of his retirement in that back yard. He was happy with his lot when he died in 1964, and he never talked about the past. When you talked to him about the past he started to cry. He never went back to his homeland, and he never kept in touch with his sisters.

My father was a man who wanted to look after his family. He wanted to make something for the future for them, and he remained with his family all the time. He was a quiet man, but he had a lot of friends, and he had his wife. She died in 1988.

83. Michele Sculli

BORN FERRUZANO, PROVINCIA DI REGGIO CALABRIA, 27 MAY 1894.
DIED FERRUZANO, PROVINCIA DI REGGIO CALABRIA, 17 SEPTEMBER 1977.

IT IS REASONABLE to assume that Michele Sculli followed his sponsor, Vincenzo Spano, to the heavily timbered Gippsland town of Erica when he arrived. Vincenzo had already settled there, and Italian timber-cutting gangs were prevalent throughout the region.

But it quickly became clear in my research that Michele's years in Australia were all too few, as there were no family or friends around who either knew him or knew of him. There was one notable exception: Michele's nephew Pasquale Sculli, who lives in the Melbourne suburb of Pascoe Vale.

Although Pasquale could tell me little of Michele's life all those years ago, he was at least able to refer me to Michele's grandson, Michele Spinella, who lived in the Sicilian town of Siracusa. I made phone contact with Michele there, and discovered that he, too, was a working journalist who appreciated this investigative side of the job. In August 1998, he sent me a copy of the book that he had written about the history of Ferruzano and dedicated to Michele Sculli. He also included the following story of his grandfather's life:

Michele Sculli was born in Ferruzano, Provincia di Reggio Calabria, on 3 May 1894 and he died in the same place on 17 September 1977. His father's name was Pasquale Sculli and his mother's Antonia Cidoni.

He was always a farmer and a breeder and he used to own pieces of land around the city of Ferruzano and neighbouring towns. He was sent to fight in the First World War and, serving as a mounted soldier, fought against the Austrians in the Veneto and Friuli regions. His actions later earned him two or three medals from the head of the Italian Republic.

Michele was married to Maria Romeo in Ferruzano in 1925, and together they raised three children — Giuseppe, Teresa and Domenico. In October 1927 Michele migrated to Australia, but returned to Italy in September 1931.

He only had a diploma from primary school and was never involved in any political activities in the city, but they all knew he was sympathetic to the cause of the Christian Democrats. He was involved in the Catholic Church as well as the Protestant and Pentecostal Churches. At sixty-five Michele retired, but carried on his farming duties anyway, continuing to produce wheat, oil, fruit and cheese.

84. Paolo Violi

BORN FERRUZANO, PROVINCIA DI REGGIO CALABRIA, 15 FEBRUARY 1897.
DIED FERRUZANO, PROVINCIA DI REGGIO CALABRIA, 16 FEBRUARY 1990.

PAOLO VIOLI DIED a day after his ninety-third birthday, having lived every one of his days as if it were his last. I know this not from the archival material I have gleaned but from the personal recollections of those who knew him, including Paolo's own son, now living in Philadelphia.

The archives reveal that Paolo Violi, the son of Domenico and Teresa Violi, was married with a daughter, Rosa, and twins, Giuseppina and Domenico, when he left Italy for Melbourne. He eventually settled at 119 Union Road, Ascot Vale — a shop and dwelling managed by his sponsor to Australia, Paolo Spano. Paolo Violi later toiled with another passenger, Giuseppe Violi (number 100), at the lush western district property known as Alvie, which was owned by J.P. Morrissy, J.P. In 1937, Paolo sought the admission of both his brother Raffaele and brother-in-law Vincenzo Gullace, then aged thirty-six and twenty-seven respectively. But there was precious little else to go by.

I resorted to the phone book for support, and after a series of phone calls I was given the name of John Ferrarro in the bayside Melbourne suburb of Black Rock. John told me that 119 Union Road, Ascot Vale, was Paolo Spano's shop and dwelling and that he vouched for all the Italian migrants coming in, providing them with work and shelter.

John, who had himself migrated to Australia from Italy in 1937, confirmed that he knew Paolo Violi and remembered the man with great affection. 'Paul Violi is dead now and he has no-one surviving him in Australia,' John told me. 'He was a hard-working fellow who did anything from digging stone to picking fruit. He came to my rescue that many times it didn't matter. We were on a tram one day and a couple of fellows tried to make fun of us because we looked different and spoke with an accent. Anyway, he got up and glared at one of these fellows. I said to him, "Please don't do anything silly, we'll end up in jail." But he just said, "Relax", because his glare was enough to shut them up. That was many years ago, and may he rest in peace.'

Another Melbourne man, Pasquale Sculli, remembered that Paolo was actually a citizen of the United States, the country to which he eventually returned with his son in the early 1950s.

Yet another local identity, Vince Tallarida, rang me back late in 1997 to advise that he had discussed Paolo Violi with a friend named John Sculli, whom he had bumped into at a recent dinner dance, and that John had told him that Paolo Violi was his uncle. (John would later help me unravel the mystery of the lives of passenger seventy, Annunziato Guida, and passenger seventy-one, Giuseppe Benavoli.) Vince gave me John's number, and on the evening of 15 December 1997 I met John at his greengrocer's store in Lloyd Street, Strathmore. John revealed that Paolo Violi had married his mother's sister, Vittoria Gullace, and gave me the following information about him:

> Paolo Violi might have actually come to Australia for a brief time beforehand, in 1922. He was a very hard-working man and he worked on farms and in quarries. I remember one day when we drove past Highpoint West he told me that he used to work there when it was a quarry. He also worked at Werribee, picking peas at market gardens.
>
> Paolo also had a brother here, named Raffaele, who never married. When I came to Australia in 1957, Raffaele was running a barber's shop in Richmond. Paolo and his wife Vittoria had one daughter and then twins, a son and a daughter. One is living in Toronto, one is in Philadelphia and the third is in Ferruzano.
>
> On many occasions Paolo went from here to Italy, back and forth. In 1955 he and his son, Domenico, moved to Philadelphia. Paolo regularly travelled between Philadelphia and Ferruzano to be with his wife and two daughters. In 1974 he returned to Australia and stayed with me at Strathmore for twelve months or so. But he had an American passport and they wouldn't let him stay, so he went back to Italy to live with his wife and daughter. He died not so long ago, at more than ninety years of age.

In the early hours of Thursday, 22 January 1998, I made telephone contact with Paolo's surviving son, Domenico, a naturalised Australian living in Philadelphia. This is his story:

My father had a brother named Ralph (Raffaele), who worked as a barber in Richmond, Australia, another brother Frank, and two sisters, Esterina and Rosina. The older one, Rosina, was a teacher, Esterina was a secretary in the council and Frank was a gardener in Calabria, by the beautiful olive trees.

My father came to Australia because they had a lot of acres of vineyards, which they sold to people. When they mentioned Captain Cook discovering Australia he wanted to go there and find out for himself. He had the money and he could travel and he had been to Montreal as a fifteen-year-old, before returning to Italy to get married.

He married Vittoria Gullace before he left for Australia, but came back after a brief stay. My oldest sister, Rosa, was born in 1929, and Giuseppina (my twin) and I were born in 1933. But he returned to Australia before Giuseppina and I were born.

He stayed in Australia, but found it difficult to get work, particularly during the War. Times were hard, but he was never interned, because he kept with the farmers and he used different names. My father returned to Italy after the War, but he loved to travel and he couldn't stay put. He used to say, 'I miss Australia' and I told him that I wanted to go with him to see for myself.

So he agreed to take me to Australia in 1946, but we had to get there via London, as there were no direct flights from Italy in those days.

We spent six months in London. I liked shoemaking, so he found me a shoe-repairing firm there, while he got himself a job in an ironworks. In the end we didn't catch a plane. We sailed to Australia on the *Orion*. We lived with a lot of *paesani* from Calabria, right in the heart of North Melbourne at the Victoria Market. I got a job at the paperworks firm of a lady in Peel Street. She had a shed out the back, which is where my father and I lived and did our cooking.

I still dream about Australia. I loved dancing and I used to go to the old town halls at St Kilda, Collingwood,

Brunswick and Footscray. These are happy memories for me and I still dream about Australia. But after a while, my father said, 'We're too far away — we're going to the United States.' He used to go backwards and forwards to the American Consulate to get permission to leave, and we were supposed to go to California in 1954, but in the end we settled in Philadelphia because my blood cousin, Bartolo Fioco, lived here.

For the next twenty years my father kept going back and forth from America to Italy, six months here, six months there. The last time he came to America I said to him, 'Dad you'll either die here or die over there — you're better off there with your wife and sisters.'

In the end he passed away there and he died happy. Dad was a great man and I miss him dearly.

85. Carmine Covelli

BORN FERRUZANO, PROVINCIA DI REGGIO CALABRIA, 16 NOVEMBER 1893.
DIED NEWPORT, VICTORIA, 21 JULY 1977.

CARMINE COVELLI'S STORY came to life after just a handful of phone calls to the five enthusiastic family members listed in the *White Pages* of the Melbourne metropolitan telephone book.

Joe Covelli confirmed that his grandfather's name was Carmine Covelli and that, after a brief stay in Australia, he later took up arms in the Spanish Civil War. Vince Covelli junior insisted that I speak to his father about Carmine, and stressed there was no time like the present. As Vince junior expressed it, 'Every time one of these old guys goes, there goes an encyclopaedia.' Vince junior's mother believed that her father-in-law was indeed the man I was looking for, and confirmed that she had heard of Paolo Violi (passenger eighty-two) and Michele Sculli (passenger eighty-three) — with whom Carmine had boarded the *Re d'Italia*.

In November 1997, in the comfort of his dining room in Moonee Ponds, Vince Covelli senior told me about his father's life:

Carmine was born in Feruzzano, Reggio di Calabria, on 5 November 1893 [although the *atto di chiamata* indicates 16 November], to Vincenzo Covelli and Agata Brancatisano. Though they never married, Vincenzo and Agata had four sons and one daughter. The first son, Domenico, died fighting for Italy in Libya in 1911. Carmine was the second. Giuseppe, born next, died in Australia, and then came another Giuseppe. The last child was a girl, Teresa.

The family were farmers who ran a mixed property — animals, fruit, that sort of thing — and Carmine used to help out. In 1917, Carmine went to fight in the First World War, at the Piave River. After the War he married Paola Laguda, from the same village. Carmine and Paola had four children. The first, Vince, was born in 1917, but died at six years of age, I think of bronchitis. Then came Victoria in 1920, myself in 1924 and Caterina in 1926.

Carmine and Paola stayed on the farm and worked until 1927, when Carmine came out to Australia on his own — the first of the Covellis to come here. On the ship with him were Paolo Violi and Michele Sculli, who were good friends of his and came from the same village.

From what I heard from him, I think he went to work in Tasmania, making railway sleepers. He worked about seven months there, got ill and returned to Melbourne to be with his brother-in-law, Paul Spano, who had arrived in 1925. My father's wife — my mother — never came out.

Carmine lived with his brother-in-law in Ascot Vale for about one month, but as there was no work, he went back to Italy in about 1928. He again worked on the family farm, and in 1929, after just one year back in the country, he had to come to terms with a personal tragedy: my mother's death. At the time she was expecting another baby, but she got caught in the rain and got pneumonia. She was thirty-three.

For two years after my mother's death, Carmine kept working and looked after the three kids at the same time. It was very hard for him, but in 1931 he married another woman from a different village, with the same Christian name as my grandmother: Agata Vigleante. They shifted to Caraffa, where my stepmother came from, and then had another son, Domenico, in 1932.

They kept working a farm there, but he was a little bit behind with the money he owed for the trip fare from Australia and, because of the money he had spent during his first wife's illness, had trouble catching up with the payments. So in 1937, as a means of making money, he volunteered to fight in the Spanish Civil War. At the time Mussolini was defending Franco's Spain and was offering good money to the Italian soldiers to fight there. My father thought, 'I need it. If I live through the war I solve my problems.' Of the war, he told me that the greatest danger was during the first few months of fighting on the front line. He told me his good friends died around him, including his *capitano*, who took a bullet from a machine gun. During the war he served as an attendant, and his tasks included looking after the horses, cleaning the soldiers' shoes — that sort of thing. But after the *capitano* died, my father, who by then was forty-three and a little bit old for the front, was put back in the kitchen to cook lunches and take them to the soldiers — a far safer exercise.

He was away for two years, and fortunately he not only came back alive, but also brought enough money with him to pay off his debts and actually buy more land. He continued to work on the farm and make a bit of wine. He was too old to serve in the Second World War.

Around this time he started to make regular contact with my uncle, Paulo Spano. My uncle had married my father's sister Teresa, who came out to Australia in 1929. My uncle and aunt had five children — three boys and two girls — and one of their sons, Vince, was the same age as my sister Caterina. During the course of my father's correspondence with my aunt, she wrote back to say they would be happy to receive Caterina to marry my cousin, Vince. Caterina and Vince then corresponded, sent each other a photo, both liked each other and married by proxy. When Caterina finally came out in 1948 she married Vince in a church, I think in Ascot Vale.

In 1949, I followed my sister to Australia after they invited me to come out. I had married Angela Suraci in Italy in 1944, but came out my own in 1949. I got my stepbrother out here in 1951, and my wife and two girls, Paola and Domenica, towards the end of 1952. My other sister, Victoria, married a man under similar circumstances to Caterina's, in Sydney, around 1953.

The whole family then got together and decided to bring my father and stepmother out, and in 1957 they got here — thirty years after Carmine's first trip here. Today, three of Carmine's children — my brother, stepsister and I — still live in Melbourne, while Victoria lives in Sydney.

Soon after their arrival, Carmine and his second wife moved in with my stepbrother at a fruit shop and dwelling in Sydney Road, Brunswick. Carmine helped out in the shop, because he was a very good workman and he couldn't stay inside. Even though he was sixty-four when he arrived here the second time, he still got work skinning sheep in Footscray.

After a while my stepbrother sold the shop in Brunswick and brought a fruit shop in Newport, at 54 Charlie Street. And that is where my father died on 21 July 1977, aged eighty-three. My stepmother passed away on 6 August 1991, and they're buried together at Keilor.

86. Francesco Taranto

BORN ALICUDI, PROVINCIA DI MESSINA, 1 APRIL 1890.
DIED THORNBURY, VICTORIA, 4 JUNE 1963.

OF THE THREE Tarantos and two Virgonas who disembarked from the *Re d'Italia* in November 1927, none were related. Yet each of the new arrivals carried the forwarding address of 499 Burke Road, Camberwell — the premises of local fruiterers and confectioners R. Costa and Sons.

Francesco Taranto, it seems, spent little time in Camberwell. Archival material confirms that as of September 1951 Francesco resided at 5 Winchester Street, Moonee Ponds, having been employed for fourteen years as a fish shop assistant for Ibrahim Aziz at 10 Puckle Street, in the same suburb.

The son of Antonino Taranto and Francesca Taranto, Francesco spent his formative years in Italy, before setting sail for the United States in 1908. But Francesco's time in America was all too brief, and after just three years he returned to his home town of Alicudi. There, on 18 October 1919, he exchanged marriage vows with Maria Francesca Taranto (no relation), who would later be reunited with him in Winchester Street.

Five years before Francesco's boarding of the *Re d'Italia*, on 5 December 1922, Francesca gave birth to their only child, Giovanna Maria. Seventy-five years later, on Sunday, 21 December 1997, Giovanna De Losa (née Taranto) told me a little bit more as we sat at the kitchen table of her home in East Brighton:

> My father had three brothers and three sisters: Bartolo (who died in the First World War), Giuseppe and Vincenzo, and Rosaria, Grazia and Giuseppina. The brothers came to Australia (Giuseppe and Vincenzo first, followed by Francesco) and ran a fruit shop in Sydney Road, Brunswick, very close to the Town Hall. Years later my father went 'fishing' for work, and ended up in the fish shop in Puckle Street, where he remained until he retired. He was seventy-three when he died after a stroke in 1963, and my mother died seven years ago, aged ninety.

'The Madman' of Messina

Passport photograph of Giuseppe Taranto, aged twenty-four, 1927.
PHOTOGRAPH COURTESY NATIONAL ARCHIVES OF AUSTRALIA, CANBERRA OFFICE.

87. Giuseppe Taranto

BORN ALICUDI, PROVINCIA DI MESSINA, 7 AUGUST 1903.
DIED FRANKSTON, VICTORIA, 29 NOVEMBER 1992.

BROOKLYN, NEW YORK, is often branded the cradle of America's gangsters. Al Capone was born there in 1899, and it was in a Coney Island bar that his left cheek found the wrong end of a switchblade — thus earning him a ten-centimetre scar and the infamous nickname 'Scarface'. By the end of the First Word War, Capone had served his apprenticeship as a Brooklyn barman and bouncer for the violent hoodlum Frankie Yale.

Meanwhile, in the world's largest seaport, neighbouring New York Harbor, a younger Italian-born Brooklynite was also descending into the murky depths of organised crime. His name was Giuseppe Taranto — known as 'The Madman'.

I knew nothing of Giuseppe Taranto's colourful past when I set out on his trail in late 1997. The first details of his life were gleaned through the Australian Archives' national office in Dickson in the A.C.T. The archives held Giuseppe's original passport, which contained a most revealing black and white thumbnail photograph of the man (shown left).

Giuseppe is depicted wearing a dark, three-piece suit, a crisply pressed white shirt and light-coloured tie. His hair is cropped close to the skull, his dark eyebrows almost meet at the top of the nose and he boasts a firm mouth and broad jawline. Moreover, his dark, piercing eyes are fixed directly at the lens in an intimidatory, 'don't-mess-with-me' manner, and it is readily apparent that Giuseppe Taranto, circa 1927, was not a man to be crossed.

The archives also held Giuseppe's naturalisation declaration, submitted to the Commonwealth on 29 April 1940. In it, Giuseppe stated that he was born on the Aeolian island of Alicudi on 7 August 1903, the son of Onofrio and Angela Taranto (née Taranto). He further declared that after arriving in Melbourne he had lived briefly in the suburbs of Brunswick and Black Rock, before settling in St Kilda and, later, Bentleigh, and that he currently ran two fruit shops in St Kilda's Barkly Street.

Giuseppe also stated in his declaration that he married in 1931 and that he and his Melbourne-born wife, Mary, became parents of a son, Ralph, on New Year's Eve 1932. In response to a question about his previous countries of residence, Giuseppe declared: 'I left Italy in 1918 for New York, America, and lived there for six years. In 1924 I returned to Italy for three years and in 1927 I came to Australia.'

But why?

The answer took some months to uncover, primarily because 'Taranto' is a common southern Italian surname — more than 150 Tarantos were listed in Melbourne's *White Pages* alone.

Compounding my problem was that fact that two other Tarantos — Francesco and Giovanni — accompanied Giuseppe on the voyage to Melbourne. It took me the best part of two years to determine that, while these three men were all born on the island of Alicudi, they were not in any way related.

A series of phone calls followed, to more than forty different Tarantos listed in the telephone book. A number of them living in and around the St Kilda area thought they knew of the man I was seeking — a man they knew only as 'Il Pazzo', 'The Madman'.

On the forty-first call, I finally secured the lead I was after. A Mr Joe Taranto of East Bentleigh told me that Giuseppe's sister, Teresa De Losa, was his godmother. I had not known of the sister up until that point, and later discovered she died of cancer some ten years before Giuseppe. Joe told me that Giuseppe had been admitted to a nursing home in the Melbourne bayside suburb of Frankston years ago and that his son, Ralph, was the proprietor of a shoe shop called Ralph's Shoes in the seaside township of Rye. Directory Assistance provided the number for Ralph's Shoes. I then made the call, only to be told that while the shop's name had been retained, Ralph had sold the business. But the shopkeeper supplied me with a contact number for the former owner. Soon I was exchanging pleasantries for the first time with Giuseppe Taranto's son.

How well I remember the initial phone conversation in October 1997. 'Hello, Ralph. My name is Tony De Bolfo. I am conducting research for a book I intend to write about what became of the 108 passengers who disembarked from the *Re d'Italia* in Melbourne in 1927. Your father was one of the passengers aboard that ship ... what can you tell me about your father's life?'

'They could make a mini-series about my father's life,' came the unexpected reply. Ralph then told me the following story:

> Dad had two sisters. His elder sister, Angelina, whom I've never met, is still living in Union Street, Brooklyn, in the United States. The other sister, Teresa, who came out here, is dead. She married Joe De Losa, a first cousin.
>
> My father had quite a colourful life before he came to Australia. At fourteen or fifteen he went to New York to live with his uncle, who worked in the stevedoring industry and controlled the harbour outside of New York. The uncle got him a job near Union Street, Brooklyn, and Dad more or less worked on the boats with him. In time Dad got his own boat on New York Harbor, which he operated for seven years, from 1916 to 1922.
>
> Dad was there during the period of Prohibition, in Al Capone's day. A lot of smuggling took place on the waterfront

and Dad got mixed up with a lot of the underworld figures involved in the practice. He used to smuggle anything and everything — alcohol, opium, even people — and as a result made quite a lot of money.

Until the Mafia got onto him.

They wanted protection money, and if you didn't do as you were told you were dead. But he wouldn't give it to them because he was so stubborn. So the Mafia planted a bomb on Dad's best friend's child, and not long afterwards went for Dad. But Dad was tipped off that someone was waiting for him at his home in Brooklyn and he went there with a loaded gun. He got in first and shot the guy five times, but the guy survived. It was written up in all the Brooklyn papers of 1922.

In the end, Dad was helped out of the States by the Brooklyn police, and a lot of his money was channelled to his mother in Italy— millions of dollars. Dad returned there for a couple of years, serving in the Italian Navy before making the voyage to Australia in 1927.

He returned to Italy again for a brief period in 1932, only to find that his mother had given the money to her younger brother, who built a palazzo in Rome. I once saw the glory box in Dad's trunk, containing all his 'I.O.U.s' and promissory notes for so many thousands of dollars. Dad's mother did give him some money, which he brought back with him to build a house in Smith Street, St Kilda, as an investment, but he was very bitter about what happened.

Dad became a greengrocer in Australia, but he was also a property developer in the St Kilda and Elwood areas. He met my mother Maria (Mary) Barrile, at the fruit shop. They married in February 1931 and I was their only child. I was conceived upstairs on the corner of Barkly and Inkerman Streets and was named Onofrio (or Norman) after my grandfather.

Dad initially lived at 100 Barkly Street, then shifted to Brighton Street, St Kilda, before building a house at 16 Sherwood Street. I was three when we moved to Sherwood

Street and we lived there from 1934 until 1954. Later he built flats in Blessington Street and we moved in there. For a while he worked in a shop nearby, in Barkly Street.

Towards the end, after Mum had been placed in a nursing home in Rosebud, I took him down to Rye and he stayed with my wife and me for about seven months. But then he developed mental problems, ended up in a nursing home at Mount Eliza. He died there at the age of eighty-nine. Mum's still alive and is going on 100.

Both parents have had healthy lives, never had heart attacks and have come through life wonderfully. Dad was a battler who came here with a suitcase off the boat. He saw the opportunities, worked hard and made the best of things. He came to Australia for opportunities, which weren't there for him in Italy.

Giuseppe Taranto's life is testimony to the quirks of fate. He emerged from a violent criminal career in New York's toughest backblocks to become a respectable old man who lived out his final days amid the relative tranquillity of a seaside nursing home.

88. Vincenzo Di Gregorio

BORN LICODIA EUBEA, PROVINCIA DI CATANIA, 22 OCTOBER 1876.
DIED SCORDIA, PROVINCIA DI CATANIA, 19 MARCH 1943.

VINCENZO DI GREGORIO married Cecilia Vita in Licodea Eubea on 2 May 1902, then Carmela Abata in Catania on New Year's Eve 1938. As you can see from his date of birth, he was the oldest passenger on the list. He was in fact over fifty by the time he boarded the *Re d'Italia*, accompanied by his friend Luigi Giarracca (passenger eighty-nine). The challenge of starting all over again at an advanced age forced him back to Italy some time in the early 1930s.

There is little recorded of his time in Australia, though the physical work required of most of the 'farm labourers', as Vincenzo's occupation was described, meant that his age would clearly have counted against him.

The most interesting sideline of the search for Vincenzo was confusing him with another Italian immigrant, Vincenzo *De* Gregorio. Arriving in the country on a different vessel in 1931, but drawn to Queensland as a cane-cutter at about the same time, *De* Gregorio's 1939 application to bring his family out was rejected. The Commissioner of Police in Ingham, Queensland, Mr C.J. Carroll, in a letter to the Federal Attorney-General's Department in Brisbane dated 24 March 1939, wrote:

> Although nothing is actually known against the applicant here, he is considered a man of doubtful character and was strongly suspected of being implicated in the bombing outrage which occurred at Ingham on the morning of 14th January, 1938, in which Vincenzo D'Agostino died as a result of injuries received. Applicant has no fixed place of abode and is only a seasonal worker.

The authorities of the day believed 'that the murder is the result of a vendetta of long standing, and may be connected with the deaths of two other Italians in 1935 and 1936'.

Unfortunately this intriguing character was not the man I was after, so I turned my attention to Italy in the hope of tracking down some answers. After completing a series of phone calls to various listings for the name 'Di Gregorio' in Licodia Eubea, I was finally referred to seventy-eight year old Sebastiano Falcone in Gravina di Catania. Sebastiano was a distant relative of Vincenzo.

In August 1999 I made preliminary telephone contact with Sebastiano, who was more than happy to cooperate. Two months later he sent me a colourful letter, which said in part:

> In 1927 there was an atmosphere of fear rather than hope among the townspeople of Licodia, because life was so difficult for them. However, among these people were two

friends who were enthusiastic about solving their problems. They were Luigi Giarracca and Vincenzo Di Gregorio.

These men were like brothers. They met every day to discuss and exchange ideas, they had a great body of knowledge between them and they acted like two philosophers. Luigi happened to own a beautiful atlas, which one day became the subject of an interesting discussion between the two men. They found a certain fascination in turning the pages one after another and commenting on the countries that they saw.

When the map of Australia appeared before their eyes they pictured a land far away, but full of wonder, full of promise and full of prosperity for those who had gone there before them. It was then and there that the two friends decided that yes, Australia beckoned them — just as she had welcomed so many other emigrants to her coasts.

When their passports were ready, Vincenzo and Luigi thought about encouraging four other Sicilians to set out with them on their voyage to Australia. These men, whose names I can only recall as Antonio, Giovanni, Jacopo and Michele, were all used to working the land, and the land would quite probably be the only source of employment for them.

The day Vincenzo and Luigi departed, their families and friends converged on the small railway station in Licodia to bid them farewell. When the train to take the men to the port picked up speed and billowed its whitish smoke, many tears were shed.

At Messina the two courageous travellers boarded the *Re d'Italia* bound for Australia. The ship set sail and these inland farm workers saw the vast oceans for the first time. They stood in great awe when, between the waves, they saw an enormous whale billowing froth as it rose from the sea before disappearing from view.

The ship ploughed through the waves, day after day, week after week, until they caught their first glimpse, from a distance, of the land they had yearned to see. It is fair to assume they experienced the feeling of finding a land never before discovered, just as James Cook had done in 1770.

For these men, disembarking in Australia was the realisation of a dream. They emerged from the ship with a great sense of joy, and together they put their hands to their lips and blew a kiss to the land on which they were about to set foot.

Once their passports and documents were checked, Vincenzo and Luigi were welcomed by the authorities, one of whom the men remembered as Colonel Fairbridge. Through Colonel Fairbridge's assistance, the two men and their four Sicilian friends ventured to a place called Cockatoo [in Victoria's Dandenongs] and worked a farm that included a weatherboard house and a stable for four horses.

A large portion of the farm was cultivated for potatoes, with thousands of tonnes picked and transported to the merchants of Melbourne. It was hard work, and the men took it in turns each week to enjoy themselves in the big city of Melbourne. In time they got to understand a bit of English, and whenever the single men met a beautiful girl they would say, 'You're very nice ... I love you ... will you come with me?'

But as the weeks and months passed, Vincenzo became melancholy. He yearned for his family and his home town of Licodia and he could not live with the tyranny of distance any longer. On the summer nights Vincenzo looked up to the stars and thought about his home, and he could not hide the tears. Luigi tried to comfort him and persuade him not to return, but Vincenzo could not bear to be without his family any more, and a deep sense of discomfort overcame him.

Soon, Vincenzo boarded a ship bound for Italy and bade farewell to his Sicilian friends in Cockatoo. They firmly believed that this error in judgment had been caused by a weakness in Vincenzo's character. For Luigi, Vincenzo's departure was a bitter blow, but he always stayed friends with

Vincenzo because he knew what sort of impact the separation from his family had made.

Life went on for those men who remained at Cockatoo, and before too long they were producing potatoes of optimum quality in record abundance. After a while the men were so grateful for their success in this blessed land that they thought of themselves as Australians. They had forgotten life in Licodia in the 1920s, because in Australia they had truly found paradise.

89. Luigi Felice Giarracca

BORN LICODIA EUBEA, PROVINCIA DI CATANIA, 5 MAY 1882.
DIED CATANIA, PROVINCIA DI CATANIA, 25 AUGUST 1969.

LUIGI GIARRACCA ACCOMPANIED Vincenzo Di Gregorio on the long and arduous journey across land and ocean, from Licodea Eubea to Melbourne. But neither would remain in the new city for long. At the time of his departure for Australia, Luigi, the son of Domenico and Francesca Giarracca (née Scordino), had been married for fifteen years to Enrichetta Gandolfo, who had given birth to their son, Angelo Maria Giarracca, on 30 June 1925.

In January 1998, with the assistance of Brunswick real estate agent Philip Giarracca, I was given a phone number for Angelo Giarracca in Catania. Angelo, who could converse in English, was happy to talk about his father and the old days:

> My father went to Australia with his friend Vincenzo Di Gregorio, but they only stayed a year or two. They were given axes to cut trees at Cockatoo in the Dandenongs. Vincenzo came back before my father. He was also a family man who had gone to Australia alone, and because he loved his family so much he felt he couldn't stay in Australia any more.
>
> In 1931, following his return, my father went to Cataggerone in the province of Catania, where he became a

country ranger who looked after the forests and the gardens. My father died many years ago and Vincenzo Di Gregorio died before him.

90. Giacomino (Jack) Casamento

Born Lipari, Provincia di Messina, 12 March 1910.
Died Warrnambool, Victoria, 6 August 1985.

GIACOMINO CASAMENTO'S FATHER originally came to Australia for work, and used to send money home to his family in Italy. But after a while the money supply started slowing down, so it was up to Jack, being the eldest of his six children, to come to Australia to assist his father. They were later joined by the rest of the family. Jack Casamento's son John recalls:

Dad came out alone in 1927 at the age of seventeen — his mother had sewed pockets in his underwear to keep his money and valuables safe! He was followed out here by his brother Frank, who also came alone.

I recall Dad telling me that he worked for a fruiterer in Brunswick for a few years just for his keep.[6] He used to go to market and load produce for his boss, and also looked after the market stall or shop.

After a while, my father decided to go to the gym to learn how to protect himself. There he met up with a couple of brothers who were professional boxers. I can't remember their names, but they became very close friends with my father. He got very interested in boxing, loved the sport, and never missed the fights on Friday and Saturday nights at Festival Hall. Above all, he became able to protect himself, his brothers, Angelo, Frank, Bob and Joe and his sister Rosie.

He also loved his racehorses, and he got his owner's and trainer's licence. He had many good country horses over the years. We have photos of them dating as far back as 1939.

He once had a horse called Gay Gambler which ran in the 1954 Melbourne Cup — a real roughy that proved to be just that, finishing last at the odds of 330 to one. That didn't worry Dad, though. He was thrilled just to have a horse start in the race.

During the Second World War Giacomino fought in New Guinea, where he was injured. His first marriage lasted only a short time — he was divorced in November 1944. After the War, on 19 February 1946, he married Jessie Harris, my mother, who is still living in St Kilda, but they were later divorced too.

Giacomino returned to Warrnambool after the War and began trading as a wholesale and retail fruit merchant. At the age of fifty-five, he was clearing boxthorn hedges surrounding a block of land he had bought to grow potatoes as a hobby, when he was struck in the eye by a piece of boxthorn and lost the sight of his left eye. All the same, he continued to supply outlying country towns with fruit until he died.

91. Giovanni (Jack) Taranto

BORN ALICUDI, PROVINCIA DI MESSINA, 13 JULY 1912.
DIED FOOTSCRAY, VICTORIA, 21 DECEMBER 1968.

IN A FRUIT SHOP at 121 Nicholson Street, slap bang in the middle of working-class Footscray, the Lopes brothers go about their business just as they did when Jack Taranto frequented the shop and dwelling more than thirty years ago. Jack's links with the Lopes family formed an important part of his life story. In fact, were it not for their assistance, little, if anything, would be known of Jack, who was a boy of fifteen when he first set foot on Australian soil.

Determining what became of Jack Taranto was always going to prove difficult, due to the fact that around 150 listings for his surname can be found in the Melbourne metropolitan telephone directory alone.

It took dozens of fruitless phone calls before the vital connection was made with a Mrs Taranto of the bayside Melbourne suburb of Brighton. She referred me to her friend, the late Maria Palamara, whom she believed to be Jack's niece. On the afternoon of 8 July 1998, Maria confirmed as much:

> Giovanni was one of three brothers. One was my father, Felice, and the other was my uncle Angelo. My father came to Australia after the Second World War, as I did in 1949, a year or so later. Giovanni died of a heart attack in 1968, my father died in 1982 and Angelo died about ten years ago.
>
> Giovanni was never married. He was a good-hearted, hard-working man, who first worked in Gardenvale for the De Losa family and later in Footscray with the Lopes brothers, always in the fruit shop. But he gambled a lot. He used to say to me, 'Never give me money', but when the time came he got it anyway and lost it all. Years ago he had an accident where he fell off his bike and was hit by a car and they had to amputate one leg. He ended up getting around with a wooden one.

Maria kindly referred me to another relative, Grace Gigliotti (née Taranto), the daughter of Jack's other brother, Angelo. Grace's memories of Jack were few by virtue of her tender years, but they more than helped to build the man's profile:

> When Jack died I was only thirteen or fourteen. I used to see him over in Footscray, always with a newspaper under his arm. You wouldn't have picked him for an Italian. He spoke perfect English and he used to back the dogs, trotters and pacers.
>
> At one stage he started taking Dad to the track. Dad won the first time, so Uncle Jack took him again. But this time Dad lost and he told Uncle Jack, 'If you come back here again I'll take off your other leg.' Dad once said to Uncle Jack, 'If you don't save money you'll end with nothing', and

Uncle Jack said, 'If I ended up without money I'd throw myself under a train.'

As I got older I'd say, 'Uncle Jack, come over', but he'd reply, 'I don't know what your Dad is going to say.' In the last year of his life he finally started coming over, and just when I was starting to get to know him, he died.

And so I turned to the Lopes brothers, Frank and John, to complete the portrait of Jack Taranto. Frank Lopes, whose family relocated to Footscray six months after his birth more than sixty-five years ago, backed up the common view that Jack struggled with a gambling problem. On the evening of Sunday, 12 July 1998, John Lopes, the owner of Lopes' Fruit Shop, reflected on the life of old Jack Taranto:

I know Jack came out as a young lad, the same as my father. He was a mad gambler and that was his pleasure. He was on a push-bike once, on his way to the races, when a vehicle hit him. This forced him to have his leg amputated and he was only in his twenties at the time.

As far as I know he worked for my uncle and aunt, Gaetano and Lina Virgona, at a fruit shop in Union Road, Ascot Vale. He left there around the late 1950s and because he was handicapped it was hard for him to get a job. Eventually he found work at the Spotswood bottle factory as a cleaner, and because he had to walk up and down stairs with a bucket and a mop, he'd get home with his leg practically red raw.

Eventually he came to us at Nicholson Street. He asked if we could give him a room, and we said yes. He didn't pay board, so he worked down in the shop, and he often said to me, 'Leave me in the shop with whatever work you want done.' So I went home and when I came back the next morning the work had always been done.

The only problem with him was that he'd bite you for £4 or £5 for baccarat, and you'd never see it again. He'd beg you for money, more often than not to pay people, otherwise he would have got belted up.

One Friday night he came home complaining about pain in the shoulder blade. In those days no-one knew as much about heart attacks, and you wouldn't think it was his heart or anything, but this particular night he went to bed without any tea. He came down the next morning all dressed up to see the doctor and off he went. But half an hour later the phone rang and it was the doctor, saying, 'I'm afraid I've got terrible news — Jack's dropped dead in Paisley Street.' He never made it to the doctor's. He dropped dead in front of the surgery.

Jack Taranto was just fifty-six when he died four days before Christmas. He is buried in the Western Suburbs Memorial Park in Altona.

Jack died as he had lived — alone — so photographs of the man were scarce. However, on the evening of 10 February 1999, John Lopes rang to say that he had happened to mention Jack's name to his uncle, Arch De Losa, as well as his interest in obtaining a photo of the man, to which Arch replied, 'I've got a photo of him.' Arch and his wife, Eunice, confirmed that Jack had worked in their Gardenvale shop for some years from the late 1930s and by then he was already incapacitated.

'By 1937 or '38 he had the artificial leg. He lost his leg when he was peddling a push-bike to Moonee Valley Races and a car knocked him over, and he was working for someone else in Brunswick at the time,' Eunice said. 'He lived with us at the shop for about four years. He was a very nice chap, but was a heavy gambler. He used to say to me, "Would you mind this money?" and gradually he'd take it all back. But he was a nice man.'

A week or two after our extensive conversation, John Lopes provided me with a terrific black and white photo of Jack (included in this book) with Arch's uncle Felix De Losa in Felix's Gardenvale back yard in about 1938. It is thought to be the only photograph in existence of the gambling man from Alicudi.

92. Michele Segreto

Born Filicudi, Provincia di Messina, 11 February 1909.
Died Camperdown, New South Wales, 27 May 1963.

The following story of the life of Michele Segreto was penned by his only child, Nancy Bartolone (née Segreto), of Five Dock, Sydney, in February 1998. Nancy was only fourteen when her father died, 'so I rely on childhood memories for the most part, and what others have told me'.

Michele Segreto was a quiet man who was comfortable among his own. He was always a little reserved amongst the *inglesi* (English), as he called the Australians in those days.

Many years ago, Michele's father, who carried the same Christian name, sought permission to marry Annunziata La Cava, a young woman from the village of Pecorine, near Michele's village of Porto on the island of Filicudi. Soon afterwards, Michele senior set off for America seeking work, and Annunziata was delighted when she later received £20 sterling through the mail. They married on his return.

Michele senior made many journeys to faraway places such as Brooklyn and Buenos Aires, and the family grew each time he returned. Twins Michele and Virginia (born in 1909) were followed by Gaetano (born in 1910), Fortunata (born in 1912), another set of twins, Maria and Angela (born in 1919) and Teodoro (who died around the age of nine, suffering from exposure after a fishing expedition).

The boys, like their father, were expert fishermen. The distance from their home to the sea was the width of the road. Michele would walk the few metres to sit on the stone wall that separated the road from the pebble beach. He would watch the sky for the weather and observe the stars at night. He knew all about the currents and where the fishing was good.

After Michele junior arrived in Melbourne aboard the *Re d'Italia* he remained there for two months, before he made the move to Sydney for a period of three years. Following the arrival of his father and his younger brother Gaetano in early 1928, they lived in the Mosman area and were supported by Michele senior's brother Antonino, who lived with his wife Giuseppina and their family above their fruit shop in Military Road. In that time they fished in Sydney and along the coast, at places such as Norah Head and the New South Wales south coast destinations of Ulladulla and Jervis Bay.

In the end, the men decided to buy a fishing boat of their own. The boat was in Fremantle, so they made the long trip across the country by train to purchase the vessel and fished in Western Australia. The Segreto men boarded with an Italian family at Pier House, Cliff Street, Fremantle. Through their efforts at sea, Annunziata and the girls in Italy were clothed and fed, and their passage money, which had been lent to them by their *paesani*, was also repaid little by little.

Talk was rife of war in Europe. Michele senior forwarded a large amount of money to his wife and remaining family in Filicudi. He warned Annunziata not to repay all debts at once, as it might be a while before more money was sent. But Annunziata, being a woman of honour, repaid everyone, and the girls survived on what was left. The end result was that the women became emaciated, and took to eating plants they had never before considered as food. Most people on the Italian islands experienced famine in the lead-up to the Second World War.

When Australia entered the War, Michele senior and Gaetano were interned in different camps as aliens. Michele junior was exempt from internment, as he had taken out Australian citizenship in 1938. He was now on his own in Fremantle, and the authorities allowed him only one more fishing trip before the boat was seized back in port. A number of Italians were informed that their boats had sunk, whereas in fact they had been either given away or sold, as the family later discovered through the Fremantle Maritime Museum. And for Michele junior and all the Segretos, this was a devastating outcome. They had actually paid off the boat and were making profits when their livelihood was suddenly taken away.

Michele senior returned to Sydney to be with his daughter, Virginia, Michele junior's twin sister, who had been the first of the family to come to Australia. Together they lived with the family of Michele senior's brother Antonino in Mosman, where Antonino still owned the same fruit shop.

Early in the War a law was passed in Australia requiring male citizens between the ages of eighteen and thirty-five to enlist for military duties. As such, young Michele served in the Citizens Military Force from February 1942 to January 1945. He served with the 21st Australian Works Company in the major country towns of New South Wales.

It was during this period that Michele junior lost his father, who died in the Royal North Shore Hospital in 1943. Michele also met his future wife, Caterina Tesoriero, during his time in the army. Caterina was the sister-in-law of Michele's cousin. In 1945, with the War nearing its end, Michele became a civilian again. He and his new wife lived with Peppino and Giovanna Lo Surdo in Leichhardt. Peppino was a fisherman who owned a boat, and regularly took Michele fishing.

Michele subsequently worked for some time at General Motors Holden in the suburb of Waterloo. He also landed a job at Fiorelli's, an importer of Italian foods, and probably the only business of its kind in Sydney in those days. The company was situated close to Central Station, in Commonwealth Street, Surry Hills.

At some point the fruit shop fraternity on Enmore Road, Enmore, convinced Michele to buy his own business, as his wife had some experience in the greengrocery trade. (She had worked for her brother, Gaetano Tesoriero, in his fruit shop at 185 Enmore Road.) Together they rented premises at 127 Enmore Road, a tiny shop front with a two-storey dwelling above. They made some progress and put down a deposit on a single-fronted house in St Peters, a nearby suburb. This house also served as temporary accommodation for many *paesani* on their arrival from Italy, and they would remain there until they secured their own homes or made other arrangements.

Caterina gave birth to a baby girl, Nancy (myself), on 14 July 1949. Michele was not present for the birth, as he had to remain behind until the shop closed. After a hard day's work, he visited his wife in hospital, then made the short walk to the nursery window down the hallway. It was there that he saw what he thought was his child with two heads (an optical illusion caused by the reflection in the glass); his vision blurred before he fell to the floor in a faint. Michele did not return to the hospital for two days, as he could not bear the thought of facing his wife in his despair at having a two-headed baby.

Michele's usual attire for the shop consisted of a clean white shirt and grey trousers. He also wore suspenders, their metal clasp bearing the word 'Fireman'. Over these he wore a heavy leather apron with different pockets at the hip and chest areas. He kept a lead pencil behind his right ear, and always moistened the tip of the lead with his tongue whenever he needed to write

Once or twice a week, depending on the weather, Michele would replace the big block of ice in the old chest. The ice dispenser was in the back streets of industrial Enmore, and Michele used to head down there, wrap the ice in a hessian bag and wheel it home on the fruit shop's trolley. This ritual ended when the Segretos bought a new Crossley electric refrigerator. Michele always kept a bottle of beer on the top shelf of the fridge in case of visitors. He rarely drank, except in their company, and even then his consumption was limited to one or two glasses.

In 1951, Michele's health began to trouble him. He was constantly tired, which prompted the family doctor, William Ward, to send him off for further tests. Preliminary results determined diabetes and the more sinister complaint of cirrhosis of the liver, which forced Michele to undergo surgery in 1953. This disease is normally associated with alcohol abuse, but such was clearly not the case with Michele. It seems that the common hepatitis virus may have predisposed him to cirrhosis. Doctors advised Michele to take a break after his operation, and he, Caterina and I took the train up to Taree. For two weeks we were guests of the Pergolizzi family, at their old rambling weatherboard with verandahs all around.

By 1958 it was impossible for Michele to work, even with support in the shop. The business and his cream-coloured Holden utility were sold to a Greek family, as was the small St Peters home, and Michele and Caterina put the proceeds towards a grand Edwardian two-storey home on the corner of Newington Road and Wemyss Street, Marrickville. The house was converted into three self-contained flats, with the Segreto flat downstairs and to the rear. The two front flats were let out, so that gradually the entire house was paid off. As there was no welfare in those days, Caterina became the breadwinner and Michele took over most of the domestic work, except for washing and ironing.

Michele still had a strong love of the sea, and set about constructing a wooden boat in his back yard. The boat slowly took shape, but his poor health unfortunately prevented its completion. Michele gradually realised he was entering the final stages of his illness. From the beginning in 1951 his prognosis was never good, but the operation had given him a few more reasonable years.

By 1962 he was wasting away. He would fall into a coma for a week or two and be hospitalised for about a month before returning home, where he would spend time in a room beside the kitchen that Caterina had converted into a bedroom.

Michele finally died in Royal Prince Alfred Hospital on Monday, 27 May 1963, at 8.45 p.m.

This was Michele Segreto's life. His birth had been on a tiny island in the Tyrrhenian Sea. He migrated to Australia at the age of eighteen. Like many others, his concern was for his family's wellbeing. He fished off the coastlines of Australia. He served his new country in wartime. He married a young Aeolian, Caterina Tesoriero, his equal in goodness of character. They raised a child, Nancy, who is grateful to them for all they did. Their union was marked by mutual support through joys and hardships. And Michele was one of the adventurers who disembarked from the *Re d'Italia* on 24 November 1927.

93. Felice (Philip) Virgona

BORN ALICUDI, PROVINCIA DI MESSINA, 16 JANUARY 1910.
DIED ASHFIELD, NEW SOUTH WALES, 28 MARCH 1979.

IT TOOK A little lateral thinking and a slice of luck to determine what actually happened to passenger number ninety-three, young Felice Virgona.

The pivotal moment came on the morning of Friday, 15 January 1999. Having exhausted all other avenues of inquiry, and convinced that Felice did not die in Victoria, I nevertheless turned to the Victorian Registry of Births, Deaths and Marriages for help. Frances Marino at the registry had no luck in locating a death certificate for the man, even though I had been able to supply her with Felice's date and place of birth and parents' names. Taking a different tack, I suggested looking for a certificate for the name 'Felix' Virgona, on the assumption that Felice might have anglicised his Christian name.

Frances called on the following Monday with the news that she could not locate a certificate for a 'Felix' Virgona. But she had made an unexpected find, having discovered a death certificate for an 'Angelo' Virgona, who died in Parkville, Melbourne, at age eighty-five, on 10 February 1983 after fifty-five years in this country. Significantly, Angelo's father and mother bore the same names as Felice's mother and father. I concluded that this could be Felice's brother. The certificate also stated that Angelo was married to Annunziata Lopes, who died at age ninety-one on 17 December 1997 and was buried with him at Cheltenham

Cemetery. Together they reared four children: Felice, Maria, Giuseppina and Giuseppe. These names dramatically narrowed the field in my search for surviving relatives.

Believing all along that Felice had lived and died outside Victoria, I hadn't bothered to contact each of the hundred or so Virgonas listed in the Melbourne *White Pages* — and how wrong I had been. For I now knew that all of Angelo's offspring were quite probably alive and living in Melbourne. So I hurriedly returned to the phone book and promptly found a number for an 'F. Virgona' in East Bentleigh.

After a couple of rings, a lady named Marie answered the phone. She explained that her husband's name was Felice, that he was indeed the son of Angelo Virgona and the nephew of Felice (or Philip) Virgona — the elusive passenger of the *Re d'Italia*. Marie explained that Philip Virgona had lived and died in Sydney, but was survived by his Australian-born wife, Ollie, who was now in her eighties and still living there quietly with her daughter.

Marie revealed that Philip was one of seven children, four brothers and three sisters. The others were Maddalena, who died in Melbourne; Francesco, who emigrated to Argentina but then returned to Italy to live out the rest of his days; Maria, who lived and died in Melbourne; Emanuele, who died in Sydney; Angelo, who of course died in Melbourne; and Angela Mirabile (née Virgona), who was still alive at eighty-six and living with her daughter Grace in the Melbourne suburb of Moonee Ponds. I made contact with Angela, who recounted the following tale:

> There was a lot of farming where we came from on the island of Alicudi — cows, wine and *capperi* (capers). I remember everyone worked their own farms by hand, as there was no electricity. I remember picking olives, grapes and capers — hard work, too. Our only break would come when we'd go dancing or do needlework or crochet, but even then the needlework was out of necessity — we made things for ourselves.
>
> I was born in Alicudi and grew up there, but when I turned eighteen I went to the island of Salina, because Maddalena,

my older sister, had gone there to pick peas, grapes and olives, and had met a man and got married. I also met my husband there. His name was Luigi Mirabile, originally from Barcellona, Sicily. He used to prune the trees under contract in Salina.

One of my brothers, Francesco, went to Argentina, but all the other brothers and sisters came to Australia. Emanuele was first, then Felice, Angelo, Maria and Maddalena. I was the last to come here, in 1965. Francesco went to Argentina because at that time they weren't taking migrants in Australia. When Australia opened up there was no work in Alicudi. Everyone said Australia was a good place, so we came here for a better life.

Down through the years the brothers and sisters always corresponded between Italy and Australia. I got most of my letters from Angelo and Maria. Felice — or 'Philip', as he was known here — married an Australian woman, and made little contact with Italy after my mother died. My father had died young, when I was only twelve, and my mother died around 1950, aged seventy-two. My mother had come to Salina to be with me after my father died, and although I always expected to see Felice and my other brothers and sisters one day, my mother never expected to see her children again.

Emanuele, who never married, originally worked in fruit shops around Melbourne, but later lived and worked on a farm in New South Wales. Eventually Felice joined him there. He then married Ollie, an Australian woman, which in those days caused problems for both families. But they had four sons and a daughter, and they were together for more than sixty years.

Felice was a down-to-earth man; he never had any anger. He was easy-going and he helped everybody. He cooked *spaghetti* every Sunday, and he liked to smoke, drink coffee and gamble. He became more of an Australian than an Italian, and he was very close to his children. Like all his brothers and sisters, he was happy with the way it all worked out.

I then traced Philip's widow, Ollie Virgona, living with her daughter Mary (Maria) Jarvis (née Virgona) and Mary's husband Barry in Bradbury, New South Wales. Mary added to the story:

> I'm afraid I don't know about his early years, because he never talked much about them. He was only fifteen or sixteen when he came here, and as far as I know he was always in Sydney. He was a chef in those early years, but whether he went straight into it I'm not sure. He certainly worked in the factories. He worked at a tin factory called Gason Hughes, another near the Children's Hospital in the city, and the last job he had was at Nestles at Five Dock, working the machines. He was there a few years until his retirement at age sixty-five. He died at sixty-nine of cancer, twelve months after he had a lung removed.
>
> The marriage prompted a split between Mum and her father, and he disowned her and all the kids. There was a bit of racial tension then. I even remember going for jobs and having people look at my name and ask if I could speak English, when that was all I could speak.
>
> But Dad's side of the family accepted Mum quite well, and together they raised four boys and a girl — Felice junior, born in 1939; Maria (me), born in 1940; then Ron, born in 1943; Robert, born in 1945; and Alan, born in 1950.
>
> Dad was a very gentle man, and he had only one bad habit. He was a bad gambler, and he used to bet on horses, dogs, anything. So bad was this sickness that Mum went out to work to support him. For the most part, though, Dad was a normal, hard-working fellow who was always there for his kids. And he always cooked lovely Italian meals on a Sunday.
>
> He died at home in Central Road, Ashfield. I believe he was happy with the way his life worked out. He was always there for his kids.

Two days later, Mary arranged for me to speak with her mother, who had been battling ill health for some time. Despite this, Ollie Virgona was pleased to be given the opportunity to say a few words.

> Philip was a good man, a nice man, and he worked hard. He was very young when he came to Australia, and he could already speak English well by the time we met. I first met him in a fruit shop in Bankstown run by relatives on Dad's side, known as Lopes. We married in Ashfield and lived in Ashfield. He was a beautiful man and I miss him dearly.

Ollie Virgona died in Campbelltown Hospital on 21 May 2001, aged eighty-three.

94. Angelo Virgona

BORN ALICUDI, PROVINCIA DI MESSINA, 15 APRIL 1913.
DIED PARKVILLE, VICTORIA, 27 JULY 1983.

GIVEN THE HUGE number of Virgonas and Tarantos listed in the Melbourne metropolitan phone book, it always seemed logical that if I persisted in making calls invariably I would eventually find a match. So it was in my search for what became of Angelo Virgona, who, as it happened, was in no way related to the other Virgona aboard the *Re d'Italia*, Felice (passenger ninety-three).

In July 1998, after a succession of fruitless phone calls, I was finally referred to a Mr Taranto of East Keilor. Mr Taranto indeed remembered the man I was looking for. 'He lived in De Carle Street, Brunswick and he never married,' he told me. 'He lived alone and he battled with cancer. I used to go around to "Uncle Ange's" place to keep him company. To give you an idea of how long ago it was, I used to take around a $7.99 bottle of Remy Martin to help him ease the pain. The doctor said he wouldn't last till Christmas, but he lasted four of them. He has another brother, Frank Virgona, still going strong in Mornington.'

At the time old Frank was basking in the warmth of the Alicudi sun on his annual trip home for the summer, so in the interim I turned my attentions to a man named Tony Alessi. Tony, I was told, had been a great friend of Angelo's. His daughter, Donna, told me the following:

> Dad was really close to Angelo. Dad owned a fruit shop in Moreland Road, Coburg, and Angelo lived around the corner at 12 De Carle Street. Angelo used to go to the shop and help out.
>
> He didn't have a lot of family. His wife passed away many years before he did and he was alone a lot, so Dad, Mum, my sister and I went over there all the time to look after him ... and he was really good to us. He was a tall man, but I think he was a smoker and he was very thin and very frail. So frail, in fact, that he had to put extra holes in his belt to hold his pants up. He was a very gentle man.

Tony Alessi had similar feelings for his old friend:

> Angelo's wife died five years before he did, and I began to see more of him from that time on. He was a pensioner then, and whenever he was by himself he'd come to the shop to give me a hand. Otherwise he'd take me to my place and we'd have something to eat. And I began to call him 'Uncle'.
>
> I had actually first met Angelo thirty-five years ago, when he worked for my brother in a fruit shop in Sydney Road, Brunswick. I bought my fruit shop in 1965, and he started coming in there about 1976.
>
> Angelo was a true gentleman. In fact there was only one thing wrong with him: his gambling. He liked baccarat and the horses. He also smoked cigarettes until the minute he died. I used to say to him, 'Uncle, please don't smoke', and he'd say, 'Too late now.'
>
> He never said much about the old days in Alicudi, and he never went back. I've been back a few times, and I used to say to him, 'Do you want to come with me?' But he'd always say, 'I've

got no-one left there, why go back?' Angelo never looked back, and he was never one for tomorrow either. He always lived for the day and he was very happy with his life in Australia.

Every Wednesday I used to take him fishing off the pier at either Flinders or Portsea. In the end, he used to say to people there, 'This is my son.'

After his wife died, I began to pay all the bills that came to his house, but I didn't mind. Then one day Angelo rang me and said, 'Nephew, what I have left belongs to you.' He left me his house in his will, which I later sold, and I looked after his funeral arrangements. He was that close to me.

Just before he died, Angelo expressly asked that only one or two people come to his funeral — myself and another friend, Tony Taranto. He was cremated at Fawkner, that was it. I miss him deeply.

On a January morning in 1999, I made the trek to the home of Angelo's surviving brother, ninety-one year-old Frank Virgona, in Alfred Street, Mornington. When I phoned Frank to arrange the meeting, he told me, 'I'm usually down at the casino, but I'll stay home if you come down.'

I arrived at Frank's modest home to find the front door ajar, but I got no response to my repeated knocking and bell ringing. A curious neighbour, sensing my predicament, told me to enter the house regardless, all the while telegraphing my arrival by calling Frank's name. I proceeded through the front door, advanced down the hallway, all the while calling, 'Francesco! Francesco!' I got to the end of the hallway, in time to see the old man awake from slumber in his bedroom and only too happy to greet me.

Frank sat me down in his kitchen and proceeded to talk to me about his life. He mentioned how, for the past sixteen years, he had spent six-monthly intervals in both the Victorian and Sicilian summers, and had never seen a winter as a result, which was a good thing as he suffered from bronchitis. He then told me about Angelo and the Virgona family:

There were ten children in the family — five girls and five boys. Each was born two years apart, in sequence — girl, boy, girl, boy, girl, boy, and so on. There was no life in Italy in those days. There was not enough to eat, it was very bad — mother and father and ten children in a small room.

I was thirty years old when I came to Australia in 1937. My first job was for Giovanni Taranto, who had a fruit shop in Rose Street, Essendon. I was there for ten years. I had already married Giovanna Taranto in Italy and she joined me in Australia in about 1950 or '51. She only died two years ago.

Angelo was a big gambler. He was a nice man, well liked. He never married and had no children.

The Little Bird of Lipari

*I wasn't afraid at all on the voyage — it was an
adventure, the chance to do something. After a while
I started to miss my mother. I thought that if I could get
work, I'd go back to see her. I used to say, 'I wish I was
a bird — I'd fly back.' But I never went back.*

— Annunziata Faralla, 1997

Annunziata Picone at nineteen years of age, just prior to her making the voyage on the
Re d'Italia. This photograph appeared on her vaccination paper.
PHOTOGRAPH COURTESY TONY AND MARIA ZIINO, MILL PARK, VICTORIA.

95. Annunziata (Nancy) Faralla (née Picone)

BORN PIANOCONTE DI LIPARI, PROVINCIA DI MESSINA, 2 FEBRUARY 1908.
DIED EPPING, VICTORIA, 6 JULY 1998.

ANNUNZIATA FARALLA (NÉE PICONE) was nearing her ninetieth birthday
when I first met her. Apart from my own relatives, she was the first
passenger I had been fortunate enough to meet face to face. A fortnight
earlier, I had attended the funeral of passenger number seventy-seven,
Francesco Lanza, whom, with the exception of an all-too-brief phone
conversation the day before he died, I never actually had the chance to
meet.

In the days after Francesco's funeral in the western Melbourne suburb of
Gladstone Park, I took up the search for Annunziata, unearthing forty-six
listings in the Melbourne metropolitan telephone book for her maiden

name of 'Picone', and was becoming resigned to pursuing a series of fruitless but interesting leads. For example, a Mrs Grace Picone revealed that her father-in-law, Giuseppe Picone, had migrated to New Zealand on the strength of an ill-fated sponsorship. 'He was only thirteen then and the family who sponsored him treated him like a slave ... so he fled to Australia, only to be taken by the Australian government and sent back to Italy,' she told me.

A few phone calls later I made contact with a man named Angelo Picone of the southeastern Victorian suburb of Wheeler's Hill. Remarkably, Angelo revealed that he had attended Christian Brothers College, St Kilda, an inner-suburban secondary school, with a second cousin of mine, Peter De Bolfo. Incredibly, he added that the woman I sought, Annunziata Picone, was in fact his *zia* (aunt). He told me that prior to the Second World War, Annunziata had arranged for the passage to Australia of her younger brothers, John and Angelo senior — the latter being his father.

Furthermore, Angelo told me that Annunziata was still alive. He told me that she could be found living quietly in the northern suburb of Bundoora — barely ten minutes' drive from my home! Angelo explained that Annunziata was in the care of her daughter, Maria, and son-in-law, Tony Ziino. He gave me the contact number, and a phone call later, Maria was on the line.

Maria told me that I had come to the right place. She informed me that her mother's ninetieth birthday was approaching on 2 February, and that her family was planning a quiet get-together to mark the occasion. 'She's got a good memory and I'm sure she'd be happy to talk about the ship. If you had rung last night you would have got Annunziata here, but she was today admitted to extended care for a week.'

Having been so close and yet so far from Francesco Lanza, and fearful of Annunziata's declining health, I begged Maria to allow me to visit her mother that very afternoon.

Maria, a gentle lady, happily volunteered Annunziata's temporary residence: Room 203, Zone Two of the Kath Atkinson Wing of Bundoora Extended Care, 1231 Plenty Road, Bundoora.

On that same afternoon, Friday, 17 October 1997 — armed with a copy of the passenger list and a photo of the *Re d'Italia* — I arrived at the wing and explained my motives to one of the orderlies. Moments later I was ushered into a television viewing room where a number of old people were gathered, including one lady sitting in a chair with her back to me.

This, said the orderly, was Annunziata Faralla.

What was most obvious to me at that moment was the full head of tight-knit white curly hair. I remember walking towards her, introducing myself to her and showing her the photograph, asking, 'Annunziata, do you recognise this ship?'

'The *Re d'Italia*,' came the swift reply.

Annunziata's eyes twinkled, which suggested to me that she would be only too happy to recount her precious memories of her long life. She rose to her feet and retired to her room. She took her place by the bed and began to tell me her story:

> I was born in Pianoconte di Lipari in 1908 to Angelo and Grazia Picone (née Biviano), and was one of ten children in the family. Two brothers are still living in Melbourne, and some are still living in Italy. I remember when I was young I used to go with the other girls and have a good time, but later on I worked, and I only had work on my mind. So I didn't want to stay there.
>
> I was the first of my immediate family to come here. I left because there was too much work and I was always at work in the house. I was the housekeeper, I had to look after the children and I had to do everything. My father and mother had a farm. They grew wheat, grapes for wine, vegetables for minestrone, everything. They wanted me to work on the farm, and things like that, too, but I didn't want to do everything, I wanted to get out a bit more [*laughs*].
>
> I'll tell you the story about why I left. One day they made me work, and I said, 'No, I'm not going to stay here.' Mother went crook, and gave me so many slaps in the face. I said to her, 'I suppose I was naughty, and I shouldn't do that to you, Mother, but you make me do that sometimes.' And I

remember like it was yesterday saying to her, 'Don't you cry for a lost friend.'

A few days later, Annunziata's daughter Maria told me about the fate that had befallen her mother in the seven decades since her arrival:

> Mum worked for some people as a housekeeper in St Kilda. After a while they got her work in a fruit shop, and she worked for them for a few years until she met my father. Mum married my father, Giuseppe Faralla, who was born in Vulcano, Lipari, in St Ignatius' Church, Richmond, on 11 March 1931.
>
> My older brother, Angelo, was born on 8 November 1931. I was born in 1933, and another brother, Giuseppe, was born in '35. Before we were born Mum and Dad had moved to a fruit shop in Malvern. Afterwards they moved to another fruit shop in High Street, Northcote, and they were there a few years before they moved to another fruit shop in Victoria Street, Abbotsford.
>
> My father was called up for military service for four and a half years during the Second World War. He was first based in Sydney, and then went to New Guinea, but when he got very sick with malaria and dermatitis he was brought back to Sydney. From Sydney they brought him back to the Heidelberg Repat, and when he recovered we brought a shop in Station Street, Fairfield, which we ran for eighteen years.
>
> Mum and Dad then bought a place in Montgomery Street, West Heidelberg, on the corner of Francis Street, and lived there for twenty-five years. Dad passed away fifteen years ago at seventy-four, and Mum came to live with me in Bundoora.

Annunziata lived out her final years with dignity in the care of Maria and Tony Ziino at their Bundoora home, which was where my future wife Kate and I paid her a visit a week or so later on the afternoon of Saturday, 25 October 1997.

That afternoon, Annunziata sat peacefully by the sunroom window gazing out into the lovely garden and reflecting on her life. Later, she showed me the beautifully embroided pillowcases she had crafted with needle and thread to help pass time during the long journey aboard the *Re d'Italia*. Before we bade one another farewell, Kate photographed Maria, one month short of seventy years since she had disembarked from the old steamship.

Annunziata's passport photo of 1927 portrays the determined, fresh face of a headstrong and independent nineteen-year-old woman. My wife's photograph of 1997 reveals the softened face of an eighty-nine year old lady, marked with the lines and wrinkles of fortune's slings and arrows, but remarkably unchanged after a full and happy life.

Annunziata (Nancy) Faralla (née Picone) died on 6 July 1998. Her funeral took place at St Damian's Catholic Church in Bundoora, where the late Father Gerry Briglia reflected on a long life well lived. Annunziata was buried with her late husband, Giuseppe Faralla, in the Melbourne General Cemetery.

96. Sebastiano Speranza

BORN LIPARI, PROVINCIA DI MESSINA, 26 APRIL 1909.
DIED TARCUTTA, NEW SOUTH WALES, 17 MAY 1972.

THE INTRICATE PUZZLE of Sebastiano Speranza's life was unravelled with the support of his brother, Camillo (Charlie), and sister, Vincenza Marmora, now living in the Sydney suburb of Castle Hill. (Coincidentally, passenger 102, Giuseppe Famularo, attended her wedding to Lucio Marmora in 1951.) She told me, 'His parents' names were Salvatore and Maria Grazia (née Paino), and he was one of nineteen children, ten of whom survived into adult life. The others were Maria (born in 1905), Maddalena (born in 1907), Giuseppe (born in 1914), Sara (born in 1916), Annunziata (born in 1919), Angelina (born in 1920), Camillo (born in 1924), Catena (born in 1931) and Vincenza, me (born in 1933).

'He was a lifelong supporter of the Fitzroy Football Club and would always listen to the footy on the radio. He would go to his shop early to get his work done so he could listen to the game.'

Sebastiano's granddaughter, Angelina, was also very helpful, after I had been introduced to her in remarkable circumstances. It happened at the Northcote home of her mother-in-law, Yvonne Mogorovich, whom I had sought for assistance in compiling the life story of another passenger, Luigi Stella (number fifty-two). Yvonne was casting an eye over the passenger list when she came upon Sebastiano's name and declared, 'His granddaughter is Angelina Mogorovich, my daughter-in-law!' Moments later, Angelina walked in the door and we were introduced.

Angelina referred me to her father, Salvatore (Sam) Speranza, whom she said would best be able to help. I phoned Sam and we arranged to meet at my Preston home. On the afternoon of Friday, 5 September 2001, Sam told me the following story:

> My father was only eighteen when he came to Australia from Lipari. I remember him telling me about the old days. He told me that he once accidentally shot himself in the leg on Vulcano, another of the Aeolian Islands, and he carried a big scar. He also told me that he had a girlfriend there, but she later married a wealthy miner on the island.
>
> More than anything else, it was a sense of adventure that brought my father to Australia. His sponsor was his older sister, Maria, who had arrived one or two years before, but it was his uncle, Vincenzo Paino, who helped fund his fare. I know that it took Dad a good two years to pay the fare back.
>
> I don't know whom Dad worked for at the beginning, but I know he cleaned out the stables behind Uncle Vince's fruit shop. Uncle Vince was also a masseur for the Fitzroy Football Club, who probably rubbed down every Fitzroy premiership player, and it was he who got Dad involved with the Fitzroy Lions. Not many people would know that Dad had two great loves — Fitzroy and opera.

He was a dedicated follower of opera and I can remember, from when I was knee-high to a grasshopper, the old H.M.V. gramophone with the big horn on top, on which he played every recording of Enrico Caruso, Richard Tauber and Beniamino Gigli. He used to sit there for hours listening to those recordings, and it was a toss-up between Fitzroy and opera as to which was his favourite.

Dad began working with his sister Maria and her husband, Dominic Raffaele, at their fruit shop in Brunswick Street. While he was there he met his first wife, Marj MacPherson (or MacPhee), who was a Fitzroy person all her life. They were together until 1935 or '36, during which time Marj gave birth to a daughter, Maria Grazia.

Dad separated from Marj and took up with my mother, Jean Florence Ford, whose ancestors were among the first settlers of the Victorian town of Benalla. At this time, around 1936, Dad got a fruit shop in Collingwood, on the corner of Johnston and Palmer Streets, and I was born there in 1937, a year before my sister Ange and six years before my brother Frank. Dad named the shop after me. It was called Sam Hope's Fruit Shop ('Hope' being the English translation of 'Speranza') and the name remained above the shop right up until the 1990s.

Later, Dad began to run another fruit shop in Station Street, Fairfield. I remember one night two blokes from the Commonwealth Investigation Branch turned up at the shop and said to Dad, 'If you're willing to pay £50 you can carry on normally and won't be interned.'

But Dad was a stubborn man. He told them where to go, and a few days later was advised by representatives of the Commonwealth to get rid of everything, including the new family house in Rathmines Street. In the meantime we were told to remove the numberplates from his van in a garage on Station Street and take them to the police station to deregister the van. Dad was then accompanied by officers on an old steam train bound for an internment camp in Beaufort. He was able to settle us into a house in Beaufort before presenting himself to the camp.

On school holidays I used to visit my father at the camp. He was in there with about 350 men, all Italian internees. All of them were well fed and well looked after, and they got on well with the person taking care of them. There was a mess hall for everybody, and every man had his own one-man tent with a little wash pan outside, which was always iced over in the mornings.

Now and then, perhaps two or three times, the men got time off from the camp. A lot of them followed Dad to our new house — men like Arturo Mennia, old Mr Laurechello, Matteo with the one arm and Tom Rinaldi. They'd spend some time at the house, then head down to the local pub and have a couple of drinks before returning to the camp.

In the camp they used to fell trees, cut them up for firewood and freight it down to Melbourne. They used to get five shillings a ton. In the last few months of his internment, Dad accidentally put an axe through his leg and spent some time in Ararat Hospital.

Dad was interned for about two years. A month or two after Italy surrendered, he and all the other men were released. Following his release, Dad arranged to take over a fruit shop in Bridge Road, Richmond, and not long afterwards, the family went back to Melbourne in a furniture van we had hired from a removalist.

We were there a couple of years before Dad and Mum separated, which in turn split up the kids. Mum shot through with Ange and Frank, while Dad took me and my half-sister Maria, the daughter of Dad and Marj. The last time I saw my Mum was when I was ten years old. I found out she was living in Rushworth, up near Echuca, and I got on the train to see her.

Dad and I lived for a time in Church Street, Richmond, while Maria lived with Dad's sister, Maria — Aunty Mary, as we called her — in Gillies Street, Fairfield. About six months later he rented a room above a shop in Bay Street, Port Melbourne, where his aunt and uncle had a fruit shop across the road.

The War had sent Dad broke. He had just enough money to get us into the house in Richmond and he was just beginning to pick up the pieces when he separated from Mum. The separation had its sequel in court, which cost Dad a lot of money, and on top of that he had one hell of an argument with his uncle, Vince Paino, which left the both of them mortal enemies for quite a while. But Dad was the type of person who asked for help from no-one. He stood alone, he was independent. I'm the same, but my half-sister Maria, with whom I was very close, found the time very hard.

He then went to work for Lever and Kitchen, making soap powder in a factory, and he worked there for about a year and a half. Some time later he bought a shop in Johnston Street, Collingwood, two doors down from Hoddle Street heading towards the station. He got rid of that shop after my half-sister Maria suffered a nervous breakdown.

The family then relocated to 91 Kepell Street, Carlton, around 1947. During our time there, Dad worked for a man named Cincotta in his de Graves Street fruit shop in the city. Dad helped Mr Cincotta with the buying of produce at market, and it was at this time, around the age of ten, that I began to help out too. Dad always believed that once you were old enough it was time to work; he never gave me pocket money, so I had to earn it by helping in the shop.

Dad spent the early 1950s working in a shop in Kew. Some time later, he agreed to help a family named Natoli run their fruit shop in High Street, Preston. Mr Natoli had actually suffered a heart attack, which meant that the shop became run down, but Dad got it up and running for Mrs Natoli.

Dad then took up a twelve-month licence to run a fruit shop owned by a Jewish man up the road in Regent, a northern suburb of Melbourne. At that time we lived with Dad at Clifton Grove in Preston. One of Dad's sisters, Aunty Catena, lived nearby, at 31 Roe Street, Fitzroy.

He then bought a fruit shop in the Broadway in Reservoir, which we opened in September 1954. A year later, on the Queen's birthday, he set sail on the *Surriento* to Italy with Aunty Angelina, my half-sister Maria and me. The voyage took thirty-seven days, during which time Maria met her future husband, a Maltese man named Leonardo Axiak. They ended up marrying in Lipari.

Throughout our time in Italy we wanted for nothing, thanks to the hospitality of the people of Lipari. Every door was open to me. If I wanted a motor boat I got a motor boat, and whatever I wanted was there. I was treated like a prince. Unfortunately, Dad had to undergo an urgent throat operation, which forced him to give up smoking and prevented him from heading to Malta to meet Len's family. So I ended up going alone. I'll never forget the day we left Lipari for Messina. Every boat lined up as ours sailed through. That was a measure of the respect that the people had, not for me or my father, but for my grandfather, whom they fondly remembered.

Aunty Ange died in 1959, on my birthday. (I married Elvira Fiume in August 1959 and my first daughter, Ange, was born on 13 August 1960. My second daughter, Nancy was born on 27 June 1966. Elvira and I divorced in 1981. I moved in with Lynette Dunn and her two sons Steven and Paul, in Nicholson Street, North Carlton, while the two girls remained with Elvira. In September 1982, Lyn gave birth to our daughter Lisa, and Lyn and I married in September 1995. The ceremony was conducted at our current home in North Coburg.)

On his retirement, Dad bought a milk bar known as The Lion's Den in Brunswick Street, Fitzroy, opposite the old Fitzroy Football Ground. His retirement was short-lived, because he wanted to take the shop on. He worked there with me for the last three years the Fitzroy team played at Brunswick Street.

We did a roaring trade on match days. Dad and my ex-mother-in-law used to set up a stall out the front and sell up to 150 dozen pies. The Fitzroy players and committee men used to come into the shop too, and we used to help them out. One year the team managed only one win, against South Melbourne, but during this time we still supplied the players with drinks and it took about six months for the club to pay us.

Dad spent his retirement years at 31 Roe Street, North Fitzroy. His uncle Vince, who had helped with his passage to Australia all those years before, lived around the corner, at 73 Delbridge Street.

I once asked him what he thought about coming to Australia and he told it to me straight. 'Sammy,' he said, 'for the first twelve months I never stopped crying, I really missed home.' But after that he settled down, and in actual fact he found his old home town strange when he went back.

In 1961, Dad returned to Italy for another holiday. There he met Maria Leopardi, and they married that very year. A year or two later, Maria gave birth to a girl, Carmelina, who was born at Richmond's Bethesda Hospital, where my own daughter, Angelina was also born in 1960.

I spent time in Sydney during the last five years of Dad's life, during which time he came up from Melbourne to see me. When he came up for the last time with Maria and Carmelina, he spent a week with my half-sister Maria, who lived just a couple of kilometres away. The following Friday he came to my place in Kingsgrove with a view to staying a further week, but on the Saturday afternoon he told me, 'I'm going home on Monday.'

On the Sunday we all went to the home of Aunty Vince, his sister. We also went to spend a couple of hours at the house of the aunt and uncle of Aunty Vince's husband Lucio Marmora, down the road. The following morning, at about seven o'clock, Dad left my house with his wife and daughter.

Four hours later the foreman at my work, together with the production manager, Gordon Vale, told me I was wanted in the office. I walked in to find the local priest and a policeman. I asked them, 'Did my father die, or did everybody die?' and they wouldn't tell me. All I can remember is Gordon turning to me and saying, 'Sam, you must have been very close to your father.'

Dad had been killed in a car accident in Tarcutta. He died immediately after the car veered off the road and nose-dived down an embankment. The sergeant of police and the priest told me that Carmelina, who had been wedged between the front and back seats, was lucky to be alive, and that Carmelina's mother had escaped with a broken collarbone.

Dad wasn't an easy father to live with, believe me, but he was a father who was terribly loyal. And he didn't have an easy life. Every time something good started to happen the rug was pulled from under his feet, and finally, just when he was starting to enjoy himself, he died.

97. Domenico Francesco Giuseppe Chiera

BORN CAULONIA, PROVINCIA DI REGGIO CALABRIA, 26 NOVEMBER 1892.
DIED CAULONIA, PROVINCIA DI REGGIO CALABRIA, 21 APRIL 1986.

THE STORY OF Domenico Chiera's life came to light after telephone contact was made with his daughter, Maria, midway through 2000. In September of that year, from her home in the northern Italian town of Turin, Maria penned a letter, which said in part:

My mother used to say that when Dad left she was pregnant, but Dad had no idea because the ship took more than forty days to arrive in Australia, and then it took more than forty days for Dad's letter to get back to Mum and another forty days for Mum's letter to get back to Dad. So it took Dad nearly four months to find out that Mum was pregnant and the child, a boy, Ilario, was born on 22 June 1928. Ilario died in September 1988.

Dad worked in Australia for four years and said that in those days all he ate was potatoes. Dad was a very hard worker and had lots of kids — eleven, eight of whom survived to adulthood. Some were miscarriages. We eight kids were brought up with a lot of sacrifices from both Dad and Mum.

Dad was only a farm worker on the land. In the first years of the Second World War, he attempted to run a grocery shop, but the War sent him bankrupt. He started working on the land again, not his own, and was paid a wage. Over time, he gave each of his four daughters a house as a dowry.

98. Giuseppe Zappia

BORN TRESILICO, PROVINCIA DI REGGIO CALABRIA, 26 FEBRUARY 1884.
DIED HILTON, WESTERN AUSTRALIA, 10 JULY 1966.

HE LIVED THE first forty-three years of his life in Italy, the last thirty-nine in Australia, and every one of them to the full. This was the story of the Calabrian farm labourer Giuseppe Zappia.

Giuseppe, the son of Domenico and Domenica Zappia (née De Giorgio), was sponsored to this country by Antonio Stillitano, who at that time lived amid the dense bushland of Diamond Creek, now an outer suburb of metropolitan Melbourne. The tranquil surrounds of Diamond Creek contrasted markedly with the rural environs of Tresilico, as his surviving son, Carmelo, whom I located in a suburb of Perth, explained:

Giuseppe was forty-three when he came to Australia, and was a farm labourer until he was seventy-one years of age. In Italy his first job was taking an ox and cart into the mountains to collect wood, which he then sold in a neighbouring town.

Between 1911 and 1912 he fought to defend the Aegean Sea against Turkey, and he also served in the First World War. He also played the *zampogna*, or Italian bagpipes, and the bugle, and he played reveille (the signal to awaken the soldiers in the morning).

Giuseppe's first wife, Carmela Zoite — who bore him three children Maria Grazia, born in 1910, Caterina, born in 1912, and Domenico, born in 1915 — herself died as a result of a very serious Spanish infuenza epidemic that hit at the end of the War. He remarried a year later, in 1919, in Tresilio, to a woman named Annunziata De Giorgio, and from this union came another three children — Carmelo (myself), born in 1920, Giovanni born in 1926, and Antonio, born in 1936.

In 1921, Giuseppe followed his dream to America, but lived there only briefly before returning to Italy. He completed the same round trip in 1925, before boarding the Australia-bound *Re d'Italia* two years later in search of work.

Not long after his disembarkation in Melbourne, Giuseppe opted to make the trek to Western Australia, where he worked on wheat farms, put up fencing and tended to oxen, sheep and cattle. In early 1935 Giuseppe again went back to Italy, but as work was not in abundance he promptly returned, disembarking from the *Montonave Remo* at Fremantle on 24 August of that year. At that time he had no relatives to greet him — only a friend, Ferdinando Gasperini, then domiciled in James Street, Perth.

In a document dated 25 August 1939 and compiled by acting inspector G. Sturcke, Giuseppe was confirmed as being in the employ of Mr T.S. Keefe at Devil's Creek, Mullewa, as a clearing contractor, averaging approximately £2 a week in earnings. 'He has £36 in account current with the Bank Of New South Wales, Mullewa,' Sturcke wrote. Acting inspector Sturcke was reporting to Canberra's Commonwealth Investigation Branch regarding Giuseppe's application for his son Domenico to be admitted into Australia. An accompanying recommendation of the Mullewa postmaster, W. Philips, describes Giuseppe as 'a very hard working and honest fellow, true to type, and spoken well of by several persons in the district by whom he has been employed during his 12 years residence here'. In an earlier letter to the investigation officer, in 1938, Giuseppe had revealed that he had also remitted approximately £70 for the maintenance of his wife and family the previous year. The appplication, however, was rejected.

A report prepared by J. Adams, the deputy director of the Commonwealth Migration Office, and submitted in May 1949 in response to Giuseppe's application for naturalisation, revealed further details. The report stated that Giuseppe had been captured at Geraldton on 21 June 1940 after police had obtained a warrant for his arrest, and that he had been interned as 'a general security measure' two days later. Giuseppe had £6/2/2d. on his person when he was brought to the Geraldton Police Station.

Giuseppe's dossier specified that his internment was based on two reasons: (1) general security, given that he had been 'employed in a district where it is considered that the internee would be in a favourable position to carry on subversive activities affecting the war effort; and (2) the fact that he had been here thirteen years, had ample time to be naturalised, and his family was still living in Italy. But Giuseppe had always declared that he had not intended to apply for naturalisation until the arrival of his wife, whom he had been unable to bring out through a lack of funds.

At some point in 1942 or '43, he was transferred to South Australia, where he spent time in both the Wayville and Loveday internment camps. Giuseppe was a member of the 'True Italian' Movement in Loveday Camp, but there is no record of his having come under any further adverse notice whilst in internment, nor of his having been a member of any subversive organisation prior to his internment. Just the same, Giuseppe Zappia, Australian prisoner of war number 12657, was regarded as 'an Italian enemy alien' by the Western Australian Deputy of Security, who recommended in November 1943 that he remain in internment. Giuseppe was finally released on 23 December 1943, and entrained on 24 December to Perth.

Following the War, Giuseppe continued to work the land as he had done for all those years in Italy. Gradually he was reunited in this country with each of his family members. He survived his second wife Annunziata, who died in 1963. He himself died three years later after suffering a stroke.

99. Giuseppe Maria Lotorto

BORN OPPIDO MAMERTINA, PROVINCIA DI REGGIO CALABRIA, 9 OCTOBER 1895.
DIED OPPIDO MAMERTINA, PROVINCIA DI REGGIO CALABRIA, 20 NOVEMBER 1951.

GIUSEPPE LOTORTO'S ODYSSEY at sea might have ended in Melbourne, but my search for what became of him ultimately ended in Sydney. Having determined that there were no telephone listings for 'Lotorto' in Melbourne, my hopes were buoyed when I discovered a number of listings in Sydney, one of which was for Anthony Domenic Lotorto, who turned out to be Giuseppe's son.

'My father was a bricklayer by profession, but when he came to Australia it was Depression time and he could not find work for his trade, so he cut the trees in the bush,' Anthony said. 'He had to go out twenty miles (thirty-two kilometres) into the bush and cut timber, which was hard. It was so tiring that one of my father's friends asked my father to cut the friend's finger to get compensation. In fact my father did the same thing to his own finger with a hammer. Times were tough both here and in the south of Italy, because there was not much industry or many factories and they relied on the land. They didn't work by clock, they worked by sunlight, and the days in winter were short.'

Anthony later wrote to me, expanding on that period of his father's life:

> ... Cutting a tree back then in rural Victoria was not like it is today. No electric saws or long, two-man saws. He had to use a small axe, which took a long time to cut the trunk. As the conditions were not favourable, work was very hard and money was insufficient, it was hard trying to survive with the money he made (if any), let alone sending money home to his wife and family.
>
> After a few years my father left Australia and returned to Italy. Unfortunately, Tony, I can't remember much, as I was young and my father did not tell me a great deal. But he was a roustabout, and always travelled for better work and money conditions. Sometimes he would travel the world to find work, for example, to France, where he had a sister he stayed with while trying to find a job.

In those early days, Giuseppe lived in Sydney, in Riley Street, Surry Hills, but he left Australia after only three years. 'He came back to Italy in 1930 to be with his wife and family, and I was born in 1931,' Anthony told me. 'I am the oldest surviving of eleven children. Six children, whose names I don't even remember, were born before me and are all gone. After me came Vincenzo (born in 1933 and now living in Sydney), Giuseppe (born in 1935 and living in Milan), Concetta (born in 1939 and living in Sardinia) and Lina (born in 1943 and living in Sydney). My father had been to war and been injured by the time he got married to Vincenza Tripodi. They brought up eleven children, five of whom are still living — one in Sardinia, one in Italy and three in Australia.

'He was in America for three or four years before he came to Australia and he had a brother, Domenico, living in New Jersey. He told me to go to Australia rather than America, because of the Mafia. I came to Australia in 1952, the year after he died.'

Anthony said that for all those years leading up to his father's death, bricklaying was his father's trade, and took him to places in France and Africa. 'In the end he died from cancer. A few years after his death, Mum came to Australia to be with me, and spent ten years here, before she herself returned to Italy. After she died in Sardinia, her body was taken back to Calabria and buried next to my father there.'

100. Giuseppe (Uncle Joe) Violi

BORN SAN EUFEMIA D'ASPROMONTE, PROVINCIA DI REGGIO CALABRIA, 20 JULY 1887.
DIED SAN EUFEMIA D'ASPROMONTE, PROVINCIA DI REGGIO CALABRIA,
9 FEBRUARY 1954.

GIUSEPPE VIOLI, THE son of Domenico and Antonia Violi (née Nocera), sought his opportunity in the lush environs of Colac in Victoria's western district. Giuseppe, along with another passenger, Paolo Violi (number eighty-four — no relation), was amongst many Italians who took up employment on the property known as Glen Alvie, then owned by the local Colac farmer J.P. Morrissy, J.P.

Morrissy's farm, according to a report filed by his solicitors, Sewell & Sewell, for Melbourne's Commonwealth Investigation Branch, comprised

'400 acres [160 hectares] of the best land in the district'. Morrissy clearly valued the Italians as honest, hard workers, for he had no hesitation in advising the Victorian Attorney-General's Department of his willingness to employ them on good wages at a time when work was generally scarce.

Given J.P. Morrissy's obvious standing in the district, it made sense to pursue the Morrissy family in endeavouring to discover something about Giuseppe Violi. In October 1998, I located a number for Peter Morrissy, an insurance agent at Cororooke. My call to Peter proved to be well worth the effort, as Peter was a kindly man who shared my interest in the local area and its history. Peter remembered that many Italians of that era came to Glen Alvie to help grow onions and garlic and that his great-uncle, Joseph Patrick Morrissy, helped provide them with cheap land and lodgings. Peter promised to make a few inquiries of his own and get back to me.

True to his word, Peter called back less than an hour later. Excitedly, he explained that he had just had a conversation with a local resident, Tony Luppino, whose late father was an Italian migrant who often talked about Giuseppe Violi, or 'Uncle Joe', as he was known. Peter passed on the number and I rang Tony myself, and he said he remembered his father telling him stories of Giuseppe Violi from Depression times.

'Uncle Joe used to get to the gate at Glen Alvie, take his boots off and walk six or seven kilometres along the railway line barefoot to the general store,' Tony said. 'He'd walk back the same way with the pack over his shoulder, get to the gate and put his boots back on, all to protect the leather.'

Tony explained that Giuseppe Violi was his mother's uncle and that his passage to Australia had been aided by fellow townsman Giuseppe Antonio Luppino. But he said that Uncle Joe soon returned to Italy to be reunited with his first wife, Domenica Delfino. 'He must have gone back three or four years later. I know that he got back to see his mother and she died in the mid-1930s.'

A couple of months after our initial conversation, Tony rang to refer me to a man named Damiano Morabito, of Heatherton, an outer suburb of Melbourne, whom he had recently met at his mother's funeral. Damiano said that he had a connection with Giuseppe through his (Damiano's) mother-in-law, Maria Flavia Violi, who was born in the same home town of San Eufemia D'Aspromonte in 1904 and who died in Melbourne in 1994.

'He [Giuseppe] passed away in Italy about forty years ago. He came to Australia, stayed about two or three years, then went back to Italy. He married three times, but had no children by any of the wives,' Damiano said. He told me that Giuseppe had a brother, Leonardo, who has since died, but added that Leonardo's grandson, Leo, was alive and well in Calabria. I wrote to Leonardo and in February 1999 received the following response from San Ferdinando in Reggio Calabria:

Dear Tony,

My name is Leo Violi. I am Giuseppe Violi's great-nephew. In 1930 my great-uncle came back to Italy and settled in San Eufemia d'Aspromonte. In this village he opened a grocer's shop and he also had a piece of land on which he sometimes grew vegetables.

He married three times because he was left a widower twice. He didn't have any children. He had three brothers and three sisters, but only my grandfather Leonardo remained in Italy.

In 1954, Giuseppe died in Reggio Calabria as a result of a road accident ...

Yours sincerely,

Leo Violi.

101. Giovannina (Nina) Famularo (née Casella)

Born Canneto di Lipari, Provincia di Messina, 3 March 1901.
Died Fitzroy, Victoria, 25 June 1961.

A SEPARATION of almost seven years was brought to a long-awaited end in Melbourne in November 1927, when Angelo Famularo was reunited with his wife Giovannina and their six and a half year old son, Giuseppe (passenger 102). Little is known of the circumstances leading to this reunion, for Giovannina and her son rarely discussed the past.

As her daughter-in-law Marie Famularo (the wife of her second son Chris) told me, 'Giovannina said she came out by boat and it was pretty horrific, but that was all she said ... she never did discuss it. She just wasn't a talker and it was like extracting teeth.'

Giovannina was born to Cristoforo and Rosa Casella (née Tesoriero) on the Aeolian island of Lipari. There she met and married Angelo Famularo and gave birth to their son Giuseppe just prior to Angelo's departure for Australia in 1922.

Angelo initially found work in the quarries at Essendon and got himself established before sending for his wife and son. On their arrival in November 1927, the family settled at 267 Brunswick Street, Fitzroy, the premises of Angelo's cousin, local greengrocer Signor Palamara. Angelo and Giovannina remained in Fitzroy for the rest of their lives, during which time Giovannina gave birth to two more children — a son, Chris, in 1930, and a daughter, Serena, in 1932. Chris takes up the story:

> Dad came from Lipari, from a place called Canneto ... it was a dot in the middle of the ocean. As far as I know, he was in the army from 1914, and when the War ended he came to Australia for a better life. He lived in Fitzroy and had the 343 and 371 Brunswick Street shops going. Seven or eight years later, Mum came out with Joe. A few years later I was born in Fitzroy.
>
> The family's first house after living with Signor Palamara was at 343 Brunswick Street, but Dad originally set up his business near Edelsten's Bike Shop, further up the street, which was where he actually died. It was a triple-fronted shop, which he used to rent, and it was between Olivers' the grocers and Wurthimes', who used to make methylated spirits.
>
> Dad used to take a hand trolley to Victoria Market and wheel the produce back. In the meantime Mum worked her tail off around the place, but she always had *comari* and *compari* (good female and male friends) to help out.

Giovannina, who was known as a gentle, soft-spoken person, survived her eldest son Giuseppe and husband

Angelo, who died in June 1958 and November 1959 respectively. They are all buried in the Melbourne General Cemetery.

102. Giuseppe Famularo

BORN CANNETO DI LIPARI, PROVINCIA DI MESSINA, 10 MAY 1921.
DIED MELBOURNE, VICTORIA, 11 JUNE 1958.

GIUSEPPE FAMULARO WAS only six and a half years old when he followed his mother down the gangway and into the waiting arms of his father, Angelo. Thirty years later that bond would be cruelly broken with Giuseppe's untimely death aged thirty-seven, which left his penniless wife Rosa to fend for their four children, all under the age of thirteen.

One of Giuseppe's sons, Pasquale (Pat) Famularo, who carried the Canneto ensign with his brother Angelo during their father's funeral procession in 1958, remembers that when the family sold out of the fruit and vegetable trade, 'the old man worked for a foundry in Abbotsford. Over the years they sponsored a lot of Italians to come out, including [political commentator] Bob Santamaria's parents.'

Joan is now living in Sydney and Mary in Perth. Pat and Angelo both live in Melbourne, as did their mother, Rosa (née Barbatano), who died on 4 June 2002. Back in November 1998, over a coffee at her kitchen table in her home in Bulleen, Rosa told me the following story:

> Joe's father brought him and his mother to Australia in 1927. Joe's brother Chris and sister Serena (Sally) were born later. My father had a fruit shop at 305 Brunswick Street, Fitzroy, and Joe's father had the fruit shop further up. I used to see him going past the shop and I first met him years before I married him. We married at St Bridget's in Nicholson Street in 1946.
>
> Joe did a couple of years of army service at the Victorian locales of Puckapunyal, Watsonia and Royal Park during the Second World War. At Royal Park he got

sick through the night and was brought to the Repatriation Hospital, and after that he never went back. He died about four years after he got out of the army. He had a bad heart, so he went in for an operation and he never came out of the hospital.

The day before he died I took our twelve-month-old daughter Mary to the hospital because he wanted to see her. He had asked us to set up a record player to play a particular record for Mary's birthday, and my sister tried to get the record, but she couldn't find it. I remember asking him how he felt that day and he said, 'I'm all right.' He never told me how bad he really was.

The next morning the Alsatian dog who used to go with him to market every day began to howl and howl. When I fed the dog he still howled, which made me think there must be something wrong. I tried to ring the hospital, but they kept telling me the doctor wasn't there, and by the time I got to the doctor at twelve o'clock he said to me, 'Oh, your husband is dead.' I got such a shock.

We had four kids at the time, but I never got any benefit when he died. I asked a priest in Hawthorn if he could help my children. He said, 'Put them in a home', and I said to the priest, 'You go in a home.'

Tony was twelve, Pat was eleven, Joan was five and Mary one, and all I was left with was one lousy dollar. For two and a half years after Joe died I was in a bad way, and I ended up having a nervous breakdown. I could have remarried and had plenty of opportunities, but my kids were more important to me than anything else.

Joe had a hard life. He went to work, he served in the army and he never had it easy. He liked to have his little bet and he played two-up, but he was a very good-hearted and happy man and I miss him a lot.

103. Domenico Loprese

BORN POLISTENA, PROVINCIA DI REGGIO CALABRIA, 28 JUNE 1889.
DIED PARKVILLE, VICTORIA, 1 APRIL 1967.

DOMENICO LOPRESE, THE son of Antonio and Lucia Loprese (née Mardocco), was a married man of thirty-eight when he disembarked from the *Re d'Italia*. He spent his first night in Australia in Melbourne's inner city, at the Gertrude Street address of Fitzroy fruiterer Signor Rosano.

Little is known of Domenico's early life either here or abroad. On 5 August 2000, my friend and interpreter Maria Monaco contacted the Polistena *comune* on my behalf — only to be advised that the *comune* building of Domenico's day had been destroyed by fire in 1942, and with it all the birth, death and marriage records. However, a marriage certificate obtained in Melbourne revealed something of Domenico's later years.

In 1962, the seventy-two year old Calabrian, then living at 107 Peel Street, North Melbourne, remarried. The bride was fifty-four year old Ruby Hickey, of nearby 149 Peel Street, with Daphne Maude Bingham and Daisy May Lauriston the bridesmaids.

Domenico died five years later, and Ruby survived her husband by twenty-three years. Her last known address was 44 Stephen Street, Yarraville — the Western Suburbs Private Nursing Home — where she died at the age of eighty-two in 1990. Domenico is buried alone in an unmarked grave in the Roman Catholic section of the Melbourne General Cemetery.

THE CHEF OF THE MELBOURNE CLUB

What was probably a passport photograph of Giuseppe Sanzaro, circa 1927.
PHOTOGRAPH COURTESY MARIAROSA SANZARO, FRANCOFONTE, PROVINCIA DI SIRACUSA, ITALY.

104. Giuseppe Sanzaro

BORN SORTINO, PROVINCIA DI SIRACUSA, 17 FEBRUARY 1894.
DIED FRANCOFONTE, PROVINCIA DI SIRACUSA, 2 JANUARY 1986.

IN 1926, A year before he set sail on the *Re d'Italia*, Giuseppe Sanzaro exchanged wedding vows with a woman named Palmira Matteucci in Rome.

It was destined to be a brief marriage. The tyranny of distance would separate wife from husband forever, although Giuseppe would ultimately be reunited with his son Alberto, to whom Palmira gave birth less than a month before his departure.

Giuseppe declared his occupation as 'mechanic' upon his arrival in Melbourne, and listed two forwarding addresses — the first that of a relative, Vincenzo Cafra, of the Pier Hotel in Frankston, the second that of a friend, Vincenzo Rossitto, of Gembrook's Rangers Hotel.

Giuseppe remained in Melbourne from 24 November 1927 to June 1935, then resided in northern Queensland from June 1935 to April 1941, and back in Melbourne from then until his departure in 1978. He worked at the Melbourne Club, Collins Street, from 1950 onwards. For a period from July 1953 he lived at 185 Victoria Street, West Melbourne, near the corner of Peel Street. From late in 1954, Giuseppe resided at 11 Crossley Street, off Bourke Street to the rear of Pellegrini's Café, and socialised with some of Melbourne's great Italian chefs, men like Tony Basile and Sebastiano di Mauro.

On 3 March 1955 Giuseppe renounced his former allegiance to Italy before Francis Palmer Selleck, the Lord Mayor of Melbourne. He continued with his duties at the Melbourne Club until his retirement in 1965, before he took up lodgings in a small room at 56 Lygon Street, and later at a dwelling in Queensberry Street, North Melbourne. There, shockingly, he was bashed one day and robbed of his pension money — a violent act that cost Giuseppe partial sight in his left eye and forced his hospitalisation.

Giuseppe later lived with one of his countrymen, Giuseppe Mure, at the latter's house in Piera Street, East Brunswick. Although Mr Mure took good care of his boarder, the bashing rendered Giuseppe fearful of his life in Australia, and on 4 April 1978, more than fifty years after his arrival aboard the old ship, Giuseppe Sanzaro, returned to the province of Siracusa aboard a modern aeroplane.

Three months later, Giuseppe penned the following paragraph in a letter to his dear friend in East Brunswick:

> Life here is very expensive. In fact, it's better in Australia than here. Despite the fact that I'm back with my family, if I were younger I would go back to Australia immediately. Unfortunately I am too old, so it's better for me to stay here.

I had learned of Mr Mure's existence when I dropped in unannounced to the Sortino Club in Scotchmer Street, North Fitzroy, on the afternoon of 26 June 1998. I had regularly driven past the club, but it took a while for the penny to drop that its members might well have known Sanzaro, given that he, like them, had hailed from Sortino.

I walked in armed with my volumes of written and photographic material, and found a group of men varying in ages from fifty through to seventy or eighty, frequenting the bar at the front of the premises. To the rear, women of the same age bracket were laying out hundreds of pieces of raw *gnocchi* by the table-load for what I later learned was the regular Friday 'Gnocchi Night' for the 200 Sortino Club members. The old chef of the Melbourne Club would have liked that.

I asked the group of men if any of them knew or had heard of Giuseppe Sanzaro. Mick Santo, the man behind the bar, said he knew of Sanzaro, and volunteered the name of a local, Giuseppe Mure, who, along with his father, had been Sanzaro's friend. Mick rang Giuseppe then and there, and set up a meeting the following Monday.

At two o'clock on the afternoon of Monday, 29 June, at his home in Piera Street, East Brunswick, the eighty-year-old Giuseppe Mure sat me down in his little lounge room. Mr Mure had made the effort to retrieve a few personal items that were once Giuseppe's — an old walking stick, the filleting knife Sanzaro carried in his coat pocket and a few precious letters sent to him by his old friend. Mr Mure also offered me a nip of whiskey, which we raised in salute to Giuseppe and all the Italian migrants. He then told me this story:

> I met Sanzaro through my father, Francesco, who came out on a different ship in 1927. I met him at a club in Lonsdale Street that belonged to Vince Catalano, from the Aeolian Islands. Catalano owned the place with a man named Barca.
>
> My father brought me down from Koo-Wee-Rup and we went to the club together. It was about 1954 and Sanzaro was living at Crossley Street. He used to socialise with the other chefs who worked at the Melbourne Club.
>
> Sanzaro worked at the club five days a week. I remember him telling me how all the rich men went there, and he cooked *ossobuco* for them. He told me that when he cooked the bones he took out the marrow jelly in the middle, rolled it in flour and turned it into *antipasto* for them. He worked there from 1950 until his retirement in 1965. After that he took the pension, but returned to the same club every day.
>
> In later years he lived upstairs at 56 Lygon Street, then he came to live with me on my retirement when I bought this

place, in Piera Street. He was a good man and a good friend, and the two of us lived here together. He liked gambling on the horses, but one time when he took me to Moonee Valley, I lost £50 and he warned me, 'Don't gamble any more.'

Through the years he kept in touch with his brother, Sebastiano, a priest at the church in Francofonte, in the same region of Sicily as his home town. He also had a sister and a son, but he never kept in touch with his wife.

I remember he was involved in a fight in Melbourne one night in 1975. He was living in Queensberry Street at the time when someone knocked at the door and punched him to steal his pension. Sanzaro was in hospital for a month, and he couldn't see properly out of his left eye. The government gave him $3000 in compensation, but I suggested to him, 'You'd better go home, it's getting dangerous.'

We arranged a passport through an agent and got a medical certificate from the doctor in Lygon Street, two doors from Nino Borsari's place. I was there with him that day, and when he took his coat off there was a huge knife in the lapel with cotton wool on the tip, which he carried with him to protect himself.

Sanzaro spoke very good English, and wrote in English too. After he went back in 1978 he wrote to me saying that he wanted to return to Australia. That was the I last time I heard from him.

Mr Mure handed me a contact address in Francofonte for Giuseppe Sanzaro's son, Alberto. I wrote a letter to that address, only to be informed by Alberto's daughter, Mariarosa, that he had died in 1997. However, Mariarosa remembered her grandfather well and was thrilled to convey her memories to me in a letter dated 20 October 1998.

> ...My grandfather Giuseppe had an eventful life. While still young he went to the United States of America and then returned to Sicily, but only for a short time. In fact, shortly afterwards he moved to Rome, enlisted in the corps of the

Reggio Guardia, and in the middle of his army career he met and married my grandmother, Palmira Maria Matteucci. He had to leave the military corps, because matrimony for these soldiers was not permitted before they had served for a certain number of years.

At this point, without work, he decided to depart for Australia, and left his wife, who was already expecting a son, Alberto, in Rome. Alberto, my father, was then born on 21 August 1928. Giuseppe's wife never forgave this sudden departure, and they were not to see one another ever again. Even when, later, he wanted his son with him in Australia, she would not allow Alberto to leave Italy. Instead, she arranged for his transfer from Rome to Sicily, in the company of an uncle (a brother of Giuseppe), who obtained a job for him. Alberto established himself in Sicily and married.

Alberto always kept in touch with his father Giuseppe through written correspondence. In 1978, my grandfather, old and tired, finally decided to return to his homeland, and my father took him into his house. He arrived in Sicily in March 1978.

Alberto used to go and see his mother in Rome frequently, but she died in 1983. Giuseppe lived his last years peacefully in Sicily and died in Francofonte on 2 January 1986. And that is all ...

Accompanying the letter was a photograph of Giuseppe, which Mariarosa believed had been taken in the United States. Dating from the late 1920s or early 1930s, it shows Giuseppe, complete with suit, tie and hat and armed with a cigarette, standing in a street and staring into the lens.

About a month after Mariarosa's letter and photograph arrived, I was driving up Brunswick Street when I caught a glimpse of the old Cox Bros building that appears to the right in that photograph. I suddenly realised that Sanzaro had in fact been photographed not in the United States, as Mariarosa had believed, but in Brunswick Street, Fitzroy, not long after he had arrived.

Some time later, my wife Kate photographed me standing in that very spot where the old chef once stood, more than seventy years ago. I forwarded the photograph to Mariarosa in Italy. (Both photographs are included in this book.)

105. Patroche Basile

BORN GREECE, CIRCA 1894. DIED ?

OF THE 108 passengers who disembarked from the *Re d'Italia* in Melbourne in 1927, all but one were Italian. The exception to the rule was Patroche Basile, a thirty-three year old married man and a telegraphist by profession, who was of Greek origin.

Patroche boarded the ship at Port Said in Egypt, with sixteen other Greek passengers who would disembark at the Australian ports of Fremantle, Port Adelaide and Sydney.

I made contact with the chairman of Port Said Shipping, Mr S.H. Hassan, to determine whether any record was kept of Patroche's boarding of the *Re d'Italia*. Mr Hassan went to great lengths to assist, because of his own passionate interest in the history of migrants. Unfortunately, he was unable to help. 'I have tried very hard, but it seems that all the records of the old shipping agents have vanished — either burnt or destroyed,' Mr Hassan told me. 'I have gone through the papers of the vessel agents, De Castro, but nothing that old could be found. The earliest records I could trace date from 1962.'

Despite seeking assistance from the various state branches of the National Archives, representatives of the Greek community and even the Egyptian Consul-General, I was unable to secure any further details of the life of Patroche Basile.

THE LITTLE KING

Michele Daniele, circa 1945.
PHOTOGRAPH COURTESY LUISA HAVYATT (NÉE DANIELE) AND RICHARD HAVYATT, CARLTON, VICTORIA.

106. Michele Lorenzo Daniele

BORN PAGO DI LAURO, PROVINCIA DI AVELLINO, 30 AUGUST 1894.
DIED SOUTH BALLARAT, VICTORIA, 3 JANUARY 1982.

BY THE TIME Michele Daniele was reunited with his wife Luisa and three children Raffaela, Giuseppina and Raffaelo in 1934, Australia was well and truly caught in the grip of the Great Depression.

'We had food, but Dad was working from six in the morning until midnight for ten shillings,' his only surviving daughter, Raffaela, told me. 'He used to shoot rabbits not far from where we lived to keep us going, which is why I growl at people now — they're never satisfied with their lot.'

But Michele, the son of a Neapolitan candle maker, graciously accepted his fate in his new country. He owned a horse, pedalled a push-bike and worked a market garden, and until the time he died at eighty-seven, never ventured from the place he had adopted, half a world away from the old land he once knew.

Michele's years in Ballarat had a profound effect on the life of Raffaela's daughter, Luisa Havyatt, whom I came to know in extraordinary circumstances. On the night of 1 July 1999, the ABC broadcast the episode of its 'Australian Story' series entitled 'In Search of Kings', dealing with my research into the passengers of the *Re d'Italia*. At one point during the twenty-minute program, the camera pans down the names of some of the passengers on the list, one of which is Michele Daniele. It prompted the following letter from Luisa three days later:

Dear Tony De Bolfo,

Imagine my surprise, emotion and delight when, while watching 'In Search of Kings', I saw my beloved grandfather's name handwritten in front of my eyes. I could hardly believe it, but there it was: 'Michele Daniele'. It even seemed to me that the camera lingered on his name to give me more time to register. I believe he was a passenger on the ship *Re d'Italia*.

The complete unlikelihood of the event makes me think that I was meant to see your program; what my grandmother Luisa would have called '*il destino*' was at work.

Why was it so unlikely? Because I was far from home in North Carlton, celebrating my fifty-third birthday on 1 July in Ayers Rock at the Yulara Resort with my husband, Richard … what a birthday present it was for me! For a moment, it seemed that my grandfather was given back to me.

My grandpa spoke very little of his early life in Australia and the voyage out. He was already a married man when he emigrated from the Naples environs. My grandmother, Luisa, joined him seven years later with their three children, one of whom was to become my mother. I loved my grandparents very much and they raised me after my parents' brief marriage ended in divorce. My grandparents lived in Ballarat, Victoria, for all their lives in Australia and both are buried in the Ballarat Cemetery.

I think your project to document the lives and fates of the passengers of that ship is a grand and wonderful one which will resonate with many — not just the particularities of the lives but the way in which they are representative of the universal experience of emigration.

It will be a great joy to talk to you in person, should you wish to know more about my grandfather. Is he one of the ones you have no information about? If he is one of your 'missing' it will be my pleasure to make him 'found'. I am eager to know more about my beloved grandpa's vanished life.

I thank you in anticipation of this opportunity and look forward to the publication of your book. To me, my grandfather Michele *was* a little 'king' and you are giving me back a part of his story.

Thank you, and please be in touch,

Luisa.

Luisa's wonderful letter served as a tremendous source of inspiration. Her sentiments reflected the spirit of cooperation and goodwill extended to me by all the descendants and gave me great confidence and enthusiasm to push on with my project.

That night I phoned Luisa to thank her for her correspondence. She told me she looked forward to talking to me more about her grandfather, and promised to do so on her return from holidays. Three weeks later, at the Havyatt family home in Carlton North, Luisa told me the following story:

My grandfather was like a father to me. I was taken to live with him and my grandmother Luisa, after whom I am named, as a baby, after my parents' separation and subsequent divorce. My grandfather was fifty-two at the time and my grandmother fifty-four.

He was indeed a little king for me. He laughed, he sang beautifully. He loved his garden, his horses, his dogs, his shooting, his food, especially fish, and company. He was very proud of me, and especially supported my scholastic achievements. He was determined I would be a scholar, not a singer like my mother, and able to support myself.

My grandfather lived in the one house for all of his life, once he'd purchased 28 Peel Street, North Ballarat, and the land to the rear of the premises, which extended the potential for a large garden. The house was a small, single-fronted weatherboard. In 1958 he built a 'sleep-out'. Our garden had grapes, and walnut, apple, nectarine and fig trees. We grew almost everything we needed for the table. He would say to me, 'Baby, go and pick a salad.'

My grandparents bottled and preserved each year; we had supplies of *salsa*, olives, onions, eggplants and salted fish. My grandfather had a *cantina* (cellar) in which he made wine and *grappa* annually. I remember the sweet, acrid smell of the *salsa* and wine-making.

My grandfather would deliver his vegetables and flowers from his horse and cart. On a separate piece of land he had purchased on the edge of Ballarat he established a market garden, where he grew mainly gladioli. He supplied Craig's Hotel and the Wattle Tea Rooms. He was famous for his Christmas lilies and did the rounds with those, too, when they were in bloom.

In the *cantina* there were rows of wine in Australian beer bottles and Cottee's and Rowland's lemonade bottles — rows and rows. The walls were festooned with salamis and sausages and swags of herbs hung from the rafters. He kept garden snails, which he fed on bran to 'clean them out', and later used for a *sugo* (sauce) for *pasta*. We were also fed on *baccalà* (dried fish) and eels which he caught.

My grandfather was a great lover of life. He did not speak much about the past. He once said to me that life was a process of happy relinquishment. He would say, 'I had the horses, which I loved, but the time came when I had to give them up — I had the accident as a trotting driver that brought a stop to that; I had the dogs, which I had to give up; and I had Italy, which I had to give up. And finally I even had to give up the bike because of my accident.' He had been eighty-five and still cycling all over Ballarat when he was knocked over by a car.

At the back of the premises we had a stable in which I remember sulkies, anvils for shoeing, and all the paraphernalia for looking after horses. Of course we had horses, but only one champion, Bezique, named after an Australian card game. As evidenced by this choice of name, my grandfather integrated very naturally with the Australian community and the racing fraternity. And he always had very strong friendships with Australians. A close friend, Mr Garlick, was a regular visitor until his death, and Mrs Garlick made a weekly visit to my grandmother.

When times were hard my grandfather worked at Ford Motors in Ballarat. The house was simple and there was never much money, but for me it was always a house of plenty. My grandparents' hospitality was enormous. They welcomed the nuns who taught me, my schoolfriends, Malaysian students for Sunday *pasta* meals, Mr Lewis the policeman who came for his bottles of wine, a chimney sweep all sooty and black who visited us regularly, and Mrs Choo, the widow of the Chinese herbalist next door. The door was always open and the table was always half-set.

I was never really aware of the age of my grandparents. They seemed timeless, really, and certainly young at heart. Yet I know that they must have experienced a great displacement as a result of coming to Australia separately. My grandfather had married my grandmother in Italy and already had three children. They did not join him in Australia until seven years after his arrival in 1927. They were a pretty dynamic couple, and I am sure there were strains as well as an abiding love.

A few years ago, Luisa penned the following poem, entitled 'My Grandparents' Cantina' — a celebration of her precious years in Ballarat:

The kitchen smelt of aromatic coffee
and comfort food was Grandma's speciality.

On cold days she would crack an egg
into the salsa bubbling on the stove,
lift it, lightly poached, onto a slice of bread,
cover it tenderly with tomato.

I liked to stab the yolk, still in its bed,
then watch the orange bleed into the red.

Grandpa domesticated alcohol completely —
recycled lemonade and beer bottles for his wines;
fiery grappa looked benign in lines
of cordial bottles labelled 'Cottee's'.

For an adolescent who looked pale
the cure was egg yolk beaten in a cup,
sugar was added, coffee, brandy.
It was a heady way to build me up.

Colds were treated with heated wine;
to sweat them out, my Grandpa said:
the fumy drink would make me dizzy,
once I slid straight out of bed.

Some practices I kept a secret:
the black eels swimming in our basin,
or worse, the bran-fed snails on sacks;
such discretion, mortification,
the price paid for a convent education.

In the dense pergola the grapes gleamed green
bred for a more exotic climate;
they would never ripen to Grandpa's satisfaction
in the watery sunlight of Ballarat.

Yet we dined most gorgeously
on sweet unopened buds in hairy chokes,
the bland flesh of the perilous prickly pear,
dainty fried zucchini flowers.

In green Depression glass containers
imprisoned anchovies layered in oil:
delicate condiments to coil,
drape like flags across vitello,
or simply swallow like small brown swords.

Salt and sweet, memory unable;
nearly as old as they were then,
now I want my grandparents back,
heart-hungry for their table.

They fed me Naples on a plate
but most of all I tasted love.

107. Giuseppe Loizzi

BORN CEGLIE DEL CAMPO, PROVINCIA DI BARI, 30 JANUARY 1886.
DIED CEGLIE DEL CAMPO, PROVINCIA DI BARI, 20 JULY 1969.

108. Pietro D'Amico

BORN CEGLIE DEL CAMPO, PROVINCIA DI BARI, 14 SEPTEMBER 1888.
DIED CAVA DEI TIRENNE, PROVINCIA DI SALERNO, 17 MARCH 1969.

GIUSEPPE LOIZZI AND Pietro D'Amico were married men of forty and thirty-nine respectively when they boarded the *Re d'Italia* at the southern Italian port of Naples.

Giuseppe spent his first night in Melbourne at the home of Giuseppe Vaccari at 90 Queen Street in the heart of Melbourne, while Pietro took up lodgings with fellow passengers Giovanni Pizzato (number thirty-six), Francesco Curcio (number sixty-five), Giuseppe Zappia (number ninety-eight) and the two Frigo boys, Marco (number fifty) and Basilio (number fifty-one), around the corner at 508 Little Collins Street, an address given by Michele Roppo, Giueseppe's brother-in-law.

What became of Giuseppe and Pietro in the days, months and years since remained something of a mystery to this author for many months. The breakthrough came in December 1999, with the assistance of the Adelaide branch of the National Archives. Archival material revealed that both men had made the 200-kilometre trek to the Neapolitan sea port from their home town of Ceglie del Campo in Bari on Italy's east coast, and it seemed fair to assume both men returned to Italy, neither having left a trace in Australia in the years beyond 1927.

A call to Ceglie Del Campo was the next step. Incredibly, Maria Monaco and I tracked down a Giuseppe Loizzi, but knew it couldn't have been *the* Giuseppe Loizzi aboard the ship, as he had been born 113 years ago. However, the Giuseppe with whom Maria chatted remembered the man we were seeking and subsequently referred her to a surviving son, Gaetano.

Gaetano revealed that his father and Pietro D'Amico were in fact brothers-in-law. He said that Giuseppe had three sisters — Grazia, Angela and Rosa — and an older brother, Francesco, with whom Giuseppe had spent twelve years working in America from 1902 onwards. Francesco worked on the railways in Chicago, while Giuseppe toiled in the coal mines of Montana.

'Giuseppe returned to Italy for the marriage of his sisters, then went to war for five years,' Gaetano said. 'He then married Maria D'Amico, the sister of Pietro. A daughter, Teresa, was born in 1920, then another two girls and a boy who all died very young. I was born in 1928, just after my father left for Australia, and Michele was born next, in 1932. Teresa has since died, but Michele is still alive.'

Gaetano informed Maria that his father and Pietro D'Amico were encouraged by the English Consulate to travel to Australia on completion of exams and work with grapevines for a six-month period. 'My father was commissioned to go to Adelaide with Pietro D'Amico to work with vines on behalf of the English government, but it appears the pair first went to Melbourne. The English Consulate in Australia had sought the asssistance of those interested in cultivating vines. My father and Pietro knew about vines and my father could also speak English, having gone to America as a sixteen-year-old, and spent twelve years there with his elder brother. Under the arrangement, the English would cover their families' expenses to Australia if the two men purchased the designated land.

'The men worked the land for six months, but discovered that the venture was not profitable ... the farm struggled badly through pre-Depression times and when the six months elapsed they were told to go it alone. But they couldn't afford to, and in 1928 they both returned to Italy after just eleven months.'

Gaetano told me that Giuseppe and Pietro worked the vines together on the Loizzi family farm until they died. The farm, which was originally established by Giuseppe's father, is sadly now stripped of the vines that the two passengers of the *Re d'Italia* tended to make a living.

109. Santo Lanteri

BORN CASSARO, PROVINCIA DI SIRACUSA, 26 DECEMBER 1905.
DIED ELWOOD, VICTORIA, 8 MAY 1976.

SANTO LANTERI HAILED from Cassaro, a small village in the hills of Sicily. The son of Salvatore and Sebastiana Lanteri (née Tartaglia), he had three brothers and two sisters. Santo's passage to Australia was ratified by a fellow countryman, Paolo Sortino, who by the late 1920s had settled in Cumbagunda, near Deniliquin, New South Wales.

'Dad settled in Robinvale in the early days,' Santo's son, Dr Ray Lanteri, told me. 'He worked as a farmhand throughout rural Victoria and New South Wales during the Depression, when things were pretty tough.'

Towards the end of the Great Depression, Santo opted to move to Melbourne. There he began work as a produce merchant at the Victoria Market, where he remained for the duration of his working life. 'Dad retired at the time the market moved to Footscray. I used to work in the market with him too,' said Dr Lanteri.

In the late 1930s, Santo exchanged marital vows with Maria Cappadona, the sister of Verona Cappadona who won the *Sun* Aria Award, a showcase for young operatic talent, in the 1950s. 'My mother's family were also Italian and they got here a bit earlier,' Dr Lanteri said. 'Maria's family ran greengrocery shops in St Kilda and they had other business interests.'

Santo and Maria raised three children, Sebastiana, Ray, and Marguerite. The family lived in Ripponlea before moving house to

Elwood, where Santo died aged seventy. Maria now resides in the Brighton area.

In 1996, the Lanteri sisters, Sebastiana and Marguerite, made a pilgrimage to Cassaro, the town from which their father hailed. There they met up with an old man who remembered the day Santo Lanteri left Italy. 'The man said that when Santo left, he embraced his mother before pushing her away,' Dr Lanteri said to me. 'I think he just wanted to get away.'

110. Carmelo Menta

BORN CASSARO, PROVINCIA DI SIRACUSA, 13 NOVEMBER 1880.
DIED CASSARO, PROVINCIA DI SIRACUSA, 13 FEBRUARY 1966.

CARMELO MENTA WAS born in Cassaro two days after Ned Kelly was hanged in Melbourne. Forty-seven years elapsed before Carmelo came to Kelly country, to the New South Wales border town of Deniliquin, where his guarantor, Paolo Belfiore, had settled some time beforehand. Why Carmelo subjected himself to this dramatic upheaval at his age is not known, but it must have been reassuring to him that Paolo would be there waiting at the bottom of the gangway at North Wharf.

In August 1999 I turned to the *comune* of Cassaro for help. With the support of my friend and interpreter Maria, I gleaned from the *comune* that Carmelo Menta was survived in the village by his grandson Carmelo, with whom I then made telephone contact. Soon afterwards, Carmelo penned the following letter:

> ...My grandfather Carmelo cut wood in his early years in Australia, but in 1943 developed malaria and returned to Italy. On his return he married Antonia Mineo, and from this marriage came two children — Paolo and Giuseppina. Paolo, my father, was doing his national service when he died in an avalanche aged twenty-seven and a half. He left behind my mother who, at twenty years old, had to fend for a son aged seventeen months.

Being orphaned of a father, I was wisely left in the care of my grandfather and my aunty Giuseppina, who didn't have children, but was married to Michelangelo Tartaglia.

I came to Australia with my mother in 1956 and lived in Melbourne until 1965. My mother died during that time. My aunt Giuseppina died in Cassaro four years ago at the age of eighty-three, and my grandfather Carmelo Menta worked and attended to his family, living until the age of eighty-five ...

Journey's End

It is eight years now since my great-uncle Igino De Bolfo first talked into my tape recorder. That was back in 1994, when my only real intention was to get my own family history on record. But Uncle Nino's story extended beyond the branches of my family tree. It prompted an interest in me to pursue what became of each of the 'kings of Italy' who, seventy-five years ago, bravely bade farewell to family and loved ones — in many instances forever — as they set off on an ageing steamer in pursuit of a dream.

Some realised their dream and some did not, but all of them, for better or for worse, responded to that great Australian ethos of 'having a go'. If I have learned anything from the lives of these men, women and children who walked down the gangway on that spring afternoon of 1927, it's that despite tremendous adversity in terms of culture, language and lifestyle, they displayed great bravery and took fate into their own hands.

I have come to appreciate the resilience of these passengers in times of great hardship. These men, women and children lived through two World Wars and the Great Depression, not to mention the great upheaval involved in leaving their homeland for somewhere new. Australia, for the most part, welcomed them onto her shores, and, for the most part, they didn't let her down.

I have also learned that *everyone* has a story to tell. The secret is to listen, and yet this is often the hardest part. So many of the descendants said to me, 'We used to hear the old stories of the past and they went in one ear and out the other. Now that they're gone, how we wished we'd paid more attention.' The remark naturally disappointed me, but it also instilled in me a resolve to pursue what became of these passengers' lives, in the hope that others might see fit to act on their own histories before it's too late.

Furthermore, through my search I have developed an even greater love for Australia. I am proud to say that I live in a country where people of diverse cultural and ethnic backgrounds in general harmoniously coexist, in a society based on the fundamental principles of democracy.

With the exception of the remarkable trio of Domenico Caffaro, Giovanni Costella and his dear mother, Maria, few members of the *Re d'Italia*'s human cargo scaled the lofty heights of the social or professional ladder. We must remember that these were manual labourers who boasted little in the way of formal education and who took on the jobs many Australians didn't want in order to somehow get ahead. For this, they deserve the utmost respect.

The 'kings' are all gone now, but their legacy lives on — not only within the pages of this book, but also within the hearts and minds of their descendants who, like me, have their forebears to thank for their own share in the freedoms and privileges of Australia.

Throughout the course of my eight-year journey, I have learned to embrace my Italian heritage. At the end of the day I am an Australian who is typical of all but the indigenous Australians, all those whose forebears somewhere down the line were immigrants to whom this great country offered answers.

And I live in a world best described by a wise man named Charles D'Aprano who, not long before he died, reminded us:

> There are many cultures, but there is only one race
> — the human race.

THE COMPLETE PASSENGER LIST OF THE *RE D'ITALIA*

THE RE D'ITALIA and her human cargo set sail for Australia on 10 October 1927, from the port of Genoa, via Naples, Messina, Port Said and Colombo. The twenty-one year old steamer was cleared by customs at Fremantle on 13 November, berthed at Port Adelaide on 19 November and sailed into Melbourne's Victoria Dock on the afternoon of Thursday, 24 November 1927. Her final port of call came four days later in Sydney.

A summary of passengers declared 523 'aliens' — comprising 506 Italians, sixteen Greeks and an Austrian, Julius Lamburger — as having been cleared by Medical Officer Ugo Pagano at Fremantle Quarantine on 13 November. A separate list was drawn up at each port of embarkation. However, the respective disembarkation lists of Fremantle, Port Adelaide, Melbourne and Sydney tally only 507, indicating that sixteen of those originally listed did not make the voyage.

A total of 124 passengers disembarked in Fremantle. (Unlike the other disembarkation lists, this one did not include details of occupation, sex, age, martial status and nationality.) A further 134 passengers followed suit in Port Adelaide and another 141 in Sydney. In Melbourne, 108 passengers, comprising 103 males, three females and two male children, disembarked, all of them having travelled third class for the forty-six day voyage.

The passengers averaged just over twenty-nine years of age when they set foot on Victoria Dock — ranging from Giovanni Giuseppe Costella at just four years, eight months and three days, through to Vincenzo Di Gregrorio at fifty-one years, one month and two days. Of the 106 adult disembarkees, sixty were listed as married.

While the Melbourne list officially records 110 passengers as having alighted from the *Re d'Italia*, two passengers, Anselmo Sist and Carmelo Spadaro, went ashore in the respective ports of Port Adelaide and Sydney and are incorrectly included. Accordingly, they are included twice in the lists that follow. Conversely, Michele Daniele, Giuseppe Loizzi and Pietro D'Amico disembarked from the *Re d'Italia* in Melbourne, despite being included with the Port Adelaide disembarkees.

Of the 108 who disembarked in Melbourne, fifty-nine had originally boarded at Genoa, eight at Naples, forty at Messina and one (the only Greek disembarkee in Melbourne, Patroche Basile) at Port Said.

Of the 106 passengers accounted for, sixty-nine lived and died in Australia. The remaining thirty-seven returned to Italy.

FREMANTLE

DATE OF ARRIVAL: SUNDAY, 13 NOVEMBER 1927

From Genoa

1. Francesco Migliore
2. Francesco Scapin
3. Domenica Perlotti
4. Caterina Rusconi
5. Maria Rusconi
6. Marcellina Rusconi
7. Albina Rusconi
8. Caleste Tagliaferri
9. Giovanni Bonzi
10. Maurizio Miotti
11. Gino Stefani
12. Pietro Capararo
13. Felice Fattorini
14. Renzo Codega
15. Giovanni Rossi
16. Michele Tuia
17. Luigi Beltrame
18. Giuseppe Bandiera
19. Attilio Bandiera
20. Emilio De Vallier
21. Giuseppe Palla
22. Pietro Bernardi
23. Maria Tomerini
24. Guido Tomerini
25. Luigi Gabasti
26. Pietro Dellebaite
27. Amilcare Dellebaite
28. Giovanni Zampatti
29. Giuseppe Ottolini
30. Domenico Biagioni

31. Achille Ferrari

32. Isidoro Dell'Avanco

33. Bartolo Pellegrini

34. Angelo Dellabona

35. Battista De Filippi

36. Massimo Polinelli

37. Marina Caligari

38. Stefano Tomé

39. Giovanni Guidice

40. Angelo Parravicini

41. Luigia Cefis

42. Battista Sacrestani

43. Giovanni Sacrestani

44. Giuseppe Recaldini

45. Carlo Bernardini

46. Agostino Pasotti

47. Attilio Urbinati

48. Emilio Della Maddalena

49. Natale Bianchi

50. Enrico Magi

51. GioBatta De Conti

52. Paolo Canarin

53. Emilio De Zotti

54. Antonio Stopar

From Naples

55. Antonio Natalizia

56. Domenico Medugno

57. Ciro Gerardo Marziale

58. Saverio Bavaro

59. Mariano Bonavolontà

60. Giuseppe Troiani

61. Clemente De Nino

62. Panfilo De Ninno

From Messina

63. Giovanni Lombardo
64. Raffaele Ditto
65. Vincenzo Ditto
66. Giuseppe Pellegrino
67. Giuseppe Spartà
68. Salvatore La Manna
69. Nicolò Licari
70. Salvatore Albano
71. Felice Iozzo
72. Antonino Crea
73. Giuseppe Roda
74. Giuseppe Giordano
75. Nicolò Casella
76. Francesco Messina
77. Pietro Rifici
78. Giuseppe Mangano
79. Pietro Calabrese
80. Nunziata Riolo
81. Nunziato Burrello
82. Carmelo Mola
83. Carmelo Ricciardi
84. Leone Pullella
85. Santo Caputo
86. Vincenzo Zappia
87. Rosario Scopacasa
88. Michele Di Nunzio
89. Francesco Fogliaro
90. Michele Ioppolo
91. Francesco Parlongo
92. Francesco Figliomenti
93. Leonardo Inocente
94. Serafino Placido
95. Cosimo Commosso

96.   Alfredo Valentini

97.   Cosimo Fereri

98.   Vincenzo Nigro

99.   Antonino Maddalena

100. Salvatore Massara

101. Giuseppe Letizia

102. Filippo Germana

103. Giuseppe Scaglione

104. Filippo Di Masi

105. Domenico Bonanno

106. Antonino Martella

107. Giovanni Schepis

108. Leo Martella

109. Giacomo Martella

110. Francesco Battista

111. Nazzareno Gagliardi

112. Filippo Tringali

113. Custodia Arrigo

114. Maria Arrigo

115. Rosa Arrigo

From Port Said

116. Naoum Stavros

117. Athanase Kleiousis

118. Basil Petron Traitse

119. Lianyos Karafilis

120. Athanase Sotiriadis

121. Christos Itlia Sanofski

122. Petros Samarge

123. Vasilios Stofanni

124. Stiglianon Traianos

PORT ADELAIDE

DATE OF ARRIVAL: SATURDAY, 19 NOVEMBER 1927

From Genoa

1. Carlo Spagnut, farm labourer, male, 24, single, Italian
2. Raffaele Zilli, farm labourer, male, 31, single, Italian
3. Agostino Squalizza, farm labourer, male, 18, single, Italian
4. Ruggero Gori, farm labourer, male, 23, single, Italian
5. Ferdinando Tiziani, farm labourer, male, 35, married, Italian
6. Erminio Castagna, farm labourer, male, 22, single, Italian
7. Filippo Vallestigara, farm labourer, male, 24, single, Italian
8. Giovanni Mazzacavallo, farm labourer, male, 23, single, Italian
9. Attilio Destro, farm labourer, male, 23, single, Italian
10. Guido Colussa, farm labourer, male, 22, single, Italian
11. Giacomino Pillon, farm labourer, male, 24, married, Italian
12. Domenico De Nardi, farm labourer, male, 24, married, Italian
13. Valentino Fuoro, farm labourer, male, 25, married, Italian
14. Gino Padovan, farm labourer, male, 17, single, Italian
15. Quinto Cavallin, farm labourer, male, 33, married, Italian
16. Gino Antonello, farm labourer, male, 24, single, Italian
17. Giovanni Satto, farm labourer, male, 26, single, Italian
18. Giacomo Cerneaz, farm labourer, male, 22, single, Italian
19. Giordano Buffon, farm labourer, male, 24, single, Italian
20. Annibale Prosdocino, farm labourer, male, 23, single, Italian
21. Giuseppe Marsiglio, farm labourer, male, 34, married, Italian
22. Vincenzo Serben, farm labourer, male, 22, single, Italian
23. Giuseppe Vincenzot, farm labourer, male, 37, married, Italian
24. Vittorio Bosa, farm labourer, male, 18, single, Italian
25. Umberto Bosa, farm labourer, male, 18, single, Italian
26. Valerio Cusinato, farm labourer, male, 24, single, Italian
27. Onorato Marcon, farm labourer, male, 17, single, Italian
28. Pietro Ferraro, farm labourer, male, 27, single, Italian
29. Antonio Ferraro, farm labourer, male, 37, single, Italian
30. Giovanni Favaro, carpenter, male, 22, single, Italian

31. Pietro Zorzetto, farm labourer, male, 22, single, Italian

32. Domenico Camilotti, farm labourer, male, 45, married, Italian

33. Alessandro Giust, farm labourer, male, 29, married, Italian

34. Egidio Del Tedesco, farm labourer, male, 22, single, Italian

35. Arsenio Pomari, farm labourer, male, 32, single, Italian

36. Vittorio Pomari, farm labourer, male, 25, single, Italian

37. Beniamino Appon, farm labourer, male, 44, married, Italian

38. Luigi Piccin, farm labourer, male, 33, married, Italian

39. Giacomo Rover, farm labourer, male, 26, married, Italian

40. Felice Rostirolla, farm labourer, male, 32, married, Italian

41. Alfonso Ravanello, farm labourer, male, 35, married, Italian

42. Giovanni Zamprogno, farm labourer, male, 42, married, Italian

43. Attilio Panizza, farm labourer, male, 18, single, Italian

44. Mauro Sandretti, farm labourer, male, 23, single, Italian

45. Eugenio Giust, farm labourer, male, 31, married, Italian

46. Antonio Moras, farm labourer, male, 40, married, Italian

47. Angelo Mattiazzo, farm labourer, male, 35, married, Italian

48. Giacomo De Simoni, farm labourer, male, 23, single, Italian

49. Alessandro Variani, farm labourer, male, 27, married, Italian

50. Giovanni Battista Matteazzi, farm labourer, male, 24, single, Italian

51. Caterino Zanocco, farm labourer, male, 22, single, Italian

52. Francesco Pizzate, farm labourer, male, 16, single, Italian

53. Domenico L. Zordan, farm labourer, male, 27, single, Italian

54. Domenico Bogotto, farm labourer, male, 24, single, Italian

55. Giuseppe Brugioni, farm labourer, male, 40, married, Italian

56. Maria Mucci, domestic, female, 30, married, Italian

57. Elsa Brugioni, child, female, two, single, Italian

58. Giacomo Brugioni, farm labourer, male, 24, single, Italian

59. Ferdinando Ciabattoni, farm labourer, male, 47, single, Italian

60. Antonio Casteletti, mason, male, 26, single, Italian

61. Giorgio Pezzutti, farm labourer, male, 21, single, Italian

62. Maria Zanella, farm labourer, female, 15, single

63. Alforisio Predebon, farm labourer, male, 17, single, Italian

64. Cristiano Rigoni, farm labourer, male, 18, single, Italian

65. Angelo Pauletto, farm labourer, male, 18, single, Italian

66. Antonio Marcon, farm labourer, male, 18, single, Italian
67. Virgilio Giuseppe Marcon, farm labourer, male, 18, single, Italian
68. Paolo Zanocco, farm labourer, male, 18, single, Italian
69. Giulio Dipré, farm labourer, male, 31, married, Italian
70. Valentino Dipré, farm labourer, male, 39, married, Italian
71. Quintiglio Dipré, farm labourer, male, 33, single, Italian
72. Primo Paoli, farm labourer, male, 40, married, Italian
73. Stefano Parisi, carpenter, male, 44, married, Italian
74. Lisinio Rigotti, farm labourer, male, 26, single, Italian
75. Giovanni Malisani, farm labourer, male, 21, single, Italian
76. Lorenzo Zecca, farm labourer, male, 24, married, Italian
77. Giovanni Panizza, miner, male, 22, married, Italian
78. Federico Marchesin, farm labourer, male, 17, single, Italian
79. Pietro Bergamin, farm labourer, male, 31, married, Italian
80. Antonio Silvestri, farm labourer, male, 32, married, Italian
81. Carlo Zecchin, farm labourer, male, 17, single, Italian
82. Angelo Sartori, farm labourer, male, 31, married, Italian
83. Placido Ganco, farm labourer, male, 26, single, Italian
84. Teodoro Borelli, farm labourer, male, 26, married, Italian
85. Anselmo Sist, farm labourer, male, 41, married, Italian

From Naples

Michele Daniele, farm labourer, male, 33, married, Italian
(Disembarked in Melbourne)
Giuseppe Loizzi, farm labourer, male, 41, married, Italian
(Disembarked in Melbourne)
Pietro D'Amico, farm labourer, male, 39, married, Italian
(Disembarked in Melbourne)

86. Giovanni Tucciarone, farm labourer, male, 23, married, Italian
87. Leonardo Antonio Mazzei, farm labourer, male, 25, single, Italian
88. Giuseppe Marino, farm labourer, male, 46, married, Italian
89. Vito Sorgini, farm labourer, male, 27, married, Italian
90. Giuseppe Acquaviva, farm labourer, male, 40, married, Italian
91. Francesco Posterivo, farm labourer, male, 30, married, Italian

92.   Giovanni Vaccaro, farm labourer, male, 55, married, Italian

93.   Giuseppantonio Tuliano, farm labourer, male, 27, married, Italian

94.   Antonio Di Stefano, farm labourer, male, 21, married, Italian

95.   Giuseppe Taddeo, farm labourer, male, 27, married, Italian

96.   Antonio Di Lorenzo, farm labourer, male, 24, married, Italian

97.   Donato Del Giudice, farm labourer, male, 22, married, Italian

98.   Vincenzo D'Orazio, farm labourer, male, 25, married, Italian

99.   Giuseppe De Commo, farm labourer, male, 23, single, Italian

100.   Diodoro De Sciscio, farm labourer, male, 38, married, Italian

101.   Domenico Memme, farm labourer, male, 29, married, Italian

102.   Antonio Puracchio, farm labourer, male, 28, married, Italian

From Messina

103.   Giuseppe Zoccoli, farm labourer, male, 51, married, Italian

104.   Paolo Camminiti, farm labourer, male, 46, married, Italian

105.   Giuseppe Chiarantano, farm labourer, male, 57, married, Italian

106.   Giuseppe Musitano, farm labourer, male, 49, married, Italian

107.   Francesco Musolino, farm labourer, male, 43, married, Italian

108.   Pasquale Romeo, farm labourer, male, 34, married, Italian

109.   Carlo Monteleone, farm labourer, male, 32, married, Italian

110.   Rosario Monteleone, farm labourer, male, 27, married, Italian

111.   Nicola Zappavigna, farm labourer, male, 32, married, Italian

112.   Vincenzo Strangio, farm labourer, male, 42, married, Italian

113.   Domenico Trimboli, farm labourer, male, 43, married, Italian

114.   Saverio Mittiga, farm labourer, male, 23, single, Italian

115.   Domenico Antonio Virgara, shoemaker, male, 34, married, Italian

116.   Rosario Zappia, tailor, male, 29, married, Italian

117.   Giuseppe Trimboli, farm labourer, male, 24, married, Italian

118.   Giuseppe Trimboli, farm labourer, male, 22, single, Italian

119.   Michele De Gregorio, farm labourer, male, 47, married, Italian

120.   Antonino Mangano, farm labourer, male, 31, married, Italian

121.   Giuseppe Mesiti, farm labourer, male, 44, married, Italian

122.   Francesco Capogreco, farm labourer, male, 30, married, Italian

123.   Francesco Mitiga, farm labourer, male, 31, married, Italian

124. Rocco Velardi, farm labourer, male, 17, single, Italian

125. Domenico Aloi, farm labourer, male, 23, married, Italian

126. Domenico Ravese, farm labourer, male, 28, single, Italian

127. Antonino Mandello, farm labourer, male, 40, married, Italian

From Port Said

128. Theothosis Micaile, farm labourer, male, 28, married, Greek

129. John Varlamos, farm labourer, male, 45, married, Greek

130. Georges Dimos Athanase, farm labourer, male, 26, married, Greek

131. Michel George Xouris, farm labourer, male, 33, married, Greek

132. Michel Nicolas Tsigros, farm labourer, male, 36, married, Greek

133. Costantin Theodore Tsonis, farm labourer, male, 39, married, Greek

134. Demetrio Anasta. Theodorou, farm labourer, male, 25, single, Greek

MELBOURNE

DATE OF ARRIVAL: THURSDAY, 24 NOVEMBER 1927

From Genoa

1. GioBatta Da Vinchie, farm labourer, male, 28, single, Italian

2. Valentino Beltrame, farm labourer, male, 39, married, Italian

3. Pietro Agostino Formentini, farm labourer, male, 28, married, Italian

4. Eugenio Basso, farm labourer, male, 24, single, Italian

5. Vittorio Borgnolo, farm labourer, male, 26, single, Italian

6. Ettore Bonanni, mason, male, 30, married, Italian

7. Luigi Dozzi, farm labourer, male, 25, married, Italian

8. Domenico Campara, farm labourer, male, 28, married, Italian

9. Giuseppe Alfonso Maria Zammarchi, farm labourer, male, 26, single, Italian

10. Luigi Tagliaferri, farm labourer, male, 21, single, Italian

11. Girolamo Deppi, farm labourer, male, 34, married, Italian

12. Angelo Brotto, farm labourer, male, 29, single, Italian

13. Ernesto Lago, farm labourer, male, 28, married, Italian

14. Giovanni Cusinato, farm labourer, male, 37, married, Italian

15. Vittorio Bonanni, mason, male, 34, married, Italian

16. Valentino Fogliato, farm labourer, male, 28, single, Italian

17. Ermenegildo Ponta, carpenter, male, 29, married, Italian

18. Antonio Cengia, farm labourer, male, 23, married, Italian

19. Angelo Menegazzo, farm labourer, male, 32, single, Italian

20. Antonio Querin, farm labourer, male, 28, single, Italian

21. Gaetano Sartori, farm labourer, male, 25, single, Italian

22. Domenico Giovanni Mario Caffaro, farm labourer, male, 25, single, Italian

23. Maria Maddalena Carbonetto, domestic, female, 28, married, Italian

24. Giovanni Giuseppe Costella, child, male, four, single, Italian

25. Francesco Benvenuti, farm labourer, male, 36, married, Italian

26. Luigi Segat, farm labourer, male, 40, married, Italian

27. GioBatta Attilio Bellò, farm labourer, male, 26, single, Italian

28. Luigi Simaz, farm labourer, male, 26, single, Italian

29. Giuseppe Conforti, male, 44, married, Italian

30. Angelo Valentino Benetti, farm labourer, male, 18, single, Italian

31. Antonio Dal Sasso, farm labourer, male, 32, married, Italian

32. Igino De Bolfo, carpenter, male, 16, single, Italian

33. Francesco De Bolfo, upholsterer, male, 24, single, Italian

34. Silvio De Bolfo, joiner, male, 25, single, Italian

35. Giuseppe Destro, farm labourer, male, 28, single, Italian

36. Giovanni Pizzato, mason, male, 24, single, Italian

37. Angelo Rigoni, farm labourer, male, 22, single, Italian

38. Tiziano Luciano Paganin (Paganini), farm labourer, male, 37, married, Italian

39. Luigi Tomaso Groppi, farm labourer, male, 22, single, Italian

40. Ridolfo Giueseppe Pasquali, farm labourer, male, 23, single, Italian

41. Gaetano Lazzarotto, farm labourer, male, 33, married, Italian

42. Giuseppe Bosa, farm labourer, male, 35, married, Italian

43. Marco Giueseppe Rizzolo, farm labourer, male, 17, single, Italian

44. Sebastiano Bonan, farm labourer, male, 22, single, Italian

45. Cristiano Rigoni, farm labourer, male, 32, married, Italian

46. Valerio Bianchi, farm labourer, male, 22, single, Italian

47. Antonio Bianchi, farm labourer, male, 21, married, Italian

48. Ampelio Acquasaliente, farm labourer, male, 23, single, Italian

49. Giacomo Sartori, farm labourer, male, 34, single, Italian

50. Marco Frigo, farm labourer, male, 17, single, Italian

51. Basilio Frigo, farm labourer, male, 16, single, Italian

52. Luigi Andrea Stella, farm labourer, male, 18, single, Italian

53. Antonio Gnata, miner, male, 19, single, Italian

54. Massimo Girardi, farm labourer, male, 27, married, Italian

55. Osvaldo Reffo, farm labourer, male, 34, married, Italian

56. Agostino Parlato, farm labourer, male, 46, married, Italian

57. Pasquino Giovanni Bertagna, farm labourer, male, 26, married, Italian

58. *Anselmo Giovanni Sist, farm labourer, male, 41, married, Italian (Disembarked in Port Adelaide)*

59. Giovanni Battista Mantovan, farm labourer, male, 32, married, Italian

60. Beniamino De Bortoli, farm labourer, male, 42, married, Italian

From Naples

61. Nicola Nicolazzo, farm labourer, male, 23, married, Italian
62. Domenico Salce, farm labourer, male, 26, married, Italian
63. Quintino Salce, farm labourer, male, 28, married, Italian
64. Antonio Carrieri, joiner, male, 35, married, Italian
65. Francesco Curcio, farm labourer, male, 26, married, Italian

From Messina

66. Antonio Italia, farm labourer, male, 44, single, Italian
67. *Carmelo Spadaro, farm labourer, male, 31, married, Italian (Disembarked in Sydney)*
68. Paolo Giordano, farm labourer, male, 29, married, Italian
69. Michele Pisa, farm labourer, male, 30, single, Italian
70. Annunziato Guida, farm labourer, male, 33, married, Italian
71. Giuseppe Benavoli, farm labourer, male, 49, married, Italian
72. Salvatore Lanza, farm labourer, male, 36, married, Italian
73. Michelangelo Italia, farm labourer, male, 23, married, Italian
74. Sebastiano Musco, farm labourer, male, 28, married, Italian
75. Luigi Mineo, farm labourer, male, 29, married, Italian
76. Gaetano Romano, farm labourer, male, 30, married, Italian
77. Francesco Lanza, farm labourer, male, 24, married, Italian
78. Paolo Corridore, farm labourer, male, 35, married, Italian
79. Domenico De Giglio, farm labourer, male, 40, married, Italian
80. Bruno Vinci, farm labourer, male, 41, married, Italian
81. Francesco Antonio Maria Pileggi, farm labourer, male, 37, married, Italian
82. Carmelo Giovanni Gattuso, farm labourer, male, 43, married, Italian
83. Michele Sculli, farm labourer, male, 33, married, Italian
84. Paolo Violi, farm labourer, male, 30, married, Italian
85. Carmine Covelli, farm labourer, male, 34, married, Italian
86. Francesco Taranto, farm labourer, male, 37, married, Italian
87. Giuseppe Taranto, farm labourer, male, 24, single, Italian
88. Vincenzo Di Gregorio, farm labourer, male, 51, married, Italian
89. Luigi Felice Giarracca, farm labourer, male, 45, married, Italian
90. Giacomino Casamento, farm labourer, male, 17, single, Italian

91. Giovanni Taranto, farm labourer, male, 13, single, Italian
92. Michele Segreto, farm labourer, male, 18, single, Italian
93. Felice Virgona, farm labourer, male, 16, single, Italian
94. Angelo Virgona, farm labourer, male, 14, single, Italian
95. Annunziata Picone, domestic, female, 19, single, Italian
96. Sebastiano Speranza, fisherman, male, 18, single, Italian
97. Domenico Francesco Giuseppe Chiera, male, 35, married, Italian
98. Giuseppe Zappia, farm labourer, male, 43, married, Italian
99. Giuseppe Maria Lotorto, mason, male, 32, married, Italian
100. Giuseppe Violi, farm labourer, male, 40, married, Italian
101. Giovannina Famularo, domestic, female, 26, married, Italian
102. Giuseppe Famularo, child, male, six, single, Italian
103. Domenico Loprese, farm labourer, male, 38, married, Italian
104. Giuseppe Sanzaro, mechanic, male, 33, married, Italian

From Port Said

105. Patroche Basile, telegraphist, male, 33, married, Greek

From Naples

106. Michele Lorenzo Daniele, farm labourer, male, 33, married, Italian
107. Giuseppe Loizzi, farm labourer, male, 41, married, Italian
108. Pietro D'Amico, farm labourer, male, 39, married, Italian

From Messina

109. Santo Lanteri, farm labourer, male, 22, single, Italian
110. Carmelo Menta, farm labourer, male, 47, married, Italian

Sydney

Date of Arrival: Monday, 28 November 1927

From Genoa

1.   Clemente Lain, farm labourer, male, 44, married, Italian
2.   Emilio Lain, farm labourer, male, 39, married, Italian
3.   Sebastiano Carboni, farm labourer, male, 26, single, Italian
4.   Nicolò Carboni, farm labourer, male, 28, married, Italian
5.   Domenico Zonta, farm labourer, male, 28, single, Italian
6.   Giambattista Busatto, farm labourer, male, 23, single, Italian
7.   Giovanni Pilati, farm labourer, male, 23, single, Italian
8.   Erminio Corradi, farm labourer, male, 29, married, Italian
9.   Gino Morcale, farm labourer, male, 23, single, Italian
10. Daniele Ragnera, farm labourer, male, 24, married, Italian
11. Albino Gaspari, farm labourer, male, 21, single, Italian
12. Giacomo Aganetti, farm labourer, male, 48, married, Italian
13. Alessandro Soster, farm labourer, male, 28, married, Italian
14. Giovanni Pasquale Carboni, farm labourer, male, 29, single, Italian
15. Leone Costa, farm labourer, male, 17, single, Italian
16. Celso Missio, farm labourer, male, 24, single, Italian
17. Giovanni Baldissera, farm labourer, male, 38, married, Italian
18. Giuseppe Giacomin, farm labourer, male, 23, single, Italian
19. Luigi Vicceli, farm labourer, male, 19, single, Italian
20. Giovanni Gomano, farm labourer, male, 22, single, Italian
21. Angelo Ferdinando Pittigher, farm labourer, male, 30, single, Italian
22. Romano Schirato, farm labourer, male, 30, married, Italian
23. Regina Pietribiasi, domestic, female, 28, married, Italian
24. Teresa Bertoldo, child, female, four, single, Italian
25. Antonio Martinuzzo, farm labourer, male, 48, married, Italian
26. Enrico Cosatto, farm labourer, male, 25, married, Italian
27. Giuseppe Danello, farm labourer, male, 35, married, Italian
28. Bortolo Bonatto, farm labourer, male, 20, single, Italian
29. Pulese Scolastica Soravia, domestic, female, 30, married, Italian

30. Carmine Cesco, child, male, four, single, Italian

31. Lelio Cesco, child, male, two, single, Italian

32. Cancian Oddone Cesco, farm labourer, male, 25, single, Italian

33. Matteo Giuseppe De Mattia, farm labourer, male, 24, single, Italian

34. Giovanni Zanatta, farm labourer, male, 41, married, Italian

35. Rosalio Zanatta, farm labourer, male, 18, single, Italian

36. Eugenio Baldasso, farm labourer, male, 18, single, Italian

37. Angelo Sartori, farm labourer, male, 25, single, Italian

38. Giosafatte Lora, farm labourer, male, 37, single, Italian

39. Angelo Albarello, farm labourer, male, 40, single, Italian

40. Aldo Mecchia, farm labourer, male, 26, single, Italian

41. Arciso Crestani, farm labourer, male, 25, single, Italian

42. Alessandro Casagrande, farm labourer, male, 49, married, Italian

43. Gino Brutto Bordignon, farm labourer, male, 27, single, Italian

44. Fortunato Marchetti, farm labourer, male, 22, single, Italian

45. Antonio Moretto, farm labourer, male, 39, married, Italian

46. Ernesto Cester, farm labourer, male, 35, married, Italian

47. Angelo Giuseppe Maestri, farm labourer, male, 38, married, Italian

48. Stefano Fanelli, farm labourer, male, 45, married, Italian

49. Sebastiano Chimello, farm labourer, male, 28, single, Italian

50. Angela Bozzo, domestic, female, 26, married, Italian

51. Florio Chemello, child, male, four, single, Italian

52. Ettore Fero, farm labourer, male, 23, single, Italian

53. Giovanni Rubbo, farm labourer, male, 28, married, Italian

54. Luigia Celloni, domestic, female, 23, married, Italian

55. Lodovico Martinelli, farm labourer, male, 24, married, Italian

56. Anselmo Pozza, farm labourer, male, 21, single, Italian

57. Gio Batta Pittin, mason, male, 26, single, Italian

58. Giuseppe De Zolt, farm labourer, male, 27, married, Italian

59. Gaspare Cesco, farm labourer, male, 27, single, Italian

60. Giovanna Meneghini, domestic, female, 37, married, Italian

61. Leonardo Dalla Fontana, child, male, 15, single, Italian

62. Mario Dalla Fontana, child, male, 12, single, Italian

63. Maria Dalla Fontana, child, female, nine, single, Italian

64. Cipriano Dalla Fontana, child, male, four, single, Italian

65.   Giovanni Dalla Fontana, carpenter, male, 17, single, Italian

66.   Giovanni Zibonda, miner, male, 21, single, Italian

67.   Giovanni Girardin, mechanic, male, 16, single, Italian

68.   Giuseppe Canderle, farm labourer, male, 16, single, Italian

69.   Eugenio De Antoni, mason, male, 35, married, Italian

70.   Antonio Della Libera, farm labourer, male, 21, single, Italian

71.   Domenico Salghetti, farm labourer, male, 34, married, Italian

72.   Francesco Martoccio, farm labourer, male, 35, single, Italian

73.   Julius Lamburger, electrician, male, 54, single, Austrian

74.   Angelo Bonnardi, shoemaker, male, 23, single, Italian

75.   Agostino Piccin, farm labourer, male, 17, single, Italian

76.   Ernesto Valbusa, farm labourer, male, 32, single, Italian

77.   Giuseppe Maggiora, farm labourer, male, 26, married, Italian

78.   Maria Rossi, domestic, female, 23, married, Italian

79.   Vittorio Botto, farm labourer, male, 31, single, Italian

80.   Andrea Bruni, farm labourer, male, 31, married, Italian

81.   Alessandro Faccin, farm labourer, male, 31, married, Italian

82.   Teodoro Meraviglia, farm labourer, male, 34, married, Italian

83.   Giuseppe Rossi, farm labourer, male, 40, married, Italian

84.   Giuseppe Costanzo, farm labourer, male, 24, married, Italian

85.   Maggiore Rollino, farm labourer, male, 37, married, Italian

86.   Francesco Laurenghin, farm labourer, male, 41, married, Italian

87.   Luigi Brescon, farm labourer, male, 28, single, Italian

88.   Luigi Marchesi, farm labourer, male, 28, single, Italian

89.   Eugenio De Amborccio, farm labourer, male, 26, married, Italian

90.   Ugo Tasselli, farm labourer, male, 27, married, Italian

91.   Ida Dadesso, domestic, female, 36, married, Italian

92.   Maddalena Bruccia, child, female, eight, single, Italian

93.   Giovanni Lando, farm labourer, male, 17, single, Italian

94.   Antonio De Lai, farm labourer, male, 21, single, Italian

From Naples

95.   Prezioso Gargaro, farm labourer, male, 23, single, Italian

96.   Giacomo Fistarone, farm labourer, male, 19, single, Italian

97. Pietro Giovanni Bonofiglio, farm labourer, male, 42, married, Italian

98. Florindo Manteri, farm labourer, male, 27, single, Italian

99. Antonino Monardo, farm labourer, male, 46, married, Italian

100. Antonio De Marco, farm labourer, male, 58, married, Italian

101. Gaetano Piscitelli, farm labourer, male, 29, single, Italian

102. Pasquale Santoponte, farm labourer, male, 27, single, Italian

From Messina

103. Vincenzo Salzone, farm labourer, male, 39, married, Italian

104. Domenico Catanzariti, farm labourer, male, 36, married, Italian

105. Antonio Sergi, farm labourer, male, 51, married, Italian

106. Rosario Catanzariti, farm labourer, male, 42, married, Italian

107. Antonio Patanisi, farm labourer, male, 36, married, Italian

108. Francesco Femia, farm labourer, male, 43, married, Italian

109. Giuseppe Femia, farm labourer, male, 40, married, Italian

110. Salvatore Sansalone, farm labourer, male, 26, married, Italian

111. Giuseppe Trimarchi, farm labourer, male, 42, married, Italian

112. Nicola Giuseppe Tipaldo, farm labourer, male, 25, single, Italian

113. Domenico Cagliuso, farm labourer, male, 22, single, Italian

114. Francesco Esposito, tailor, male, 27, single, Italian

115. Vincenzo Cirillo, shoemaker, male, 21, single, Italian

116. Leonardo Basile, farm labourer, male, 16, single, Italian

117. Giacomo Cosenza, farm labourer, male, 30, single, Italian

118. Damiano Cutri, farm labourer, male, 50, married, Italian

119. Bartolo Virgona, farm labourer, male, 47, married, Italian

120. Giuseppe Virgona, child, male, 10, single, Italian

121. DomenicoVozzo, farm labourer, male, 31, single, Italian

122. Filippo Marano, farm labourer, male, 23, single, Italian

123. Vita Concetta Marano, tailor, female, 25, single, Italian

124. Santo Marano, child, male, two, single, Italian

125. Domenico Di Carlo, farm labourer, male, 22, single, Italian

126. Giuseppe Sciuto, farm labourer, male, 23, single, Italian

127. Anna Sciuto, domestic, female, 26, single, Italian

128. Carmelo Pennisi, farm labourer, male, 19, single, Italian

129. Antonino Vassallo, farm labourer, male, 18, single, Italian
130. Salvatore Lo Monaco, farm labourer, male, 27, married, Italian
131. Rosario Veochio, farm labourer, male, 23, single, Italian
132. Rosario Tomarchio, farm labourer, male, 41, single, Italian
133. Orazio Cassaniti, farm labourer, male, 23, single, Italian
134. Domenico Romeo, farm labourer, male, 32, married, Italian
135. Alfio Maccarone, farm labourer, male, 28, married, Italian
136. Alfio Torrisi, farm labourer, male, 32, married, Italian
137. Filippo Micale, farm labourer, male, 46, married, Italian
138. Giuseppe Pafumi, farm labourer, male, 18, single, Italian
139. Venera Parisi, domestic, female, 40, married, Italian
140. Carmelo Spadaro, farm labourer, male, 31, married, Italian
141. Domenico Bonanno, farm labourer, male, 32, married, Italian

Index of Passengers

ENDNOTES

Chapter Two — Recollections

1. 'Ozzie's place' was the fish shop and dwelling of Uncle Andy's cousin, Ozvaldo Mattea, at 257 Bridge Road Richmond. But Igino found short-term work with Andy Mattea instead, at a fish shop at 197 Victoria Street, West Melbourne, near the Elizabeth Street corner, before separating from his brothers to take up employment in the coastal town of Rosebud. As Uncle Nino recalled, 'It was a shop owned by two Spaniards, and Andy and I lived upstairs. We worked there together, and I got £2 a week.'

Chapter Four — The Voyage

1. On 25 October 1927, the Italian liner *Principessa Mafalda* sank in the Atlantic Ocean off the Brazilian coast, as a result of an explosion in the boiler room of the vessel. A newspaper report of the following day conveyed the following details of the tragic event as follows:

   ITALIAN LINER SINKS; 1170 OF 1238 SAVED

   October 26, 1927. Carrying more than 800 Italian immigrants bound for the promised land of South America, the Italian liner *Principessa Mafalda* now lies at the bottom of the Atlantic Ocean off the Brazilian coast. Rescue vessels have saved all but 68 of the 1238 passengers and crewmembers. Anticipating their arrival in Rio de Janeiro, the immigrants aboard the *Mafalda* began to celebrate after last night's supper. When the ship ground to a halt following an explosion in the boiler room, the high spirits turned to tears and trembling as the passengers hit the main deck in frantic quest of lifeboats and life preservers.

   — from *Chronicle of the 20th Century*, Chronicle Publications, Mount Kisco, New York, 1987.

2. It is possible that the passengers' hands were checked to ensure that all their fingers were intact for work purposes. Archival information reveals that Agostino Costella (husband of passenger twenty-three, Maria Costella, and father of passenger twenty-four, Giovanni

Costella) was permitted to disembark from the SS *Caprera* in Melbourne on 22 November 1925, despite being stopped by the Italian Emigration Commissary at Genoa, 'as it was noticed that he had lost the index and middle fingers of his left hand'.

The author has also learned that some Italian timber cutters felling trees in Victoria's Gippsland region actually opted to chop off their own fingers, successfully claim accident compensation and later return to Italy with their proceeds.

3.   Ampelio first stayed at 91 Canning Street, Carlton, the premises of Mr G. Scapin. Mr Scapin was quite probably the owner of a boarding house, one of many dotted in and around the Carlton area at that time.

4.   Note the discrepancy between the price paid by Igino De Bolfo for his fare — 1500 *lire* — and the 5000 *lire* paid by Annunziata. Assuming that their recollections are correct, we can only guess that Annunziata had a better class of cabin, and hence paid more.

Chapter Six — The Passengers

1.   Inter-camp correspondence, National Archives of Australia, Series A367/1.

2.   Kathleen Gorham, O.B.E. (1931–1983) was a principal dancer in the Australian Ballet's first season of 1962. Upon her death, Edward H. Pask wrote in the magazine *Dance Australia*: 'A curtain has fallen, and the world of dance mourns the passing of Kathleen Gorham, who was the first Australian-trained ballerina to become a national celebrity and whose name was a household word for more than 30 years. A brilliant artiste, a dedicated teacher, a kind and generous adviser and a dear friend — for me, Kathleen Gorham was all of those; to dance and dancers, she gave openly the fruits of her experience and the deep-rooted love of her chosen art.' Sir Robert Helpmann said: 'Kathleen Gorham was my favourite Australian ballerina and the creator of my ballets *The Display* and *Yugen* for the Australian Ballet. Not only was she a great performer, but a very great person and friend — I shall miss her.'

3.   Toni related the following tale about one cinema outing, when she and John saw the 1935 Cecil B. De Mille film *The Crusades*. 'The soldiers and horses kept getting shot, and as I walked home I was in tears. He said to me, "What's the matter with you? The lead characters are only actors, they're not really dead", and I said, "It's not the actors I'm worried about, it's the horses!"'

4.   The Mauthausen concentration camp, located twenty kilometres from the city of Linz in Austria, was established on 8 August 1938. Mauthausen was a so-called 'Category Three Camp'. This was the fiercest category, which for its prisoners meant *'Ruckkehr unerwünscht'* (return not desired) and *'Vernichtung durch arbeit'* (extermination by work). On 5 May 1945, units of the American 11th Armor Division liberated the main Mauthausen camp, and discovered the bodies of 15,000 people buried in mass graves. A further 3000 died in the weeks that followed the liberation through disease and starvation. In total, 150,000 men, women and children are thought to have died in Mauthausen.

5.   Michelangela Ganci (or 'Gance', according to Luigi's death certificate).

6.   This may have been the premises of A. Russo, greengrocer, frequented by Annunziata Casamento, who was listed as Giacomino's sponsor.

TYPES OF ITALIAN MIGRANTS who arrived yesterday in Melbourne by the Re D'Italia, which berthed at 19 North Wharf with passengers and cargo from southern European ports.

How Melbourne's now-defunct *Sun News-Pictorial* reported the previous day's arrival of the *Re d'Italia*, in the edition of Friday, 25 November 1927. The identities of the five passengers are not known.